D1473003

Handbook of Feminist Therapy

Lynne Bravo Rosewater, Ph.D., is a licensed psychologist in private practice in Cleveland, Ohio. She focuses on reframing roles for women and men in her work with individuals, couples, families, and groups. Dr. Rosewater is one of the founding members and the current chairperson of the National Feminist Therapy Institute. As a national expert on both domestic violence and the Minnesota Multiphasic Personality Inventory (MMPI) profile for battered women, Dr. Rosewater prepares personality assessments for use in court with battered women who have killed their batterers. She is currently working on a book about the process of change in therapy.

Lenore E. Auerbach Walker, Ed.D., A.B.P.P., is a licensed psychologist in independent practice at Walker & Associates in Denver, Colorado. She does psychological assessments and provides psychotherapy in a general practice with a specialization in women and children who have been victims of men's violent behavior. She often testifies in courts around the country, documenting psychological injury and speaking on behalf of battered women who kill their abusers. Dr. Walker previously has authored *The Battered Woman* (1979) and *The Battered Woman Syndrome* (1984) and edited *Women and Mental Health Policy* (1984). She is a frequent contributor of book chapters and professional journal articles and speaks nationally to groups who work with women victim/survivors of violence. She presently is working on a new book, tentatively titled *Getting It All: Women in the Eighties*.

Handbook of Feminist Therapy:
Women's Issues in Psychotherapy

Lynne Bravo Rosewater, Ph.D.
Lenore E. A. Walker, Ed.D.
Editors

Section Editors:
Patricia Spencer Faunce, Ph.D.
Carolyn C. Larsen, Ph.D.
Lorna P. Cammaert, Ph.D.
Iris Goldstein Fodor, Ph.D.
Elizabeth Rave, Ed.D.
Doreen Seidler-Feller, Ph.D.
Laura Brown, Ph.D.
Hannah Lerman, Ph.D.
Natalie Porter, Ph.D.

Editorial Contributions by
Patricia G. Webbink, Ph.D.

Springer Publishing Company
New York

Springer Publishing Company, Inc.
536 Broadway
New York, New York 10012

85 86 87 88 89 / 10 9 8 7 6 5 4 3 2 1

Library of Congress Cataloging in Publication Data

Main entry under title:
Handbook of feminist therapy.
  Includes bibliographies and index.
  1. Feminist therapy—Congresses. I. Rosewater, Lynne Bravo. II. Walker, Lenore E.
RC489.F45H36   1985   616.89′14′088042   85-4782
ISBN 0-8261-4970-7

Printed in the United States of America

Contents

■ ONE
A Feminist Philosophy of Treatment   1
Patricia Spencer Faunce, Editor

v

■ TWO
Introduction to Feminist Psychotherapeutic
Techniques and Practices   **47**
Carolyn C. Larsen and Lorna P. Cammaert,
Editors

■ **THREE**

Women's Issues across the Lifespan: Transcending Sex Roles 131
Iris Goldstein Fodor, Editor

■ **FOUR**

Violence against Women: An Overview 199
Elizabeth Rave, Editor

Contributors

Joan R. Saks Berman, M.A., currently is employed as a clinical psychologist by the Indian Health Service. She earned her doctorate from Northwestern University, after receiving a B.A. from the University of Chicago and an M.A. from Indiana University. She is a native of Chicago and at one time was in private practice as a feminist therapist there. She also has experience teaching women's studies, adult basic education, and English as a second language. She was a founding member of the Chicago Women's Liberation Union and the Association for Women in Psychology, as well as the Feminist Therapy Institute. In 1970 she cut sugar cane in Cuba as a member of the Venceremos Brigade and in 1973 she traveled to the People's Republic of China with a special all-women delegation.

Lilian Bern, M.A., is a marriage, family, and child counselor and a certified neurolinguistic programmer. She has been in private practice in Sebasstopol, California since 1979. Lilian is also an instructor in the women's re-entry program at Napa Valley College, as well as founding member and co-director of Chrysalis Counseling Services for Women, Inc. Her special areas of interest are domestic violence, lesbian families, and the therapeutic use of feminist fairytales.

Laura Brown, Ph.D., received her doctorate in Clinical Psychology in 1977 at Southern Illinois University at Carbondale. She is currently a licensed psychologist in private practice in Seattle, Washington and is Clinical Assistant Professor of Psychology at the University of Washington. Her major interests include lesbian psychology, ethical issues in feminist therapy, feminist therapy theory, women survivors of sexual and domestic violence, and eating disorders.

Beverly Burch, M.S.W., is a psychotherapist in private practice in Berkeley, California and a consultant to the Women's Therapy Training Project in El Cerrito, California. She also has an M.A. in English Literature. Her particular areas of interest are clinical work with lesbians and the interweaving of object relations and feminist theories. She has published fiction, poetry, and book reviews in small press journals as well as papers on lesbian issues in the psychotherapy literature.

Vasanti Burtle, Ph.D., is in private practice in Encino, California. Her treatment focus is on the holistic functioning of women in society, alcoholism, borderline personality disorders, and workers' compensation. She has a B.A. in English Language and Literature from the University of London; an M.A. in Experimental Psychology from the New School for Social Research, New York; and a Ph.D. in Professional Psychology from the California School of Professional Psychology, Los Angeles. She is a member of the English Bar and a past Fellow of the Institute of Psychiatry, Law and Behavioral Science, University of Southern California. Previous experience includes 11 years' research on employment conditions of women and young workers at the International Labor Office, Geneva, Switzerland. She has co-edited *Women in Therapy: New Psychotherapies for a Changing Society* (1974) and has edited *Women Who Drink: Alcoholic Experience and Psychotherapy* (1979).

Marylou Butler, Ph.D., is a counseling psychologist who is currently the Director of Special Services and Associate Professor of Psychology at the College of Santa Fe. She is a certified psychologist in New Mexico and Pennsylvania and is currently in private practice in Santa Fe, New Mexico. Dr. Butler completed her master's degree at the University of Wisconsin-Milwaukee in 1968 and her doctorate at Arizona State University in 1973. She was a member of the Feminist Therapy Collective, Inc. in Philadelphia from 1973 to 1978.

Lorna P. Cammaert, Ph.D., currently holds a dual appointment as a professor in the Department of Educational Psychology, University of Calgary, Alberta, and as a counselor at the University's counseling services. She received her Ph.D. in Counseling and Developmental Psychology from the University of Oregon. Her interests encompass female sexuality, sexual harassment, assertiveness, decision making, and self-esteem groups for women. Dr. Cammaert has served as the national coordinator of the Canadian Psychological Association Interest Group on Women and Psychology and is a coauthor with Dr. Carolyn Larsen of *A Woman's Choice: A Guide to Decision-Making.*

Aphrodite Clamar, Ph.D., a clinical psychologist, received her doctorate from New York University and currently is engaged in the practice of psychotherapy in New York City. She has done research and published widely in the area of unusual families (adoptive and stepfamilies, for example) and in areas of concern to women.

Doris C. DeHardt, Ph.D., earned her doctorate from Michigan State University in 1961. She currently is Professor of Psychology and Director of the Psychology Clinic at California State University, Long Beach. She began her professional life as an experimental psychologist but gradually shifted her focus to expanding the contributions of women's experience to the profession of psychology. As a clinician in private practice, she is particularly interested in helping women to balance their desire for intimacy with their struggle for identity and self-validation.

Mary Ann Douglas, Ph.D., received her doctorate in Clinical Psychology from the University of Utah. She is currently Assistant Professor in the Department of Psychology, Nova University, Ft. Lauderdale, Florida, where she teaches in the clinical psychology program and is the founder and director of the Family Violence Clinical Research Program. The program provides for clinical training, research, and direct clinical service. Her research interests include woman-battering, incest, and power in intimate relationships. Her clinical practice involves the application of feminist principles to work, primarily with women in individual therapy and with couples and families.

Judy Eron, M.S.W., is a clinical social worker in private practice in Nashville, Tennessee. She received her B.S. in Occupational Therapy from the University of Pennsylvania in 1970 and her M.S.W. from the University of Tennessee in 1976. In addition to her work as a feminist therapist, Judy is a songwriter and performer of women's music. The songs on her album, "I Can't Believe That Was Me," reflect her concern for women's well-being. She performs across the country for social and psychological organizations.

Patricia Spencer Faunce, Ph.D., holds her doctorate in Counseling Psychology. At the University of Minnesota, she is Professor of Psychology and Women's Studies and a feminist therapist with the Student Counseling Bureau. Dr. Faunce has developed and teaches numerous courses about women on each of the following topics: feminist therapies; women's psychological development; personality; achievement motivation; work; power; and feminist research methodologies. Her research includes work in these areas as well as dramatizing the lives of our foremothers in psychology, mind-body interaction, and feminist pedagogy/teaching/scholarship. The class-action sex discrimination suit against the University of Minnesota has felt the impact of Faunce's active involvement as an organizer, strategist, and claimant.

Iris Fodor, Ph.D., received her doctorate in Clinical Psychology from Boston University. She is Professor of Educational Psychology at New York University, where she trains psychologists for schools and is a member of the Women's Studies Commission, which has developed a program for women in the human services. She is also a therapist who has lectured and written extensively about women's issues and mental health.

Maureen Calista Hendricks, Ed.D., is a graduate of the School of Educational Change and Development, University of Northern Colorado, and a licensed clinical psychologist in private practice in

Denver, Colorado. She is the author of *The Marriages and Marital Adjustment of Resigned Roman Catholic Priests and their Wives*. She also is a support group leader for Resolve of Colorado and a member of Woman Church Speaks and the Women's Ordination Conference of the Roman Catholic Church.

Doris Jeanette, Psy.D., received her doctorate from Baylor University and since has studied with Joseph Wolpe, M.D., Jean Houston, Ph.D., and Irwin Yalom, M.D. In addition to her private practice, Doris has supervised at Rutgers University, Temple Medical School, and the Feminist Therapy Collective in Philadelphia. She has consulted for such diverse institutions as Jefferson Medical School, Swarthmore Women's Center, and the Armed Forces. Among the numerous groups and workshops that Doris teaches is "Playshops," which she created to free the brain, the body, and the heart. Currently, Dr. Jeanette is writing a book, from which her contribution to this book is taken, about her process, her reality, and her freedom.

Sharon E. Kahn, Ph.D., is Associate Professor of Counseling Psychology at the University of British Columbia, where she supervises counselor training and teaches a course in gender-role issues in counseling. She received her doctorate in Counseling Psychology from Arizona State University. Her research has been published in such journals as *Personnel and Guidance, Counselor Education and Supervision, Canadian Counsellor*, and *Sex Roles*. She has been the Coordinator of the Interest Group on Women and Psychology of the Canadian Psychological Association. Her recent research interests are in the area of women's career development.

Carolyn C. Larsen, Ph.D., is a psychologist at University Counseling Services, University of Calgary, Alberta, in private practice, and a consultant to community women's programs. She received her doctorate in clinical psychology from Indiana University. Recently she has coauthored, with Lorna Cammaert, *A Woman's Choice: A Guide to Decision-Making;* and is collaborating with Jean Pettifor and Lorna Cammaert on the development of ethical guidelines for counselling/therapy with women for the Canadian Psychological Association. She also is a coauthor of *Therapy and Counselling with Women: A Handbook of Educational Materials*.

Ella Lasky, Ph. D., is a psychoanalyst in private practice in New York City working with individuals and couples. She supervises doctoral candidates in clinical psychology at both the City University of New York and Yeshiva University. She was instrumental in the formation in 1972 of the Women's Psychotherapy Referral Service, a nonprofit feminist organization located in New York City, and has been a member of Who's Who of American Women since 1975. She has published an anthology of articles on sex-role issues, *Humanness: An Exploration into the Mythologies about Women and Men,* and has published several articles on women's self-esteem and achievement issues.

Hannah Lerman, Ph.D., is in private practice in Los Angeles. She received her doctorate in Clinical Psychology from Michigan State University in 1963 and has written about women's issues in therapy and feminist therapy for the past 10 years. She currently is writing a book on Freud and women's issues and serves as President of the Division of the Psychology of Women of the American Psychological Association.

Lauree E. Moss, M.S.W., Ph.D., is a licensed psychotherapist in the San Francisco Bay Area. She also is on the psychology faculty and is an advisor and codirector of the Feminist Therapy Master's Degree Program at Antioch University West, San Francisco. She is an associate member of the Gestalt Institute of San Francisco and has been in private practice for over 12 years. Over the last nine years, she has been offering training and consultation for therapists who want to learn how to integrate body therapy into verbal therapy.

Natalie Porter, Ph.D., is Assistant Professor of Clinical Psychology and Director, Psychological Consultation Center, University of Nebraska-Lincoln. Both her clinical and research interests center on the supervision process.

Elizabeth Rave, Ed.D., received her doctorate from the University of Southern California. She is presently Professor of School Psychology and Women's Studies at the University of Northern Colorado. She has worked with and learned from survivors of interpersonal violence for over 10 years.

Mary Resh, Ph.D., is a clinical psychologist in independent practice in Boulder, Colorado. She is the same age as Elizabeth Taylor.

Joan Hamerman Robbins, M.S.W., is a feminist therapist in private practice in San Francisco. She earned her M.S.W. from the University of California at Berkeley and is a coeditor of *Women Changing Therapy: New Assessments, Values and Strategies in Feminist Therapy* (1983). Ms. Hamerman Robbins is on the editorial board of the feminist quarterly, *Women & Therapy;* and she has lectured, written articles, and presented workshops and papers at national conferences of mental health professionals which reflect her deep commitment to integrating a feminist consciousness into the practice of psychotherapy.

Doreen Seidler-Feller, Ph.D., received her doctorate in Clinical Psychology from Ohio State University. She is currently on the staff of Cigna Healthplans, Los Angeles, as a staff psychologist. In addition, she maintains a private practice devoted to individual, couples, family, and sex therapy. Her research interests center on the development of a feminist perspective within various areas of applied clinical psychology.

Sara Sharratt, Ph.D., is Associate Professor of Counseling, Sonoma State University, Rohnert Park, California. She is a founding member of Chrysalis Counseling Services for women, which she still continues to codirect. She has been in private practice part time for the last 12 years and currently is the chairperson of the Counseling Department at Sonoma State University, where she has taught for the last eight years.

Rachel Josefowitz Siegel, M.S.W., is a clinical social worker in private practice in Ithaca, N.Y. She is on the editorial board of the journal, *Women & Therapy*, and on the executive board of the Women's Studies Program at Cornell University. She has recently coedited *Women Changing Therapy: New Assessments, Values and Strategies in Feminist Therapy* (1983).

Ruth F. Siegel is a feminist therapist in private practice in Chicago, Illinois, and a founding member of the Feminist Therapy Institute. She

xviii : : *Contributors*

has been a camp director, a teacher and assistant director of a nursery school, and a feminist therapist for 11 years. Having gone through her own life awakening in her fifties, she now spends her time enabling women to reclaim their own power. She also gives workshops and presentations on anger, power, and changing life roles.

Adrienne J. Smith, Ph.D., received her doctorate in Clinical Psychology from the University of Chicago in 1966, but it was not until six years later that she began to develop a feminist consciousness. Since then she has worked extensively with women as a feminist therapist and has presented numerous papers and workshops on women's power issues and on feminist therapy. A founding member of the Feminist Therapy Institute, she continues to work with women to enable them to reclaim their own power and now is interested in teaching other therapists.

Linda K. Stere, M.S.S.W., is a clinical social worker in a private feminist therapy practice in Nashville, Tennessee. For the past two years she has chaired the Women's Issues Committee for NASW in Tennessee, a group that has planned regular, continuing educational programs and workshops designed to improve the quality of services to women. She also has taught a course titled "Women and Treatment" at the University of Tennessee School of Social Work.

Gisela M. Theurer, M.A., received her master's degree in Counseling Psychology from the University of British Columbia in 1981. Her professional work includes five years as an assistant director of a psychiatric home for women in Germany, and contract work and research assistance in counseling in Vancouver for the last three years. Presently she is studying the issue of unemployment, from the inside.

Laurie Weiss, M.A., has been practicing and teaching psychotherapy since 1972. She and her husband, Jonathan B. Weiss, Ph.D., practice together in Littleton, Colorado and are internationally known teachers of psychotherapy. Laurie consults with organizations about human relations and conflict management, focusing on the creation of situations where everybody wins.

Introduction—
Feminist Therapy:
A Coming of Age

LYNNE BRAVO ROSEWATER AND
LENORE E. AUERBACH WALKER

This volume grows out of the First Annual Advanced Feminist Therapy Institute, a gathering of 60 experienced feminist therapists who shared their exciting and innovative work. It was held in Vail, Colorado, in April, 1982.

The chapters in this book reflect the growing edge of feminist therapy and, as such, mirror the maturity of thinking about psychotherapy with women. As women working together with women, these therapists have gone beyond the realization of psychological theory based on male developmental norms and have come to understand its inadequacy in explaining the female experience. While several authors previously have examined gender-based developmental psychological differences (Gilligan, 1982; Sturdivant, 1980) and the implications such differences have for mental health workers (Brodsky & Hare-Mustin, 1980; Franks & Rothblum, 1983; Rawlings & Carter, 1977) and mental health policy (Walker, 1984), little has been written about the clinical application of such principles, especially for the advanced psychotherapist.

The development of feminist therapy as a specific technique has grown since its first appearance in the late 1960s. Simultaneous to the emergence of the new wave of the women's movement, the process of therapy and its impact on women's lives was examined. Chesler (1972) found that women were encouraged to adapt to unconscionable situations and often fed tranquilizers to make their pain more bearable. Soon therapists all over the country began experimenting with new ways to help strengthen women's abilities for making the changes necessary to continuing their psychological growth. Without talking to the others, each therapist on her own, calling herself a feminist therapist, began the journey with her clients to separate personal issues from those collective issues that arise from being a woman in a society that invalidates women as a class. Finally, in the 1970s, feminist therapists began to meet each other, slowly at first, at various professional meetings, and then in large groups at the Association for Women in Psychology Conferences. They began to discover the differences between good, nonsexist therapy and that which has a more political stance supporting the re-empowerment of women in a society that does not encourage such strength.

Although papers dealing with these issues have been presented at numerous meetings, feminist therapists' written work rarely has been published. This book helps to fill that gap by adding to the documentation of the advanced clinical application of psychotherapeutic techniques with women.

The principles of feminist therapy—a commitment to political, economic, and social equality for both women and men and a commitment to an equalitarian relationship between therapist and client (Rawlings & Carter, 1977)—remain unchanged. The chapters in this book reflect the expansion and reinterpretation of these principles. The diversity of techniques in feminist therapy becomes apparent from the range of chapters in this book, a range that spans discussions of psychotherapy with such diverse clientele as older women, women with limited income, and lesbian couples. Part of the maturation process of therapy is an expansion of the integration of traditional psychotherapeutic concepts and practice to meet the criteria set forth for feminist work. In addition, new topics are raised that previously have not been seen as feminist therapy issues, such as spirituality, stepparenting, and conflicts over fees. With feminist theory accepted as a valid application to therapy, issues also arise regarding training of and supervision by feminist therapists.

The topics discussed at the Vail Conference and reported here are all separate entities, but together they form a cohesive reflection of the current state of the art of psychotherapy with women. Missing, however, is a presentation on the application of feminist therapy with minority women. Unfortunately, such a presentation also was absent from the Vail Conference reflecting the ambivalence within the minority women's community toward embracing a feminist philosophy that may not reflect their concerns adequately. It is hoped that subsequent conferences and volumes will make greater efforts to obtain a full exploration of these issues and to present relevant written material.

The ideas expressed in this book represent the expanding scope of feminist thinking. In the beginning, feminist therapists all tried to stay within the politically correct mandate. Now that feminist therapy has been an acceptable process for over 10 years, such limitations no longer are seen as necessary and have been lifted. Arguments abound in this book. Comfortable with policy process and finding it helpful, Butler lists guidelines for feminist therapy and comments on the usefulness and rationale for such guidelines. Jeanette, on the other hand, writes a scathing critique of feminist therapy in which she chides, "[Sister], you are no better than your brother," illustrating her belief that *any* policy is control and therefore oppressive.

The need to make feminist therapy available to a wider spectrum of women is also discussed in this book. Resh addresses the different needs of the woman client over 50, who grew up in one world and now finds herself in another, and discusses how to be both cognizant and tolerant of these differences. Larsen and Cammaert discuss another group of women whose needs differ: women on welfare and lower-income women, who are both intimidated by feminist rhetoric and ambivalent about how much change they wish to create in their lifestyles. Pointing out the need for feminist therapists to move at their client's pace, Larsen and Cammaert discuss the work they have done with poorer women and the insights they've gained from this experience.

REFLECTIONS ON AND RE-EVALUATION OF POWER

"The personal is political" has been an essential element describing the feminist commitment to using individual understanding about oneself as a basis for understanding the oppression of all women. While the concept of feminist therapist as advocate is not new, the specifics and sophistication of such advocacy and how it relates to the more objective process of therapy are delineated clearly in this volume. Walker, in her chapter on feminist forensic psychology, discusses the importance of expert testimony in the courtroom as a way of heightening awareness of sexism in the law and attempting to create new policy resulting in greater justice for women. Rosewater, in a similar vein, argues for the importance of feminist test interpretations, saying that it is the interpretation, not the test, that presents difficulties for feminist therapists. Further, such woman-oriented interpretations of widely used tests can be powerful tools of advocacy. Other writers discuss ways of integrating a political stance while allowing clients the freedom to use therapy to grow at their own pace.

Advocacy issues heighten the recognition that the therapist does have power. An equalitarian relationship between therapist and client then becomes one in which equality is viewed as equal worth rather than equal power. Douglas discusses the inequities of power in a therapy situation and urges that the different combinations of power differentials be explored more fully. Brown, accepting that the therapist has greater power and privilege, suggests an ethical commitment to use such power and privilege in the client's behalf. Rosewater uses similar arguments in her plea for the development of feminist test interpretations. Walker discusses ways to re-empower the woman victim to become a survivor of violence. The importance of re-examining the valuing of female traits also is explored by Smith and Siegel. They argue that part of the process of teaching women how to be more powerful includes helping them value the power they already possess; hence, covert power is seen neither as second class nor as manipulative, but rather sometimes as an effective way to get results.

The direction of therapy with women was re-examined by the 60 clinicians at the Vail Conference. While Weiss makes a plea for the importance of women learning to say no, both Fodor and Stere are critical of the direction assertiveness training has taken. Fodor questions if women really have a deficit in assertiveness skills or if, rather, there are simply female ways of being assertive that differ from male ways. Why, Fodor questions, are the things that women value and for which they take a strong stand (e.g., developing relationships) any less valid than the things men value? Concerned about the pitfalls of assertiveness training as traditionally practiced, Stere offers an alternative model that she considers more feminist in practice.

THE GROWING EDGE OF
PSYCHOTHERAPEUTIC PRACTICE

In order to understand female development better, Lerman believes that we need to develop a feminist theory of personality. In her chapter she discusses some of the barriers to developing such a feminist theory. As she argues, much psychoanalytic thought pervades literature on women and psychotherapy, and several other authors also question some of these traditional psychoanalytic concepts in their chapters. Robbins, from her experience in private practice, questions what traditionally have been labeled "resistance issues" in therapy and discusses the benefits of having clients assume greater personal power, such as by setting their appointments according to their own perceived needs.

Moss is critical of those traditional therapists who avoid all touch; she argues that touch is an important and vital part of therapy. Sharing her concept of feminist body psychotherapy, Moss discusses how feminist therapy can integrate touch into feelings of nonsexual wholeness and intimacy. Seidler-Feller critiques traditional sex therapy as being nonfeminist and exploitative of women clients. She defines the sexist assumptions that underlie the treatment procedures for sex therapy.

Even more critical of the concepts underlying couple/family treatment are Sharratt, Bern, and Burch. Most approaches to couple or family work have not taken into account a sizable segment of the population, lesbian couples and lesbian families. Pointing out the differences in a couple where both partners are women, they discuss the critical importance of understanding the more intense and more diffuse boundaries women have with one another. The points they raise indicate the error of believing that work with lesbian couples presents the same dynamics as those found with heterosexual couples. Further, their criticism that nonlesbian women have been insensitive to these issues is often true. Many of their suggestions can be integrated easily into a feminist conception of family systems theory.

Addressing the issue of our own homophobia is covered in Siegel's chapter. Describing her work with a lesbian women's group Siegel shares her own growth process and offers suggestions for ways that other therapists can confront their prejudices and fears. The whole notion of what relationship is "right" for a woman is discussed by DeHardt, who raises a provocative question: Is helping a woman to stay in a dysfunctional heterosexual relationship consistent with the empowerment ethic of feminist therapy? DeHardt gives a series of questions that a woman client can use to explore the dynamics of her relationship with a male partner. Such questions allow the decision process to reside with the client, while at the same time conveying a feminist conceptual analysis of heterosexual relationships.

NEW FRONTIERS

Many issues discussed in this book are topics not previously found in the feminist literature. For example, Lasky talks about the unique problem fees pose for women therapists. Women tend both to undervalue themselves and to undercharge for their services. Feminist therapists prefer to have some form of adjustable fees in order to provide services for women at all economic levels. Lasky argues for clarity about such policies that addresses confusing values about money. Brown furthers this discussion by raising the issue of business ethics consistent with feminist principles. The relationship between client and therapist is addressed by Saks Berman, who argues that dual relationships are not always avoidable or unhealthy, if handled in a sensitive manner. Citing the special problems of small towns or isolated rural communities, she states that, if the client wants a feminist therapist, overlapping relationships may be unavoidable. She points out that the ethical constraints of the American Psychological Association against dual relationships are not always feasible, so modifications may need to be spelled out, especially for the feminist therapist.

Two different chapters look at new issues concerning women and motherhood. Clamar discusses the role of the stepmother, the bias against her, and the need for feminist mentoring to help the stepmother to adjust to her new role. Hendricks talks about the woman unable to become a mother and the therapeutic issues such women and their partners face.

Although women are reclaiming their spirituality, little has been written about how to combine it with therapy process. Hendricks discusses the inherent contradictions between patriarchal religion and feminist theory and looks at the options for women who are both religious and feminist. In presenting her alternative to the fundamentalist religious dogma, she argues for women not to give up all spirituality.

While violence against women is a very old topic, feminist research on the causes and consequences of such violence and the treatment for survivors of violence is only about a decade old. Rave discusses the impact of pornography and traces its underpinnings to all violence against women. Citing newer research as a contrast, Rave points out the inadequate methodology of the President's Commission on Obscenity and Pornography (1970), which found no link between pornography and criminal behavior. She suggests the objectification of women originates and is reinforced by such misogynist views of sex acts and violence.

The relationship between violent behavior and increased emotional distress is discussed by Rosewater, who presents her research with battered women. Rosewater found a significant correlation between the severity of violence and the clinical scale elevation of the MMPI. The composite MMPI profile for these battered women was similar to a composite MMPI profile for chronic schizophrenic women, leading her to question whether women previously diagnosed as schizophrenic or borderline were not, in fact, battered women.

Walker discusses how to know when therapy is needed and presents clinical techniques for use with victims of men's violence. She points out the unique problems of survivors of sexual, physical, and psychological assault and suggests techniques for the client to use, including establishing and rehearsing an escape plan in case the violence recurs.

TRAINING ISSUES

Given the success of feminist therapy as a treatment philosophy, it becomes necessary to provide training for new therapists. Faunce shares her teaching of feminist therapy, especially the problems of a feminist instructor developing curriculum in a traditional setting. Her analysis of critical scholarly thinking and applications to the feminist therapy classroom are outstanding. Kahn and Theurer discuss how to evaluate the effectiveness of such courses in the counseling of women. They share the method they have used to do such an evaluation, and they cite its limitations and make suggestions for more in-depth study. Porter relates the need for feminist supervision and shares the problems and rewards of being a feminist therapist supervisor in a traditional psychological graduate program.

CONCLUSIONS

The idea for a feminist therapy institute, where like-minded therapists could meet with each other and grow professionally and personally because of the contact, has been in the hearts and minds of groups all over the country. There were several starts and stops over the years, some in Colorado, so it seems fitting that the organizational structure that finally created the First Advanced Feminist Therapy Institute was based in Vail. The first symposium sponsored by the Feminist Therapy Institute, from which the chapters of this book are taken, was planned for several years by a large and changing group of organizers. It was decided that each woman attending would be validated for her own expertise in the field by presenting her work and then dialoguing with others. Although this format prohibited an in-depth study of each area, it did give the opportunity to sample the diverse, rich variety of the activities of self-labeled feminist therapists. The sense of camaraderie and joy experienced by the 60 or so attending, through this process of sharing, was substantial. The chapters selected for this book represent some of the most exciting of the papers presented. The Institute's symposium has since been repeated on a yearly basis, with new papers presented each year. We believe it will continue to be an important part of the Feminist Therapy Institute's training program.

A commitment to helping feminists publish grew out of this first conference. Those with more writing skills and experience volunteered to be section editors, tediously editing every chapter and giving suggestions to the authors. As a result, some exceptional clinicians have finally been able to pass on their work by writing about it here, revealing the uncharted waters while at the same time addressing the important issue of the clinical application of feminist theory.

Lynne Bravo Rosewater
Lenore E. Auerbach Walker

REFERENCES

Brodsky, A. M. & Hare-Mustin, R. (Eds.).(1980). *Women and psychotherapy*. New York: Guilford Press.
Chesler, P. (1972). *Women and madness*. New York: Doubleday.

Franks, V., & Rothblum, E. (Eds.).(1983). *The stereotyping of women: Its effects on mental health*. New York: Springer.

Gilligan, C. (1982). *In a different voice*. Cambridge, MA: Harvard University Press.

Rawlings, E. I., & Carter, D. K. (Eds.).(1977). *Psychotherapy for women: Treatment towards equality*. Springfield, IL: Charles C Thomas.

Sturdivant, S. (1980). *Therapy with women: A feminist philosophy of treatment*. New York: Springer.

Walker, L. E. (Ed.).(1984). *Women and mental health policy*. (*Women and policy series, Vol. 9*.). Beverly Hills, CA.: Sage Publications.

President's Commission on Obscenity and Pornography. (1970). *Report*. Washington, DC: U.S. Government Printing Office.

Principles Concerning the Counseling and Therapy of Women*

PREAMBLE

Competent counseling/therapy processes are the same for all counselor/therapist interactions. Special subgroups require specialized skills, attitudes and knowledge. Women constitute a special subgroup.

Competent counseling/therapy requires recognition and appreciation that contemporary society is not sex fair. Many institutions, test standards and attitudes of mental health professionals limit the options of women clients. Counselor/therapists should sensitize women clients to these real-world limitations, confront them with both the external and their own internalized limitations and explore with them their reactions to these constraints.

* Prepared by the American Psychological Association Division on Counseling Psychology, Committee on Women. These principles were endorsed unanimously by the American Psychological Division 17 (Counseling Psychology) Ad Hoc Committee on Women, the Executive Committee of Division 17 during the August 1978 meeting of APA in Toronto as necessary for responsible professional practice in the counseling and therapy of women. It appeared in *The Counseling Psychologist*, Vol. 8, No. 1, 1979 and is reprinted with Division 17's permission.

The principles presented here are considered essential for the competent counseling/therapy of women.

1. Counselors/therapists are knowledgeable about women, particularly with regard to biological, psychological and social issues which have impact on women in general or on particular groups of women in our society.

2. Counselors/therapists are aware that the assumptions and precepts of theories relevant to their practice may apply differently to men and women. Counselors/therapists are aware of those theories and models that prescribe or limit the potential of women clients, as well as those that may have particular usefulness for women clients.

3. After formal training, counselors/therapists continue to explore and learn of issues related to women, including the special problems of female subgroups, throughout their professional careers.

4. Counselors/therapists recognize and are aware of all forms of oppression and how these interact with sexism.

5. Counselors/therapists are knowledgeable and aware of verbal and nonverbal process variables (particularly with regard to power in the relationship) as these affect women in counseling/therapy so that the counselor/therapist-client interactions are not adversely affected. The need for shared responsibility between clients and counselors/therapists is acknowledged and implemented.

6. Counselors/therapists have the capability of utilizing skills that are particularly facilitative to women in general and to particular subgroups of women.

7. Counselors/therapists ascribe no preconceived limitations on the direction or nature of potential changes in counseling/therapy for women.

8. Counselors/therapists are sensitive to circumstances where it is more desirable for a woman client to be seen by a female or male counselor/therapist.

9. Counselors/therapists use nonsexist language in counseling/therapy, supervision, teaching and journal publications.

10. Counselors/therapists do not engage in sexual activity with their women clients under any circumstances.

11. Counselors/therapists are aware of and continually review their own values and biases and the effects of these on their women clients. Counselors/therapists understand the effects of sex-role socialization upon their own development and functioning and the consequent values and attitudes they hold for themselves and others. They recognize that behaviors and roles need not be sex based.

12. Counselors/therapists are aware of how their personal functioning may influence their effectiveness in counseling/therapy with women clients. They monitor their functioning through consultation, supervision or therapy so that it does not adversely affect their work with women clients.

13. Counselors/therapists support the elimination of sex bias within institutions and individuals.

 **one**

A FEMINIST PHILOSOPHY OF TREATMENT

PATRICIA SPENCER FAUNCE, Editor

> Courage to be is the key to the revelatory power
> of the feminist revolution.   —*Mary Daly*

Feminism is the value system around which new conceptualizations about therapy with women have been developed. Feminist therapy has no "name" leader, but considerable congruency exists among we feminist therapists (Greenspan, 1983; Rawlings & Carter, 1975; Sturdivant, 1980) as to what constitutes this value system. This therapy stresses our philosophical concerns: the significance of therapists' attitudes, values, and beliefs on the therapy process and outcome. Important is the philosophy that determines the attitudes with which techniques are used and theories supported. When we describe ourselves and our work, we speak most often of our visions of what women can be, our beliefs about what therapy for women should be, and our attitudes toward therapy.

The explicit commitment to feminist values as a basis for conceptualizing therapy is what distinguishes feminist therapy from others. Simply to be nonsexist and to attempt modification of existing approaches is inadequate. What is necessary is a critical recognition of sociocultural

1

agents and factors as generating emotional distress in women, and the development of special expertise in working with women's issues and concerns.

So we have translated our feminist belief system, our feminist philosophy of life, into a philosophy of treatment for women (Sturdivant, 1980). This philosophy of treatment provides a necessary bridge between concern about the role of values in psychotherapy and most issues in treatment, on the one hand, and a conceptual framework that portrays how these issues are integrated into the therapeutic process.

A feminist belief system affects all treatment dimensions, including nature of women and mental illness definitions, women's psychological distress etiology, symptom interpretation, therapeutic interventions foci, therapist role, therapist–client relationship, and therapeutic goals. The belief in the sociocultural roots of women's emotional distress commits us to a feminist growth/developmental model of therapy within which both personal and social change are significant therapeutic goals, and political action an integral part of therapy.

Some believe feminists have created a revolution within the psychotherapy profession. Certainly there is now a new philosophy of treatment—one that is connected with the feminist value orientation—for working with women. Within this mental health revolution it is important continually to re-examine and rebuild beliefs and assumptions about the range of possibilities for women, about female psychology and personality, and about the nature of women.

The chapters in this theory section are a part of this ongoing re-examining and rebuilding process. In Chapter 1, Lerman addresses barriers to the conceptualization of a feminist theory of personality. She describes two primary reasons why psychotherapists and psychologists have not developed a feminist theory of personality: (1) the seductive influence of psychoanalysis and psychoanalytic assumptions on the thought processes and (2) our insufficient recovery, to date, from the mental set associated with our second-class status. While urging us to "move forward to our own self-acceptance," Lerman encourages us to explore more vigorously our own feminist framework, values, and assumptions as possible avenues for theoretical advancements. The intriguing idea of extrapolation from the "personal is political" concept to move us toward a more general theory of personality is offered as an appetizer for further creative and courageous reconceptualizing.

Smith and Siegel concern themselves in Chapter 2 with the redefinition of power in both the personal and interpersonal realms. They first review and re-evaluate views of power and status and stress the critical significance of redefining power for women. They then illustrate, in three therapeutic process stages, their belief that feminist therapy, through this redefining process, can facilitate women's learning and risking the use of new power modes.

In Chapter 3, Robbins provides us with a fresh look at women's separation–individuation struggles as seen through the therapy appointment process. One of the consistent patterns that Robbins has observed in her clinical work with women is the client's move to modify the weekly appointment routine, that is, to reduce the appointment frequency established in her therapeutic relationship with the therapist. Through a rethinking process, Robbins comes to see the arrangement restructuring as serving a meaningful purpose, one of unraveling the knotted separation–individuation threads of an earlier piece of female development. The client once again is taking charge of becoming an autonomous person in the context of a caring relationship, and the therapy dyad provides an opportunity to rehearse that process.

Butler, in Chapter 4, offers a discussion of eight guidelines for feminist therapy that are a potential tool for identifying mental health professionals who are feminist therapists in a community and for educating prospective consumers of feminist therapy. Each stated guideline is followed by the author's evaluation, based on her review of feminist therapy philosophy and her 10 years of experience as a feminist therapist.

Finally, in Chapter 5, Jeanette contemplates feminism and its future, especially whether or not feminism can change and expand with and for women. She writes of her life-long journey toward freedom and addresses "truths" about which she believes feminists have been silent; the fear of ourselves and how we avoid, rather than confront our fear; how judgment and love have been used to control us and others; how women have been "shot down" not only by sexism but by other women and feminism; and how the use of only the left brain by some feminists stifles and destroys the creativity, spirit, and courage in us. Jeanette states her belief that "now I need to let go of feminism so that I can move on and embrace more of myself" and she implores us to "Live the truth. That is [our] power."

REFERENCES

Greenspan, M. (1983). *A new approach to women and therapy*. New York: McGraw-Hill.

Rawlings, E. I., & Carter, D. K. (Eds.).(1975). *Psychotherapy for women: treatment toward equality*. Springfield, IL: Charles C Thomas.

Sturdivant, S. (1980). *Therapy with women: a feminist philosophy of treatment*. New York: Springer.

1

Some Barriers to the Development of a Feminist Theory of Personality

HANNAH LERMAN

An overt assessment of psychological theory was not part of the first wave of the twentieth-century Women's Movement. At that time, psychological theories were largely academic and had not yet permeated the public consciousness; the authority and perspective of the entire masculine-based body of scientific knowledge and thought remained relatively unchallenged; and psychoanalysis, which was just appearing on the scene, even seemed to have a potential for positive impact upon women's lives.

Both feminism and psychoanalytic theory arose out of similar roots during the first part of the twentieth century, and both were attempting to deal with similar underlying social dynamics (Firestone, 1971). Both at once were responses to centuries of increasing privatization of family life, the extreme subjugation of women, and the sexual repressions and subsequent neuroses this caused.

Shulamith Firestone (1971) calls Freudianism "the misguided feminism" (p. 41). Freud, she says, had grasped the notion that sexual repression was the most crucial problem of the modern era. Society, however, chose psychoanalysis and used it to contain "the immense social unrest and role confusion that followed in the wake of the first attack on the rigid patriarchial family. It is doubtful that the sexual revolution could have remained paralyzed at the halfway point for half a century without its help; for the problems stirred up by the first wave of feminism are still not resolved today" (p. 70). Firestone further describes the process of how feminism, which had no explicit psychological component at that time, was overpowered socially:

> Freudianism was the perfect foil for feminism, because though it struck the same nerve, it had a safety catch that feminism didn't—it never questioned the given reality. While both of their cores are explosive, Freudianism was gradually revised to suit the pragmatic needs of clinical therapy: it became an applied science complete with white-coated technicians, its contents subverted for a reactionary end—the socialization of men and women to an artificial system. But there was just enough left of its original force to serve as a lure for those seeking their way out of oppression—causing Freudianism to go in the public mind from extreme suspicion and dislike to its current status: psychoanalytic expertise is the final say in everything from marital breakups to criminal court judgments. Thus Freudianism gained the ground that Feminism lost: It flourished at the expense of Feminism, to the extent that it acted as a container of its shattering force. [p. 70]

Along with the influential rise of psychoanalytic theory among professionals, psychoanalysis itself has greatly influenced the society as a whole in very diverse and often hidden ways. Both theory and practice have become major factors in society's rationale for women's oppression (Firestone, 1971).

In contrast, the second wave of twentieth-century feminism evoked the consensus among feminist psychologists that the pervasive effects of psychoanalysis needed to be countered. Feminist therapy, from its start, has created its own alternative to psychoanalytic and other male-model theories, which have contributed to the maintenance of society's hierarchical sex-role orientation. Feminist therapy emphasizes sexism as a reality in our present system and, along with past events, a contributor to women's misery. Feminist values and techniques promote equalitarian rather than hierarchical relationships; respect for the client's expertise about herself, rather than denial or negation; and acceptance of negative feelings as normal, expected responses to oppressive conditions.

The literature reflects this emerging perspective. Sturdivant (1980) describes much of the early ferment between feminism and traditional psychological theory and the evolutionary process of feminist therapy. Gilbert (1980) gives a clear summary of the two significant principles that have emerged within feminist therapy: that the personal is political and that the therapist–client relationship is viewed as being equalitarian. The first principle incorporates the concept that oppression has not just existed but has become part of our view of ourselves, and this principle must be brought to awareness in order for change to occur in ourselves and in our world.

What was not acknowledged during the early period of feminist theory is the impact and hold that psychoanalysis has upon our thought processes in this psychologized society. One may move away fairly easily from the specific content of psychoanalytic theory as it applies to women's lives. Many feminist theorists have done that. One cannot, however, move away as easily from the fundamental, underlying precepts of psychoanalysis, because we may not even recognize how much they permeate our thoughts and assumptions.

Possibly we may not wish to discard ultimately every single one of the underlying psychoanalytic (metapsychological) assumptions we hold. An important process, however, is to examine those assumptions that are present implicitly in our thought and to make them explicit. Often, those many individuals, including feminists, who have not been schooled directly in psychoanalysis do not know or consider that such concepts as "the unconscious" and "psychological determinism" came directly into the mainstream of psychological thought from Freud.

Except for the most extreme behaviorists, probably few would wish to deny that anyone's behavior today may be understood in relationship to the occurrences in that person's yesterdays or that the connection might involve more than a simple learning paradigm. To the extent that we maintain these views, we are holding to psychoanalytic concepts at a metapsychological level. The same is true if we believe that any one of us does not necessarily know, herself, the full motivation for any particular bit of her behavior. The difficulty exists not in this, but when we try to explain specifics in a given case.

Compared to psychoanalytic theory, which in retrospect seems to enter easily into the explanation of human behavior, other available theoretical frameworks provide merely partial interpretations and often fall short of providing full understanding. Whenever, within some other given perspective, explanation can go no further, psychoanalytic theory then beckons seductively with its purported deeper and fuller interpretation. Such seduction is, indeed, one important reason for its popularity. Having been seduced, one may then believe that she has reached further within her own system when, instead, she has reached into unacknowledged prior assumptions that have their base in psychoanalytic concepts.

Despite the active feminist ferment in concept and technique, feminist psychotherapists and psychologists have stopped short of the full development of a feminist theory of personality. Our lack of progression comes, in part, from our lack of recognition about how much psychoanalytic theory continues to color our thinking. Nonrecognition of this thought corruption cannot be indicted as the only reason for our lack of progress in the development of a feminist theory of personality. Jean Baker Miller (1976) points out that

> It is only because women themselves have begun to change their situation that we can now perceive new ways of understanding women. It is only because many women have, once more in our time, said, "We refuse to be second class," that we begin to see all of the meanings that second class status has contained—not only for women themselves, but for the entire structuring of the human mind and for our attempts to understand how that structure comes about. [p. 135]

Just as individuals brought up in a two-dimensional spatial world cannot imagine or comprehend three-dimensional space, we probably have not yet recovered sufficiently from the mental set associated with second-class status to develop, as Rae Carlson (1972) challenged, "a genuinely adequate theory of personality [that] could provide a comprehensive view of total human functioning" (p. 29). Along the way, we need to recognize, that

> theoretical orientations in personality-psychoanalytic theory, social learning theory, role theory, cognitive-developmental theory, third force humanistic psychology—despite major controversies concerning the kinds of constructs and observations deemed relevant—are united in presenting a general, universalistic (and largely masculine) account of personality. Thus

the problem of accounting for feminine deviations from universal principles has been almost equally embarrassing to (and ignored by) all major
theorists. [Carlson, 1972, p. 29]

We must not ignore, however, that, at least in part, we have developed a theory. How a problem is defined determines how and where
one looks for a solution (Rawlings & Carter, 1977). We have started with
a redefinition of the problem and, out of that, have evolved new techniques and attitudes with which to approach women clients. We have
not stated a theory separately from our practice. Theory is embedded in
our practice, and, at this moment, theory remains incomplete. Most of
us who have been involved in the feminist approach to psychological
theorizing know that the path has not been easy. The blindness and
unconcern of the majority of theorists remain. The larger psychological
community still questions and challenges us about our basic assumption—that we suffer emotionally in any degree from second-class citizenship and that assumptions about female second-class nature are built
into the very fabric of the major psychological theories. We who wish to
promote our own theoretical autonomy find it difficult to keep ourselves
centered and focused in the midst of such onslaughts. The constant
battle also drains off energy that otherwise could go toward theoretical
development.

Thus, psychoanalytic theory and practice continue to hold a high
status position, even among the disenfranchised (Lerman, 1981). Our
continuing wish to be acceptable and mainstream is apparently what
brings someone like Nancy Chodorow, an avowed feminist, to accept
psychoanalytic theory uncritically (Chodorow, 1978) and to fail to recognize, as Rubin (1975) has pointed out, the need to differentiate between
the use of psychoanalytic theory to provide a description of female oppression and the use of the theory to rationalize such oppression.

Despite her sociological background, Chodorow has retained psychoanalysis' key stance that the psychological is not informed by any
sphere other than its own. Chodorow is stuck with the premise that
personal development never encompasses more than the family and
that actions of the parenting figures are never influenced by the envi-
rons, either social or physical, in their interactions with the child.
Despite lip service to the role of society, nothing in Chodorow's theory
tells us how different cultures produce adults with differing personality
configurations. Most importantly, she does not deal with the highly

biased presentation of supposed psychoanalytic "evidence" that confuses data with interpretation. Fisher and Greenberg (1977), who are relatively sympathetic to psychoanalysis, conclude in their review of psychological research that "one is almost forced to conclude that Freud's Oedipal theories, as they apply to women, remain either largely untested or already contradicted in certain significant respects" (p. 409).

Yet Chodorow uses uncritically the presumptive data and does not deal with the research external to the analytic situation, research that bears upon the psychoanalytic view of women. Instead, she reiterates and reinterprets the very same concepts that many feminist psychologists have discarded because they perpetuate women's oppression.

The most important feminist theorist who accepted psychoanalysis before Chodorow was Juliet Mitchell (1974), who maintained that Freud's theory described, but did not advocate, the patriarchy that existed at his time. She, however, has not acquired the following that Chodorow has, and on that basis has less significance for discussion of our theoretical development. Chodorow's acceptance of psychoanalytic theory and her re-introduction of it into the realm of theorizing about women has enabled other women to re-accept it and even to re-embrace its therapeutic principles, perhaps with a renewed hope of being able to have higher status endowed upon them. Feminist therapists have begun to enter psychoanalytic institutes. The institutes' hierarchical structures, along with their emotional isolation and lack of support for feminism, cannot help but take a toll on those feminist therapists within their walls. Equally critical is the effect on their ability to remain centered and focused on the need to continually examine all theoretical formulations for the degree to which women are considered psychologically equal (or unequal) to men.

When one considers all extant theories, women's second-class and inferior status is embedded most clearly in the very fiber of psychoanalytic theory. It is extremely difficult to imagine psychoanalysis as emerging with an acceptable view of the place of women, despite the present patching and revising going on within psychoanalysis itself as a response to the criticism and theorizing of the past 10 years (e.g., see Eissler, 1977; Schafer, 1974).

One possible avenue for feminist theoretical advancement is implicit within our present feminist framework(s). If we would wish to move toward a more general theory of personality that could encompass more than our present theory, could we not extrapolate further from the concept that the personal is political? We do believe that women's ills in our world are related to their internalized oppression, to "the enemy outposts in our heads" (Kempton, 1973). By implication, men's sex-role socialization contributes to their internalized oppression. Could we not investigate just how broadly the personal-is-political concept is applied? In my view, a strong possibility exists that, whatever the cultural set-up, emotional ills might arise most easily in the conflict between what a society says that a woman (or a man) ought to be and what is actually the potential of that particular person.

Other general concepts also could emerge if we explored more closely and vigorously our own values and assumptions, rather than attempting to reinterpret and reintegrate other theories, particularly psychoanalysis. As feminist therapists we must avoid concepts that, at base, remain alien to ourselves.

Jean Baker Miller (1976) reminds us that we must "refuse to be second class" (p. 135). Refusal of second-class citizenship must continue to influence our theorizing. Since the probability is high that no personality theory ever will be susceptible totally to verification in strictly scientific terms, the purpose of any theory has to be in its relevance and its usefulness. No point at all exists in falling back on any theory whose very bases presume the inherent inferiority of female human beings. We must move forward toward our own self-acceptance.

REFERENCES

Carlson, R. (1972). Understanding women: Implications for personality theory and research. *Journal of Social Issues, 28,* 17–32.

Chodorow, N. (1978). *The reproduction of mothering: Psychoanalysis and the sociology of gender.* Berkeley, CA: University of California Press.

Eissler, K. R. (1977). Comments on penis envy and orgasm in women. *The Psychoanalytic Study of the Child, 32,* 29–82.

Firestone, S. (1971). *The dialectic of sex: The case for feminist revolution.* New York: Bantam Books.

Fisher, S. & Greenberg, R. P. (1977). *The scientific credibility of Freud's theories and therapy.* New York: Basic Books.

Gilbert, L. (1980). Feminist therapy. In A. M. Brodsky, & R. Hare-Mustin (Eds.), *Women and psychotherapy: An assessment of research and practice.* New York: Guilford Press.

Kempton, S. (1973). Cutting loose: A private view of the women's uprising. *Esquire, 80,* 251–254.

Lerman, H. (1981, December). Psychological theories that look at women's lives: How far have we come since Freud? Paper presented at the First International Interdisciplinary Conference on Sex Roles, Haifa, Israel.

Miller, J. B. (1976). *Toward a new psychology of women.* Boston: Beacon Press.

Mitchell, J. (1974). *Psychoanalysis and feminism: Freud, Reich, Laing and women.* New York: Random House.

Rawlings, E., & Carter, D. (Eds.). (1977). *Psychotherapy for women: Treatment toward equality.* Springfield, IL: Charles C. Thomas.

Rubin, G. (1975). The traffic in women: Notes on the "political economy of sex." In Rayna R. Reiter (Ed.), *Toward an anthropology of women.* New York: Monthly Review Press.

Schafer, R. (1974). Problems in Freud's psychology of women. *Journal of the American Psychoanalytic Association, 22,* 459–485.

Sturdivant, S. (1980). *Therapy with women: A feminist philosophy of treatment.* New York: Springer.

2

Feminist Therapy: Redefining Power for the Powerless

ADRIENNE J. SMITH AND RUTH F. SIEGEL

Empowerment is usually understood as the process of helping a powerless individual or group to gain the necessary skills, knowledge, or influence to acquire control over their own lives and begin to influence the lives of others. As feminist therapists with nearly 10 years of practice, we have become aware of another form of empowerment for women, namely, helping women to gain awareness of power they *already* have but have not recognized as such.

The term "power" is used here to include both personal and interpersonal power. Interpersonal power is the ability to influence others who have access to essential resources, with the aim of convincing them to provide one with those resources. (For more detailed definitions, see Kipnis, 1976.) Personal power, or the ability to determine one's own life, is similar to Roberts' definition of freedom as "the right . . . to conceive of time and space as belonging to the self and to experience a sense of being able to control and direct one's own movement through the short span of human life" (1976, p. 15).

Because women[1] have been denied direct access to formal power—
access to essential resources and authority, including political, financial,
and familial authority—we usually have been described as a group *lacking
in power* (Johnson, 1976). In fact, powerless groups do exercise interpersonal power, but in forms different from that of the dominant group.
Specifically, the power exercised by women tends to be covert, indirect,
"ladylike." When women are encouraged to recognize these tactics as a
form of power—one that is determined by our lack of formal power—we
can become more aware of our own strengths and move to use and acknowledge overt interpersonal power tactics. Overt tactics, in turn, will
render us more personally powerful and more in control of our lives.

Viewing oneself as powerless leads to feelings of impotence, rage,
and depression. As feminist therapists we are in a position to empower
the woman, that is, to enable her to reclaim her own power by renaming
certain aspects of her behavior, especially that called manipulative or
crazy, as attempts to achieve the goals of control and influence under
given societal constraints. In our process of validating her perceptions,
sharing our own experiences, and introducing her to feminist writings,
we facilitate reduction in our client's feelings of difference and inadequacy and introduce her to her own strengths.

STATUS AND POWER

Increasing evidence indicates that the differences between women and
men in their expression of power are due to status rather than sex. According to Frieze, Parsons, Johnson, Ruble, and Zellman (1978, p. 304)
status is "a hierarchy of inferiority and superiority on some dimension or
set of dimensions." Because "male in itself means higher status" (p. 305),
the two variables of gender and status are almost completely confounded.
Unger (1979), in an extensive review of the literature on status, gender,
and power, shows that "male–female relationships are essentially similar
to relationships between high and low status individuals and thus status is
a more parsimonious explanation than gender" (p. 6).

Women "get what they want" through indirect, covert influencing
techniques, often using the assigned sex-role-appropriate behaviors of

---

1. Although we have worked with several women of color, the observations and hypotheses discussed in this paper are based on our experiences with the majority of our
   clients who are white, middle-class, American-born women. We cannot assume that the
   principles of underground power are similar across race and class lines.

helplessness, dependency, coyness, and appeal to emotions. Under the oppressive constraints of patriarchy, women, who are low-status people, use second-class power tactics that usually are not acknowledged as power (McClelland, 1975). Even when women achieve their objectives, therefore, both sexes continue to see a woman as powerless. The frequent attribution of women's successes to luck and men's successes to skill is evidence that neither sex believes women have sufficient abilities to control their own lives.

The indirect forms of interpersonal power—what we call "underground power"—are used to resist or refuse when overt refusal would invite retaliation. Retaliation can range from physical violence to financial deprivation, shaming, and/or capitalizing on the woman's own internalized belief that she is bad, unnatural, an unloving mother, or a "castrating bitch."

Envision the woman whose husband wants her to have sex before going to a party. She knows an outright no will bring punishment, perhaps in the form of moodiness or anger or some other behavior that, at best, will ruin her evening and, at worst, will cause her physical harm. Rather than refuse, she acts with cunning: "Gee, honey, I'd love to but wouldn't you rather have me fresh for your boss (client, friends) tonight? You know I want to make you proud of me. It's never too late when we get home." These tactics enable her to influence his behavior in such a way that he believes she is interested in his welfare. He remains powerful and she remains safe.

The woman who finds herself in this situation may be aware that she gets results, but, more than likely, she attributes this to "feminine wiles," not to power. Relying on tactics that emphasize her dependence and subservience to her husband reinforces her lack of self-esteem. Further, since all definitions in a culture dominated by men are filtered through what Roberts (1976) calls "the masculist screen," women accept men's definition of them as "inferior" and "other." "To coexist as unequals within circumstances of the greatest intimacy women must come to believe the physical, economic, and political inequities are just and justifiable. . . . Intellectual life, as institutionally organized, must transmit patterns of inequality so that people will believe that the subordinate position of women is only 'natural,' that their shrunken time and space are not only proper but even protective" (Roberts, 1976, p. 16). With this imprinting we, as women, feel guilty, evil, and unnatural if we dare question our assigned roles.

At some level of consciousness every woman is aware of the

discrepancy between her perceptions of the world and the masculist world view; but without validation from other women we are unable to risk defining ourselves. Unvalidated, our perceptions lead to feelings of despair, madness, and occasionally suicide—as has been documented by Chesler (1971) and fictionalized by Gilman (1973) and Chopin (1971).

A focus of feminist therapy is to empower women to become self-defining. As the therapist gives positive acknowledgment of women's needs, needs not approved of by the dominant male culture, women's self-esteem rises and they begin to explore the risks involved in using power more directly. Becoming aware of their "womanpower," in other words, can lead to more-overt behavior that gives them more real power, both interpersonal and personal, and greater ability to direct the course of their own lives.

Awareness of the conflict between our needs and that which we have been taught is appropriate behavior often brings women to therapy. Traditional therapy has attempted to reduce this conflict by "adjusting" women to their correct roles. Women's reality is invalidated and the power differential between women and men is reinforced in both the traditional therapeutic process and in our daily lives (Schaef, 1981). Since subordination to what is dominant is seen as woman's proper place, her distress is reduced by "helping her accept" and enjoy her subordinate position. The notion of dominance over her is usually transmitted and modeled by a male therapist who possesses automatically attributed higher status due to his being male and an "expert," and who may well be biased against activity in women (Bowman, 1982).

The source of conflict, rather than being acknowledged as existing between the woman and societal demands, is referred back to the woman herself. "Blaming the victim" leads to further internalization of what is, in actuality, an external conflict.

Feminist therapy deals with the woman's side of the conflict: acceptance of the woman's needs and perceptions as appropriate for her, given her situation. Society's attempts to fit her into an impossibly narrow role lead to symptom formation. The symptoms themselves may represent her best possible attempt to survive under the circumstances. The therapist, not only by supporting the woman's perceptions, but also by helping her see the forms of power she has been exercising in her "powerless" state, can better assist the woman's process of self-discovery and growth.

REDEFINING POWER

Redefining power for women in therapy is similar to the use of communication theory and positive connotation described by Palazzoli, Cecchin, Prata, and Boscolo (1978). Working with schizophrenic family systems, the authors redefine individual symptoms as maneuvers designed to maintain systemic equilibrium. Defining "sickness" in terms of moves in the family game allows the therapist to acknowledge the purpose and meaning of seemingly meaningless behavior. "Craziness" is placed within its context as consisting of moves within a power structure and is revealed to be the best possible solution to the problem as perceived by the family and the individual. By pointing out the goal-directedness of the behavior, the therapists allow the clients to choose other means of reaching those or other goals.

Similarly, feminist therapy places the woman's behavior in context and positively connotes it as the only possible response to the alternatives as seen by the client. The context is the sexist society, as it affects and filters through the couple or family structure in which the woman is living. Her goal—the goal of all human beings—is to exercise as much personal power and mastery over her life as possible. The woman, however, must do this within a system that denies her overt power. The obvious solution to this double bind is to exercise power while denying it; to reach toward a goal while pretending, to oneself and others, not to want it; to act upon others without knowledge that one's actions have any effect; and, in general, to be manipulative, sneaky, underhanded, and devious.

In the so-called "doctor–nurse game" (Stein, 1971), the woman is usually conscious of the maneuvers by which the nurse offers advice and suggestions to the doctor so that she (the nurse) leads him (the doctor) to believe the information originates with him. On the other hand, when these maneuvers are unconscious, the woman and everyone in her environment define her as bad and crazy. The "dilemma for women," as the 1970 study by Broverman, Broverman, Clarkson and Rosenkrantz concludes, is "the conflict between having to decide whether to exhibit positive traits considered desirable for men and adults and have femininity questioned, or to behave in the prescribed feminine manner and accept second-class adult status" (p. 6). Each of the choices in a woman's life demands that she either adhere to a too-rigid role or rebel against it, and, as Chesler (1971) points out, in either direction lies madness.

Redefining power for women means affirming the power inherent in either choice: the invisible, "feminine" power or the assertive, visible "masculine" power. The function of feminist therapy is to help the woman see that what was wrong in either case was the constraints of the stereotyped role, not her response. The more she is able to perceive herself as exercising some form of power, the more she will be able to expand that power and claim new forms, that is, become empowered in more effective and satisfying ways that broaden her choices and therefore her ability to define herself.

PROCESS OF FEMINIST THERAPY[2]

Feminist therapy can be divided into three stages. The first stage enables the woman to recognize the social etiology of her so-called pathology, that is, to understand that the personal is political. The second stage introduces the woman to her own strengths by redefining her use of power and modeling an equalitarian relationship with the therapist. The third and final stage supports the woman as she experiments with new, more effective behaviors in her personal and work environments.

During the first stage of therapy, feminism identifies those sociopolitical or interpersonal forces that may impact differentially on women and men. Thus, we validate the woman's experience of rage as she becomes aware of her training for second-class status throughout childhood. She recognizes the pain of being treated as more fragile and less capable than boys; of seeing Mother continually catering to Father's greater power; of having her dreams and ambitions discounted while boys' are encouraged—in short, of learning what is a "woman's place."

Such discriminatory treatment continues throughout a woman's life, in all areas from public media through private jokes and subtle put-downs at home and work. By a continual interweaving of childhood memories and current circumstances, therapy facilitates the validation of past behavior and feelings and enables the woman to distinguish between behavior that was essential to her state as a powerless child and behavior that is appropriate to her current adult status.

As American society is currently structured, women often have to choose between family or career, between a "feminine" or a "masculine" identity. Because achievements are identified with masculinity, men do

2. For a more detailed explanation of the process of feminist therapy, see Gilbert (1980), Greenspan (1983), and Sturdivant (1980).

not experience conflict as women do, when they achieve. Feeling like an imposter (Clance & Imes, 1978) or ascribing one's accomplishments to "luck" rather than "skill" are techniques by which many women resolve their conflict between feminine and masculine identities and at the same time protect themselves against expected punishment or ostracism. Because feminist therapists, as women, also have experienced these feelings, we are able to share our awareness of the social pressures and internalized fears that prevent us from acknowledging our achievements. By affirming the social context of her feelings, we enable the woman to recognize her fears of leaving the familiar world of dependent females to risk the judgments of the establishment, both female and male, as she enters the world of achievement.

The second stage of therapy is focused on those aspects of female development that become distorted through over- or under-emphasis: power, dependency, and responsibility. Client and therapist work together to determine the underlying purposes of the client's behavior and to redefine it. The woman learns, during therapy, to recognize the conflict between autonomy and dependency as it was evidenced in her particular family dynamics, and in general, as she grew up. By redefining her childhood behavior as the best possible solution within her perceived environment, the client's guilt is reduced and her perception of herself begins to shift from victim to survivor. Through an understanding of the purposes of both past and present behavior, the client recognizes the choices she had as a child and the different choices she now has as an adult. As her awareness of the societal impact on her growth increases, she expresses long-repressed hurt and rage, further enhancing her feelings of strength. In addition to encouraging the woman to define her own behavior rather than accept society's definitions, the therapeutic relationship itself serves as a model of greater equality. By sharing our personal experiences of women's oppression; our struggles to overcome internalized fears, doubts, and anger; and our growth to our present consciousness, the client begins to realize the lack of distinction between "sick" client and "healthy" therapist as the client learns more effective coping mechanisms.

The therapist also demystifies the therapeutic process. Rather than labeling her behavior, we encourage the client to search with us for the underlying purposes of her actions. We reduce the discrepancy between the therapist's skills and the client's skills and therefore reduce the client's dependency on the therapist and encourage her to take greater control over her own life. The feminist therapist helps to contradict the life-long encouragement of female dependency by consistently sharing her power and control through empowering the client.

During the third and last stage of therapy, the woman synthesizes what she has learned and begins to practice new behavior. As her fear of deviating from the rigidly polarized stereotypes lessens, she is increasingly able to recognize the legitimacy of her needs and to establish her personal balance. Shifts from her previously polarized position of either over- or under-dependency lead to shifts in the equilibrium she had established in her relationships. Therapy focuses on the risks and responsibilities of change at this point. While we stress the social and cultural etiology of the individual's personal pathology, we also emphasize her responsibility for choice and change. Clients are encouraged to determine their own lives within the limits of reality.

In summary, feminist therapy, as we practice it, is based on our belief that American women share many of the characteristics of an oppressed people; thus, we must become aware of our own power in order to initiate and participate in our own liberation.

CONCLUSION

As Johnson states, "Women have less access, in reality and in expectations, to concrete resources and competence, leaving them with indirect, personal and helpless modes of influence" (1976, p. 99). Such styles of power leave women feeling weak and guilty; weak because they do not see themselves as having or using power, and guilty because the tactics they use are labeled manipulative and bad. Indeed, women need wide access to more overt forms of power (Johnson, 1976). Recently, emphasis has been placed on teaching women how to use overt power. Books, assertiveness training, mentorship, and women's networks for support and information exchange are some of the teaching techniques used. Before women can learn to use overt power modes effectively, however, we must recognize that we have been exercising power covertly in conformity with societal demands. Feminist therapy, by redefining power, can aid women in learning new power modes and risking their use.

REFERENCES

Bowman, P. R. (1982). An analog study with beginning therapists suggesting bias against "activity" in women. *Psychotherapy: Theory, research and practice, 19*, 318–324.

Broverman, I. K., Broverman, D. M., Clarkson, F. E., Rosenkrantz, P., & Vogel, S. R. (1970). Sex-role stereotypes and clinical judgements of mental health. *Journal of Consulting and Clinical Psychology, 34*, 1–7.

Chesler, P. (1971). *Women and madness*. New York: Avon Books.

Chopin, K. (1971). *The awakening*. New York: Avon Books. (Original published in 1899).

Clance, P. R., & Imes, S. A. (1978). The imposter phenomenon in high-achieving women: Dynamics and therapeutic intervention. *Psychotherapy: Theory, Research and Practice, 15*, 241–247.

Frieze, I. H., Parsons, J. E., Johnson, P. B., Ruble, D. N., & Zellman, G. L. (1978). *Women and sex roles*. New York: W. W. Norton.

Gilbert, L. A. (1980). Feminist therapy. In A. M. Brodsky and R. T. Hare-Mustin (Eds.), *Women and psychotherapy*. New York: Guilford.

Gilman, C. P. (1973). *The yellow wallpaper*. Old Westbury, NY: The Feminist Press. (Original published in Boston, Small, Maynard, 1899).

Greenspan, M. (1983). *A new approach to women and therapy*. New York: McGraw-Hill.

Johnson, P. (1976). Women and power: Toward a theory of effectiveness. *Journal of Social Issues, 32*, 99–109.

Kipnis, D. (1976). *The powerholders*. Chicago, IL: University of Chicago Press.

McClelland, D.C. (1975). *Power: The inner experience*. New York: Irvington.

Palazzozi, M. S., Cecchin, G., Prata, G., & Boscolo, L. (1978). *Paradox and counterparadox*. New York: Jason Aronson.

Roberts, J. I. (1976). Pictures of power and powerlessness: A personal synthesis. In J. I. Roberts (Ed.), *Beyond intellectual sexism: A new woman, a new reality*. New York: David McKay.

Schaef, A. W. (1981). *Woman's reality*. Minneapolis, MN: Winston Press.

Stein, L. I. (1971). Male and female: The doctor–nurse game. In J. P. Spradley & D. W. McCurdy (Eds.), *Conformity and conflict: Readings in cultural anthropology*. Boston: Little, Brown.

Sturdivant, S. (1980). *Therapy with women: A feminist philosophy of treatment*. New York: Springer.

Unger, R. (1979). Status, power and gender: An examination of parallelisms. In J. Sherman & F. Denmark (Eds.), *New directions in research on women*. New York: Psychological Dimensions.

3

The Appointment Hassle: Clues about Women's Themes of Separation-Individuation

JOAN HAMERMAN ROBBINS

> No one ever told us we had to study our lives,
> . . . that we should begin
> with the simplest exercises first
> and slowly go on trying
> the hard ones, practicing till strength
> and accuracy became one with the daring
> to leap into transcendence, take the chance
> of breaking down in the wild arpeggio
> or faulting the full sentence of the fugue.
> —*Adrienne Rich* (1978, p. 73)

A FEMINIST PERSPECTIVE

The substance of feminist therapy—the complex unfolding of a woman's story woven back and forth through present and past experiences, set in the context of a patriarchal culture—provides us with a richness and depth of female life previously neglected. A female therapist listening to a woman's story with care shares with her client an awareness of the cultural and psychological constraints that *both* women have experienced growing up female in a male-defined and structured society.

Out of the stories of women's lives come the tools to build a model of feminist therapy. We must develop the issues that emerge and create our own explanation for our lives.

My feminist therapy model is based on the powerful effects of cultural oppression on women's lives; the myriad and subtle ways in which female character is profoundly shaped by the stereotyped expectations of women and men in our society. Room is made here for the impact of early experiences that inform a female child's character within the context of the social, economic, and political realities into which she is born.

Some aspects of personality development growing out of object relations theory (Horner, 1979; Masterson, 1981) may have relevance in a feminist therapy perspective. The feminist clinician, however, must remain constantly cognizant of important limitations inherent in these and other traditional formulations, since they are based on a male model of development that does not take into account the conditions that are unique and special to female development, and since they view the mother as an instrument for the gratification of the infant's needs and the organizer of all her early experiences. Rarely is the mother seen as a person with her own life needs, rights, and ambitions. Minimal attention is paid to the father and his influence on the child. I am influenced further by the writings of other feminists who address the issues of women's oppression and by the strength we find together for creating new options for ourselves (Caplan, 1981; Flax, 1978; Miller, 1976; Rich, 1976).

THE APPOINTMENT-MODIFICATION THEME

My clinical work with women affords me the special opportunity to observe and identify themes and patterns that consistently appear in the therapy process. One pattern that began to intrigue me was a client's move to modify the weekly appointment routine long after the establishment of the therapeutic relationship. At the time a desire for modification is expressed, she and I are at work on an important issue; we appear to be on the edge of new understanding and resolution. We both are clear that therapy is not over. Nevertheless, she wishes to reduce the frequency of appointments.

This pattern's repetition with a single client, as well as with many clients seen over the course of years, provoked my attention. The themes and issues that emerged did not fit with traditional explanations of appointment hassles, which generally had been interpreted as client resistance to therapy. As I worked with this phenomena I became aware that my client was not resisting therapy but, rather, was restructuring the arrangements between us to serve a deeper purpose. We were engaged in reworking an earlier piece of female development. She was taking charge of rehearsing the becoming of an autonomous person in the context of a caring relationship—a piece of her development short-circuited in childhood.

THE FEMALE DILEMMA OF BECOMING A PERSON

According to Mahler, Pine, and Bergman (1975), children seem to experience a period in toddler development called the rapprochement phase when, from approximately 15 to 21 months, the toddler experiments with separateness from the mother by practicing being close and not close to her. These separateness experiments are beginning experiences with themes of "me" and "not me," and do I still exist if Mother is not present? Since how the toddler integrates these experiences can influence the concept of self as a separate person as she works out future developmental tasks, we must place them in the cultural context in which a young female grows. A girl is encouraged to remain in relationship with the mother as she matures; boys are encouraged to move away and shift to a relationship with the father and the larger nonfamily world. Acknowledging the impact of male values on psychological theory, we can understand why traditional theory places a high value on separating from the mother as one key to individuation and independence.

Girls develop in the same culture as boys but receive different messages; nevertheless, according to traditional theory, we are expected to accomplish the same tasks they do. Some of the culture's messages to little girls are to be quiet, compliant, and "ladylike" and not to be assertive, aggressive, self-initiating, smart, or quick. Helpless and dependent behaviors are encouraged and rewarded, reinforcing our dependency on

Mother for a sense of self and safety, and on Daddy (men) to help us maneuver through life. While very young, a girl learns to imitate her mother in her caretaking role, quickly learning that nurturing others is more highly rewarded than speaking up for one's own needs. Clearly these dictates stifle a girl's sense of a self that is separate, autonomous, differentiated, and able to survive in the world. In addition to this social reality is the fact that female children are frequently molested and raped (Butler, 1978), which provides further reinforcement for her believing that it is dangerous to be autonomous out there in the world.

We also are taught that we must relinquish our "claim" to Mother, who presumably has met all our needs, and shift our affectionate and erotic feelings to Father, that is, males. Erotic feelings for Mother, along with our age-appropriate feelings of dependency, vulnerability, and the need for female nurturance can become deeply buried. At no point are we presented with an opportunity to work through this loss of Mother. The female child begins to distance from these powerful unresolved feelings *and* from Mother, who becomes the symbol of this primitive chaos. Thus, two major developmental tasks appear to become intertwined: the shift to Father begins to mean separation and autonomy, and Mother must be left behind in order to grow up. Father now appears on the scene with vigor and becomes identified with the surge toward movement, cognition, growth, the urge to discover and explore the world—to become a person. The pulls are out of balance. Centuries of oppression have taken their toll. How can a devalued mother, exhausted by the daily responsibilities and demands of child care and homemaking, compete with the father's role in the family? He does not stay home, he does not participate in the daily care of the female child, but he does offer her access to a world beyond the home.

The little girl senses the power imbalance: Mother has less power than Father; to bond with Mother would be to acknowledge their sameness and her own lack of power. The daughter views identifying with Father's goals and expectations as a way to escape "becoming like Mother." Thus, she will follow Father's invitation to enter the world of adequacy, autonomy, independence. Clearly, she follows Father at the expense of resolving her issues with Mother and identifying with her as a female. No matter how hard the daughter tries to model herself after the father, neither of them can really ignore that important difference— she is female.

The presumption that a heterosexual choice will be made in early femalehood further encourages the daughter's turning to her father to meet her needs for affection. Additionally, the deep-seated homophobia in our culture helps to short-circuit mother–daughter bonding (Caplan, 1981), thereby reinforcing female dependence on males for affection and modeling for autonomous behavior.

But some fathers have limitations that interfere with their ability to give to their daughters. Patriarchy trains males to expect females to attend to male emotional needs. Because of this training, the father expects to be taken care of; he is unaware of the need to reverse the roles and of his daughter's need to be nurtured. The father, instead, uses the daughter to meet his own needs for affection and adulation. Therefore, the father is not a nurturing, caring parent who supports his daughter's individuation and helps her to fashion a more adequate sense of self.

Primitive and overwhelming feelings are buried in working out these developmental dilemmas. Themes of separation and individuation, a core experience for all of us, are played out over and over in our development.

These themes may be played out differently in those families of today where there may exist an experience of equality between partners and a growing appreciation for a woman's right to a life of her own. Nevertheless, our female clients may still carry childhood conflicts that reflect the oppressed, devalued status of women and the paucity of strong, positive female role models.

THE CLINICAL EXPERIENCE

The Clients

The women clients I describe grew up in the traditional Caucasian middle-class family of 35 years ago. The daughters perceived their mothers as quite different from their fathers. Fathers were hard working and successful, providing adequately for their families. When at home, fathers were affectionately present for their little girls. The mothers were wives/mothers/homemakers; most had three children within five years of marriage. They were depressed and unhappy; tired and lacking zest for their lives; cold, needy, and withholding.

In general, the daughters, now adult clients, come from families composed of female children; frequently they are the youngest of two girls. In their adult lives they are college educated, often successful professionals, but sometimes in a job that does not express their true creative potentials. Some are married or in long-term relationships with women or men; fewer have children.

Making the Connections

Let us return now to the pattern that originally caught my attention: The therapy relationship has been well established, a piece of important work is close to new understanding, and the client expresses the wish to come to therapy less often. Sometimes the request coincides with my vacation or hers, the summer, money problems, or an increase in pressures at work, school, or home.

A basic tenet of feminist therapy is that the client is in charge and knows what is best for herself. For too long we have allowed others, namely men, to define our experiences and our feelings. We must define ourselves. I respect the client's right to determine the course of her therapy. Nevertheless, at times I experienced anxiety and confusion when my client expressed her desire to alter the regular pattern of appointments. I felt concern when my "clinical" judgment did not match her "personal" judgment.

If feminist therapists are going to be sensitive to what is different in women's experiences, we need to acknowledge that our client is trying to teach us something. This awareness has increased my respect for the client's ability to know herself and has deepened my trust in the therapy process, the crucible wherein we search together for enlarged understanding.

I have come to believe that the client has been exploring new territory when she expresses the wish to attend therapy less often. As a woman becomes more adequate, competent, and autonomous, she will begin to differentiate and feel more integrated. These feelings promote the desire to practice this new awareness in the world beyond the therapy room. The client also is aware that we are involved in a meaningful connection that supports her struggles to grow and define herself; she wants to remain connected to this supportive experience. Rapprochement is being practiced in a new context: Am I okay while in your view? Am I okay out of your view?

For many women, this practicing phase of individuation within a close female relationship was interrupted in childhood as the daughter turned away from the mother and toward the father as the solution to her struggle to differentiate, become autonomous, and separate from the mother. The daughter's early mistrust of female closeness, too, is an issue. Originally, in girlhood, she may have assumed that the only way to become her own person was through distancing and detaching affection from her mother. She felt as if she could not have both: her sense of a separate self *and* her mother. In the therapy dyad we have an opportunity to extend and expand the practicing period, to accept fuller expression of the themes of closeness in a caring relationship, differentiation of self from the other person, and individuation on the way to becoming one's own person.

The Case of Julie

I first met Julie 10 years ago when she joined a mothers' group I was leading. Years later she became, briefly, a client for individual therapy. In 1980, Julie separated from her husband and became engaged in a prolonged, hostile battle with him over child custody and money. These events led her back into therapy. In our work together Julie has stated repeatedly that she is afraid to feel her feelings. "Expressing feelings is like a slide board: you gotta go down, no brakes, no holding, no help."

We had worked together for 12 months when I took a vacation that would overlap with Julie's vacation. When we resumed meeting, Julie announced that she wanted to stop therapy, saying, "I need all my energy to maneuver through the next several months." Julie was conducting her life well, and I supported her decision while also suggesting she come in once a month for a few months so we could keep our connection alive; Julie readily agreed. A month later she missed our first appointment; she totally forgot it.

When Julie finally came back, we both were clear that she was not managing well; she was blanking out on her feelings and devaluing herself vis-à-vis her ex-husband and the child-care arrangements. As we talked she expressed reluctance: "I don't want to be here; it's too hard to open up and then go on alone. I have too much to handle; I can't do this too." I was supportive; I agreed that she was managing a lot.

Julie continued, "Give me some answers, I want some tools from you."

I responded, "I don't know what's best for you; only you know what's best. I respect your decision. Whatever you decide will be right. We have stopped and started up before; we know it works. The themes and issues are not lost; they just go underground. When you are ready, we can resume therapy."

Julie decided to continue, but three months later the issue reappeared. Julie stated, "I want to cut back because of the pressures in my life; I am fearful I can't manage them and express more of my feelings." We were back to square one: Holding it all in was the only way to handle feelings. "If I let it out I won't be able to function," she said.

This time I pointed out our experience together: Julie had increasingly expressed her feelings in therapy and had managed an intense and hectic time in her life. I stated clearly that I did not believe we should cut back at that time; our work together was important and should continue on a weekly basis. Julie took a week to decide; she chose bi-weekly appointments. In that hour she began to talk about her fear of losing control and the need to recover immediately: "I can't risk this! I need to stay in control, yet feelings are sometimes taking me by surprise."

Julie's behavior raised important issues for me: Had I been using good clinical judgment in accepting her modification of appointments? I believed in the importance of Julie experiencing her own power and making decisions, yet I was uneasy. When we worked in the regular pattern of weekly meetings, Julie maintained her balance but avoided her feelings; when we changed the pattern, Julie opened up.

Julie's behavior pushed me into a crisis of confidence. I wanted to trust her judgment, but my clinical judgment was being threatened by the client's taking control. Were we into a power struggle? Was I avoiding using my power because I did not want to disagree with my client? I began to monitor our work more closely, trusting the answers to lie in the process. I discovered that in each bi-weekly session Julie had taken charge of what we had discussed, keeping the threads in her own hands from one meeting to another.

Through working in the bi-weekly pattern, more of Julie's inner world opened. When the divorce was almost final, Julie was able to experience some of her sadness and pain at the ending of her marriage: "I want to see Steve one more time and tell him that I love him in spite of all we have been through. Only then can I separate. It is the same with my father. I need to tell him that too, but I am scared I won't be able to separate. I want to walk away face-to-face. I don't want to turn my back on him—that's not really separating, is it?"

Then Julie shared an image: "I am on a very narrow mesa, almost like, but wider than, a tightrope. It spans two shores, like a canyon. It is empty below and I am someplace in the middle. I dare not turn around. I can only go forward. As I see ahead it doesn't look so great. I can barely see the other side, it looks like an arid desert. I am scared. I don't know if I will like it there, or if I can survive there."

In this image I clearly observed the issue of female autonomy. I expressed my confidence in Julie's ability to go across to the other side without everything being known. In time, she would sharpen the skills and tools she needed for managing more adroitly her life. Trusting herself seemed the most vital lesson for Julie to learn. My belief in her ability to discover her own direction added to her new sense of self.

REFLECTION

Together, my clients and I are grappling with the creation of new models of female individuation. We are explorers of the unknown; frequently we do not know what will work. However, the trust we have in our experiences together, the caring and respect we have for one another, are helping us find our way. In the therapy dyad, we are unraveling the threads of female development that became knotted up years ago; she is learning to become a separate person capable of standing on her own while remaining in a caring relationship with a woman.

Our childhood training, both intraphysically and culturally, clings heavily to us; we are sensitive to our issues of helplessness and dependency. Sometimes we defend fiercely against acknowledging these feelings because they threaten our fragile sense of self. Patience, understanding, persistence, and practice are definitely prerequisites for explorers.

REFERENCES

Butler, S. (1978). *The conspiracy of silence: the trauma of incest*. San Francisco, CA: New Glide Publications.

Caplan, P. (1981). *Barriers between women*. New York: Spectrum.

Flax, J. (1978). The conflict between nurturance and autonomy in mother–daughter relationships and within feminism. *Feminist Studies, 4*, 171–189.

Horner, A. (1979). *Object relations and the developing ego in therapy.* New York: Jason Aronson.

Mahler, M., Pine, F., & Bergman, A. (1975). *The psychological birth of the human infant: symbiosis and individuation.* New York: Basic Books.

Masterson, J. (1981). *The narcissistic and borderline disorders: an integrated developmental approach.* New York: Brunner-Mazel.

Miller, J. B. (1976). *Toward a new psychology of women.* Boston: Beacon Press.

Rich, A. (1976). *Of woman born: motherhood as experience and institution.* New York: W. W. Norton.

Rich, A. (1978). Transcendental étude. In *The dream of a common language.* New York: W. W. Norton.

■ 4
Guidelines for Feminist Therapy

MARYLOU BUTLER

Although much has been written about feminist therapy, determination of who is a feminist therapist other than through self-definition is difficult. The identification issue makes it problematic for consumers to make thoughtful selections of feminist therapists and for mental health professionals to make appropriate referrals to feminist therapists. While the selection problem is mitigated somewhat by the availability of written consumer aids (Bloom, Cohen, Curran, Edwards, Klein, Robson & Zarrow, 1975) and by such national referral lists as the Feminist Therapy Roster of the Association for Women in Psychology, these materials have not been widely disseminated.

This chapter is an evaluation of a set of guidelines for feminist therapy (Fondi, Hay, Kincaid, & O'Connell, 1977) that were developed by a task force of members of the Feminist Therapy Collective, Inc. of Philadelphia and feminist therapists in private practice in Philadelphia. The guidelines were developed for use in screening feminist therapists in the Philadelphia area who wished to be placed on a feminist therapy referral list maintained by the Women's Center at the University of Pennsylvania. The task force conducted group interviews with each therapist in which she was asked to read and respond to these guidelines, indicating areas of agreement and disagreement. Each therapist was evaluated informally by the task force, for clarity and consistency of her own thinking regarding feminist therapy and an ability to indicate how her view of feminist therapy works in actual practice with clients. The guidelines outlined here are offered as an aid to consumers and mental health professionals who wish to identify feminist therapists in their own communities. A formal system for interviewing and rating feminist therapists based on these guidelines has not been developed yet.

In the remainder of this chapter, each guideline is spelled out and followed by the author's commentary, based on (1) a review of some of the theory of feminist therapy that has emerged since the guidelines were developed and (2) her experience as a feminist therapist over the past 10 years. Clearly, total agreement on the theory and practice of feminist therapy does not exist yet. It is hoped that these guidelines will be a further stimulus for clarification of what we *can* agree on, so that this information can be disseminated to consumers of feminist therapy.

GUIDELINES AND COMMENTARY

Guideline 1

The basis for feminist therapy is a recognition of the harmful effects of the sexist society in which we live. Real oppression of women based on gender as well as class and race is the basis for the conflicts, low self-esteem, and powerlessness reported by many women who seek therapy.

Comment: This assertion appears to be agreed upon by most feminist therapists, despite other philosophical differences (Rawlings & Carter, 1977). In fact, the development of feminist therapy has grown, in part, out of a search for an alternative to traditional therapy, which functions "as a mechanism of social control, preserving the status quo and protecting the patriarchal structure of society by perpetuating sex-role stereotypes in both its theoretical stance and practical application" (Sturdivant, 1980, p. 66).

Guideline 2

Feminist therapy explores with clients the inherent contradictions in the prescribed social roles for women. Rejected is the medical model of psychiatry, which locates the source of human conflict within individuals, that is, in a vacuum, with no relationship to the socioeconomic system within which we live. Emphasized is a sociocultural and systems approach to psychological growth and change.

Comment: The focus on intrapsychic conflicts as the source of psychological distress, the use of diagnostic labels that connote sickness, and the authoritarianism of a traditional therapeutic relationship are opposed by feminist therapy. The focus in feminist therapy on environmental stress as a major source of pathology is not used, however, as an avenue of escape from individual responsibility; rather, clients are helped to understand the sources of their oppression through careful sex-role analysis and to draw on the philosophy of feminism to help them conceptualize alternatives.

Guideline 3

Feminist therapists support women in an exploration of their inner resources and capacity for nurturance and self-healing. They encourage the process of individual goal setting and support those client goals that transcend traditional sex-role stereotyping. They encourage the exploration of various lifestyles and sexual orientations and support the acquisition of skills for self-directed and interdependent living.

Comment: Useful here is a comparison of two different models of change, one growing out of the medical model and the other coming from preventive mental health theory (Ivey, 1976):

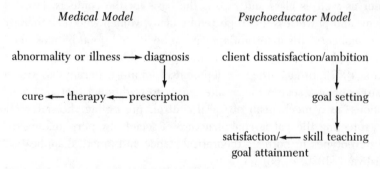

Figure 4.1 Models of Therapeutic Change

The psychoeducator model focuses on clients as learners rather than as patients and underscores the role of the therapist as a consultant in the client's change process rather than as one who is responsible for the client's cure. The process of identifying problem areas, setting goals, and evaluating treatment outcomes is a cooperative one between therapist and client, and it occurs throughout the therapeutic process.

Guideline 4

Feminist therapy distinguishes itself from traditional therapies by its nonsexist frame of reference. Feminist therapists utilize appropriate existing therapeutic modalities and develop new techniques compatible with the underlying philosophy of feminist therapy.

Comment: Feminist therapy is both nonsexist and political in its use of sex-role analysis and differential-power analysis as cognitive tools for helping women to differentiate between internal and external sources of distress. Feminist therapy employs these techniques to help women restructure their beliefs about themselves, about women as a group, and about their life situations. For example, depression and lack of assertiveness may be viewed as a result of the powerlessness of the female sex role, rather than as inherent personal deficits; rape is seen as a tool of male domination of women, rather than a result of female seductiveness. Difficulties on the job often are viewed as a function of sexual harassment and discrimination, rather than personal inadequacy. Lesbianism is viewed as a choice to make a commitment to and love another woman, rather than as the expression of unresolved dislike for men. This kind of cognitive restructuring enables women to avoid engaging in a process of blaming themselves for being victims (Ryan, 1971).

Guideline 5

Feminist therapists work on demystifying the power relationship inherent in any therapeutic situation. Doing so requires a feminist therapist to be open about her own values and attitudes.

Comment: The need for equalitarianism in the therapist–client relationship is generally agreed upon by feminist therapists; less consensus exists on how to achieve this goal. Orienting techniques that are helpful include

1. Disclaiming the position that therapists are experts about their clients (Gilbert, 1980)
2. Informing clients of their rights and privileges and encouraging them to ask questions regarding therapist attitudes and values,

fees and time schedules, and the nature of therapy (Hare-Mustin, Maracek, Kaplan, & Liss-Levinson, 1979)
3.   Modeling by the therapist, including appropriate self-disclosure

The purpose of therapist self-disclosure is to help foster a sense of communality of experience shared among women rather than to assert therapist superiority or to meet the therapist's own therapeutic needs. Feminist therapists have a responsibility to seek their own therapy or professional supervision when that will help them avoid interfering with their client's change process.

Guideline 6

Feminist therapy affirms that matching women clients with women therapists is often the most therapeutic choice for women. Feminist therapists use both individual and group approaches to therapy. Affirmed, in particular, is the value of an all-women's group therapy model. The group model enables women to (1) validate each other's strengths, (2) develop mutual support systems, (3) break down their isolation from each other, and (4) help each other perceive various possibilities for growth.

   Comment: A number of reasons underscore the position that the most effective feminist therapy is done by female therapists. While male therapists may espouse equalitarian attitudes and values, these may not be transmitted behaviorally in working with their female clients. The female feminist therapist has the potential to serve as a role model for clients, to feel greater empathy with women because of her shared experience of being a woman, and to avoid the usual power differential of male expert and female patient. These factors, along with the phenomenon of female passivity in the presence of males, indicate that female therapists who are feminists may do more to facilitate female clients' growth than male therapists (Sturdivant, 1980).

   An all-female, group therapy model can provide a resocialization experience for women in which they shift from identification with a male-defined social system to a female-oriented one where they learn to love each other and themselves. The group experience helps women to further their own individuation and complete unfinished developmental tasks in the areas of interdependence, assertiveness, and autonomy.

Change is fostered by the alternate frame of reference created in the therapy groups where "women exist apart from men . . . ; it is permissible . . . for women to bond strongly to each other . . . ; women are worthwhile and have valuable contributions to make to one another; men have no monopoly on power and importance" (Sturdivant, 1980, p. 144).

Guideline 7

Feminist therapy requires that a therapist (1) conduct an ongoing evaluation of her practice; (2) make provision in her practice for low-income clients; (3) examine her lifestyle and values as they relate to her therapeutic approach; (4) identify with the goals and philosophy of feminism; and (5) examine her race, class, and sexual orientation as they may lead to therapeutic blind spots with clients.

Comment: The therapist's own personal development and the way she conducts her practice are also criteria for feminist therapists. In her private life a feminist therapist should be working toward optimal functioning, with equality, mutual understanding, and respect as the basis for her personal relationships. She should be engaged in an ongoing consciousness-raising process in order to continue to bring an evolving feminist awareness to the therapy process. She also should be an expert on the psychology of women and women's mental health by participating in continuing education and supervision activities that focus on the growing body of knowledge on women's development and mental health needs (Johnson & Richardson, 1981). Lastly, a feminist therapist should be engaged in social change efforts that promote women's equality.

Guideline 8

Feminist therapists acknowledge that therapy per se is not a cure-all, and they encourage women to consider other avenues for growth and support instead of or in addition to a therapeutic experience.

Comment: Although conversion of clients to political feminism is not a goal of feminist therapy, feminist therapists must become aware of community resources for women and make referrals to women's centers, CR groups, and feminist organizations, when that would be therapeutic for clients.

CONCLUSION

Feminist therapy is not only good therapy but is also a radical departure from traditional therapy because of its affirmation of a feminist value orientation and its use of equalitarian practices throughout the course of treatment. The guidelines for feminist therapy presented here are potential tools for identifying mental health professionals who are feminist therapists in a community and for educating prospective consumers of feminist therapy. The next step is to develop a systematic procedure for interviewing and rating the responses of therapists, in order to assess whether various components of their therapeutic approach are feminist or not.

REFERENCES

Bloom, S., Cohen, D., Curran, D., Edwards, G., Klein, P., Robson, E., & Zarrow, M. (1975). *Off the couch: a woman's guide to therapy*. Somerville, MA: New England Free Press.

Fondi, M., Hay, J., Kincaid, M. B., & O'Connell, K. (1977). Feminist therapy: a working definition. Unpublished manuscript, University of Pennsylvania.

Gilbert, L. A. (1980). Feminist therapy. In A. Brodsky & R. Hare-Mustin (Eds.), *Women and Psychotherapy*. New York: Guilford Press.

Hare-Mustin, R., Maracek, J., Kaplan, A., & Liss-Levinson, N. (1979). Rights of clients, responsibilities of therapists. *American Psychologist, 34*, 3–16.

Ivey, A. (1976). Counseling psychology, the psychoeducator model and the future. *Counseling Psychologist, 6*(3), 72–76.

Johnson, M., & Richardson, M., with Courtois, C., Farmer, H., Kincaid, M., Nickerson, E., Christian, L., & Wolleat, P. (1981). *Models for training counselors of women: Report of Division 17 Committee on Women Task Force on Training for Counseling Women*. ERIC document no. 208 271.

Rawlings, E., & Carter, E. (1977). Feminist and nonsexist psychotherapy. In E. Rawlings and D. Carter (Eds.), *Psychotherapy for women: Treatment toward equality*. Springfield, IL: Charles C Thomas.

Ryan, W. (1971). *Blaming the victim*. New York: Random House.

Sturdivant, S. (1980). *Therapy with women: A feminist philosophy of treatment*. New York: Springer.

5

Feminism, The Future of?

DORIS JEANETTE

I remember two nuns, with their backs to me, sitting on a park bench, high on a hill overlooking a waterfall. The moment I saw them, their energy totally captivated mine. Their presence overtook me, stunned and pleased me. They were in love. I dropped to my knees. The feeling emitting from their white-and-black personas was one of pure serenity and union. It is the closest and most intimate I have ever experienced two people being in public. They were not looking at each other, not touching. They were in peaceful, pulsating rapture, united by a vision, a moment, a hard stone park bench and their love.

Their radiating, loving energy pulled me toward them. I let myself go to them—to be with them, to feel what it was like to be inside of them. I was taken by their essence, so calm and vulnerable on one hand; a gift for anyone who took the time to notice two nuns sitting with their backs to the world. Yet, as my being entered them, I was overcome with conflict, confusion, and awe. Twisted inside, hidden deep, knots of disguise lay heavy, waiting.

Their love of religion hated their love of each other. Who they were hated who they were; a conflict in the self. A challenge to the heart. They would have to choose. To deny, repress, forget, sneak, pretend, hide. Or could they? Would they face themselves, honestly and sincerely?

For them to acknowledge their feelings openly, to reach out and physically touch each other, to throw away their black-and-white gowns —this would be for them to embark upon a complete overthrow, a complete rejection, of all they had built their lives around. Everything they were and every way they lived would have to be open to question and examination. They would have to have great courage to turn around and face the fact that who they were and what they believed in was no longer valid—for them. They would have to have great courage to acknowledge that they had become someone they once hated.

The nuns' present choice was obvious. They were two black-and-white gowns sitting on a stone park bench high on a hill looking at a magnificent waterfall with their bodies perfectly in tune, their visions of beauty united—not touching, not yet taking the step into confusion. Not yet ready to say that all they believed in, organized their lives around, trusted, fought for and lived for was no longer valid—for them. Not yet choosing to let their foundation be shaken, their habits exposed, the truth about themselves revealed. Not yet choosing to be in a time and a moment of change.

But I am in a time and a moment of change. All my life I have been on a journey headed for freedom. Lusting to love myself. Wanting to feel alive and present for all of my previous moments. Wanting the freedom to be who I truly am outside in the world. Wanting the freedom to expand and create and become all that I can become. Wanting the freedom to founder and fall. My desire and my passion. Freedom.

Everything I think, do, feel, or create reduces itself to this. I do not want to be controlled. By anyone. I want to be free. Whether I am accommodating or rebelling, my goal is the same. Whether I am conscious or unconscious, my goal is the same. I want to feel free. This is my core and this is my essence. Freedom. The freedom to be me.

I do not believe I am so different from other *Homo sapiens*—be they female or male. I believe every action and reaction in the entire world can be reduced to this desire for freedom. That which is true at the individual level is also true at the group level, is also true at the world level. We all want the same thing. And we all are scared. Because we are scared, and because it is not in vogue to be sacred or kosher or even normal, very few of us admit how frightened we are, how frightened we are of ourselves.

Instead, we have devised a thousand different ways to avoid our fear. We deny it par excellence. We repress it, depress it, dress it up in pretty clothes, stiff smiles, and chatter. We exaggerate it and blow it up until it is meaningless. All of these façades keep us from feeling, from knowing our fear and our life. I call these distant delusions Control. Control is anything that is used to keep you away from your authentic feelings. Control is very different from freedom. Control is what our two nuns must use in order not to be in a time and a moment of change. Control is what I must let go of if I want to be free.

One of the primary means that human beings have created for controlling themselves and others is a thing called Judgment. When I start to fly, take to the skies, to soar so, so high—I always feel shot down, like one of those clay pigeons that are tossed into the air and shattered with a single shot. It is a feeling I have come to expect. It is one of those realities one must come to terms with. One can call it criticism, sexism, or feminism. By any name, it impacts upon me, and I crumble. It is control. It is judgment. It is someone putting me down for being myself.

It doesn't matter how adequate I feel or how much I don't believe the attack or judgment. I hurt and fall. I feel. My body bleeds when my flesh has been cut and my feelings hurt when my being has been insulted. I can no longer pretend that I don't care. I definitely care. I definitely feel. I am a most sensitive creature. I am a woman.

I have come to expect the bullet, dodging, prepared for all the shots that come from known enemies. The side where I know they hate me and judge me. The side where sexism resides. And then, to be shot in the back. To be discredited and destroyed. To be shot down on the side unexpected. The side where I thought they loved me. The place where women reside. The side where feminism flourishes.

As if it were me. As if I were doing something wrong. As if I could not be trusted. As if where I needed to go was not somehow right. Not politically correct enough, not self-sacrificing enough, too powerful. As if my expertise were a judgment against others. As if my ability, strength, and beauty took something away from others, instead of giving others something. As if my direction were less valid than others.

Feminism, in this way, seems like my mother. To judge me as if there were a right way—a perfect way—to be a feminist, a good daughter. A way to be what I should be, defined by someone else's needs, not by my own. My mother holds on. Controlling. Feminism holds on. Controlling. Judging me. My mother loves me. My sisters love me.

To me, the pain is somehow worse when I am judged in the name of love. Love controls me with a grip much stronger than hate or rejection. I need love every day. I need love as much as I need water and air. To have love associated with and connected to control is painful, indeed.

To be controlled by love is to doubt my very own experience. I doubt my entire worth. I stop. I wait. Holding back my energy and spirit—instead of flying. I feel as if I should be controlled. And so, I control myself. How quickly and insidiously I destroy myself. Time and time again, I succumb to judgment.

To Pass Judgment. To proclaim that it is either good or bad. Wrong or right. A success or failure. Your praise is as judgmental and controlling as his criticism.

Two nuns perched on the brink of human change, not yet choosing to step into confusion. My desire and lust for freedom, symbolic of all of our desire, shot down by judgments from feminists, sexists, and mothers. The process of change unfolds. The process of human change for two nuns, for me, for feminism, and for you. All of us, evolving or extincting. Living or dying. Changing or stuck. Our life is a process. What kind of life are we creating? What are we as women giving birth to? What are we as feminists giving to life?

Vail, Colorado, spring 1982. The Advanced Feminist Therapy Institute. To see what is there. In a room without windows in the middle of those gorgeous Rocky Mountains, from early in the morning until late at night, using the brain—using, mostly, entirely, the left brain. We see women sitting on straight chairs, unconscious of their bodies, talking:

"You have a sliding fee scale—good. You don't—bad."

"You touch your clients—bad. You don't—good."

"And what is a true feminist? Definitely not too straight or too rich or too sexy. Definitely not too radical or too poor or too insensitive. Now let's see—what does that leave us?"

"You don't want to hear what I say? You do want to hear what I say?"

The left brain exalted, as usual, in its own structure, in isolation, without the right brain, without the body, without the spirit. The current question on the floor for discussion is, What do you do when a client is involved in a relationship with a man that is not good for her? Do you (a) tell her the truth or (b) tell her the truth or (c) tell her the truth or (d) tell her the truth? Feminist therapists spending a lot of time discussing important questions, looking for important answers. Unfortunately, they are looking for answers in the same place everyone else has always looked for answers. Outside. In judgments. In control. In authority.

And ah, how the aspens do dance in the wind for those who sit at their base and stare at the sky. In a room without windows. And how the mountain water pebbles become pleasure for those who can imagine themselves one.

The left brain, in isolation, stifles, destroys, controls that which is most womanly about me—my unconscious, my creativity, my body, my breath. My courage to face death and pain. My courage to be honest and different. My courage to challenge the foundation upon which I have stood. My courage to give birth. To change. To know nothing. That which is deep inside me. Ignored by the world. Ignored by feminist therapists. Ignored. Who I am is not valued or validated. Nowhere do I see my pain. Nowhere do I see my fear. Nowhere do I see my depths. Nowhere do I see my passion. Nowhere.

Feminism, the future of? Can Feminism change and expand with and for that special creature called Woman? I am not sure. That is like asking, Can Mother change and expand with and for that special person called Daughter? One is not quite sure of the answer. My mother does not let herself express what she feels, or speak what she thinks, or do what she wants. She is silent. Her silence is our silence. As women, our silence slices through our lives so insidiously and consistently that we easily miss our own absence. We do not even recognize how little we exist. There is no reflection of me in the mirror of my world. My truth is silent. And you do not want to hear.

And I have the choice. A thousand times a day. The choice to control myself and remain silent. The choice to blame others. The choice to victimize myself again and again. The choice to see the truth, feel the truth, and set myself free. The truth that hurts to see. The fears that are real. There is always the choice.

Philadelphia, fall 1982. Feminist Therapy Collective. Case conference. For the third time in a row the presented woman is being discussed as a "borderline." I have said everything I wanted to say twice already about this. I feel like no one is listening to me. I think I am going to puke. For six years I have been fighting this judgment. I am screaming inside. But not a word comes out. I may explode. Last year I did say out loud that I was an obsessive personality and so there, stuff your labels. I was ridiculed by one and not supported by any. So there. What's the use? They haven't been listening to me. Am I not saying what I'm saying? Do you not want to hear? Now I am screaming.

Do not judge her any more. When you do not have what someone needs, you call them needy. When you feel controlled by someone's dependency, you call them borderline. No human being needs anything they don't need. They need it because they need it, and if you can't help them meet those needs, tell them the goddamn truth. Don't put it on her any more. You may not have what she needs—say so. Confess the truth. Tell her you are limited. Tell her you are scared, tell her you don't know what to do. Don't tell her any more lies. Don't hide your fears and inadequacies by using her any more. Tell her you don't know what to do, either.

Stop it. You must stop it. I am definitely screaming. Stop victimizing in the name of feminism. There is no one here to diminish. There is no one here that is less capable and competent at being a human being than you. There is no one here with different needs than you. There is no one here to feel sorry for. There is no one here to treat humanistically or feministically. Take your one-up patronizing feminist bullshit and scram. To victimize someone in the name of feminism is to be victimized with a bond as deadly as that of patriarchy.

You do not get any points for being a noble, condescending feminist. To blame by feeling holier than is yet another way to control. To feel sorry for a woman if she is not a feminist. To feel sorry for all the borderlines of the world. To disrespect. To discuss ways to get a woman to do what you think is good for her. To discuss ways to get a woman off your back. Puke, puke, puke. Control in any disguise is control. Feminist therapists, you are doing exactly the same thing as patriarchal therapists. You think you know the answer better than they. You are acting like an authority on the subject. You are doing the same diminishing number; it looks different because it is around the circle, but it is a circle and it is the same controlling defense. You are putting yourself on a pedestal, safe and protected from the needy. You are no better than your brother. You are hiding behind the defense of feminism. I repeat: You are no better than your brother.

To feel the truth deep down inside. To say the truth when no one wants to hear. To expose the truth that no one wants to feel. I hate what I see; I hate what I feel; I hate what I am. Disgusted and sick, I revolt. I want to puke when I see and feel what women have done in the name of Feminism. I hate what mothers do in the name of Love. Control. I hate how I used people to meet my own unclaimed needs. I hate how I distanced myself from the dirt and the filth of human vulnerability. I hate how I thought I was better than them—because I was a feminist or competent or composed. Most definitely competent and composed. To feel the truth deep down inside. I hate what I have hidden behind. Disgusted and sick, I revolt and succumb; letting myself bathe in the truth. I let go. I become the truth. I feel the truth.

I am not Mother's perfect daughter. I am not the perfect feminist therapist. I am not superior to sexist men. I am not packageable or pleasant. I am no longer controlling myself. I am real. And my truth is not always pretty and what I feel is not what you want me to feel. Sometimes I do not like what you do. I hate your denial and your lies. The truth that it hurts to see, and feel, and expose.

To be in time and a moment of change. To be headed for freedom. To be wanting trust that does not betray. Safety that is not an illusion. Power that is as comfortable as wearing nothing in the summer sun. Lusting to love yourself. And when we feel the truth we set it free.

Feminism, the future of? Can we change? Do we even want to change? Do we desire freedom and space? Do we long? Will we satisfy our longing? If feminism cannot let go—of us—we must let her die. If our mothers, therapists, or lovers cannot let go of us—help us with a push—we must be the ones to let go. We must truly separate ourselves—unto ourself. Feminism must die, so that Woman can be born.

Feminism is a large, socially acceptable box no longer needed for those of us who intend to be free. What was once a necessity is now a burden. I needed feminism just as the nuns needed religion. Now, I need to let go of feminism so that I can move on and embrace more of myself. The conflict in the self is resolved; I have become someone I once criticized. Again and again the process is the same. To be in a time and a moment of change.

And there will always be the doubt. And there will always be the choice. The choice to feel or not to feel. The truth.

Without feminism, without my protective defense, how will I be safe? I have been burned at the stake for less than this. My being, my power scares the socks off of bankers. Construction men act like monkeys. Black men hoot and holler. Feminist therapists and humanists will try to save me as they did the witches. I am only "imagining" my crime, they say. But you and I know that WE ARE the crime. Imagining—hell. We have not defended for nothing. We have not hidden for 2000 years because we are imagining our crimes. Our power, springing from our truth, alive and full, is the crime. And everyone is scared and no one will admit it and we are at the beginning again. Yes, my dear, you will be attacked, of that you can be sure. People will try to control you. People will criticize and judge you; sexist men and feminist women will do the honors. And you—you will attack yourself. And you—you will choose what to do.

> With the death of feminism, Woman was born. Woman was the creature that awakened the world, calmed the fears, and created a new way of being. They were especially equipped, deep down inside, for giving birth to new creations. So it was only natural that they were the ones to evolve into a new and wonderful being. Their power was real and authentic, humble and strong.

No one is going to give you power; nobody has it to give you. Men do not have power, all they have is control. Power springs naturally from integrity. There is nothing you have to do, except live it. Live the truth. That is your power. Power by its nature is never over or under anything or anyone. It is real and moves toward life.

We will create new protections, which value our total being. We will allow ourselves to respond as needed. We are not by nature either passive or aggressive. We are by nature survivors. We will do what we must do to survive—physically, emotionally, and spiritually. We will not be only brains and minds and heads. We will not need to control. We will only need to be ourselves.

> And so, the women began to take on their own names. The father of the child became as important as his involvement with the child. Women started to show themselves as they truly were; their energy, loving but very, very firm, came out for all to see, hear, touch, and feel. The world was embraced with the truth. And so, Patriarchy was over before most people even noticed.

I need you. To tell me the truth. I want you to be with me. I want you to walk tall and proud beside me. Love me in my confusion, with no answers. Love me strong and soaring. Tell me how beautiful and sexy I am. Tell me how cold and critical I can be. Tell me how creative and delightful I can be. Tell me how foolish I sound, yelling from the pedestal. Give me your truth. Please. See me as I truly am. Come PLAY with me.

> And so, a new age dawned, creating a new way of being, as human beings impacted upon the earth in yet another movement toward life. And again, that movement was led by the women and the children.

■ two

INTRODUCTION TO FEMINIST PSYCHOTHERAPEUTIC TECHNIQUES AND PRACTICES

CAROLYN C. LARSEN AND
LORNA P. CAMMAERT, Editors

The chapters comprising this section represent a broad scope of topics, concerns, and methods. Most of the authors begin their papers with critiques of current psychotherapeutic practice and then proceed to suggest more effective and congruent ways to function as feminist therapists. What becomes evident throughout this section is the struggle to make basic assumptions explicit and to examine the fundamentals of feminist therapy and how it is practiced.

Many of what now seem the more obvious issues in psychological theory, such as sex-role restraints and the failure to recognize women's uniquenesses, have been raised and examined within other writings. The contribution of these chapters is that they go beyond what have become obvious issues, to pose some deeper questions about the translation of feminism into psychotherapeutic practice and how best to serve clients from a feminist perspective. There are refreshing reviews of some old issues (e.g., assertiveness training, anger) in context with some unique and tested developments, and there are previews of some newer strategies (e.g., lesbian couples therapy, staff training) that are proving effective.

Feminist therapists have not developed an original set of techniques as much as they have adopted, modified, and extended techniques from many psychotherapeutic approaches. The uniqueness of feminist therapy techniques, therefore, stems from political and philosophical values (Rawlings & Carter, 1977) that are not linked to any particular set of therapeutic techniques but have profound effects on what techniques are selected and how they are applied. Being aware of how these techniques impinge upon women clients, what their meaning is in terms of a feminist perspective, and what implications they have for the nature of the changes our clients seek is crucial to the advancement of feminist therapy.

The following chapters advance our thinking about our techniques and practices by their questioning stance, their challenges to existing techniques, and their search for new approaches. The underlying and unifying theme explicit in the chapters in this part is that feminist therapists must maintain a critical attitude toward their practice. Fine examples of this attitude are presented here.

Linda Stere begins her chapter by summarizing critiques of traditional assertiveness training (AT). She proceeds beyond these critiques with a detailed description of a program in self-esteem training (SET) for women.

In a related chapter, Laurie Weiss uses a Transactional Analysis context to analyze and treat women's depression. Weiss' seven-step assertiveness training program, which can be used in individual or group therapy, teaches women to say no, to make requests of others, and to negotiate to get their individual needs met.

Anger is the focus of Chapter 8, by Vasanti Burtle. After a critical analysis of recent writings about anger, Burtle describes some specific treatment procedures with women. The aims of these procedures are to encourage women's awareness, expression, and constructive use of their anger.

Nonverbal methods of increasing awareness of feelings and integrating mind and body are the themes of Chapter 9, by Lauree Moss. Central to her therapy is the importance of touch and the use of a less stressful, nurturing approach.

Chapters 10 and 11 focus on therapy with lesbian couples. Sara Sharratt and Lilian Bern, a feminist lesbian couple, are cotherapists with lesbian couples. In their chapter, they criticize heterosexism in feminist psychological writings, which they view as denying lesbian existence. Specific problems lesbian couples bring to therapy and the elements of their cotherapeutic approach are elaborated by the authors. In Chapter 11, Beverly Burch elaborates on merger, a dynamic common to lesbian relationships, which she finds can be a destructive or healing force. Burch traces aspects of women's development as a means for understanding conflicts about separateness and merger, and she illustrates how these issues are worked through in therapy with a lesbian couple.

Chapter 12, by Carolyn Larsen and Lorna Cammaert, describes the format, clients, staff, funding, and process of a decision-making program for women. The issues that arise in supervising the staff of these programs is the central theme. Using examples, the authors examine two issues that emerge: whether and how to encourage women participants to engage in social action and how to handle reactions of staff if participants choose to reject feminist principles.

Doreen Seidler-Feller's chapter completes this section. She summarizes ideology and practice and presents an alternate conceptualization of sexual complaints and a feminist approach to intervention.

REFERENCES

Rawlings, E. I., & D. K. Carter (Eds.).(1977). *Psychotherapy for women: Treatment toward equality*. Springfield, IL: Charles C Thomas.

■ 6
Feminist Assertiveness Training: Self-esteem Groups as Skill Training for Women

LINDA K. STERE

In response to criticisms of traditional psychotherapy with women in the early 1970s, feminists within the helping professions began offering innovations such as consciousness raising groups, a feminist model of psychotherapy, and assertiveness training groups for women as primary modes of feminist therapeutic practice (Zukerman, 1979). Assertiveness training groups as skill training groups seemed particularly attractive because behavior modification techniques appeared to offer greater potential neutrality with regard to social values (Blechman, 1980). At face value, assertiveness training also appeared to be a most effective and logical means for treating the problems of women that arose from or were reinforced by limited female sex-role stereotypes (Jakubowski, 1977).

In spite of efforts to adapt assertiveness training (AT) to meet the special needs of women, questions regarding the effectiveness of AT for women have been raised recently by several behavior therapists/ researchers (Fodor & Epstein, 1983; Kahn, 1981; Linehan & Egan,

1979). All of these writers raise and challenge the implicit assumptions that women have a deficit for which they must seek training in large numbers, that women are generally inappropriately assertive, that how women should be effectively assertive is obvious and can be taught easily, and that if women learn appropriate assertive techniques they will become more interpersonally successful.

One author cites research that shows that appropriate assertive behaviors by women may be labeled aggressive by others, and that many women who express effective assertive behaviors also experience high degrees of anxiety accompanying their assertive responses (Kahn, 1981). In one study of AT groups, the results showed that women who might gain the most from AT groups, namely, those restricted by the demands of a traditional female role stereotype, were typically the dropouts of the class, while the feminist-identified women benefited most on all measures of assertiveness (Ellis & Nichols, 1979). How clinicians and trainers address the needs of these AT dropouts and whether or not the feminist "successes" are actually more empowered and respected in the world are questions that must be explored.

There are two ways feminist therapists might respond to the potential pitfalls and inadequacies of AT groups for women. One way is to seek to move beyond the limitations of a change technique that is aimed at individuals and women and focus more on working with social structures and men (see Chapter 23 of this book). The other response is for therapists to offer even better services to women seeking personal change. The focus of this chapter is to examine briefly the potential clinical pitfalls of AT groups as traditionally practiced and offer an alternative model that illustrates guidelines for ensuring that assertiveness training is truly feminist practice.

CLINICAL PITFALLS OF ASSERTIVENESS TRAINING

Many of the pitfalls of ineffective AT groups arise from overemphasizing the expert status of the leader, while neglecting the resources within and the unique situations of the individual members of the group. This is usually done for the sake of efficiency in teaching AT material or for the sake of research uniformity, or by inexperienced leaders. The following is a brief summary of ways in which the leader may reinforce her "expert" status, with suggestions for alternate methods in each area.

Defining Assertiveness and Evaluating Responses. When definitions and evaluations are used, women may become preoccupied with making a "correct" response, reinforcing their tendencies for perfectionism and looking outside the self for the "correct" way to interact. Given the complexity of human interactions, with different situations demanding a range of responses from accommodation to intimidation, or from passionate emotional expression to absolutely calm rationality, trying to talk about appropriate assertion in general is probably ineffective and potentially misleading. "Discrimination training" (Kahn, 1981), which helps women to discern how to act in a variety of settings and situations, should be included; and group members should be tapped as a valuable resource for suggestions.

Implying that Assertiveness Leads to Successful Interpersonal Interaction. By omitting a discussion of the limitations and difficulty of individual change and by failing to explore the possible negative consequences of becoming more assertive, the leader creates an expectation that reinforces the tendency for the woman to blame herself if the interaction fails. Failure to discuss the difficulties of overcoming the social inequities of a world in which people generally are not oriented toward taking the needs and interests of women seriously, leaves the woman isolated and self-blaming.

Handing Out Lists of Basic Human Rights. Defining personal rights is a complex cultural and religious matter. Women who strongly adhere to traditional sex-role values may leave AT groups as a result of the cognitive dissonance between their beliefs and the values introduced by the leader (Ellis & Nichols, 1979). However, introducing the notion of "personal rights" often has a dramatic effect on women. Rights lists should be suggestions or worksheets to be voted on, discussed, or debated by members, or created by the members themselves. Consequences of different beliefs should be explored, and focusing on arriving at a consensus should be avoided.

Handing Out Lists of Irrational Beliefs. Leaders commonly present a list labeled "irrational beliefs," as if there is one basis for judging rational action and therapists know what it is. Although the leader may be trying to address catastrophic thinking, she risks reinforcing one of the most common avenues women take to invalidate themselves and their feelings. How the beliefs are stated is critical; for example, Irrational Belief #1 from Bloom, Coburn, and Pearlman (1975) may not be so irrational: "If I assert myself, others will get mad at me." Probably the word "irrational" should be avoided when examining beliefs and values with women.

Rehearsing Leader-contrived Role Plays. Utilizing the real-life situations of the members is the heart of the therapeutic value of all-women AT groups. Practicing contrived situations has questionable generalization to other situations (Fodor & Epstein, 1983) and is symptomatic of leader-centered groups.

Dealing with Power Tactics. Another potential pitfall is the leader's failure to deal responsibly and realistically with the consequences and ethics of using power tactics with others. The AT best seller, *When I Say No I Feel Guilty* by Manuel Smith (1975), has been criticized by several AT writers for promoting power tactics for manipulation, rather than teaching mutually respecting, assertive communication (Alberti & Emmons, 1978; Kelley, 1979). Teaching techniques that enhance the probability of a power struggle without also teaching conflict resolution techniques could be deemed irresponsible to the individual and her relationships. The leader and the members should be clear about the purpose of the training and differentiate between learning assertive communication, learning to ventilate anger, and learning to use power tactics to achieve one's goal.

AN ALTERNATIVE MODEL: SELF-ESTEEM TRAINING

Some of the preceding potential pitfalls are less critical when working with women who already have a fairly strong sense of self, are oriented to feminism, and primarily need support and an opportunity to practice ways they wish to change. However, a woman who has rather low self-esteem and is constricted by a rigid female role stereotype may require a more comprehensive approach that helps her to increase her self-awareness, her self-confidence, and her self-acceptance before tackling the interpersonally conflictual AT material. The following is a description of the content of self-esteem training (SET), which was designed to address the needs of these women.

In order to be comprehensive SET groups should include self-awareness exercises, esteem- or strength-building exercises, relaxation techniques, cognitive techniques to counter negative self-statements, exploration of belief systems that devalue women, and an exploration of the potential consequences of change, positive and negative. The focus of the skill building is primarily on the woman's dialogue with herself, rather than on the interpersonal skills commonly practiced in AT groups (such as refusing unreasonable requests, responding to others' criticism or manipulation, and making requests). Improving self-esteem is presented as a matter of learning certain personal skills and is subdivided into the following four components.

1. **Accepting my feelings as rational and valid**
   a. Validating my feelings of guilt and resentment by tracing their sources; recognizing that strong feeling does not necessarily mean being out of control
   b. Trusting my feeling reactions as my genuine and unique response to something real
   c. Being able to express my feelings to others as I so choose
2. **Being able to please myself**
   a. Knowing what I like, want, need
   b. Feeling important and worthy enough to say what it is I want
   c. Taking action in my own behalf; making requests
3. **Identifying my strengths**
   a. Revaluing my feminine skills and qualities
   b. Feeling the courage to be as successful and capable as I can be
   c. Making positive statements about myself, to myself and others
4. **Knowing and accepting my imperfections and being gentle with myself**
   a. Having realistic expectations of myself and manageable ideals to inspire me
   b. Feeling calm in the face of criticism
   c. Being able to state what my shortcomings are

These definitions of self-esteem skills provide a framework for setting concrete and specific goals for change, and they also differentiate skills into thought, feeling, and action components. General goals such as "liking myself better" or "being more confident" are avoided. In addressing these SET goals, group leaders could design a variety of exercises and activities, and this author encourages others to be creative in utilizing ideas from the rich resources available, from which some of the following exercises were taken (e.g., Jongeward & Scott, 1976; Kelley, 1979; Lange & Jakubowski, 1976; Osborn & Harris, 1975; Phelps & Austin, 1975).

Self-esteem Training Exercises

The following is a summary of the exercises and presentations of SET, first presented through the personal growth program of a local YWCA and advertised as follows:

> BECOMING YOUR OWN BEST FRIEND: Low self-esteem in women is the source of many unfortunate conditions—shyness, underdeveloped talents, depression, guilt, and loneliness. Learn specific exercises and readiness for becoming more caring and respecting toward oneself and for telling the difference between selfishness and positive self-attention. Mondays, March 1–March 22, 7:00–9:00 P.M., YW Bldg. $40.00

The following activities are presented in the order in which they are introduced in the course, which is composed of four, two-hour, weekly sessions.

Self-esteem Scale. Creating a scale that divides self-image into several components (e.g., emotional self, social self, intimate self, physical self) provides a pre- and postgroup self-reflection for each woman. Changes may be noted in the degree of liking or disliking for each category, and the scale presents one way to begin specifying goals.

Defining Sources of Low Self-esteem. The general sources of low self-esteem are described as (1) a continuing experience of having one's needs not satisfied or one's thoughts and feelings invalidated, and (2) a significant loss, failure, or disappointment(s). The development and maintenance of low self-esteem from blocked needs and feelings is described in greater detail, utilizing the theories of Karen Horney (1945,

1950). The step-by-step process is outlined whereby the desire to avoid conflict and disapproval causes emotions to be blocked, deemed wrong, and eventually repressed, resulting in the creation of rigid self-ideals that maintain the repressed need or emotion by expressing characteristics that are direct opposites of the hidden feeling. For example, repressed hostility is transformed into the self-ideal of being and acting totally loving and dutiful toward others, repression of dependency needs leads to an ideal of total self-reliance; repression of tenderness leads to a glorification of toughness (Horney, 1950).

Two implications of this theory are emphasized throughout the group. In order to re-establish lost self-esteem, a woman must rediscover the disowned need or emotion and recognize that perhaps the most difficult aspect of change is giving up the positives, namely, exaggerated and unrealistic self-ideals. To illustrate this process, it is suggested that the reason battered women resist changing is not because they enjoy suffering, but because they continue to be busy trying to be perfect wives and mothers and blame themselves for not achieving their ideals.

Perfectionism Exercises. Members are asked to explore their idealistic beliefs about a perfect world, perfect others, and a perfect self. An adaptation of Ellis's "irrational ideas" (Ellis & Harper, 1974) is utilized for voting and debate, and the list is renamed "Ideas that Undermine Self-Acceptance." Members also rate themselves on a brief "Perfectionism Scale" (Burns, 1980) and reflect on the results.

Countering Negative Self-statements. Members continue to work on perfectionism and self-criticism by completing a worksheet called "A Devaluation List," which categorizes common roles and activities of women. Negative self-statements are elicited first, by members completing a sentence under each category, beginning, "I should be (shouldn't be). . . ." The beliefs in each category are then translated into feeling statements by completing the sentence, "I feel guilty that. . . ." Finally, the women transform these statements into feelings of frustration and anger, completing for each thought, "I resent that. . . ." An example of a complete series is (1) "I should be a more patient and loving mother," (2) "I feel guilty for yelling at my kids so often," and (3) "I resent all the constant demands my children make on me and that my husband never helps with them." Much time for discussion and sharing follows this written exercise.

Defining Social and Cultural Sources of the Devaluation of Women. The ideas of Elizabeth Janeway (1971, 1974) and Jean Baker Miller (1976) are utilized in presenting a graphic analysis of American culture that illustrates specific social and cultural barriers that inhibit women from gaining and maintaining self-esteem. Brainstorming and blackboard illustrations complete a visual image of a world divided into male and female, masculine and feminine values, homeplace and work-place values, and finally, godliness and evilness. The overlay of adjectives and activities that emerges on this divided board in the three-part discussion makes painfully evident the confusing and conflicting values present in our culture and the particular pitfalls for women who lack awareness of this social milieu.

Modeling Exercises. Members list three women, real or fictitious, and describe what they admire or appreciate about them. Next they list phrases, positive and negative, describing their mothers. They also list messages of approval or disapproval from their fathers. In discussion, they reflect on which qualities they may be glorifying or denying in themselves, and they strive to define realistic ideals and models as inspirations for themselves.

Guided Imagery. The leader takes the total group through an ego-enhancing description of themselves, suggesting a world in which their hopes for themselves are manifest and describing in detail many expressions of self-confidence. Then she suggests that they imagine the reactions of others to their changes. Discussion afterward focuses on consequences of changing.

Self-appreciations and Compliments Exercise. After listing skills, accomplishments, qualities, or interests that they like in themselves, each woman hands her list to a partner, who gives each compliment back to her as if she were her best friend. After each woman receives her own positive statements, she shares her thoughts and feelings during the exercise.

Boasting. Using her list of self-likes if necessary, each woman stands in front of the group and boasts about herself for three to five minutes. This exercise is first modeled by the leader, who also may act as a coach during the exercise. Following each speech, the listeners applaud the boaster. This exercise can be completed in small subgroups and possibly repeated with a larger number of listeners. Occasionally, a woman will insist on sitting down, in her reluctance to do the exercise.

Homework Tasks. Suggestions for weekly practice begin with sensory focusing exercises, relaxation exercises, and ritualizing time with oneself. Each week, new tasks are added that structure giving tangible and intangible gifts to oneself. Positive, reassuring self-talk, spoken aloud, is recommended for countering anxiety-arousing situations; also encouraged is keeping a daily journal of negative self-talk, to raise awareness of continual subliminal negative dialogue with self. A self-appreciation and personal successes journal is introduced in the last session of the group.

Group Process Guidelines in Self-esteem Training

As the preceding sequence of exercises reveals, each group is designed to ensure that the women are guided first to focus inwardly and make clear contact with themselves, then to uncover their compelling ideals and habitual negative messages, and finally to experience the positive strength-building exercises. Early in the group, women may connect unexpectedly with deep residues of anger and sadness, even in the course-type format, and the response and support of other members is usually spontaneous or easily coached. Having revealed many of their worst thoughts and fears about themselves, the positive work that comes later has a genuineness and power it would have lacked earlier in the group. Most exercises are conducted in small, self-selected subgroups of two or three women who come to know one another well in a relatively short time. More than half of the group time is devoted to their sharing themselves with one another. Evaluations consistently reveal that the most valued aspect of the course is hearing the thoughts, feelings, and experiences of other women. In the final class, a fifth skill is added to their skills list, namely, forming and maintaining a network of support with other women. Personal independence is redefined, not as not needing others, but as the ability to find companionship in which one can be most openly and honestly oneself.

The leader offers all groups the option of continuing in a self-support group, which she may assist in organizing for one or two sessions. The course that follows the "Best Friend" group is recommended to them. It deals with anger and fair fighting and includes typical AT exercises as well as a focus on styles of expressing anger and on guidelines for fair fighting. Many women choose to take this follow-up course, although earlier they had avoided such conflict-laden material.

Offered by itself or in a sequence of assertiveness training procedures, self-esteem training for women can be another group tool for empowering women to act in their own behalf by becoming more actively self-determining and accepting and respecting of their unique needs, feelings, and desires.

REFERENCES

Alberti, R. E., & Emmons, M. L. (1978). *Your perfect right* (3rd ed.). San Luis Obispo, CA: Impact.

Blechman, E. A. (1980). Behavior therapies. In A. Brodsky & R. Hare-Mustin (Eds.), *Women and psychotherapy: An assessment of research and practice* (pp. 217–224). New York: Guilford Press.

Bloom, L. Z., Coburn, K., & Pearlman, J. (1975). *The new assertive woman*. New York: Dell.

Burns, D. D. (1980, November) The perfectionist's script for self-defeat. *Psychology Today*.

Ellis, A., & Harper, R. A. (1974). *A guide to rational living*. North Hollywood, CA: Wilshire Book.

Ellis, E. M., & Nichols, M. P. (1979). A comparative study of feminist and traditional group assertiveness training with women. *Psychotherapy: Theory Research, and Practice, 4,* 467–474.

Fodor, I. G., & Epstein, R. C. (1983). Assertiveness training for women: Where are we failing? In P. Emmelkamp & E. Foa (Eds.), *Failures in behavior therapy* (pp. 132–154). New York, John Wiley.

Horney, K. (1945). *Our inner conflicts*. New York: W.W. Norton.

Horney, K. (1950). *Neurosis and human growth*. New York: W.W. Norton.

Jakubowski, P. A. (1977). Assertive behavior and clinical problems of women. In E. I. Rawlings & D. K. Carter (Eds.), *Psychotherapy for women: Treatment toward equality* (pp. 147–167). Springfield, IL: Charles C. Thomas.

Janeway, E. (1974). *Between myth and morning: Women awakening*. New York: William Morrow.

Janeway, E. (1971). *Man's world, woman's place*. New York: William Morrow.

Jongeward, D., & Scott, D. (1976). *Women as Winners*. Reading, MA: Addison-Wesley.

Kahn, S. E. (1981). Issues in the assessment and training of assertiveness with women. In J. D. Wine & M. D. Smye (Eds.), *Social Competence* (pp. 346–367). New York: Guilford Press.

Kelley, C. (1979). *Assertion training: A facilitator's guide*. La Jolla, CA: University Associates.

Lange, A. J., & Jakubowski, P. A. (1976). *Responsible assertive behavior: Cognitive behavioral procedures for trainers*. Champaign, IL: Research Press.

Linehan, M., & Egan, K. (1979). *Assertion training for women: Square peg in a round hole?* Paper presented at Symposium on Behavior Therapy for Women, Association for Advanced Behavior Therapy, San Francisco, CA.

Miller, J. B. (1976). *Toward a new psychology of women*. Boston: Beacon Press.

Osborn, S. M., & Harris, G. G. (1975). *Assertive training for women*. Springfield, IL: Charles C Thomas.

Phelps, S., & Austin, N. (1975). *The assertive woman*. San Luis Obispo, CA: Impact.

Smith, M. J. (1975). *When I say no, I feel guilty*. New York: Dial Press.

Zukerman, E. (1979). *Changing directions in the treatment of women: A mental health bibliography*. Rockville, MD: DHEW.

■ 7

Getting to "No" and Beyond

LAURIE WEISS

This chapter describes a set of assertive techniques that have been demonstrated, in the author's experience, to be effective in helping women overcome the problem of depression. These techniques have been designed specifically, according to principles derived from a Transactional Analysis approach to developmental theory (Babcok & Keepers, 1976; Levin, 1974).

Eric Berne (1966) has proposed a direct link between feelings of depression and an inadequate supply of recognition—"stroking," in Berne's terms. Steiner (1974) and Levin (1974) elaborated this idea further in describing how early patterns of learning lead to lovelessness, depression, and lack of assertiveness in adults. The process of development of these patterns in early childhood is described in some detail by Babcock and Keepers (1976) and by Levin (1974).

Independently of these Transactional Analysis-based theories, the popular literature on assertiveness (e.g., Alberti & Emmons, 1975; Bloom, Coburn, & Pearlman, 1975; Fensterheim & Baer, 1975) proposes a variety of methods for teaching assertiveness skills. These skills are intended to help individuals communicate directly, honestly, and effectively, in order to avoid unwanted commitments and to make clear what they do want. This chapter shows how the systematic teaching of certain assertiveness skills can help women learn or relearn to identify what they need and want, and to be effective about getting it, thus alleviating depression and establishing a workable method for preventing its recurrence. Suppression of natural assertive behaviors creates the conditions for "stroke" deprivation and subsequent depression. Specific assertive techniques are related to the relevant developmental stage in which assertive behaviors are originally learned or suppressed.

DEVELOPMENTAL ORIGINS OF DEPLETION AND DEPRESSION

Many women who have come to therapy in distress show symptoms not only of depression but also of unresolved anger and bitterness. Often their complaints are along these lines: "I take care of everybody, I think about what they need, and I give them what they need. But when I want something for myself, nobody notices. I'm doing everything I was taught to do to be happy. Why isn't it working?" These distressed women are found in all sorts of situations and roles. What they have in common is the belief that a woman's role is to take care of others. Further, each believes that if she takes care of others long enough and well enough, her turn will come—and with it her reward. This, of course, rarely happens, and women continue to give until they are seriously depleted. Finally, when there appears to be no prospect of obtaining what they need from their relationships, they seek help.

These caretaking women fail to make clear requests concerning their own needs and wants because they believe that getting what they want would deprive somebody else. On the rare occasions that they do make requests, they experience feelings of guilt that serve to reinforce their belief in the necessity of giving to others. A part of the woman says, "See how bad you feel when you take what you want? How can you be so selfish? It's not really worth it, is it?" Because feeling guilty feels worse than doing without what they want, and because they do care about others, these women continue to exist on whatever positive crumbs fall their way. It does not occur to them that they may be carrying more responsibility than is necessary or appropriate.

People "know" what they are supposed to do because of early

socialization and adaptation to role models readily visible to them as they mature. Transactional Analysis developmental theory (Babcock & Keepers, 1976; Levin, 1974) suggests that much of "knowing" can be traced directly to patterns of transactions that occur at specific stages of child development. Most of these transactions take place between children and their "parenters." A parenter is any person providing parenting, not necessarily a biological parent. Once the transactional patterns are set, they tend to recur throughout life. From this framework (Berne, 1972; Steiner, 1974), the aim of therapy is to help the client identify and change fixed patterns that limit autonomous adult functioning.

Most of the patterns that cause problems for depressed women originate between the ages of nine months and three years (Levin, 1974). These dysfunctional patterns then interfere with attempts to learn other healthy patterns during the preschool and grade-school years.

An important developmental task between nine months and 18 months of age is to learn about the environment through active exploration. The transactional response a child needs during the exploratory stage is for a parenter to be available and responsive to the child's initiative. Ideally, the parenter provides protection by making sure the environment is safe for the toddler and by offering distraction from unsafe situations, while leaving the child free to entertain herself with independent exploration. Often, however, the parenter is upset by the toddler's "getting into everything" and tries to limit her exploration by restraining her unnecessarily and, at the same time, keeping her entertained. Inappropriate distraction teaches a child to ignore her own exploratory impulses. Perhaps because of the parenter's expectations, or because of more rapid maturation, many little girls tend to be extremely responsive to this type of stimulation. Instead of exploring on their own, they learn to respond to the external stimulation and approval provided by the parenter. They learn to be "good little girls" before the age of two (Levin, 1974).

An important developmental task for the two year old is to break early symbiotic attachments and establish a sense of independent identity. Transactionally, this is accomplished in two stages. First, the child attempts to experiment with being separate by being oppositional to whatever the parenter suggests; hence, the no-saying, "terrible twos." The appropriate transactional response to this is for the parenter to allow the child as much freedom as possible and not to get particularly upset about the child's oppositional behavior. After the child has been oppositional for some time, usually months, the parenter reaches a point of extreme frustration and the child signals that she is ready for more responsibility. The next stage commences when the parenter insists that the child take care of some of her own needs in a way that also considers the wishes of the parenter; for example, the child is expected to use the potty instead of the diaper, pick up the toys herself, and so forth. After a struggle, the child decides that it is to her own advantage to act independently. The parenter approves, and both win. The child begins to see herself as an important individual in a world of others who are also important.

Often, the "good little girl" is too involved with earning approval from parenters even to attempt to become separate. In never occurs to her to say no or to attempt any opposition. She does get toilet trained and does learn to take responsibility, but this is done in order to please grownups, rather than to please herself. There is little struggle involved, and she rarely experiences her own strength and autonomy.

The "good little girl" asks few questions. Instead, by quiet observation, she figures out what is expected of her and does it. During the school years she is usually no problem: She does not argue or insist on knowing the reasons for rules. She may rebel for a time during adolescence, but during adulthood she usually reverts to the model she learned during childhood. The early parenting patterns, which taught her to ignore her own impulses, serve to keep her unaware of her needs. Because she does not even know what she needs, it is only by accident that she ever gets her needs met. She learns to adapt and to do what is expected of her throughout her life, and then she wonders why she feels empty. She experiences "the problem that has no name" (Friedan, 1963). Often, she lacks a sense of her own individuality and believes she must take care of others in order to be complete (Steiner, 1974). Constant deferral of her own needs to those of others leads to the suppressed anger that, combined with a severe "stroke" deficit, leads to depression (Berne, 1972; Steiner, 1974; Wyckoff, 1977).

"YOU" OR "ME"?

The erroneous idea that people get their needs met only at the expense of others is a cultural problem as well as an individual one (Steiner, 1974, 1981). Our society teaches us to focus on "you" *or* "me"; seldom do we take ourselves and others into account at the same time. Women usually focus on "you"; men often focus on "me." Obviously, both sexes take both positions at different times; women, however, are socialized to focus on "you" in stereotyped ways, such as in making sacrifices for their families. The solution is not to have women focus on "me" instead of on "you," but rather to teach them to focus on "you" *and* "me" and how both can negotiate for what they want (Wyckoff, 1977). Therapy focuses on helping a woman to find analogous ways to relive the transactional developmental experiences so she can achieve new outcomes, learn to take into account what she wants as well as what others want, learn that she is an important individual in her own right, and learn to deal with other individuals in new ways.

SEVEN STEPS TO SAYING NO

Almost always, a former "good little girl" has trouble saying no to the requests of others, and her unwillingness to refuse requests has led directly to her present depleted state. To engage her in the treatment process, the therapist comments, at some point during the initial discussion, "It sounds as if there are very few things you say no to," or "It sounds like you are always saying yes." After she has agreed that saying no is a problem, a seven-step treatment plan is followed.

The seven steps described here focus on specific developmental issues. They do not necessarily take place in the order listed, but all must be accomplished to assure that the depression will not recur. These seven steps can be done as homework and practiced during individual and/or group treatment sessions.

Step 1

During this stage, the client gains practice in saying no, aloud but in private. It may be suggested, as a homework assignment, that she say no 20 times a day, including variations such as, "I don't want to" and "I won't." When she is at home alone, she is to say no about everything she does not want to do: "No, I don't want to make the bed." "No, I don't want to clean up." "No, I don't want to call the repairman." While saying these no statements, she does do the tasks. She continues this process throughout the day, whenever she is alone, and is especially encouraged to say no to things she knows she needs to do and has been putting off.

This formal procedure is used to help the client begin to experience the natural rebelliousness of a two year old beginning to engage in a separation process. It gives the client permission to acknowledge, overtly, feelings she has been attempting to suppress. This procedure is relatively safe because she can do it in complete privacy; it involves no transactions with anyone else.

Step 2

After the client has had a week of practice in saying no in private, she is encouraged to enter into a contract to say it semipublicly. She agrees to tell certain close associates what she is learning about herself and to ask them whether they are willing to help her practice making changes. If so, she and they agree that, for a period of time, she will automatically say no to everything they ask her to do and then discuss with them whether or not she really is willing to do the task. During this stage, most women quickly reconsider their no and do whatever is asked of them.

This stage is riskier than Step 1 because it involves transacting with others. It simulates the beginning of the separation stage of development by providing benign "surrogate parenters" who will listen to the woman's "rebellion" without getting upset, while continuing to stroke her. Simultaneously, it reinforces the position of the client as a responsible adult who does not automatically enjoy the rights of a two year old but must contract with adults for this special treatment.

Step 3

The task here is to say no and mean it, in situations where it is relatively safe to refuse. The client continues to say no semipublicly and consider how she feels about each request. If it is something that she strongly does not want to do, she is encouraged to refuse to do it and to negotiate with the person who made the request. The outcome of the negotiation will be either that the task will get done some other way or that both of them will be satisfied, even if the task does not get done. The important gains here are learning how to negotiate and how to consider the other person's feelings and desires while maintaining her own right to refuse the request. The purpose of saying no at this stage is to recognize and validate the part of her personality that has wanted to say no and has not done so because of her fear of unpleasant consequences.

This procedure encourages the client to use two-year-old rebellion in a healthy, grown up way. She must acknowledge her own dislikes, which is often easier than discovering her likes, and give herself enough consideration to refuse to engage automatically in unpleasant activities.

Negotiation is a skill that a "good little girl" often lacks. During the grade-school years, when less-adapted children began learning to negotiate by arguing incessantly with parents and peers, she remained passive and compliant. To overcome this lack of practice, the client may be encouraged to negotiate with the therapist or others in the therapy group, about meeting times, phone calls, homework assignments, and the like.

Step 4

This important stage of treatment involves going beyond no. First, the client is asked to create a "wish list" or "I want" list. She agrees to carry several index cards with her each day. Every time a fleeting wish occurs, she will write it down and capture it. Once the list is compiled, she agrees to take action on some items. It does not matter whether the item is large or small; the important thing is to take action.

This step recreates the exploratory stage and helps establish a natural pattern of recognizing a desire and doing something active to attain it.

Step 5

During this stage, the client learns to ask other people for what she wants. This is often a frightening step. Few women have had much experience in making direct requests for strokes, appreciation, help, or anything else. Most are used to giving hints about what they want and hoping that someone will respond. Asking directly is threatening, usually due to the fear of being refused. This fear may be alleviated by pointing out that, if she is refused, she will be no worse off than she was before she asked. A client may need lots of time to rehearse her requests and to make plans carefully about who to ask first, who to ask if the first person says no, who else to ask if the second person says no, and so on. An analogy is often useful in helping women pass this barrier: What do they do when a store is out of an everyday item they want? They simply search for it in other stores until they find it.

This procedure takes the client back to an even earlier developmental sequence. Infants and toddlers make direct demands and insist on a response. "Good little girls" are trained to manipulate others in order to obtain what they want, instead of asking for it directly. Many clients feel helpless to get what they want. This step is extremely important in helping the client establish a sense of her own power to control her destiny and to avoid future depression.

Step 6

Here the client breaks her habit of mind-reading what others want. Her instructions are: When you suspect that people want something, ask them what they want instead of guessing and automatically getting it for them. Ask your husband whether he wants you to get a cup of coffee for him, instead of automatically bringing it to him. When your children give you long tales containing invitations for you to help them in some way, ask them why they are telling you about the situation, or ask what they would like you to do about it. After others have made their requests, decide whether you are willing to do as they ask.

Uninhibited preschool children ask many questions in their attempts to understand the world. What they need in response are clear, honest, and age-appropriate answers. "Good little girls" do not like to bother grownups, so, instead of asking, they try to figure things out for themselves. As adult women, they are highly intuitive. Problems arise, however, because they seldom check to find out whether their intuitive perceptions are correct. The tasks of Step 6 reestablish questioning others as a way of getting information and checking out assumptions.

Step 7

The final stage of treatment involves teaching the client how to negotiate and reach consensus in high-risk situations when her wants seem to be in direct conflict with the wants of others. To avoid the unfortunate situations created by people who settle on a "proper" solution to a problem that has never been defined, she is first taught to define the problem clearly and to determine what each person wants, before attempting to settle her conflict. Then she is taught how to state her own needs and wants clearly, how to ask questions that clarify the needs and wants of others, how to discover mutual and complementary needs, how to clarify areas where disagreement exists, how to generate several options that might resolve the disagreement, and, finally, how to choose an alternative that allows each party to achieve satisfaction.

The processes of Step 7 challenge the cultural perception that if one person "wins"' what she wants, another has to lose. Few children are taught to focus on negotiating so that everybody can win. The development of negotiation skills that consider "you" *and* "me" is a task for adults who are aware of themselves as separate individuals with their own important needs and wants and who also recognize that the needs and wants of others are equally valid. This task can be accomplished only after all the other developmental tasks have been completed.

CONCLUSION

When a woman has learned to recognize what she does want, to say no to what she does not want, and to ask others for strokes and support, she no longer is engaging in the learned behaviors that led her to depression. She no longer automatically does what she is "supposed" to do. She thinks about her own needs as well as those of others. She negotiates and creates situations in which everyone wins. She gets what she needs in most situations and begins to be aware of her own autonomy. Her depression lifts as she takes charge of asking for what she wants, turning down what she does not want, and getting an abundance of strokes.

REFERENCES

Alberti, R. E., & Emmons, M. L. (1975). *Stand up, speak out, talk back: The key to self assertive behavior*. New York: Pocket Books.

Babcock, D., & Keepers, T. (1976). *Raising kids OK, Transactional Analysis in human growth and development*. New York: Grove Press.

Berne, E. (1966). *Principles of group treatment*. New York: Grove Press.

Berne, E. (1972). *What do you do after you say hello?* New York: Grove Press.

Bloom L. Z., Coburn, K., & Pearlman, J. (1975). *The new assertive woman*. New York: Delacorte Press.

Fensterheim, H., & Baer, J. (1975). *Don't say yes when you want to say no*. New York: Dell.

Friedan, B. (1963). *The feminine mystique*. New York: W. W. Norton.

Levin, P. (1974). *Becoming the way we are: A transactional guide to personal development*. Berkeley, CA: author.

Steiner, C. (1974). *Scripts people live*. New York: Grove Press.

Steiner, C. (1981). *The other side of power*. New York: Grove Press.

Wyckoff, H. (1977). *Solving women's problems through awareness, action, and contact*. New York: Grove Press.

∎8
Therapeutic Anger in Women

VASANTI BURTLE

Acted-out anger is socially and legally censured in virtually every culture. Women in cultures that foster rigid gender-role demarcations have found that the proscription against acting out extends even to the experiencing of anger. The "normal" woman is thus perceived socially as passive in terms of acted-out behavior and passionless in her inner experience of an important human emotion.

Such an attitude is obviously unacceptable to the clinician who believes that therapy with women is truly effective only when the client gains access to the full repertoire of her emotions and learns to work with those emotions in healthy ways. Like men, women are entitled to the experience of anger and they need to use it in ways that do not injure themselves or others. The experience and healthy use of anger can serve as a significant therapeutic tool in the treatment of women, and the feminist clinician needs to examine how the client's personality and the socialized suppression of anger intermesh as catalysts for pathology.

MENTAL HEALTH PROFESSIONALS AND
WOMEN'S ANGER

The cultural image of the "good," angerless woman has had its most insidious effects in the hands of mental health professionals. Before the advent of feminism, the course of therapy for women clients was largely guided by Freud's doctrine (1933) that masochism is "truly feminine" in that it binds erotically destructive tendencies that have been turned inward. That position was reinforced further by Deutsch's (1944) identification of the "feminine core" as passivity, masochism, and narcissism. The main thrust of therapy, then, was to help women to endure their suffering rather than to remove its cause or promote personal growth.

Later, women were helped to deal with emotional problems by iatrogenic masking or suppression of anger through overuse of antidepressants, anxiolytics, tranquilizers, and the organic changes associated with electroconvulsive shock treatment. Anger also was controlled through the covert encouragement of the use of prescription drugs and alcohol. The chemical management of women is still promoted actively as a means for maintaining the illusory ideal of womanhood.

Contemporary literature shows little understanding of anger in women. When Madow (1972), for example, criticizes feminists for "seeming unduly hostile and aggressive," or when he describes rape in terms of a teasing woman inciting the rape and then showing her anger by having her attacker severely punished, he makes no comment on the quality of anger typical of the dispossessed or of the victim of a crime. Blum (1976) shows less insensitivity when he states that women cannot be expected to function in a "good-enough mothering role" if they have resolved the problem of aggression only in masochistic ways. His statement, as Nadelson, Notman, Miller, and Zilbach (1982) underline, implies that aggression in women is acceptable only in the service of others.

Carol Tavris (1982) summarily dismisses the connection between anger and depression in women (Chesler, 1972; Weissman & Paykel, 1974) and cites Beck's cognitive therapy, but without reference to the statement made by Beck and Greenberg (1974) that "women are in fact no more predisposed to suffer from depression than are men. What distinguishes male from female depression is simply that the events which typically trigger depression tend to be sex-typed" (p. 129). Tavris sees no difference between men and women in either the experience or expression of anger, save that women are more reluctant to express anger in public places. She fails, however, to examine what factors in society or in family socialization may contribute to that difference. Citing a study in which Hokanson (1970) "created masochism in his laboratory," she reports,

> Hokanson noticed something that most of his fellow psychologists were ignoring in the 1960's: Women. They were not behaving like men. When you insulted them, they didn't get belligerent; they generally said something friendly to try to calm you down. When Hokanson wired them up to a physiological monitor to see whether they were secretly seething with rage, he discovered that . . . for men, aggression was cathartic for anger; for women, *friendliness* was cathartic. [p. 124]

Tavris makes no effort to reconcile this finding with her twin arguments that (1) the expression of anger can only create more anger (and is therefore not cathartic), and (2) there is no difference between men's and women's experience and expression of anger. Nor does she apply her emphasis on learning theory to a discussion of Hokanson's results.

When Broverman, Broverman, Clarkson, Rosenkrantz, and Vogel (1970) published their landmark study, they reported that mental health practitioners perceive the healthy woman as different from the healthy man; that is, being more submissive, more easily influenced, more excitable in crises, more emotional, more conceited about appearance, having feelings more easily hurt, less independent, less adventurous, less objective, less competitive, and less aggressive. While those criteria of health are all too often accepted as the goal of therapy for women and the resolution of anger is never approached, a new attitude is beginning to emerge.

Anger is a major feminist issue; and consciousness-raising groups have played a critical role in helping women "find their anger" (Cherniss, 1972; cited in Kirsh, 1974). With increasing sensitivity to women's disadvantaged position in society, anger is identified, expressed, and allowed to reach a catharsis, so that personal and social change are facilitated.

Novaco's (1975) cognitive treatment approach to anger management is admirably conceived but exemplifies some of the pitfalls that feminist clinicians working with women need to avoid. Novaco proposes that making a nonantagonistic response to provocation will cause individuals to believe that they are not angry; indeed, Novaco had developed a series of self-statements designed to regulate anger in this way. The danger is that many of these suggested self-statements can serve to help oversocialized women deny anger totally. For instance, the self-statement, "For someone to be that irritable, he must be awfully unhappy," is an open invitation for an oversocialized woman to rescue and nurture the person who is attacking her.

Those mental health professionals who have addressed the issue of anger in women for the most part have concerned themselves with the management of anger, either through masochistic and submissive ways or through cognitive and behavioral procedures. Appropriate anger management is indeed an essential component of emotional maturation, but, in the present writer's opinion, it needs to be founded on a therapeutic process whereby the woman client is enabled to look at her experience of anger, accept it without guilt or loss of self-respect, and eventually learn to express it or use it in ways that foster healthy growth and self-esteem and facilitate good relationships and effective functioning in the community.

A NEW TREATMENT APPROACH

The following observations are based on the writer's approach to anger as a treatment tool for women. It has helped to resolve problems of underlying anger in women with clinical depression, panicky anxiety attacks, explosiveness, and alcohol or drug abuse; and has proven useful for women seeking emotional growth and effective participation in personal and professional relationships.

The Clinician's Attitude

The feminist clinician working with women clients has no need for traditional professional stereotypes. Clinician and client relate on a first-name basis, with both sitting at a close but comfortable distance (with the determination of intervening space left to the client), and without furniture cluttering the emotional and physical space between them. The clinician in such a setting is an ally, capable of sharing the client's anger and of turning its energy into adaptive channels. She is real, and she is a role model.

For these reasons, she has to exercise special care to avoid the client's covert invitations to blame or censure; for, as scapegoat, the client is on familiar territory. If, for example, the client expresses a rageful desire to kill her child, the clinician will reassure herself as to the safety of the child. Then, she will not place the client in the stereotype of the "bad mother," but rather will sort out what, in that statement, is fantasy, self-hate, helplessness, hurt, inadequacy, and/or emotional impotence.

Aspects of Anger Therapy

Validating the Anger Experience. The angry self-image, while negative for many men, is often abnormal or grotesque to women. For example, a client described herself when angry as a "diabolical noncreature who goes about in this twisted, inhuman way, causing destruction and being wild and untamed and generally diabolical." The acknowledgment and validation of anger is important in modifying such a self-image. From the outset, the client needs to learn not to back off from her anger, to understand that it is a vital element in the repertoire of human emotions, a mechanism designed to ensure survival, with potential for positive action. She must be convinced that the energy aroused by the anger response need not be used to hurt either herself or others but can be used for appropriate self-assertion, maintenance of good relationships, and creativity.

Examining the Anger Experience. Whether the client is in outright denial of anger or whether she presents with a history of inappropriate acting out and expression of anger, she may find it virtually impossible to verbalize the quality of that anger. She may need help in seeing that anger is not a unitary emotion and in identifying what feelings of helplessness, hurt, frustration, or outrage underlie the overwhelming feeling of aroused anger. Focusing on those feelings becomes the core of the therapeutic process.

To facilitate the examination of the anger experience, it is often useful to have clients draw their feelings. Graphic expression results in a wide range of representations, some showing turmoil in a tangle of colored scribbles, others persisting in denial through drawings of flowers or smiling faces, and others reflecting the black hues and trapped configurations of depression. When women choose to draw themselves, they may produce a stereotypically seductive female outline, with red flames blazing in the midsection and tears flowing down the face or draw themselves as grotesque witches and vampires.

Once the client is convinced that she will not be condemned for whatever extremes of anger she has illustrated, she usually will be ready to discuss the drawing. In so doing, she is enabled to describe her actual feelings of anger as well as the feelings from which anger emanated.

Anger Management. Once the experience of anger has been acknowledged and its quality identified, it is important to provide the client with a growing mastery over that anger, prior to learning appropriate expression of it. Three approaches have been useful in moderating the high energy and overwhelming emotion associated with anger arousal: a physical workout, an emotional intermission, and the transfer of power.

A physical workout tends to dissipate high levels of adrenalin in the system. Exercise, swimming, jogging, bataca work, simply pounding pillows, and screaming in some private place have all been useful.

Complete change of focus also has been effective, provided anger has been owned and validated first. An emotional intermission, with attention focused on routine, sequential tasks, often can restore a sense of mastery that is the first step in dealing with the source of anger. A similar result is achieved through imagery that takes the client's attention out of the mousetrap of the moment and transposes it to a wide-range perspective in which her immediate problems are seemingly reduced in magnitude. The effect is often a sense of restored competence.

Yet another approach involves the symbolic transfer of power from the other to the self. The "bag and shelve" exercise requires the client to imagine her opponent standing in front of her and shrinking until he or she is small enough to put into a supermarket bag, which the client then imagines herself folding at the top and placing on a high shelf. Completely based on imagery, the effect of this exercise is that of canceling out the feelings of helplessness, frustration, and hurt that underlie anger. Another approach requires the client to give her adversary a small, symbolic gift, without the latter's knowledge. She may choose, when angry feelings supervene, to give a penny that is placed in a special box or bowl. As the number of pennies grows, so anger diminishes, because gift giving is a powerful act that restores a sense of mastery over the environment.

Clearing the Way for Considered Action. Drawing out and defusing anger circumvents depression and acting out and allows the client freedom from the interference that anger imposes on attention and information processing (Novaco, 1975; cf. Bogen, 1969), so she can maintain the objectivity necessary for correcting the injuries done to her.

Now it becomes important for the client to examine her values, as few women have given systematic thought to personal ideology. Values determination sows the seeds of identity, facilitates the decision-making process, and facilitates the use of power in appropriate ways.

Although not endorsing McClelland's (1975) comments on power in women, this author has found that his four-stage paradigm of power offers a useful model for putting the client in touch with the different ways in which she can be effective in expressing her anger and at the same time gain insight into ways in which she uses power inappropriately. In stage 1, power is derived from dependency: "They are dependent because it makes them feel strong to be near a source of strength" (p. 15). In stage 2, power comes through self-control, self-management, and autonomy of thought and behavior. For women, usually, the pathological aspects of stage 1 will have to be worked through in treatment and the acceptance and practice stage 2 facilitated.

Stage 3 involves power through impact on others, including helping behavior. "For help to be given, help must be received. And in accepting a gift, or help, the receiver can be perceived as acknowledging that he is weaker . . . than the person who is giving him help" (McClelland, 1975, p. 18). Certainly, both in family life and in the economic sector, women's giving is often perceived as the receiver's right, and women must value their own giving before it is valued by others.

Stage 4 is an aspect of duty. McClelland notes that "the self drops out as a source of power and a person sees himself as an instrument of a higher authority which moves him to try to influence or serve others" (1975, p. 20). Women who come into therapy frequently find it extremely difficult to see themselves as instruments of any authority higher than parents, husband, children, or employers, if personal values remain indeterminate.

Once the client has identified maladaptive and unhealthy uses of these four aspects of power, she learns to practice them appropriately. As described by McClelland, "Maturity involves the ability to use whatever mode is appropriate to the situation. Immaturity involves using

78   : :   Feminist Psychotherapeutic Practices

perhaps only one mode . . . or using a mode inappropriate to a particular situation" (1975, p. 24).

Thus, self-assertion (Alberti & Emmons, 1978; Butler, 1983; Fensterheim & Baer, 1975) takes on a more meaningful dimension because it is predicated on the most appropriate use of power and one's personal value system. It no longer will be an imperative on women, emanating from an external locus of control, but a self-evolved and very personal style of assertion that constitutes a positive outcome of anger therapy.

CONCLUSION

The experience of anger—an ordinary and "normal" emotion—cannot be given indiscriminate expression through inappropriate verbalization or confrontation while in a state of anger. The suppression or repression of anger, on the other hand, may trigger emotional problems; and this is particularly true of women whose socialization, by excluding both the experience and the expression of anger from the feminine role, has frequently been the forerunner of severe psychological sequelae. Appropriately used, therefore, anger therapy can play a significant role both in the treatment of clinical pathology and in the emotional maturation of women clients.

REFERENCES

Alberti, R. E., & Emmons, M. L. (1978). *Your perfect right: A guide to assertive behavior*. San Luis Obispo: Impact Publishers.
Beck, A. T., & Greenberg, R. L. (1974). Cognitive therapy with depressed women. In V. Franks & V. Burtle (Eds.), *Women in therapy: New psychotherapies for a changing society* (pp. 113-131). New York: Brunner/Mazel.
Blum, H. (1976). Female psychology, masochism, and the ego idea. *Journal of the American Psychoanalytical Association, 24*(5), 305–351.
Bogen, J. E. (1969). The other side of the brain, II: An appositional mind. *Bulletin of the Los Angeles Neurological Societies, 34*(2), 135–162.
Broverman, I. K., Broverman, D. M., Clarkson, F. E., Rosenkrantz, D. P., & Vogel, S. R. (1970). Sex-role stereotypes and clinical judgments of mental health. *Journal of Consulting and Clinical Psychology, 34*, 1–7.
Butler, P. (1983). *Self-assertion for women*. New York: Harper & Row.
Cherniss, C. (1972). Personality and ideology: A personalogical study of women's liberation. *Psychiatry, 35*, 104–125.

Chesler, P. (1972). *Women and madness*. New York: Doubleday.

Deutsch, H. (1944). *The psychology of women*. New York: Grune & Stratton.

Fensterheim, H., & Baer, J. (1975). *Don't say yes when you want to say no*. New York: Dell.

Freud, S. (1933). *The psychology of women*. New York: W. W. Norton.

Hokanson, J. E. (1970). Psychophysiological evaluation of the catharsis hypothesis. In E. L. Megargee & J. E. Hokanson (Eds.), *The dynamics of aggression*. New York: Harper & Row.

Kirsh, B. (1974). Consciousness-raising groups as therapy for women. In V. Franks & V. Burtle (Eds.), *Women in therapy: New psychotherapies for a changing society* (pp. 526–534). New York: Brunner/Mazel.

Madow, L. (1972). *Anger*. New York: Scribners.

McClelland, D. C. (1975). *Power: The inner experience*. New York: Irvington.

Nadelson, C. C., Notman, M. T., Miller, J. B., & Zilbach, J. (1982). Aggression in women: Conceptual issues and clinical implications. In M. T. Notman & C. C. Nadelson (Eds.), *The woman patient* (vol. 3: Aggression, adaptations, and psychotherapy) (pp. 17–28). New York: Plenum Press.

Novaco, R. W. (1975). *Anger Control: The development and evaluation of an experimental treatment*. Lexington, MA: Lexington Books.

Tavris, C. (1982). *Anger: The misunderstood emotion*. New York: Simon & Schuster.

Weissman, M. M., & Paykel, E. S. (1974). *The depressed woman: A study of social relationships*. Chicago: University of Chicago Press.

Feminist Body Psychotherapy[1]

LAUREE E. MOSS

THE TOUCH TABOO

The use of touch and other nonverbal techniques in psychotherapy has
been controversial since the inception of the psychoanalytic movement.
In an article entitled "The Value of Touch in Psychotherapy," Jean
Wilson (1982), a nurse and psychotherapist, traces the history of therapists' attitudes toward touching:

> Before Freud's time, psychiatry was essentially the application of various
> physical therapies . . . to the body in an attempt to influence the mind.
> Freud postulated the structure and dynamics of the psyche but kept the
> body and its systems as a frame of reference. His theory had its basis in
> physical medicine. In his early work on hysteria, Freud was impressed by
> the apparent power of touching and massaging patients who were dis-

1. The author acknowledges with gratitude the assistance of Marny Hall, Maggie Rocklin,
   Alana Schilling, and Tedi Dunn in the preparation of this chapter. Also, the suggestions
   of Lynne Bravo Rosewater, in the beginning, and the editorial assistance and support of
   Carolyn Larsen and Lorna Cammaert have been greatly appreciated.

traught. For a time, in his practice, he stroked the patient's head and neck for stimulative effect. He also allowed patients to touch him.

As the art of psychotherapy evolved, many clinicians considered touch to be detrimental to the therapeutic relationship. Wolberg, Menninger, Render and Weiss forbade any touch in therapy for fear that touch may arouse sexual feelings and bring forth outbursts of anger. [p. 66]

Even though feminist therapists have taken a nontraditional approach to many therapeutic issues in their practices and writings, they have not challenged this "touch taboo" to any significant degree. Wilson's article suggests that therapists who use touch do not speak of it for fear of misunderstandings or repercussions. For feminist therapists, the concept of touching may raise the specter of sexual exploitation of female clients by male psychotherapists. Even when client and therapist are both women, touch may evoke troublesome sexual feelings or boundary issues. These concerns are legitimate, but to avoid any discussion of touch and its utilization as a therapeutic technique is a classic example of baby and bathwater going out together.

THE CONSPIRACY OF SILENCE

The formal training of psychotherapists typically excludes touch as an integral part of therapy. The nonverbal techniques of movement, breathing, and energy work usually are absent from the psychotherapy curriculum also, although the more humanistically oriented schools present these therapies as elective courses. More often, however, these subjects are discounted as "touchy-feely California" therapies, grouped with Reichian and bioenergetic body therapies, or labeled as radical or avant-garde.

The fear of being considered a less-than-reputable practitioner prevents many therapists and students alike from viewing body therapy as a viable therapeutic approach. Not only are therapists inhibited in the use of touch, but this self-imposed censorship prevents discussion of the subject by students who might otherwise express an interest in nonverbal work. Fearing that touch and other nonverbal methods of working will raise more difficult issues and/or create additional transference and countertransference problems, too many therapists deny themselves and their clients the opportunity to contact and experience such deep-seated and long-repressed emotions as rage, pain, longing, sexual fears, terror, and grief.

Nevertheless, it is becoming more and more apparent that verbal therapy alone is not bridging the gap between body and mind (Mander & Rush, 1974; Moss, 1981). It does not, and cannot, address the estrangement that people feel from their bodies. In fact, working with the mind and feelings and not paying attention to the body actually can reinforce the pathology of the mind/body split. This split, or self-alienation, is one of the major problems that therapists must work toward healing, in themselves as well as in their clients. Many psychological, sociological, and political factors, arising out of the patriarchy, are both cause and effect of this schism. Women especially are beginning to recognize this split as a major factor in their denial of self-love and personal power. As Adrienne Rich (1977) states:

> I know no woman—virgin, mother, lesbian, married, celibate—whether she earns her keep as a housewife, a cocktail waitress, or a scanner of brain waves—for whom her body is not a fundamental problem: its clouded meaning, its fertility, its desire, its so-called frigidity, its bloody speech, its silences, its changes and mutilations, its rapes and ripenings. There is for the first time today a possibility of converting our physicality into both knowledge and power. [p. 290]

The specific issues that feminist therapists address are all familiar ones: power, assertiveness, intimacy, autonomy, sexuality, self-esteem, and the awareness and expression of anger. Because divisions often lie at the core of these issues—divisions between mind and body, between "right" and "wrong" versions of self, between self and others—these divisions are more fully explored and overcome within the context of an integrated mind/body approach to therapy. By facilitating a new linkage between feelings and bodily sensations, body therapy helps women to begin to reclaim their bodies. Accompanying this experience of unity is a new sense of empowerment.

FEMINIST BODY PSYCHOTHERAPY

Body therapy encompasses an understanding of body language and employs breath awareness, movement, voice work, and touch. The theories and techniques of body psychotherapy can be utilized by any therapist, regardless of her therapeutic approach. To integrate verbal and body therapies within a feminist perspective, this author blended the theories of two traditional body therapies with less well-known theories and techniques developed by several German women. For example, work with the voice often is used to aid expression of emotions such as anger, sadness, and joy; and touch can be used to work with energy and with chronically tight muscles, as well as to nurture, support, and console the client. This new model is also influenced by psychodynamic theory and gestalt therapy.

Influences

Traditional body therapies are well represented by the theories of Wilhelm Reich (1967, 1971, 1972) and Alexander Lowen's bioenergetics (1967, 1975). The work of these men "focuses on the linguistic, postural, muscular, and gestural characteristics of the individual" (Moss, 1981, p. 24) and is based on the belief that the body holds repressed thoughts and feelings. Thus, the body can provide important and useful access to unconscious materials and unresolved conflicts. Attention to such body characteristics can help the client to identify and release painful and blocked emotions. The body therapy techniques developed by Reich and Lowen and their followers, however, involve much stressful and often painful work, such as hitting, kicking, screaming, intense breathing, stress-inducing positions and movements, and deep pressure applied to tight musculature, referred to as one's body armor.

In dramatic contrast to this approach is the body work developed by a few German women, including Elsa Gindler, Magda Proskauer, Marion Rosen, Ilse Middendorf, and Doris Breyer (Moss, 1981). Their work promotes mind/body awareness and integration using such techniques as movement, touch, natural breathing, sensory awareness, and voice work. Although relatively unknown in the United States, these women and their work have gained attention in the last few years (Kogan, 1980; Moss, 1981; Rush, 1973, 1979) because of their nonstressful and nonpainful practices. Initially trained in the physical therapies, each of these women subsequently has pursued psychological studies or training or has worked with psychological consultants to increase her knowledge and understanding of human behavior.

Although feminist body psychotherapy has been influenced significantly by the work of Reich and Lowen, it diverges from their theories and practices in important ways. First, the literature of Reich and Lowen, like most of the psychological literature of Freud and his followers, does not consider the changing social and cultural roles of women in society. Traditional body therapies are laden with Freudian assumptions and value judgments about women and are filled with uncompromising attitudes about homosexuality. Second, the pushing and straining emphasis of the techniques, which are often experienced as painful and stressful, are an aggressive and frequently inappropriate way to help a woman become aware of and sensitive to the different sensations and expressions of her body.

The *nonpainful, nonstressful* body work practices of Gindler, Proskauer, Rosen, Middendorf, and Breyer are integrated into a nurturing approach for working with the same issues and problems noted in the traditional body therapies (Moss, 1981). The feminist body psychotherapist teaches her client how to love herself, including her body, how to use her body to express her feelings instead of blocking them, and how to listen to her body's physical messages to gain understanding of her needs and desires for release, expression, and contact. An underlying assumption of feminist body psychotherapy is that all lifestyles and sexual identities (such as lesbian, bisexual, celibate, heterosexual) are valid and should be affirmed in therapy.

Integration

Feminist Body Psychotherapy enhances physical and emotional awareness through techniques that integrate verbal exploration with the techniques already mentioned: gentle movements, soft energetic touch, natural breathing, and voice work. To use this work in therapy, the therapist must form a therapeutic alliance with the client before introducing these nonverbal methods. Typically this can take four to six sessions and in some cases much longer. The therapist must trust her clinical judgment and intuition about the appropriate time to use touch or other body therapy techniques.

A basic principle of feminist body psychotherapy is *"Don't push the river"* (Sevens, 1970). Nudge, gently encourage, support, and allow time for personal change to occur (Moss, 1981). Within a benign, safe environment, the organism can work naturally and beautifully to achieve peace and balance. With therapeutic intervention, the individual can increase her awareness of chronic tension, repressed feelings, and habitual posture patterns. As she does so, her organism slowly will free itself of its restrictions—without excessive pain, force, or stress.

Clinical Examples

Two clinical examples of feminist body psychotherapy will illustrate these concepts.

Sara. A 40-year-old therapist, wife, and mother, Sara came for body therapy with chronic shoulder pain, having had extensive verbal psychotherapy. Formerly an active, independent feminist, over the last decade she had devoted herself more and more to traditional wife and mother roles. On returning to work as a therapist, she felt competitive and one-down professionally in relation to her husband.

During our third session, I suggested that Sara lie down and begin to notice where in her body she felt the rise and fall of her breath. Using a simple technique of inhaling and exhaling with a pause after exhalation, Sara relaxed and became conscious of the novelty of the sensation. Since she exercised regularly, she was surprised to discover she had felt tension everywhere in her body.

With her permission, I put my hand on her belly for a few minutes as she breathed naturally. I removed my hand and asked what she felt. She reported a softness in her belly which for once she did not experience as flabbiness. It felt warm and soothing. She remarked that my hand felt gentle and comforting, permitting her to experience those feelings. After she consciously inhaled and exhaled for a few minutes, I asked Sara to resume natural breathing and to focus on whatever sensations she experienced. She reported sadness emerging from her belly and a sense of not being soft with herself. This sadness reminded her of her right shoulder, which had been hurting and now hurt less.

Asked what her sadness meant, Sara reported that simply lying down and breathing had so relaxed her that she realized how little time she spends with herself. As tears welled up, she said that she had always pushed herself to be a perfect wife, perfect mother, perfect therapist. She sobbed as she expressed her disappointment with herself: She thought she already had worked these issues through in her previous therapy.

When her crying eased, Sara said she could see that she had never really given up her striving to be perfect. As she spoke, I put one hand above her shoulder and my other under it, holding and cradling her shoulder. I felt her shoulder release and rest in my hands. I asked her to say what she was experiencing. She connected the relaxation in her shoulder and the lessening of pain with the nurturance she felt from my hands. She saw her chronic pain as a message from her body to take better care of herself, to retain some nurturance for herself.

A few weeks later, noting increased body tension in a stressful and potentially dangerous situation, Sara began using the breathing exercises to relax and become more centered. She purposely made time for herself for this nurturing activity. As a result, she was more effective in handling this difficult situation. Now Sara uses her body's signals—that is, her body tension and/or pain in her shoulder—as barometers of her need for self-nurturance. The nonverbal techniques used throughout our sessions gave Sara some tools for reducing and eliminating pain in her shoulder and for becoming more loving toward herself.

Iris.   A young college woman who had struggled for years with issues of body weight and size, Iris sought help from me because of my work with women on such issues. Iris was feeling proud of having recently lost weight. She also was angry at the society that made her hate her body and wanted to learn about fat liberation so she could learn to accept her body.

We spoke at length about the oppression of fat people and the forms of discrimination they experience. Despite my interest in the fat liberation movement, she questioned my ability to understand her struggles since I was not fat. She reported difficulty in talking about her feelings to women smaller or thinner than herself. I supported Iris' desire to talk with women her own size. I told her about local resources for fat women—a fat women's theater group and fat liberation support groups. Potential involvement in fat liberation aroused both fear and excitement in Iris.

I worked verbally with Iris until the day she arrived at a session feeling very anxious and angry. She had just eaten lunch but still felt hungry and was afraid that she would go home and binge after our session. She found this upsetting, since she recently had begun to feel good about her eating habits.

I chose to explore her feelings of hunger and asked Iris to try an experiment. She agreed to close her eyes and report whatever she was aware of in her body, from head to toe. She reported a feeling of tightness in her chest and throat and a pressure around her eyes, which I associated with a desire to cry.

I asked Iris to talk more about what had gone on at the lunch with her lover, who was one of her most important friends and constant companion. Her lover was distraught because of a death that required that she return home indefinitely. Iris, after briefly comforting her, drove her to the airport and then came to therapy.

I suggested to Iris that her lover's unhappiness and sudden departure must be very upsetting, that perhaps she was not feeling hungry at all but felt like crying. This indeed was the case, and she began to weep. As Iris' weeping intensified, I encouraged her to let her voice out and to not hold her breath. I asked her if she wanted to be held. Iris shook her head no, and I told her that if she changed her mind she should let me know. With her sobs increasing and breathing deepening, Iris spontaneously lay down in a fetal position on the couch.

When her crying ceased, Iris reached out to hold my hand, saying she felt differently now. She reported the sensations in her throat and chest were gone and she was very aware that she had been breathing minimally. She connected holding her breath to holding back her tears. She said that when she was crying at the beginning, she felt tense and hopeless, but when I reminded her about her breath, her crying had deepened and she had begun to feel less tense and desperate. We discussed the connection between minimal, controlled breathing and blocked emotions.

This examination of her bodily sensations, crying, and awareness of her breath helped Iris to contact her sense of grief and her feelings of helplessness about her lover's situation and her own loss of daily support. She also learned the important connection between breath and emotional expression. She saw the value of developing a support system outside of the home and recognized that hunger and compulsive eating were often connected to situations in which she actually felt like crying.

Eventually, through therapy and participating in a fat liberation support group, Iris began to accept her body, irrespective of weight gains or losses. At the same time, she focused on getting in touch with her actual feelings and on learning to handle stress in her life without falling apart or going on a food binge.

These two greatly abbreviated examples highlight certain common issues that women bring to therapy and their satisfactory resolution through an integration of verbal and nonverbal approaches. I have selected examples where touch and other nonverbal techniques have supplemented feminist therapy. The *process* of feminist body psychotherapy, however, is as difficult to describe as are most psychotherapeutic processes. Examples of women who have characterological problems or who have been in therapy for more than two years were not included because of the difficulty of describing long-term psychotherapy briefly. A long-term treatment approach is compatible with feminist body psychotherapy, provided the therapist has a good sense of timing about intervention and the clinical judgment to decide which techniques are appropriate in each situation.

Becoming a Feminist Body Psychotherapist

The therapist wanting to integrate body psychotherapy into her work must begin with an examination of her own mind/body split and her feelings about her own body. Before she can help clients to utilize nonverbal techniques, the therapist must have some direct experience with these techniques herself. In addition to familiarity with techniques that promote greater body awareness and increased mobility and motility and permit fuller and more open breath, she must have a sensitivity about variations of touch, including pressure-point work, massage, stroking, and holding.

To gain this familiarity and sensitivity, the therapist needs to acknowledge and explore her reservations and fears about touching per se and about using touch in therapy. Comfort with touch often can be acquired through massage workshops and by talking and working with colleagues and friends who have had body therapy experiences. Intensive training is valuable but not essential. There are many books on the market today about the body, some of them already cited in this chapter. Weekend workshops, consultation, and supervision are other invaluable aids for helping the therapist increase her knowledge of the body and how it works. Then, together with other therapists, she needs to talk about her fears— and theirs. Therapists must examine both how fear inhibits the use of touch and how therapy promotes or discourages the mind/body split.

SUMMARY

Feminist body psychotherapy is essentially an integrative process. It encompasses feminist values and beliefs and draws on the theoretical orientations of Freud, gestalt therapy, bioenergetics, Reichian therapy, and the nonstressful and nonpainful approaches developed by several German women body therapists. Many of the theories and tools from these methods are used by feminist body psychotherapists to focus on the issues that emerge during therapy. The body therapy techniques per se emphasize the female way of working. With discussions, training, and consultation, body therapy techniques can be integrated into feminist therapy to help heal the mind/body split in ourselves and our clients.

A quote from Adrienne Rich (1977) provides a meaningful conclusion and future direction:

> In arguing that we have by no means yet explored or understood our biological grounding, the miracle and paradox of the female body and its spiritual and political meanings, I am really asking whether women cannot begin, at last, to *think through the body*, what has been so cruelly disorganized—our great mental capacities, hardly used; our highly developed tactile sense; our genius for close observation; our complicated pain-enduring multipleasured physicality. . . .
>
> We need to imagine a world in which every woman is the presiding genius of her own body. In such a world women will truly create new life, bring forth not only children (if and when we choose) but the visions, and the thinking necessary to sustain, console, and alter human existence—a new relationship to the universe. Sexuality, politics, intelligence, power, motherhood, work, community, intimacy will develop new meanings; thinking itself will be transformed.
>
> This is where we have to begin. [pp. 290, 292]

REFERENCES

Kogan, G. (1980). *Your body works: A guide to health, energy and balance*. Berkeley, CA: Transformation Press.

Lowen, A. (1967). *Language of the body*. New York: Collier.

Lowen, A. (1975). *Bioenergetics*. New York: Coward, McCann and Geoghegan.

Mander, A. V., & Rush, A. K. (1974). *Feminism as therapy*. New York: Random House.

Moss, L. E. (1981). *A woman's way: A feminist approach to body psychotherapy*. Ann Arbor, MI: University Microfilms International.

Reich, W. (1967). *The sexual revolution*. New York: Farrar, Straus, and Giroux.

Reich, W. (1971). *Selected writings: An introduction to orgonomy*. New York: Farrar, Straus, and Giroux.

90   : : *Feminist Psychotherapeutic Practices*

Reich, W. (1972) *Character analysis* (3rd ed.). New York: Farrar, Straus, and Giroux.

Rich, A. (1977). *Of woman born*. New York: Bantam.

Rush, A. K. (1973). *Getting clear: Body work for women*. New York: Random House.

Rush, A. K. (1979). *The basic back book: The complete manual of back care*. Berkeley, CA: Moon Books/Summit Books.

Stevens, B. (1970). *Don't push the river*. Moab, UT: Real People Press.

Wilson, J. M. (1982). The value of touch in psychotherapy. *American Journal of Orthopsychiatry, 52*, 65–72.

10
Lesbian Couples and Families: A Co-Therapeutic Approach to Counseling

SARA SHARRATT AND LILIAN BERN

HETEROSEXISM IN PSYCHOTHERAPY

In spite of the growth and wealth of feminist psychological writings in the last decade, much of our current thinking continues to be painfully heterosexist. In the much-praised work of Miller (1976), Dinnerstein (1976), Chodorow (1978), and Brodsky and Hare-Mustin (1980), there is no mention of lesbianism and/or lesbian relationships.

Rich (1980) brilliantly analyzes the compulsory nature of hetero-sexuality, exposing the heterosexist assumptions contained in much feminist thought: "We can no longer have patience with Dinnerstein's veiw that women simply collaborated with men on sexual arrangements of history . . . heterosexuality has been forcibly and subliminally imposed on women" (pp. 652–653). The assumption that most women are innately heterosexual continues to be reflected in our attempts at creating a new psychology of women.

Nevertheless, there has been an increased awareness that many women couple with other women in committed relationships and that many raise children in lesbian families. The resistance to dealing with other than heterosexual arrangements reflects the continuing presence of heterosexism and homophobia; and, while we as feminists examine homophobia, we are less willing to challenge heterosexism.

Nowhere are heterosexism and homophobia more evident than in the field of family therapy. This is apparent in feminist analyses of couples' adjustments (Laws, 1975) and marital and family conflicts (Gurman & Klein, 1980) outlined in textbooks dealing with women and psychotherapy.

Hare-Mustin (1978), in advocating a feminist family therapy approach, still holds onto a traditional heterosexual definition of family and familial arrangements. Out of a total of 49 references, this article, which was given the outstanding achievement award by the Association for Women in Psychology, cites no work about or for lesbians.

It is not surprising to find that psychotherapy for lesbians has not been readily available, especially sexual, couples, and/or family therapy. Also, the minimal writings for and work with lesbians in psychotherapy have been done predominantly by lesbians themselves, who, due to their own lifestyles, could not join in the myth that all families and/or couples are heterosexual (Escamilla-Mondonaro, 1977; Hall, 1978; Riddle & Sang, 1978; Sang, 1977).

While it is imperative that, as lesbians, we write about our own experience, it is just as imperative that our heterosexual sisters begin to examine their basic heterosexism and their oppression of lesbians—that is, their denial of lesbian existence in their writings. They must engage actively in confronting these issues with each other (Beck, 1982; Katz, 1978). Lesbians have been carrying the burden of doing most of the consciousness raising, teaching, and advocacy.

Signs of this oppression are evident in therapeutic practice. The assumption is often made that a heterosexual female therapist requires no additional training in working with lesbian clients. Conversely, the lesbian therapist is often asked to examine possible countertransference issues, especially around men and heterosexuality. Lesbian therapists sometimes complain about not being recognized as psychotherapists because their identity as lesbians takes precedence over their identity as psychotherapists.

LESBIAN RELATIONSHIPS

Most women come to therapy with relational problems, and lesbians are no exception (Anthony, 1982). Yet, for lesbians these difficulties are compounded, for the following reasons:

1. Lesbian relationships do not receive the recognition, validation, and support that are given to heterosexual relationships (Hall, 1978). We live in a highly homophobic, heterosexist society, where lesbians continually face the risk of severe losses: loss of job, loss of family support and approval, loss of children, loss of heterosexual friends, loss of status and respect in the community. Furthermore, legal marriage is not available to lesbians as proof of their commitment to each other in the eyes of society. These factors increase the interdependency and the expectations that the partners have with one another, which of course bring additional stresses to the relationship.

2. This lack of recognition and validation is also common within the lesbian community, as a result of the internalization of homophobia (McCandish, 1982). Long-lasting partnerships are difficult to maintain. Often lesbians will see other lesbians as available, even when in a relationship. A lesbian relationship is not seen as a viable, solid entity with boundaries defined by mutual, lasting commitment.

3. The combined inner and outer homophobia and heterosexism affect the lesbian's self-concept and her position in the world, yet the finding of no particular psychopathology in lesbians has been validated throughout most of the literature (Freeman, 1971, 1975; Mannion, 1981; Oberstone & Sukoneck, 1976). This in itself is surprising, given the oppression of lesbian existence, and it speaks to the ego strength and inner psychological resources of lesbians as a group. Nevertheless, the difficulty in integrating one's lesbian identity into social and cultural functioning often leads to problems such as alcohol abuse (Diamond & Wilsnack, 1978), stress overload (McCandish, 1982; Riddle & Sang, 1978), and depression (Mannion, 1981).

Specifically, the five most common relational issues that bring lesbians into therapy are

1. In contrast with men—who experience themselves according to their deeds—women experience themselves relationally, that is, as con-

nected to the world in terms of other people (Miller, 1976). When Miller talks about women's difficulties with separateness and their wish for increased intimacy, she fails to note that this can exist only in relation to men's desire for separateness and their avoidance of intimacy. Hence, when two women couple, the potential for increased intimacy and fusion is indeed multiplied. It follows, therefore, that the intimacy level in a lesbian relationship is likely to be greater than in a heterosexual one. Yet, what can be a source of joy and fulfillment also can create strong difficulties with issues of separateness and individuality (Burch, 1982). This results in feelings of being stifled, separation anxiety, poor boundary setting, and difficulty in working out disagreements. Differences are perceived as threatening, and needs for fulfillment outside the relationship are confused with abandonment and rejection. Ultimately, the two are unable to remain as autonomous individuals while enjoying intimacy and togetherness.

2.   The other side of the same dilemma is the dread of the intense merging, fearing the possibility of eventual engulfment and disappearance. This often results in endless conflicts and disagreements that serve to insure separateness and independence. The couple deals with the fear of fusion by avoiding intimacy and closeness, or by having predictable sequences of intimacy followed by violent disagreements, followed by intimacy—ad infinitum.

3.   Lesbian couples sometimes also bring to therapy the polarization of this continuum of the relational self and the individual self, where one woman fears the engulfment while the other fears the aloneness. Often this dilemma is accompanied by sexual dysfunction—lack of desire, infrequency of contact, or strong disparity in expressed wishes for sexual contact—which often are taken as signs of rejection and create tension, withdrawal, and fighting.

Clearly, the therapeutic work is toward establishing a balance between the need for intimacy and the need for aloneness. In addition, women need to learn to become less other-oriented, so they develop a sense of self-worth through their being and through their doing, rather than just through their relationships.

4.   In addition to intimacy, lesbians struggle with the issue of power. The inequality of power between women and men has been amply documented (Polk, 1974). The feminist movement has sought to end this existing power imbalance, and certainly the equalization of power is of central value to feminist psychotherapy (Kaschak, 1981).

Lesbian relationships do not have built into them the asymmetry of this power differential and thus are more congruent with the feminist value of equalitarianism in human relationships. Yet the paucity of these new models within a patriarchal structure and the lack of experience in living with them can create difficulties for lesbians.

While trying to attain and maintain a balance of power, lesbians can become caught in symmetrical escalations: runaway competitiveness to remain on at least an equal footing with the partner (Bodin, 1981). In this process, the move of one partner conflicts with the successive move of the other, in that each claims the one-up position. This may be a result of defensive maneuvers against familiar feelings of powerlessness.

5. The other side of this coin is that often, as women, lesbians are unfamiliar with feelings of power and can become fearful of their expression in the relationship. There is often denial on the part of the woman who feels more powerful (even if it is temporary or circumstantial), followed by maneuvers to take the one-down position and get taken care of by the partner, such as by getting sick, having accidents, or coping poorly with work or family demands.

The therapeutic work is to help each woman feel comfortable and secure enough with her own power that she will be willing to accept its relativity and fluctuation within the relationship, as well as the necessity for its expression.

CO-THERAPEUTIC APPROACH

In our work with lesbian couples, the following elements are present: (1) we are a co-therapy team working with another team, (2) we are two feminist women working with two women, (3) we are two lesbians working with two lesbians, and (4) we are a lesbian couple doing therapy with a lesbian couple. There is a progressive potential for identification and modeling (Bandura, 1969). The advantage of cotherapy work with couples and families has been extensively documented (Luthman & Kirschenbaum, 1974; Whitaker & Keith, 1981).

Yet there are areas that need to be worked out before the cotherapy team becomes an effective one. As Luthman and Kirschenbaum (1974) suggest, the first is the intimacy level between the cotherapists. A lesbian relationship, as previously mentioned, can reach a level of intimacy that is potentially higher than that of a heterosexual or a male homosexual relationship. As two women and as a lesbian couple, we can model a level of intimacy and closeness that is *appropriate* for lesbian couples, whereas there is a danger that a therapist using the heterosexual dyad as a norm, who is unaware of the uniquenes of the dynamics of lesbian relationships, may view lesbian couples as fused or merged.

The first mode in which we express our sharing is the stylistic one. Our knowledge of one another allows us to support and enhance each other's interventions. One sits back and observes while the other one challenges the couple's system; when necessary, the observer may come in to challenge the other, changing the course of the interventions.

The second mode bears more directly on the content of what we share with the couple in treatment. The following are specific examples of the manner in which we incorporate aspects of our personal relationship into the therapeutic process:

1. When appropriate, we share a relevant story about the other. We also use this approach to tell of our similarities and differences.

2. We share with clients specific teachings that we received from the other.

3. We share our own difficulties in understanding the other one's cognitive map of the world, and we reframe our differences in terms of complementarity, as opposed to polarity.

4. We share specific ways in which we have learned to improve our communication.

5. We share some of our ongoing struggles and vulnerabilities. This aspect is particularly important, as we want to dispel the myth that we are a "perfect couple" and counteract the tendency of clients to idealize their therapists.

6. We share our feelings of affection for each other, both verbally and nonverbally, thereby giving permission to the women to do the same in the presence of others.

As Luthman and Kirschenbaum (1974) state: "The second area of concern in the development of the cotherapy relationship has to do with making room for each other's differences" (p. 199). As a lesbian couple, we have struggled and worked toward a balance of separateness and autonomy that is functional for us and which we model as co-therapists.

We do this by having different styles (one more confrontive, one more supportive), by sometimes stating differences of opinion or views on particular situations, or by predicting different outcomes for our clients' difficulties (e.g., one optimistic, one pessimistic). Each one of us at times takes sides with a different member of the couple, maintaining that alliance for several sessions, then switching.

In addition to making some of these interventions, we model the acceptance of each other's differences, hence dispelling two myths: (1) that because we are lesbians we think and feel alike; and (2) that differences are dangerous and need to be avoided.

Luthman and Kirschenbaum (1974) mention another major area of development in the co-therapy relationship, that of decision making, which has to do with whether both therapists are operating as equals, or one is operating as an assistant therapist. In feminist language, this is about the distribution of power in the relationship.

This has been the area of greatest difficulty for us. In our personal relationship we have maintained an equality of power which, because of our personal attributes, comes naturally. Professionally, however, one of us has more years of training and experience. Here an asymmetrical relationship could come naturally, but, because of our values, we strive for a symmetrical one, which is not always easy to maintain.

In our case, we have not attained a fixed position or permanent resolution. Most of the time, we operate as equals: The opinions of each carry the same weight and both are equally responsible for actions taken and outcomes attained. Occasionally, under high stress or when facing the demands of a delicate or unfamiliar situation, we lapse into a competitive rather than cooperative stance, and seniority temporarily takes over. At this point, we renegotiate and take the necessary steps to re-establish symmetry.

CONCLUSION

Our concerns as a couple are similar to those of other lesbian couples in our culture; our concerns as a co-therapy team of two women parallel some of the concerns encountered by women in relationships with other women. Therefore, we have an affinity with our lesbian-couple clients that allows us to offer them validation and modeling in the following areas:

1. Understanding the struggle and pain of being a woman living in a misogynistic society
2. Valuing lesbianism as an acceptable, healthy alternative to heterosexuality
3. Seeing the commitment of two lesbians in a couple as a viable, rewarding lifestyle
4. Becoming comfortable with strong needs for intimacy and closeness, as well as needs for separateness and individuality
5. Becoming comfortable with our own personal power, as well as with that of other women
6. Developing a cooperative attitude that stems from self-knowledge and self-esteem and thereby developing a balance of these needs.

REFERENCES

Anthony, B. (1982). Lesbian client–lesbian therapists: Opportunities and challenges in working together. In J. C. Gonsiorek (Ed.), *Homosexuality and psychotherapy: A practitioner's handbook of affirmative models* (pp. 45–59). New York: Haworth Press.

Bandura, A. (1969). *Principles of behavior modification*. New York: Holt, Reinhart, & Winston.

Beck, E. T. (1982). *Nice Jewish girls: A lesbian anthology*. Watertown, MA: Persephone Press.

Bodin, A. (1981). The interactional view: Family therapy approaches of the Mental Research Institute. In A. S. Gurman & D. P. Kniskern (Eds.), *Handbook of family therapy* (pp. 267–309). New York: Brunner/Mazel.

Brodsky, A. M., & Hare-Mustin, R. T. (Eds.) (1980). *Women and psychotherapy: An assessment of research and practice*. New York: Guilford Press.

Burch, B. (1982). Psychological merger in lesbian couples: A joint ego, psychological and systems approach. *Family Therapy, 9*, 201–207.

Chodorow, N. (1978). *The reproduction of mothering. Psychoanalysis and the sociology of gender*. Berkeley, CA: University of California Press.

Diamond, D. L., & Wilsnack, S. C. (1978). Alcohol abuse among lesbians: A descriptive study. *Journal of Homosexuality, 4*, 123–142.

Dinnerstein, D. (1976). *The mermaid and the minotaur. Sexual arrangements and human malaise*. New York: Harper & Row.

Escamilla-Mondonaro, J. F. (1977). Lesbians and therapy. In E. I. Rawlings & D. J. Carter (Eds.), *Psychotherapy for women: Treatment toward equality* (pp. 256–265). Springfield, IL: Charles C Thomas.

Freeman, M. (1971). *Homosexuality and psychological functioning.* Belmont, CA: Brooks/Cole.

Freeman, M. (1975, August). Far from illness: Homosexuals may be healthier than straights. *Psychology Today,* pp. 28–32.

Gurman, A., & Klein, M. (1980). Marital and family conflicts. In A. M. Brodsky & R. T. Hare-Mustin (Eds.), *Women and psychotherapy: An assessment of research and practice* (pp. 159–188). New York: Guilford Press.

Hall, M. (1978). Lesbian families: Cultural and clinical issues. *Social Work, 23,* 380–385.

Hare-Mustin, R. T. (1978). A feminist approach to family therapy. *Family Process, 17,* 181–194.

Kaschak, E. (1981). Feminist psychotherapy: The first decade. In S. Cox (Ed.), *Female psychology: The emerging self* (pp. 387–401). New York: St. Martin's Press.

Katz, J. (1978). *White awareness: Handbook for anti-racism training.* Norman, OK: University of Oklahoma Press.

Laws, L. J. (1975). A feminist view of marital adjustment. In A. S. Gurman & D. G. Rice, *Couples in conflict* (pp. 73–123). New York: Jason Aronson.

Luthman, S., & Kirschenbaum, M. (1974). *The dynamic family.* Palo Alto, CA: Science & Behavior Books.

Mannion, K. (1981). Psychology and the lesbian. In S. Cox (Ed.), *Female psychology: The emerging self* (pp. 256–274). New York: St. Martin's Press.

McCandish, M. B. (1982). Therapeutic issues with lesbian couples. In J. C. Gonsiorek (Ed.), *Homosexuality and psychotherapy: A practitioner's handbook of affirmative models* (pp. 71–79). New York: Haworth Press.

Miller, J. (1976). *Towards a new psychology of women.* Boston, MA: Beacon Press.

Oberstone, A. V., & Sukoneck, H. (1976). Psychological adjustment and lifestyle of single lesbians and single heterosexual women. *Psychology of Women Quarterly, 1,* 172–188.

Polk, B. B. (1974). Male power and the women's movement. *Journal of Applied Behavioral Science, 10*(3), 415–431.

Rich, A. (1980). Compulsory heterosexuality and lesbian experience. *Signs, 5*(4), 631–660.

Riddle, D. I., & Sang, B. (1978). Psychotherapy with lesbians. *Journal of Social Issues, 34*(3), 84–100.

Sang, B. (1977). Psychotherapy with lesbians: Some observations and tentative generalizations. In E. I. Rawlings, & D. K. Carter (Eds.), *Psychotherapy for women: Treatment toward equality* (pp. 266–275) Springfield, IL: Charles C Thomas.

Whitaker, A. C., & Keith, V. D. (1981). Symbolic-Experimental Family Therapy. In A. S. Gurman & D. P. Kniskern (Eds.), *Handbook of Family Therapy* (pp. 187–225). New York: Brunner/Mazel.

■11

Another Perspective on Merger in Lesbian Relationships[1]

BEVERLY BURCH

One of the important contributions of feminist therapy is the exploration of lesbian relationships from a perspective that validates rather than pathologizes lesbianism. We now have a developing body of literature to which we can turn and from which we can build a deeper understanding of both lesbian relationships and women's psychology. Because the primary difference between lesbian relationships and all other couple relationships is that they are created by two women, they help us to understand more about the psychological nature of all women.

Lesbian relationships are often characterized by the dynamic of merging, also called fusion or enmeshment, in which the two partners think, feel, or act as if they are almost the same. They experience a pull toward this kind of unity that can make their growth as individuals more difficult. Sometimes the relationship must end in order for one or both

1. This paper comes out of the community in which I live and work, and I am indebted to other women who have shared their own ideas and related experiences. I am especially grateful to Nina Ham, Linda Heine, Joan Hamerman-Robbins, Maggie Rochlin, and Ellie Waxman for their contributions to my thinking.

100

women to individuate. The negative effects of merging have been described by several writers who also address the issue of how to help the couple use therapy to become more separate from each other without ending their relationship (Burch, 1982; Krestan & Bepko, 1980; Nichols, 1982).

This chapter continues this discussion of merger and adds another perspective to it. While fully understanding the potential destructiveness of merger, we also can see another side, its positive effect as part of an ongoing developmental process. To understand how merger can support rather than restrict individual growth, we must turn to some of the newly emerging theories of women's development.

SEPARATENESS, RELATEDNESS, AND GENDER IDENTITY

Traditional conceptualizations of mental health have maintained that separateness—that is, the experience of self as a totally separate person—is the keystone to psychological maturity. The task of separation–individuation is perhaps the most crucial one in early development, and successful passage through later developmental stages is utterly dependent upon success in that one. Not until feminist theorists began to look at those early stages, however, was it noticed that little girls and little boys go through very different experiences during that time.

During its first three years, the child gradually emerges from an early period of symbiosis and moves through stages of increasing awareness of herself as distinct from mother, a separate person and an individual one (Mahler, 1975). Through this process of development the mother holds an unconscious identification with her daughter because she is female like herself. This identification keeps the mother and daughter in a more complex, more prolonged state of merger than occurs with mothers and sons (Chodorow, 1978). The daughter's capacity for relationship develops more fully; her sense of herself includes a self-in-relationship. Her sense of her own boundaries is less firm as a consequence, and her sense of herself as a separate person is both less secure and less rigid. Her capacity for empathy and intuition, that is, nonverbal and unconscious perception, is enhanced.

The son, on the other hand, has more sense of separateness and also needs more of it. His early identification is with his mother. When he begins to see himself as male, he must establish himself continually as separate from his mother in order to be securely male (Chodorow, 1980). Separateness is a precious quality to him in that sense, one that he holds on to throughout his life. To maintain this separateness, he must keep the female-identified parts of himself in repression, including, to some extent, his capacity for empathy and his sense of self-in-relationship. A daughter can continue her identification with her mother while she develops her gender identity as female.

From this perspective, it seems that the notion that separateness and maturity are the same thing is a male-oriented value. Psychological theories have been developed primarily by men; it is not surprising, then, that separateness would be elevated to a high status. As has been noted many times before, our traditional psychology is a psychology of white, upper-middle-class males, and all variations from that standard have been labeled deviant or pathological (Blake, 1973; Broverman, Broverman, Clarkson, Rosenkrantz, & Vogel, 1970; Lerner & Fiske, 1973). We need to enlarge the picture so we can understand that separateness is one pole of an axis, and the other pole is relatedness. These two poles seem to be populated unequally by men and women.

Understanding this basic difference in gender identity is the first piece of the puzzle of understanding merger. With this awareness, we can see how it is that merger could occur so easily in an intimate relationship between two women. Both partners in the couple are more or less rich in relational capacity; both have less of a psychic boundary between them. In a relationship between a woman and a man there is usually a division of emotional roles among these lines: the woman provides the relatedness and the man provides the boundaries. With two women these roles are not built in. There is more possibility for deep connectedness, and there is also more difficulty with finding the boundary between them. Merger occurs more easily.

DEPRIVATIONS IN FEMALE DEVELOPMENT

The second piece of the puzzle is understanding the nature of female development in a patriarchal culture. Under the conditions of patriarchy, the needs of women are pushed aside. The predominantly female capacities for relatedness, emotional attunement, and nurturance are devalued. Child care is women's work, so the child's development occurs in relation to a woman who has learned more or less adequately to be attuned to and nuture the needs of this child, yet who also knows that these essential capabilities are not considered important or useful in the "outside" world, the "real" world. This enormously difficult and demanding task of helping her child grow up is considered to be a simple one, second-nature to her. Finally, a part of her task is to raise her daughters to do the same for others, to know more about others' needs than their own.

Again there is the unconscious identification of a mother with her daughter, only now we can appreciate that this identification must be an ambivalent one. The mother's inevitable conflicts about being a woman are evoked in this identification and are passed on to her daughter through the ways she nurtures her (Flax, 1978). She can give to her son in a less ambivalent, more direct way. With a daughter, nurturance is likely to be complicated. Perhaps she gives too much at some times and nothing at others, as she unconsciously acts out her own sense of deprivation and neediness alternating with a sense of unworthiness. Physical contact and nurturance are complicated further by the mother's internalized taboo against homosexuality (Caplan, 1981; Flax, 1978). The sensuality of physical contact will stir not only her prohibitions against incest, as with her son, but also will stir her homophobia.

As the daughter moves from symbiosis into differentiation, difficulties continue. The mother has been teaching the daughter to forego her own needs. Now she teaches her to attune herself to others by expecting her to meet the mother's own neglected needs for relatedness (Caplan, 1981). She holds on to her daughter rather than supporting her on her path toward autonomy during the period of separation-individuation. Thus the child feels insecure as she ventures out and is more in need of connection with her mother. Individuation holds the threat of abandonment, while going back holds the danger of engulfment, of falling back into the union with her mother and losing her budding sense of self.

We see these pitfalls for the girl's development all along the way. She grows up feeling undernurtured, her needs denied or misinterpreted, and carries conflicts about separateness and closeness in relationships. She nevertheless has an enriched capacity for empathy and deep relatedness if it has not been too disturbed by these troubles. Keep in mind that we are looking at "normal" women's development, normal children and normal mothers, not "bad" or pathological mothers or unusually traumatic development. Some of the consequences of this process are problematic, however, and some are labeled pathological per se. Again, these gender differences raise questions about the distinctions between pathological and "normal" for both women and men.

MERGER AND GROWTH

With this understanding of women's development as background, a broader perspective on merger can be seen. Aware of its potential destructiveness to individuality, we can see its possibilities for growth or healing as well. When we drop the idea that separateness and maturity are the same thing, a relationship that allows more intimacy can be perceived as more of an asset. Such a relationship can help to assuage the early deprivations a woman may have suffered.

All intimate relationships probably include some element of merger, either frequent or occasional. A lesbian relationship allows a woman a new experience of merger with another woman and to some degree evokes the early parent–child merger. Men also experience this in heterosexual relationships; often, however, it arouses defenses that reinforce their separate stance. Women in lesbian relationships alternate between similar defenses and lack of them, between fear of merger and the wish for it. The intensity of this new intimacy also arouses old vulnerabilities, allowing them to be re-encountered and worked through in a new way, altering the old configuration of needs and defenses. In the adult relationship she may find nurturance that was withheld from her as a child. Later nurturing does not replace what she missed as a child, but it does affect her sense of self-worth, her basic self-image as too needy or unlovable. It can, in effect, enlarge her capacity to receive.

Regaining the experience of merger in a lesbian relationship can be joyful and satisfying. When a woman first begins the relationship, she may seek more and more until it unsettles her, stirring up fears of loss of self. Then she reacts oppositionally to her lover. She finds herself fighting a lot or needing to disagree constantly, marshaling her resistance to her lover's ideas or influence. She sets boundaries in whatever ways she can: She withdraws sexually, she talks about leaving, she has an affair. Perhaps she does leave, only to re-experience the same dilemma in her next relationship. Gradually she understands that it is her own autonomy that needs strengthening. Now she begins another passage through the dangerous waters of separation–individuation and rediscovers her fear of abandonment. Her experience has come full circle, and she goes back and forth between separation and merger, encountering the fears each brings up.

In individual therapy women often need another woman as therapist to allow this process to develop. The therapist must be able to let merger occur between them and to tolerate her client's related fears as she goes back and forth, working through the fears. Of course the working through process will stir the therapist's own related issues, sometimes very deeply.

In couple therapy another dynamic emerges: The woman's lover acts out the opposite side of the drama. They are partners together in this play, only they have both convinced themselves that they are different in nature, according to their own fixed character traits: one needs to have more separateness, the other needs more connection. Almost as a corollary to this polarization, the more separate woman feels critical of her partner. Unconsciously she experiences her lover as part of herself that needs to be kept under control. The lover represents some part that is disowned, perhaps a facet of the desire for merger, which she fears.

The therapist's job is to help the couple understand the process better themselves and alter their perceptions of each other. Almost always, one sees women who are struggling with the pull of merger acting out these different roles in the relationship. This most obvious level is deceiving: The more separate partner would change her role if her lover began acting more separate. Without understanding this dynamic, the therapist may conclude that she is dealing strictly with individual pathology. Sometimes this conclusion is accurate; often it is not.

A clinical example is helpful here. Let us use Kate and Allison, who have been lovers for three years. They come to therapy because Allison feels Kate's cycles of passivity and dependence are a problem. She values independence highly and is critical of Kate. She keeps pushing Kate to be more aggressive and more independent of her and the relationship. Kate begins to say no; she is not interested in becoming more aggressive; she wants closeness and feels she is independent enough. She has established some separateness in that act of refusing to change to be more like Allison. She is paradoxically making an active choice to accept the passive side of herself, and she is not dependent on Allison's approval of this choice.

Allison cannot see this aspect of Kate. She is focused on herself.

She insists that Kate take on her values and perspective. On a behavioral level Kate appears to be trying to maintain a merger—and even says that is what she wants—but she resists merger at the same time by keeping her own identity and values. Underneath her more independent-seeming behavior, Allison is the one who cannot accept their differences and allow them to coexist. She demands they be alike. Who is really trying to remain as one? Both are, though in different ways. Neither is truly separate, for they are partners engaged in a complex, multilayered struggle to manage both closeness and a definite boundary between them. Each is just as dependent on the other to play her role in the drama, and neither perceives the potential they have for exchanging these roles.

The task is not to try to establish a permanently separated state between them, but to help each understand this process and its underlying meaning for them individually. Rather than seeing them as constantly at odds with each other, we can see them as engaged in a complicated and delicate balancing act which they must do together—creating both separation and connection. At the same time, each is allowing the other to do part of her work for her and protect her from her own fears. Allison attempts to establish more autonomy, but she does not see any contradiction with trying to take Kate there with her. She is stuck in the struggle and must begin where she really is, by confronting her wish for merger and her fear of losing herself in it. She must accept both her own passivity and dependence as well as Kate's before she can come fully into her own self. In this process she begins to experience herself as more whole and solid, less in danger of engulfment. Kate is a constant reminder of what she is afraid of in herself.

Kate's focus in primarily on the relationship, allowing her to avoid herself. She discovers that beneath her desire for merger she is really afraid of being alone with herself. Nevertheless she is attracted to separateness as the direction in which she needs to go—that is part of why she is attracted to Allison. She takes some steps into real separateness, and she feels empty, frightened, and abandoned but discovers that she survives her worst fears. She slowly comes to know herself more deeply and discovers she has a self that is stronger than she thought. For each one of them, it is a process of finding that part of herself she resists when she sees it reflected in the other. For both, merger is an experience of participating in what they most fear.

Exploring either of the polarities of separateness or merger, one encounters fears of engulfment *and* abandonment; they are opposite aspects of the same experience. Allison is afraid of engulfment so she draws boundaries to secure herself. But she cannot go too far into separateness either without the fear of being totally alone there, thus she tries to make Kate go with her. On the other hand, Kate is also terrified of closeness, in spite of her expressed desire for it. She has chosen Allison so that someone will draw the boundaries for her, to keep her away from this fear. As Kate becomes stronger in herself, she begins to be able to open her capacity for relatedness. She can choose to be with Allison then out of a deep sense of being with herself. Both of them are learning to be more at ease with relatedness and separateness simultaneously.

This example is just one variation of a pattern that must have almost infinite permutations. The process of growth in a relationship turns out not to be about establishing separateness per se, but about establishing one's self, finding, nurturing, and strengthening it. Chodorow (1980) makes the point that, for women, "the strength, or wholeness, of the self does not depend only or even centrally on its degree of separateness." The experience of merger can be a part of this process of growth: finding one's self inside the merger and keeping one's self through the transition back out of it. Trust in the self is built by learning that one can love deeply and not have one's self devoured or abandoned. Through alternating merger and separation, a woman begins to trust that she has a resilient self that can be hurt but not destroyed in the vicissitudes of a relationship. It is because she has this strength that she will not lose herself altogether to her lover, nor will she die if she is left.

Our culture has a belief in "rugged individualism" embedded in it. This belief says that strength is a matter of standing alone and that one builds strength by pushing oneself on into independence, without help from others. Winnicott (1965), the British object-relations theorist, understood it differently: "The basis of the capacity to be alone is a paradox; it is the experience of being alone while someone else is present." At first this person is literally present; eventually her presence is incorporated psychically so that the person may be actually alone in the physical sense. The basis of aloneness, however, is always relatedness.

Another cultural assumption in psychodynamic theory is that fear of engulfment and fear of abandonment are signs of rather severe personality disturbance, the borderline states (Masterson, 1981). Now we are seeing that these are women's issues in a much larger sense and we must broaden our conceptions. The basic dilemma of mother–daughter relationships under patriarchy is that the relationship is likely to en-gender these fears. Difficulties in adult relationships with separating or with merging are a replay of that early dilemma. These fears are dredged up by the relationship and can be dealt with by using the greater resources of one's adult self and those of the therapist. Of course it is important for the therapist to assess the severity of those fears and move accordingly. Some clients may not be able to tolerate merger or loss of merger and may need psychotherapy to develop greater ego strength before they can deal with these vulnerabilities. In any case it is probably our cultural fear of these issues that has led us to cast them in such a negative light.

Finding one's own individuality and distinctiveness at a new pace and with new support allows a woman to begin to heal those early wounds. We can understand merger as part of this process, the develop-mental process of relationships. Merger is not destructive per se; only when a relationship is fixated in merger has the process gone awry (Burch, 1982). For women, connectedness to others is an important part of the sense of self. Therapy requires facilitating the ongoing process of merger and separation, both of which will continue to recur at their own pace. The task is finding one's self in all phases of this process, both in connection with the other and in separateness, alone with oneself. The back-and-forth movement of this process is perhaps an essential part of the lifelong development of individuation.

REFERENCES

Blake, W. (1973). The influence of race on diagnosis. *Smith College Studies in Social Work, 43,* 184–193.

Broverman, I. K., Broverman, D. M., Clarkson, F. E., Rosenkrantz, P. S., & Vogel, S. R. (1970). Sex-role stereotypes and clinical judgments of mental health. *Journal of Consulting and Clinical Psychology, 34,* 1–7.

Burch, B. (1982). Psychological merger in lesbian couples: A joint ego psycho-logical and systems approach. *Family therapy, 9,* 201–207.

Caplan, P. (1981). *Barriers between women.* New York: Spectrum.

Chodorow, N. (1978). *The reproduction of mothering: Psychoanalysis and the sociology of gender.* Berkeley, CA: University of California Press.

Chodorow, N. (1980). Gender, relation, and difference in psychoanalytic per-spective. In H. Eisenstein and A. Jardine (Eds.), *The future of difference* (pp. 3–19). Boston: G. K. Hall.

Flax, J. (1978). The conflict between nurturance and autonomy in mother/ daughter relationships and within feminism. *Feminist Studies, 4,* 171–189.

Krestan, J., & Bepko, C. (1980). The problem of fusion in the lesbian relationship. *Family Process, 19,* 277–289.

Lerner, B. & Fiske, D. W. (1973). Client attributes and the eye of the beholder. *Journal of Consulting and Clinical Psychology, 40,* 272–277.

Mahler, M. (1975). *The psychological birth of the human infant.* New York: Basic Books.

Masterson, J. (1981). *The narcissistic and borderline disorders.* New York: Brunner/Mazel.

Nichols, M. (1982). The treatment of inhibited sexual desire (ISD) in lesbian couples. *Women & Therapy, 1,* 49–66.

Winnicott, D. W. (1965). *The maturational processes and the facilitating environment.* New York: International Universities Press.

■ 12

Feminism at the Grassroots

CAROLYN C. LARSEN AND
LORNA P. CAMMAERT

For over a decade women in Calgary, Alberta have been participating in three innovative group counseling programs called Contemporary Woman: Options and Opportunities. These programs were designed to help women learn about themselves and their options for the future, and to develop the skills and self-esteem that increase the probability of realizing their personal goals.

While looking for new directions, the participants are largely from traditional social backgrounds and from marriage/family/career orientations that were and are conventional. Despite these conservative, non-feminist attitudes and values held by the participants, the program was developed on a feminist philosophy. The objectives of the planners in designing the goals and format for the program were to provide the opportunity for women to become stronger, more independent, and responsible for making decisions about their own lives. Keeping in mind these objectives and the conservative participants, the program content and process are tailored to allow each woman to consider and use them at the level she finds acceptable.

The program goals for the women are

1. To meet and know others who, like themselves, are seeking expanded opportunities and meaningful experiences
2. To obtain professional group counseling, receive encouragement and gain confidence in order to formulate their own realistic goals and take the first step toward achieving them
3. To acquire a realistic appraisal of the skills, training, and time required in order to reach various goals and objectives, whether in education, employment, creative, or service spheres
4. To assist in the development of a more fulfilling lifestyle.

DESCRIPTION OF THE PROGRAMS

The first contemporary woman (CW) program was offered in 1971 to women who were self-selected by responding to public advertising and who could afford the fee (then $50, now $125). The program sessions are held two mornings or two evenings per week for 10 weeks. There is a maximum of 32 participants in each program, and they meet as a full group for sessions of information and skill building. The large group divides into four small groups for a number of sessions, so more attention can be given to individual concerns and decision making. About 1000 women have participated in these CW programs.

The staff of each program consists of a coordinator, four small-group leaders, and a test administrator/interpreter. Various resource people are brought in to present the information and lead the skill-building sessions.

Having demonstrated the responsiveness of women to this type of program, a second set of programs was initiated in 1972. These programs are designed for women on social assistance; one is for women who have been on assistance for less than two years and the second for women on assistance more than two years. These free, seven-week programs meet three full days per week. The staff for each program consists of a coordinator and social worker. Typically, there are 15 to 20 participants per program, referred by their social workers and screened by the CW staff social worker. (For a more complete description of these programs, see Larsen and Cammaert, in press.)

The authors of this chapter were responsible for designing the format and content of all three programs. They continue to be actively involved as consultants, recruiting and training staff, providing ongoing quality control, implementing innovations, and evaluating.

THE CLIENTS

The majority of women who choose the fee-paying program are from 25 to 55 years old, married, worked before having children, and have been and are full-time homemakers. They come to the program to find more satisfaction in their lives and/or to plan for the time when their children leave home.

Women attending the free programs range in age from 19 to 55 years. Characteristically, the mean age of women on short-term assistance is 30 years and on long-term assistance is 38 years. Women in the short-term assistance group have been receiving assistance for less than two years and usually are in crisis, that is, recently deserted, going through divorce procedures, and/or involved in custody battles. Women on long-term assistance have been receiving assistance for two to 16 years, with a mean of seven years. The young women in this group are usually unwed mothers or from a family of origin that also received assistance.

Although there are many similarities among the women of all three groups, and although their needs for greater self-esteem and skill development are more similar than different, it has been extremely useful to have three separate groups. Women who come to these programs lack the qualities of confidence and self-esteem, do not believe that they have choices about how their lives develop, and lack information about themselves and their community. However, the specific needs and abilities of each group are very different.

Another aspect that is common among the women of all groups is their basic conservatism. Frequently they are alienated or have purposely disassociated themselves from other women, stating women are superficial and have limited interests and that they cannot make contact with other women on a meaningful level. They express great fear in attending the first session, express some distaste for being with so many women, express trepidation over being with these women for so many hours, and are quite vocal about not wanting to be "bra-burning" feminists. Feminism is for those "other" women who are radical, who march, who rant and rave, and whose behavior is quite suspect. Nevertheless, the motivation of the participants for personal change and to receive constructive help is high. Often by attending the group, the women have exhibited tremendous personal strength and courage.

THE PROGRAM PROCESS

While there are differences among participants and in the content and intensity of these programs, the participants' experiences of the process are essentially the same. The program is designed to allow women to engage each other immediately at a very personal level, and permission is given to disclose thoughts, feelings, and perceptions at a more meaningful level than most of these women have experienced previously. As a result, they meet other women in a rewarding, affirming, and often joyful manner that changes attitudes toward women generally and themselves as women specifically. They begin valuing other women and thus themselves. The supportive atmosphere that develops is a significant part of the process that occurs. A belief emerges that "women are okay, and I am okay."

As the women examine their own interests, values, decisions, and strengths; learn about community resources; and develop or significantly improve skills in communication, assertiveness, interviewing, and parenting; they grow personally. The women evaluate their current lifestyles for satisfactions and also consider new possibilities for themselves. With this self-evaluation comes the ability to develop realistic goals for themselves and to implement an action plan to accomplish these goals.

The effects of the program may or may not result in observable social action. A few women have worked to bring changes to certain public institutions whose policies have limited women's opportunities. An example of this is a woman who insisted on being allowed to take a usually full-time technical program on a part-time basis. Other women have become active in community or church organizations and represent women's viewpoints.

The greatest observable effect of the program occurs in the personal interactions the women have with their husbands and partners, children, family, and friends. They have a fresh outlook, a new or renewed confidence, and new or revived skills, and these influence their interactions. This is a grassroots effect that has the power to expand the women's perceptions and attitudes on a very personal basis. It is potent in its effect, although it is not social action as usually defined in feminist literature.

THE ISSUES

As feminists, how do the leaders in the programs approach and interact with the conservative women who attend the programs? As Sturdivant (1980) has stated, the "appropriate function of the feminist therapist is to facilitate personal problem-solving, growth toward self-actualization, and the resocialization process" (p. 153). However, two major issues arise for the staff. The first revolves around the feminist guideline that clients are to be encouraged to engage in social action on their own behalf (Gluckstern, 1977; Rawlings & Carter, 1977; Sturdivant, 1980). The second is that, at the very time the staff is teaching the women decision-making skills, helping them to increase their self-esteem, and encouraging them to take responsibility for their lives, the leaders must be prepared for the possibility that the women may decide against adopting a feminist philosophy.

Social Action

The concept that clients be encouraged to engage in social action on their own behalf appears to negate a tenet that, for these authors is more pre-eminent. The tenet is to approach clients therapeutically where they are in their socialization rather than where the staff might like to see them. An essential aspect of this is to use language that the women understand and accept rather than psychological and feminist jargon. While working from a feminist philosophical base, the feminist ideas and principles expressed in the program are presented gently and gradually to these conservative women.

This approach is explained by Wilson-Schaef's levels of truth concept (1981). The first premise in her concept is that every issue has its own level of truth. Levels of truth move in a progression. As one grows and increases in awareness, her or his levels of truth move from the superficial to the more profound.

Many of our clients are virtually unaware of the issues confronting women today. These women would be at level 1 concerning this truth.

Women who are motivated to attend the CW groups are beginning to be aware of some of the issues and are motivated to find a possible alternative for themselves, through personal examination. This is level 2. As mentioned earlier, they are definite in not wanting to become or to be associated with feminists.

Women enter level 3 with new awareness of the externally imposed restraints and barriers to women that impinge on them personally. Depression and anger are two common emotions at this level. Having worked through this level, the women enter level 4, where they begin to gain perspective, learn skills, and see that they can take responsibility and can effect change in their lives. They put these awarenesses, skills, and changes into action on a personal level. It is expected that the women have reached this level before the group ends.

Having worked at level 4 for some time, the women may move to level 5, where they become more aware of and angry about the larger institutionally based restraints and barriers. A constructive resolution of the anger felt at level 5 usually will result in developing the necessary skills for taking social actions. This happens at level 6.

It is expected that the leaders, who are at level 4, 5, or 6, had better "understand the concept itself and the levels of truth others are at concerning it" (Wilson-Schaef, 1981, p. 153). One of Wilson-Schaef's observations is that everyone will fight for the "rightness" of her level of truth, but the vehemence and intensity of that conviction tends to decrease as the person moves along the levels. Thus people who have gone through more levels of truth tend to be more tolerant and open-minded and less likely to attack those who are still at lower levels. This understanding is essential for the leaders to have, if they are going to follow feminist principles in accepting women at whatever level they are and if they are going to work effectively with the women entering the groups who are at level 1 or 2. The leader may be prepared to implement social action, as they are at level 6, but the women in the program are not yet at this stage.

Reactions to Feminism

A value conflict that arises for the leaders revolves around their personal tenets of feminism, one of which states that each woman is her own best expert about herself. After helping a woman in a program to develop her decision-making skills, encouraging her to take responsibility for herself, and thus increasing her self-esteem, it is difficult for leaders to see the woman decide against a feminist alternative. This value conflict most often centers around traditional marital/family situations, which the leaders may view as creating and maintaining a dependency paradigm (described more completely by DeHardt in Chapter 17 of this book). Even so, it is essential that leaders be sensitive to the socialized environmental and situational constraints that the woman may experience. While the leaders can open doors and help the woman generate and explore her alternatives, the leaders cannot and should not attempt to shove her through a particular door. Such an action would defeat the feminist tenets of valuing the woman and her strengths, expertise, and self-sufficiency in making the best decision possible for her at this point. Also, it would be against the tenet of valuing the woman's right and responsibility to make her own choice. Two examples may help illustrate the value conflicts.

Rita was depressed and debilitated when she first attended the program, as she had just emerged from a battering relationship and was on assistance. During the program, Rita made phenomenal leaps in self-confidence, becoming a bright and lively group dynamo. She had evolved a plan to divorce her husband and to return to school on her way to becoming financially independent. In the last week of the program, Rita announced she and her husband were reconciling. The staff were dismayed and felt that all the gains Rita had made would be smashed. These reactions were conveyed to Rita, but she thought the gains she had achieved would make her stronger in the relationship, and she would not live with her husband until they had completed marriage counseling. Even so, the leaders doubted that the gains of seven weeks were consolidated enough to combat successfully the interaction pattern built over years. Contact with Rita since the program ended has confirmed her position: She *was* stronger, the marriage counseling *did* help, the relationship is much different and much better, and Rita has continued the other part of her plan to become employed. Rita knows she has the strengths and the skills to leave the marriage, should the battering recur.

Another example is of Jan, a vivacious woman who had been an elementary school teacher before having her children 10 years ago. She considered returning to her profession throughout the program, struggling with her preference for remaining as a homemaker and her knowledge that she had much to contribute as a teacher. Her decision was to stay at home and expand her involvement in sports. Jan's small-group leader thought the best alternative for Jan was to return to work, where she had found so much satisfaction, and the leader found herself pushing Jan in that direction rather than allowing Jan her own choice.

In both examples, it was difficult for the leader to allow the woman concerned the freedom and the trust to make her own decision, even though it was contrary to the leader's beliefs about what gains were feasible. Although it is personally very difficult, the leaders do learn to place more emphasis and faith on the feminist tenet that each woman is her own best expert, realizing that what the leader does can facilitate a process that may only begin during a program. Over the brief program period, the women may change dramatically, but their starting position, readiness, motivation, and eagerness are factors in how dramatic and how quickly changes occur. As the woman leaves the program, consolidates her learnings, and initiates new behaviors, undoubtedly the learning process and the changes continue.

One function of staff meetings and of having a program consultant who is skilled in group process is to help staff deal with these issues. When the staff's personal values or professional opinions conflict with the decision a woman makes for herself, these differences are worked through and the goals and basic philosophy of the program are refreshed. The support of other staff and the consultant are central to this process. In the example of Rita, the staff had several extensive discussions that helped to alleviate their concerns about her choice and enabled them to continue working with her in a positive, supportive manner, helping her to be realistic in her expectations about the reconciliation.

SUMMARY

The contemporary woman programs are based on a feminist philosophy, both in program design and content. This philosophy is presented and modeled in a moderate manner. As the participants are mostly conservative in outlook and lifestyle, a goal is to introduce or expand feminist concepts at a level these women can consider and perhaps adopt. Two issues that this approach raises for the program staff are whether and how to encourage women to engage in social action and how to handle their feelings and reactions if participants choose to reject feminist philosophy. These issues have been managed by providing ongoing staff training. The basic concern is always for the individual woman and for encouraging her to reach her own choices. Emphasis can be placed on the effects of the woman's more effective functioning in her immediate environment as a form of grassroots social action. As in any therapeutic endeavor, the client must make choices for herself in light of her own resources, socialization, and current circumstances. Given the relatively short time frame of the program and the readiness of the participants, the hope that the women will embrace a feminist philosophy must be moderated. The temptation is to be overzealous in our impatience for women to develop in a feminist direction. It is crucial to acknowledge the right of each person to choose her own options, make the best of her opportunities, and move at her own pace.

REFERENCES

Gluckstern, N. (1977). Beyond therapy: Personal and institutional change. In E. Rawlings & D. Carter (Eds.), *Psychotherapy for women: Treatment toward equality* (pp. 429–444). Springfield, IL: Charles C Thomas.

Larsen, C. C., & Cammaert, L. P. (in press). For women on social assistance: A brief, intensive, effective group counseling program. In C. Starke-Adamec & P. Caplan (Eds.), *Sex roles II: Feminist psychology in transition*. Montreal: Eden Press.

Rawlings, E. I., & Carter, D. K. (Eds.).(1977). *Psychotherapy for women: Treatment toward equality*. Springfield, IL: Charles C Thomas.

Sturdivant, S. (1980). *Therapy with women: A feminist philosophy of treatment*. New York: Springer.

Wilson-Schaef, A. W. (1982). *Women's reality: An emerging female system in the white male society*. Minneapolis, MN: Winston Press.

■13
A Feminist Critique of Sex Therapy

DOREEN SEIDLER-FELLER

In effect, the publication of Masters and Johnson's *Human Sexual Response* (1966) and *Human Sexual Inadequacy* (1970) established contemporary theory and practice in brief, behaviorally oriented sex therapy. Not only did sex therapy develop as a field of scientific inquiry and professional specialization, but the old claim of the helping professions to entitlement as arbiter of sexual ideology, philosophy, and ethics was reinstated, too. Masters and Johnson's influential treatment paradigm has undergone innumerable adaptations, refinements, and critiques (Seidler-Feller, 1980; Zilbergeld and Evans, 1980); however, the question of sex therapy's adequacy from a feminist perspective seldom has been broached.

Approaches to female sexuality and sex therapy are important for a variety of reasons. First, sexuality is a significant part of most women's lives and, given women's sexual socialization (Brown, undated; Kerr, 1977; Stock, 1983), it often is a conflict-laden part. Second, because of socialization effects, traumatic life history experiences (e.g., incest, rape), and changing social preference and custom, women increasingly are requesting remedial sexuality services. Third, much remains to be learned regarding the nature of female sexuality and the means of increasing sexual adjustment and satisfaction.

This chapter represents an initial examination of the question, What does feminism demand of sex therapy? In order to address the question, a summary of ideology and practice in sex therapy is followed by a presentation of alternative conceptualizations of sexual complaints. A feminist approach to intervention concludes the paper. In this paper, many relevant issues—such as language, diagnostic conventions, and the use of pornography and surrogates in sex therapy—are excluded. Moreover, the focus is confined to heterosexuals, since the data base on them is broader and more widely disseminated. For discussions of sex therapy with lesbians, the reader is referred to Brown (undated) and Brown, Larson, and DeWolfe (1979). Finally, the reader is referred to Brodsky and Hare-Mustin (1980) and Rawlings and Carter (1977) for essential introductions to the premises and principles of feminist therapy, as well as to other parts of the present volume.

SEX THERAPY: IDEOLOGY AND PRACTICE

As a branch of behavior therapy, brief sex therapy is consistent with positivist approaches to human behavior. It is prized for its brevity, its pragmatism, its mechanics and techniques, and its proximity to medicine, biology, and physiology (Tiefer, 1981). These features make sex therapy vulnerable to the lure of the "technological fix" (Berkeley Sex Therapy Group, 1980) and to the "medical ceremonializing of sex" (Szasz, 1981). Szasz argues that sexual freedom and sexual behavior have come under therapeutic definition and control and, in the process, human diversity and freedom have been compromised. The social control of human sexuality is deeply relevant to a feminist approach to sexuality and sex therapy since, as Gilbert (1980) suggests, evaluating the influence of sex roles and statuses along with a therapeutic orientation to personal and social change are central tenets of feminist therapy. Who defines the problem(s)? With what assumptions, values, and interests? To what end(s)? In short, what are the latent and manifest functions of sex therapy for women? Overtly, its purpose is to free individuals from sexual disinterest and dysfunction to the extent that a behavioral technology allows. Its latent purposes are several.

Szasz (1981) argues that therapeutic management of human sexuality is a potent means of social control, a means well suited to a modern secular age. In this view, individuals surrender their freedom, dignity, and privacy to an instrumentality that represents and enforces the prevailing general values and sexual ethic of the patriarchal state. Owing both to the spirit of the positivist approach and the influence of biologically based explanations of human sexuality (Tiefer, 1981), therapeutic direction is directed away from sex-role psycho- or sociodynamics. In overall terms, sex therapy takes the structure and values of sexual encounters as givens. Where heterosexuals are involved, this often means implicit reinforcement of normative sex roles and the power differential between the sexes that underlies them (Johnson, 1974, 1976). Sex therapists seem to assume that normative sex roles are either (1) the basis for sound functioning, (2) of small moment in understanding psychosexual functioning, (3) relatively immune to brief behavioral intervention, or (4) some combination of the three. Such patriarchal bias renders illusory the sexual and sex-role equalitarianism evident in much sex therapy writing.

Szasz (1981) cites the Masters and Johnson practice of rehabilitating the "sexual underdogs" (women and homosexuals) by claiming the oppressed to be sexually and therefore morally superior. This way of thinking is manifestly romantic and propagandistic since it is *not* accompanied by sex-role analysis. The sexual status quo remains undisturbed. New sexual information, as exemplified by Masters and Johnson's *Human Sexual Response* (1966), to say nothing of new sexual ideology, such as *Homosexuality in Perspective* (Masters and Johnson, 1981), do not, of themselves, address sex-role tensions and inequities.

In the sexual realm, the lack of attention to power and sex roles (as restructuring devices) promotes treatment interventions and goals based upon the sexual encounter as men experience it. Male power informs treatment imagery and idiom, even if the presenting complaint involves the female. For example, LoPiccolo and Lobitz (1972) generated an influential nine-step masturbation program for women that involves two (male) experts declaring the woman "out of touch" and ignorant about her body and its beauty in step 1 and exhorting her, by various degrees, to masturbate to orgasm, until step 7, where the focus automatically shifts to "enabling her to experience orgasm through stimulation by her husband." Latter steps are devoted to bridging techniques enabling the "wife" to experience orgasm under her "husband's" control, either concomitant with intromission or independent of it. Despite the detailed do's and don'ts, and the apparently scientific, systematic nature of the masturbation sequence, their own results indicated its unreliability. Indeed, orgasm could occur at "almost any step in this program" or outside it altogether. The authors overlook the potential of their highly variable results as a means for understanding female orgasm and their attempt to systematize orgasmic attainment. While some recent publications also have addressed female orgasmic variability, the data were available then but required a feminist eye to interpret. It also should be noted that this program assumes coupling, heterosexuality, marriage, and a sex-typed script. These assumptions enhance the status quo rather than women's control over their bodies. In later work with two women psychologists (Heiman, LoPiccolo, & LoPiccolo, 1976), LoPiccolo has produced work that is freer of such assumptions and more sensitively integrates female sexual experience, variation, and preference into treatment. Barbach (1975, 1980), in all her major work, is the acknowledged pioneer in developing programs for women that free them from sex-typed sexual choreography.

As sex research and critical awareness improve, treatment for women appears to be improving. Ellison (1982), in a paper detailing the harmful consequences of sex therapy, cites four beliefs intrinsic to the field which she regards as potentially hazardous. These beliefs are that (1) a right way to experience sexual response exists, (2) good sexual function means having the right kind of orgasms, (3) the client should change if she or he does not fit the program and its values (e.g., regarding the value of masturbation); and (4) outcome is measured in terms of a particular function or skill (e.g., solo orgasm).

While these beliefs are applicable to both sexes, they seem to apply to women with special force, given women's greater response variability and the controversies surrounding their variability over the decades. Of special note here is the last-cited belief, because it refers to the impact of the positivist, male-identified success criteria used (sometimes exclusively) in standard sex therapy, criteria that usually do not recognize the couples system or other larger ecological considerations (Ellison, 1982).

These observations dovetail with recent research findings on differential (male versus female) sexual socialization and its impact on female sexuality. Stock (1983) summarizes these distinctions as follows: control versus helplessness; genitally versus generally focused sexuality; objectification, fixation, and conquest versus love and/or romance orientation; and performance versus process orientation. The former descriptors refer to standard male socialization, while the latter refer to female social-ization. The function-oriented outcome criteria (Ellison, 1982) are iden-tifiable with the performance orientation Stock describes as masculine in nature, and they depend upon the uniformity-of-sexual-response-beliefs prevalent in the field.

Mainstream sex therapists rarely ask questions that challenge exist-ing definitions, such as, What is a sexual stimulus, a sexual situation, a sexual response? What reinforces female sexual expression? Which situa-tional factors inhibit it? What effects do variables such as premenstrual syndrome, pregnancy, lactation, surgery, infertility, and so forth have on female sexual desire and function? Or, as Tiefer (1981) has asked in the context of sex research: What is the psychological role of foreplay acts? Is genital response the best measure of sexual response, and for whom?

The genital intercourse bias has been described by Rossi (1973) as a "phallic fallacy" that serves to demean and subordinate nongenital sexu-ality through language contrasting foreplay with sexual intercourse. These values inhibit the development of foreplay variations (with thera-peutic potential) and the idea of foreplay for its own sake. Tiefer (1981) sees such masculine biases as consistent with a "hot sex framework" and implies that the framework is, possibly, antagonistic to women's sexual interests.

In this connection as well, Jayne (1981) argues that psychological satisfaction and related variables are ignored in much sex research on women. This persists despite the early data indicating that female satis-faction is inversely related to orgasmic intensity (Masters and Johnson, 1966) and that most satisfaction is tied to relationship status and activity (Gebhard, 1966). These and other data have suggested quite consistently that relationship variables have salient impacts on aspects of female sexual function. Power distribution is an added relevant variable here. Rainwater (1966) and Hatfield, Greenberger, Traupman, and Lambert (1982) have reported more sexual and relationship satisfactions among couples in equitable relationships. Moreover, Kirkpatrick (1980) found an inverse relationship between sexual satisfaction and sex-role identifi-cation, with the feminist subsample reporting greater satisfaction.

As the early data of Masters and Johnson (1966), Rainwater (1966), and Gebhard (1966) reveal, much of this data has been available for some time, even as it has been reasserting itself in the work of current researchers. What was lacking was a sex-neutral or woman-oriented interpretive framework, perhaps a "cool sex framework," to expand on Tiefer's (1981) metaphor. Cumulatively, those blind spots cited in this section, as well as the larger framework problem, have tended to reinforce sexist sexual values and, therefore, to have weakened treatment, theory, and practice.

ALTERNATIVE WAYS OF VIEWING "SEXUAL DYSFUNCTIONS"

Brief sex therapy implicates a host of variables in the etiology of functional sexual disorder. These include religious orthodoxy, homosexuality, hostility, other sexual dysfunction, marital problems, early sexual trauma, depression, anxiety, misinformation about sex, illness, surgery, and lack of sexual skill and knowledge (Hogan, 1978). Many of these variables depend upon learning and invoke large-scale social processes with implications for sexual behavior. Yet in mainstream literature there is little recognition of the potential contribution of sex-role issues to the understanding of female sexual complaints. Recently, Stock (1983) and Kerr (1977) have produced articles that focus explicitly on sex-role socialization, sexism, and sexual dysfunction. Freiberg and Bridwell (1975) have suggested that female sexual complaints are related to the historical interpretations that women's sexual role(s) have been given by male theorists. Subsequent discussion in this chapter, then, will be an elaboration of the idea that sexual dysfunction reflects sexual politics.

Female sexual dysfunction may be viewed as a general status protest, making reference to the unacknowledged, "natural" power differential between the sexes, or particular partners, or both. Conflict between the sexes as interest groups is well documented in intimate interpersonal relationships (Raven, Centers, & Rodrigues, 1975; Raven & Kruglanski, 1970; Scanzoni, 1972). Moreover, it is important to recognize that the power differential has a multitude of consequences—economic, political, social, and moral. Salient among them is the proprietary interest the male has in the female body, that is, his sense of ownership and entitlement. In a culture that tolerates male sexual aggression and confounds sexuality with aggression, and where brief sex therapy ignores and thereby sanctions it, a woman's best defense against a sexual ritual of subordination may be "sexual dysfunction." From adolescence onward, the language of male sexual contact has a pronounced element of exploitation, game playing, conquest, even sadism (Lawrence, 1975; Littewa, 1974). It surely is part of the legacy of sexuality for Western women. Thus, "vaginismus," "dyspareunia," "general sexual dysfunction," and "disorders of desire" may each be viewed, in part, as reflections of present and/or past male status displays.

In a new empirical study, Stock and Roberts (1982) found that power conflict was correlated positively with sexual dysfunction development, and wives contesting the conjugal power balance had husbands who developed "sexual dysfunction," the net effect of which was to reduce the wife's conjugal power challenge. These data suggest that sex-role-based power issues may be implicated in "sexual dysfunctions" and that, where either female or male dysfunction exists, the therapist ought to look for unacknowledged power conflict intended to preserve or alter power relations.

Looked at in a slightly different context, "sexual dysfunction" may be seen not merely as resistance to male superiority and aggression, but as expression of self-ownership and right to privacy. The "dysfunctions" women present may represent struggles around sexual access and attempts to challenge rules regarding male sexual rights. The controversial nature of the idea that women have an inalienable right to control over their bodies is evidenced in the ongoing struggle for the full spectrum of reproductive rights and in the extensive feminist critique of general medical, psychiatric, and gynecological practice. Yet curiously, power-based or sex-role explanations are largely absent from mainstream sex therapy literature of women's disorders.

Another context for understanding female "sexual dysfunction" is that of the female reproductive cycle and conflicts generated out of it. Sex therapy generally pays little attention to the impact of these transitions (birth, menarche, premenstrual syndrome, menopause, lactation) on sexual feelings and behavior. Part of the crisis involved at each of these points is the necessity of role adjustment and the possibility of resulting power loss. For example, Rice and Rice (1977), Hare-Mustin (1978), and others have observed that the birth of a child to a heterosexual couple results in power and relationship changes that adversely affect women. "Sexual dysfunction" thus may be a prophylactic measure!

Similarly, "sexual dysfunction" may involve a dispute or strike over working conditions. A majority of American women work at two full-time jobs, struggling to meet and balance a multitude of demands. For women with partners, conflicts in this arena may appear in sexual terms. More research is needed on the effects of fatigue and role stress.

These are just some of the symbolic directions in which sexual complaints may be understood, resulting in better treatment of current or future clients. Even brief sex therapy can ill afford to bypass sexual politics. Existing professional ways of viewing "sexual dysfunction" are not inherently inconsistent with a feminist approach but seem naively to ignore the history of Western sexual conflict and compromise alive in each of us.

TOWARD A FEMINIST SEX THERAPY

The foregoing critique has implications for feminist intervention and change. First, how we define human sexuality determines what and how we treat. Because the values of current sex therapy incorporate masculine biases into the perception and definition of sexual behavior, the first level of feminist intervention involves asking anew the apparently simple questions, for example, What is a sexual stimulus?

Tiefer (1981) suggests assessing the nature of the partner's commitment and the woman's body image, self-esteem, previous experience with forced sex, and attitutes toward the exchange value of sex. To these should be added the following: How does she react to the treatment situation and setting, including the potential presence of a male cotherapist? What is (are) her latent purposes for entering treatment? For example, is she responsible for correcting a relationship difficulty? Does she want to become a sexual superstar? Is she trying to alter or reinstate the power balance? What are her sexual politics? Her partner's?

The protocol should inquire how she uses sexual, interpersonal, and emotional vocabularies; how she defines sexual pleasure and pain, what patterns, both explicit and implicit, emerge in her sexual decision making, and what kinds of power and power deficits exist that may be amenable to modification (Seidler-Feller, 1976).

These kinds of questions imply a challenge to the merely mechanical and technical approach in standard assessment. Introduced here is a variety of cognitive, affective, ethical, social psychological, anthropological, and political dimensions that flesh out the feminist premise that *the personal is political.* A feminist approach needs to be attentive to and thoughtful about mainstream values that link sex and aggression; reinforce menstrual, pregnancy, and menopausal taboos and prejudices; underscore sex-role assignments in sexual encounters; and overvalue sexual outcome at the expense of sexual process. Feminist philosophers and ethicists (Lawrence, 1975) stand to make an invaluable contribution in this area.

Feminist sex research, both basic and applied, will be of inestimable help in this area. Feminist research and development will produce treatment materials and modalities consistent with a feminist approach. Barbach (1975, 1980), for example, has made a vital contribution in the development of group methods for preorgasmic women. Not only does the group provide the critical possibility of getting and giving feedback, group solidarity, and other dynamisms associated with group process, it also *contextualizes* women's sexual problems, and it does so in a way that provides an alternative to the heterosexual context.

However ideal the group modality may be, it will not always be available for women seeking treatment. Whether on an individual or couples basis, feminist sex therapy must be oriented toward the principles of feminist therapy and toward shifting around existing sex stereotypes or other problematic sexual arrangements. Sexual and metasexual tasks and responsibilities (e.g., contraception, sex initiation) may be reordered, thus reordering sex-role elements. Modeling competent and effective sexual talk is important, especially around taboo sexual topics.

Validating women's subjective reports of their sexual experiencing and sexual diversity, both within and without treatment, is necessary. This can be transformed usefully into a series of treatment materials (scrapbooks, albums) that are based upon diverse women's experiential reports. In this way, aspects of other women's intimate experience become available to women in therapy.

Finally, as Hare-Mustin (1978) observes, a treatment contract is entirely consistent with a feminist approach.

CONCLUSION

The broad, ecological view offers the possibility of correcting perceptual and conceptual biases in the field of sex therapy. New lines of inquiry, as suggested here, will promote new etiological formulations, along with revisions in diagnosis and labeling. With the enlarged and improved data base resulting, assessment and treatment are bound to become more informed and effective.

REFERENCES

Barbach, L. G. (1975). *For yourself: The fulfillment of female sexuality: A guide to orgasmic response.* Garden City, NY: Doubleday.

Barbach, L. G. (1980). *Women discover orgasm: A therapist's guide to a new treatment approach.* New York: Free Press (Macmillan).

Berkeley Sex Therapy Group (1980). *Expanding the boundaries of sex therapy* (rev. ed.). Berkeley, CA: Author.

Brodsky, A. M., & Hare-Mustin, R. (Eds.).(1980). *Women and psychotherapy: An assessment of research and practice.* New York: Guilford Press.

Brown, L. S. (undated). *Internalized oppression as an issue in sex therapy with lesbians.* Unpublished manuscript.

Brown, L. S., Larson, R., & DeWolfe, D. (1979). *Sex therapy and education with lesbian and bisexual women: A model for intervention.* Paper presented at the Fourth World Congress of Sexology, Mexico City.

Ellison, C. R. (1982). *Harmful effects of sex therapy.* Paper presented at the Annual Convention of the American Psychological Association, Washington, DC.

Freiberg, P., & Bridwell, M. (1975). An interdisciplinary approach to female sexuality. *Counseling Psychologist, 5*(1), 106–111.

Gebhard, D. (1966). Factors in marital orgasm. *Journal of Social Issues, 22,* 88–95.

Gilbert, L. (1980). Feminist therapy. In A. M. Brodsky & R. Hare-Mustin (Eds.), *Women and psychotherapy: An assessment of research and practice* (pp. 245–265). New York: Guilford Press.

Hare-Mustin, R. (1978). A feminist approach to family therapy. *Family Process, 17*(2), 181–195.

Hatfield, E., Greenberger, D., Traupman, J., & Lambert, P. (1982). Equity and sexual satisfaction in recently married couples. *The Journal of Sex Research, 18*(1), 18–32.

Heiman, J., LoPiccolo, L., & LoPiccolo, J. (1976). *Becoming orgasmic: A sexual growth program for women.* Englewood Cliffs, NJ: Prentice-Hall.

Hogan, D. R. (1978). The effectiveness of sex therapy: A review of the literature. In J. LoPiccolo & L. LoPiccolo (Eds.), *Handbook of sex therapy* (pp. 57–84). New York: Plenum Press.

Jayne, C. (1981). A two dimensional model of female sexual response. *Journal of Sex and Marital Therapy, 7*(1), 3–30.

Johnson, P. (1974). *Social power and sex role stereotyping.* Unpublished doctoral dissertation, University of California, Los Angeles.

Johnson, P. (1976). Women and power: Toward a theory of effectiveness. *Journal of Social Issues, 32*(3), 99–110.

Kerr, C. (1977). *Sex for women who want to have fun and love relationships with equals.* New York: Grove Press.

Kirkpatrick, C. S. (1980). Sex roles and sexual satisfaction in women. *Psychology of Women Quarterly, 4,* 444.

Lawrence, B. (1975). Four-letter words can hurt you. In R. Baker & F. Elliston (Eds.), *Psychology and sex.* Buffalo, NY: Prometheus Books.

Littewa, J. (1974). The socialized penis. *Liberation Magazine, 18*(7), 10–17.

LoPiccolo, J., & Lobitz, W. C. (1972). The role of masturbation in the treatment of orgasmic dysfunction. *Archives of Sexual Behavior, 2,* 153–164.

Masters, W. H., & Johnson, V. E. (1966). *Human sexual response.* Boston: Little, Brown.

Masters, W. H., & Johnson, V. E. (1970). *Human sexual inadequacy.* Boston: Little, Brown.

Masters, W. H., & Johnson, V. E. (1981). *Homosexuality in perspective.* Boston: Little, Brown.

Rainwater, L. (1966). Some aspects of lower class sexual behavior. *Journal of Social Issues, 22,* 96–107.

Raven, B. H., & Kruglanski, A. W. (1970). Conflict and power. In P. Swingle (Ed.), *The structure of conflict.* New York: Academic Press.

Raven, G. H., Centers, R., & Rodrigues, A. (1975). The bases of conjugal power. In R. E. Cromwell & D. H. Olson (Eds.), *Power in families.* New York: Sage.

Rawlings, E. I., & Carter, D. K. (1977). *Psychotherapy for women: Treatment toward equality.* Springfield, IL: Charles C Thomas.

Rice, D. G., & Rice, J. K. (1977). Non-sexist "marital" therapy. *Journal of Marriage and Family Counseling, 3,* 3–10.

Rossi, A. (1973). Maternalism, sexuality and the new feminism. In J. Zubin & J. Money (Eds.), *Contemporary sexual behavior: Critical issues for the 1970's.* Baltimore: Johns Hopkins University Press.

Scanzoni, J. (1972). *Sexual bargaining: Power politics in the American marriage.* Englewood Cliffs, NJ: Prentice-Hall.

Seidler-Feller, D. H. (1976). Process and power in couples psychotherapy: A feminist view. *Voices, 12,* (45), 67–71.

Seidler-Feller, D. H. (1980). *A comparison of group and self-directed treatment formats in the management of premature ejaculation in single males.* Unpublished doctoral dissertation, Ohio State University, Columbus, OH.

Stock, W. E. (1983). Sex roles and sexual dysfunction. In C. Widom (Ed.), *Sex roles and psychopathology.* New York: Plenum Press.

Stock, W. E., & Roberts, C. W. (1982). Power conflict in sexually dysfunctional couples. Manuscript submitted for publication.

Szasz, T. (1981). *Sex by prescription.* New York: Penguin Books.

Tiefer, L. (1981). The context and consequences of contemporary sex research: A feminist perspective. In S. Cox (Ed.), *Female psychology: The emerging self* (2nd ed.). New York: St. Martin's Press.

Zilbergeld, B., & Evans, M. (1980, August). The inadequacy of Masters and Johnson. *Psychology Today,* pp. 29–43.

 **three**

WOMEN'S ISSUES ACROSS THE LIFESPAN: TRANSCENDING SEX ROLES

IRIS GOLDSTEIN FODOR, Editor

Throughout their lifespan, most women try to fulfill their social sex-role prescriptions, that is, achieving the stereotypic feminine goals of marriage and motherhood. However, as women go through life they find that the traditional goals may not be so easy to obtain or sustain and, even if achieved, may not be satisfying. Life doesn't always turn out according to the script. Sometimes motherhood is evasive or comes in a nontraditional form; sometimes a good man is hard to find or an intimate marital relationship remains elusive. Many women seek therapy for these disappointments and frustrations, for help in fulfilling their dreams or for coming to terms with their disappointments. For such women, therapists need to challenge the assumptions underlying these old dreams, encourage new goal setting, and provide a supportive atmosphere for experimenting with new scripts and roles.

The chapters in this part address these lifespan issues. Each author discusses an aspect of woman's struggle to transcend her original sex-role programming. The therapist/authors are available as guides who enable their varying clientele to chart their own courses.

Chapter 14, on feminist spirituality, by Hendricks, spells out the Western religious legacy of patriarchy. God is a man. Man was created in God's image. Women can reach God only through serving men. When rules are violated there is retribution and wrath. Some special women can achieve the direct route to salvation by remaining celebate and sacrificing their lives for God. (In the Catholic tradition there is an actual marriage ceremony.) Most women choose the indirect route. Through mortal marriage and motherhood, they receive devotion and atone for Eve's sin. Further, in Catholic theology, women are presented with a madonna image, a virginal model of ideal virtue and goodness.

These religious teachings still permeate Western culture. Religious women in particular are vulnerable to these messages. Hendricks discusses the crisis of religious women who come for help, fearing God's wrath for trying a different path. She also reviews some of the recent work in feminist theology. There are two trends: one movement is toward the liberalization of traditional teachings and a restoration of the balance between the sexes, while the other seeks to revive the goddess as a focus for feminist spirituality. Further, Hendricks emphasizes the importance of therapists in correcting some of the madonna-image messages. They can model for patients ways to be of service to others, without subservience.

In Chapter 15, Hendricks discusses the crisis experienced by women who cannot fulfill the motherhood imperative. She decribes them as having "uterine socialization": "That the ultimate purpose in life is conception and motherhood. They feel stripped of their self-worth if they cannot conceive. They will not accept other choices." Work with such women and their spouses consists of presenting them with other viable options to having a "birth child."

While some women worry about the lack of a "birth child," many other women struggle with the stress inherent in having a stepchild. Given the high divorce and remarriage rate, more and more women are assuming the role of stepparent. Clamar addresses this issue in Chapter 16, estimating that 50 million people are involved in stepparenting. Unlike the pure, good madonna image of the birth mother, stepmothers come with their own sets of mostly negative myths. Clamar quotes a 10-year-old stepchild: "When I think of a stepmother, I think of someone mean." The concept of the wicked stepmother reaches far back in human history; thus a contemporary stepmother, according to Clamar, is "enveloped in a hostile atmosphere created not by her own actions, but by folklore." Clamar proposes a two-pronged intervention in stepparenting issues: "mentorship" and feminist therapy. She envisions a network of mentors, "stepmothers emeriti," available for the new stepmother. They, like feminist therapists, can help validate all the pushes and pulls and the multiple roles and demands of the stepmother. Further, they can help the woman adapt to the realities of the situation, set reasonable goals, and refocus on the pleasures inherent in the role.

In these changing times, more and more women are questioning traditional choices. Women are coming to therapy for help in deciding whether or not to stay in an unsatisfactory relationship or for guidance about finding a suitable mate. DeHardt, in Chapter 17, discusses some of the limitations in male-defined relationships (heterosexual mating). She states that "women often become less than, rather than more than, the persons they are capable of being when struggling to develop or maintain a relationship with a man." Thus she raises a dilemma for feminist therapists: Is woman's traditional role in a heterosexual relationship at variance with self development? To help therapists and clients alike, she has constructed a set of questions one should ask in considering a man for a serious relationship, as well as questions the woman should ask herself about her own motivations for being with such a man. She concludes that a good man with feminist values is hard to find. She hopes to help her clients to rethink the typical belief that the search for a man is "the pivotal adventure in a woman's life." Instead, she issues a plea for women to "place self-development above such a search."

Many women have reached DeHardt's conclusions. They wish for more than the limited relationships that most males and females have. She cites Bernard (1981), who points out that married heterosexual intimacy is the exception rather than the rule. Rather than stay with the limitations inherent in so many male-defined relationships, many women are bonding in lesbian relationships, although such lesbian bonding is still relatively uncommon. Most women will settle for the heterosexual imperative and its privileges (even if unhappy), rather than find the courage to explore lesbian alternatives, mainly because they are homophobic. In Chapter 18, Rachel Siegel addresses the issue of homophobia in women and talks about lesbian issues. Siegel states that the lesbian therapist's goal should be "to overcome her own ignorance and fear of lesbian reality, to lift the veil of invisibility imposed by the male heterosexual power structure, and to break the taboo of silence that helps to perpetuate the myths and distortions surrounding our love of women and our fear of that love."

Siegel believes that heterosexual therapists must work on their own homophobia, and she presents four ways of educating them: (1) personal therapy, (2) reading literature, (3) supervision and sharing with lesbian colleagues, and (4) the special learning that comes from being open to learning from lesbian clients. Thus, for Siegel, therapists are not free to support clients' choices unless they are themselves educated in various life options.

All of the chapters discussed so far assume that women coming for therapy are struggling with unhappiness about their own choices or needing help and support to re-plan or get on with a new life. Resh's chapter, however, describes another kind of client, the over-50 woman, who followed the script but finds that times have changed and she is in culture shock. This woman may present with depression, anxiety, or somatic complaints and be confused about her issues. Resh dramatically presents the historical context necessary for understanding such a woman, by describing the case of Lucille, a product of the Depression, who is not a member of the "me generation" but rather the "I-should club." Resh's therapeutic approach is similar to the other approaches described in this part. The client needs to shift gears from focusing primarily on serving and being dependent on others to working on her own self-development. Resh stresses the need for understanding the cultural context of these older women's concerns, in order to provide a compassionate treatment.

Of course, there are other lifespan issues with which women struggle and seek a therapist's help. The chapters in this part provide a broad analysis of how to separate a woman's individual issues from the reality of the larger social context. These techniques have been a cornerstone of feminist therapy that have differentiated it from other therapies.

REFERENCE

Bernard, J. (1981). *The female world*. New York: Free Press.

14

Feminist Spirituality in Jewish and Christian Traditions

MAUREEN CALISTA HENDRICKS

RELIGION AND SPIRITUALITY

Religion and spirituality are two dimensions of a belief system that follow one another. *Religion* may be described as a specific belief system that attributes, to a being or beings of a higher order than humankind, the creation and ordering of the universe from its beginnings through the present time. The deity or deities that a religion proclaims usually are acknowledged as having power over human beings in one or more specific areas of life. They are, therefore, to be respected and obeyed. In the early stages of the development of a religion, a certain person or persons proclaim that the deity has revealed to them norms of behavior for all believers. Laws that are based on the norms of behavior are proclaimed by the religious leaders as being the will of the deity. From these initial laws many finely detailed rules and regulations may be developed. Penalties for failure to observe the laws, rules, and regulations are prescribed and attributed to the command of the deity. Reward for obedience may be defined as a happy life, prosperity or good fortune

135

in this present life, or a life after death. Failure to obey may be said to result, conversely, in unhappiness, misfortune, and misery in the present life, as well as in an afterlife.

Spirituality is the manner in which a person chooses to respond to a specific religion or to a nonspecific, broad understanding of the meaning and purpose of life. A spirituality continuum can be conceptualized as containing a broad spectrum of responses to a specific religion or to a nonspecific belief system. It is, therefore, possible that this response to religious values could result in a legalistic form of spirituality that would emphasize the adherence to the minutiae of religious rules and regulations, or in a wholistic form of spirituality that would look beyond the letter of the law to the sense of meaning of life as understood in light of the belief system. How spirituality develops among religious groups profoundly influences their basic attitudes toward and relationship to the members of these groups.

THE JUDEO-CHRISTIAN DEVELOPMENT OF RELIGION AND SPIRITUALITY INTO A PATRIARCHAL MODE

Judaism and Christianity both reverence as the word of god a series of books of scripture that recount the early understandings of there being one god ("monotheism") and of the evolution of the image of this god as both powerful and male. Genesis, the first book of the Bible, contains three traditions that have been and still are very important to its interpretation: (1) Yahwist, the earliest and most symbolic, (2) Elohist, and (3) priestly, characterized by law, ritual, and theology (Hunt, 1960). The Yahwist and priestly traditions each present a separate account of the creation of the world and of humankind. In the priestly tradition, women and men are created equally at the same time: "Male and female he created them" (Genesis 1:27). In the Yahwist tradition, woman is created from the rib of man and then is named by him: "She shall be called woman for from man she has been taken" (Genesis 2:23). The Yahwist account also tells us that woman, Eve, is the cause of misery for all humankind to come, therefore, she is to bear children in pain and be under her husband's domination (Genesis 3:1–24).

From this early part of scripture onward, regardless of which tradition authored the content, the history of the Jewish people is told in terms of male relationship to God and the continuity of the tribes as enumerated by male lineage. Women are named sporadically and usually in relationships to men, either father, brother, husband, or son. The story of Moses contains a genealogy that clearly demonstrates the pattern used (Exodus 6:14–25). The use of male sacrifice, male priests, male elders, predominantly male inheritance, and a god referred to as "he" demonstrate the early establishment of patriarchy in Judaism. Kertzner (1978), in his explanation of contemporary Jewish practice among Orthodox, Conservative, and Reform branches of Judaism, gives repeated examples of how persistent, except among Reformed Judaism, the patriarchal pattern still is.

The Christian tradition, departing from or ignoring the feminist teachings of Jesus, slowly, through its first five centuries, evolved into a patriarchal mode similar to Judaism (*New Woman*, 1982). Along with the patriarchal mode revival was the development of a theology based on the Yahwist Genesis tradition that has been and continues to be used to oppress Christian women. All Roman Catholic clergy and most Protestant clergy are male. God is referred to as "he" in the religious literature and acts of faith that Christians profess. The current "Moral Majority" Christians especially use the Yahwist account of creation and "the fall" to claim the need for male dominance over females in all aspects of life.

PATRIARCHAL RELIGIOUS OPPRESSION OF WOMEN

Though McGrath (1976) speaks of the oppression of women in non–Judeo-Christian traditions and O'Faolain and Martines (1973) give even greater detail about some of the traditions throughout history, here we will focus mainly on the patriarchal Judeo-Christian traditions as they affect women and their spirituality. Eve, the cause of the fall of humankind from the Garden of Eden, according to the Yahwist tradition (Genesis 3:1–24), apparently was not used in Jewish patriarchal tradition to oppress women. This may be because the priestly tradition, which discontinues at Genesis 2:3 and then picks up again at Genesis 5 (Hunt, 1960), does not mention Eden or a banishment. It was Christian theologians who later capitalized on the Eve story to oppress women (Clark & Richardson, 1977, p. 29).

In Judaism it was the childbearing function of the women that led to oppressive rules and regulations about sexual behavior and menstrual uncleanness. McGrath (1976) speaks of the male fear of menstruation that is found even today among primitive peoples. The concept of uncleanness, directly related to menstruation and childbirth among Jewish women, was the cause of most of the oppressive laws that controlled women's lives (Leviticus 15:19–30). McGrath (1976) also reports the post–Mosaic times as those in which the connection was established between uncleanness and moral transgression. By the time of the Essenes, about the same time as the life of Jesus, "woman was both guilty and contemptible" (p. 17). Sheinfeld's (1982) poignant description of the distress experienced by infertile Orthodox Jewish women who ovulate before the period of ritual uncleanness has ended, is a testament to the persistence of this oppression in some forms of Judaism, even today.

Yet another form of oppression was experienced by Jewish women: Until the seventh century the rabbinic tradition perpetuated the myth of Lilith, a demon who was said to have evil power over children. Plaskow (1979b, p.199) reports that Lilith, the first wife of Adam, was created equal to him and ran away because she could not tolerate him.

Porter and Albert (1977) report on the complexity of values within contemporary Judaism in regard to the role of women: "The religious role of women is to provide the proper home atmosphere for Jewish life" (p. 347). Ritual and ceremonies clearly define the division of labor. At the same time, women, like men, are encouraged to develop the self and expand their education and effective coping with life. The Porter and Albert study found that Jewish women had the least adherence to the traditional role model of woman solely as a homemaker, when compared with several groups of Christian women.

Christian women have fared not much better than their Jewish sisters in the patriarchal oppression their churches both allow and promote. As noted earlier, it was Christian theologians in the early Church who promoted the Eve myth as a proof of women's inferiority. Thomas Aquinas in the thirteenth century began to speak of women as defective males who were able to reach God only through men. As early as the third century, Tertullian had called women the "devil's gateway" and occasions of sin for chaste men (O'Faolain & Martines, 1973, p. 132).

Another mythological oppression has been imposed on Christian women to control their "Eve-ness." Mary, the mother of Jesus, is presented in traditional Roman Catholic teaching as a perpetual virgin. Mary is the only acceptable role model for a Christian woman, who is supposed to spend her life repenting her "Eve-ness." In the Roman Catholic Church a woman is either a celibate nun or married with children (childbirth helps to pay the Eve debt). The virgin nun has been held in higher regard and respect than the married woman. Marriage is traditionally, for both Catholic and Protestant churches, the only acceptable place where a woman is allowed sexual activity, which is permitted in order that she may pay her Eve debt through childbirth.

In explaining her understanding of the Eve myth as compared to the Mary myth, Janeway (1980) states, "Mary is never going to let Eve enjoy herself without waking up to a guilty morning after" (p. 576). That statement illustrates her explanation of the Protestant Victorian attitude toward women, which was devised in a male-dominated society and persists to this day. We have seen the early Christian teachings that laid the foundation for the Protestant version of the Eve and Mary myths. The Protestant churches, some of which denied the virginity of Mary as taught by the Catholic Church, chose to focus on the motherhood of Mary. Marriage was the saving grace for sensual men. The wife provided a safe outlet for the husband's sexual appetite while serving as a role model of virtue for him. By having children, the wife not only satisfied her husband but allowed both spouses to satisfy the command of God. Women were seen as void of passion and solely meant to serve as receptacles of male sperm and the children thus conceived.

PATRIARCHAL RELIGION'S PATHOLOGICAL EFFECTS ON WOMEN

In today's society the conflict between the Eve and Mary myths is losing its power as women become more conscious of their personhood. The remnants of that myth, however, are still present and still wreak havoc on women's mental health as well as their spirituality. The male-controlled so-called Moral Majority in the United States contains a strong Evangelical fundamental Christian ideology that can be quite traumatic to women. Meadows (1980) details the harmful effects of the female subordination to male authority in marriage required by these religious tenets.

In a study of depressed homemakers, Stoudenmier (1976) found that many women who chose to adhere to the submissive-wife doctrine became depressed. He sees their depression to be related to four factors: "suppressed anger, poor body image, an absence of reinforcing events in life, and an interpersonal anxiety that includes feelings of excessive dependency and inferiority" (p. 62). Given the Eve and Mary myths, with their negation of the woman as a person, it is not hard to see how such depression occurs. A woman who is socialized into the myths may believe she must choose submission, yet may find it intolerable because it is an extrinsic, male value. If a woman is placed in a "Catch-22" situation in her faith's tradition, she cannot be both "a normal woman and a normal human being" (Janeway, 1980, p. 575), for her submissive stance does not allow for growth and individuation. Since degree of religious involvement is not a sure safeguard against suicide, a deeply depressed "submissive wife" or nun is a high-risk client (Beit-Hallahmi, 1975).

THE CHOICES: SHEDDING OF PATRIARCHY OR EMBRACING THE GODDESS

As Jewish and Christian feminists come to terms with the reality of the powerful patriarchy of their faiths' traditions, two main avenues of response are being chosen by those who do not abandon all forms of spiritual life. One avenue is working for the liberation of the tradition from all oppression and its restoration to a balance of sexual equality as stated in the priestly tradition of Genesis 1:27: "Male and female [God] created them." The other avenue is reviving and recreating the goddess as a focus of spirituality.

Jewish feminists focus on revising ritual through change in religious language, attempting to balance the forms of address to the deity via the use of female terms, to make the language nonoppressive (Gross, 1979). Sabbath prayers have been rewritten with reference to God as a woman ("she") (Janowitz & Wenig, 1979). Rituals to celebrate the birth of a female child and her initiation into the covenant community of Israel have been developed (Plaskow, 1979a). A revised Haggadah has been developed that reflects the importance of Jewish women in the history of Israel (Cantor, 1979). While Greenberg (1981) questions Orthodox Judaism about its treatment of women, Reformed Judaism is ordaining women as rabbis (Kertzner, 1978, p. 32).

Christian feminism is based more on theology than ritual and seeks to restore full humanness to Christianity. Christian feminist spirituality deals with "enablement, empowerment and mutuality . . . [and the issue of] the bonding of women across barriers of color, sexual preference and life style . . . " (*New Woman*, 1981, pp. 4–5). Christian feminists attest to the feminist messages of Jesus that presented women as equal to men, especially in religious matters (McGrath, 1976).

Other feminist concerns, such as changes in sexist language, have been an issue for almost a decade in the Roman Catholic Church and most other churches as well; these changes are coming about slowly, frequently with a great deal of resistance. Ministry is denied women in varying degrees throughout the Christian church. The Roman Catholic denies women ordination to the priesthood because they are not male and therefore do not look like Jesus. Other denominations admit women to various levels of ministry, even ordination, yet tend to keep them in teaching rather than management positions.

Within the Roman Catholic Church, women in religious orders (nuns) have been kept segregated from other women. The Women's Ordination Conference of the Roman Catholic Church is working to break down those separation barriers, as is a newly formed group called the Association for the Rights of Catholics in the Church. All Christian feminists are attempting to bond with women of color and diverse ethnic backgrounds. The Daughters of Sarah is an Evangelical feminist publication that also has attempted to facilitate this bonding.

Some feminists, however, consider the liberation work inadequate. For example, in order for women to be free of "patriarchal policemen," C. P. Christ (1979, p. 197) claims that they need to abandon the Judeo-Christian traditions altogether and turn to the goddess to proclaim their long-denied power, beauty of body, will, and heritage. The goddess is seen as a symbol of affirmation of the female power as independent and competent in being and acting without men. In the goddess belief system, the cyclical function of the female body is revered for its life-giving ability, in contrast to the uncleanness attributed to it by patriarchal beliefs, while the affirmation and assertion of female willpower overcomes the sin of self-negation of women in these systems. This feminist spirituality proclaims "wholeness, healing love, and spiritual power not as hierarchical, as power 'over,' but as power 'for', as enabling power. It proclaims the goddess as the source of this power . . . " (Fiorenza, 1979, p. 137). Finally, the bonding of women in the sharing of their common heritage is encouraged, especially that of mother and daughter, where the mother can pass to the daughter the "herstory" of their heritage (Christ, 1979, pp. 273–286).

Janeway (1980) sees the goddess as just another form of the Mary myth and a way of keeping women's identity focused on their reproductive capacity. Wilson-Kastner (1982) reports on the concern of Christian feminists that the goddess focus will simply promote another form of sexism where females are superior and males are inferior. Collins (1981) sees this form of feminist spirituality as dealing only with white middle-class women and causing a further division of women among themselves, as well as between women and men.

ISSUES IN THERAPY

Affirmation of her client's personhood by a feminist therapist is what I see to be the focal point of therapy with women dealing with religious issues. Role modeling of female ability to be of service to others, which the woman frequently sees herself called to, while not being male dependent or submissive, is another function of the feminist therapist and very important for the client's growth (Miller, 1976).

Women who present themselves for help in dealing with current religious conflict or the impact of past religious conflict are similar only in the harmful impact that patriarchy has had on them. Some have abandoned religious practice in their late teens or early twenties and come to therapy in their early thirties to find meaning in life and heal the wounds of patriarchal oppression. Others are active in ministry in their church and are trying to deal with their sexist experiences and/or decide whether or not to resign their ministry. A third group comprises women who are active members of a patriarchal religion and are in conflict because of its oppressive tenets.

One of the first assessments I make in the initial stages of the therapeutic process is the woman's god image. It is almost always male, usually an old man, who has very conditional love, a "perform or else" love where the "or else" is harm to the person. One client imaged God as an old man dealing a deck of cards and giving her an Ace of Spades, telling her that she was creating her own hell. This client had long ago abandoned the faith of her childhood, but the impact on her current life was precipitating panic attacks.

An assessment of the most significant male is the woman's childhood, often the father or grandfather, usually reveals a connection between their behavior and her god image. Much can be worked through in both relationships simultaneously, as this connection becomes clearer to the client. Depression and acute anxiety over god's wrath are found regardless of the woman's current religious affiliation. Those women in ministerial positions who feel externally controlled or oppressed by men usually are growing in feminism and experiencing a great deal of conflict. Actively religious women become acutely anxious when thoughts of abandoning their faith arise as patriarchal oppression becomes more apparent. What I have termed the "zapping-God" phenomenon can be quite powerful, especially for women in ministry. This phenomenon is based on fire and brimstone teachings about God's punishment, which could strike at any time (Matthew 24:42), and about the final judgment, at which time the unfaithful will be cast into eternal punishment (Matthew 25:41). Once these teachings are firmly believed and a woman begins to question her faith's tradition, her fear of God's punishment can be overwhelming.

The "Mary syndrome" in Catholic women, especially nuns and ex-nuns, is one in which the woman can never accept herself as a person because she can never meet the perfection criteria of Mary, who has been given to her as a role model. When a Catholic woman has both the zapping-God fear and the Mary syndrome, her anxiety and depression can be quite intense. Nuns and ex-nuns are the women most likely to experience the least affirmation and the greatest conflict (Hart, Ames, & Sawyer, 1974). These clients need to be affirmed as sexual beings and helped to look at what choices are available to them and to decide which choices they can live with. The process is usually fraught with both anxiety and depression as the old powerful messages of Eve versus Mary complicate it. These myths need to be acknowledged and then demythologized by the client, with the support of the therapist and good Christian feminist literature. Dream work, in which the client's conflict and growth can be seen and utilized for working through and affirmation, is most helpful.

Jewish women face a unique set of circumstances in that, for many, rituals with clearly defined norms are a part of everyday life, depending on the form of Judaism that they observe. Sabbath meals, dietary regulations, and ritual baths following periods of uncleanness are examples of the scope of their religious observances outside the temple or synagogue. Support for the client's spiritual quest, along with the actual therapy sessions, can be found in the writings of Christ and Plaskow (1979) and Greenberg (1981). A publication called *Lilith*, a magazine for Jewish women, is also available. As part of a minority group, it may be more difficult for a Jewish woman to allow herself to make choices in spirituality that could alienate her from her familial/religious support systems. The therapist's respect for both the client's pace in her quest and her ultimate choices is essential.

Obviously the issues are both diverse and powerful. Whether the client is a distressed homemaker, an oppressed minister, or a nonpracticing (of religion) woman, the commonality of patriarchal oppression and/or the zapping-God syndrome results in varying degrees of anxiety and depression. Unless these oppressive issues of spirituality are acknowledged and carefully worked through, they will continue to disturb the client, for they are often at the core of her distress.

Last, although an effort was made to deal with ethnic diversity in this paper, the only reference dealing with black women and religion found in the current literature is by Murray & Harrison (1981), who see the church as a place of growth for black women in the future. Although they refer in passing to sexism in the churches, they still see the church as the place where black women will affirm each other and provide bonding through supportive activities.

CONCLUSION

Patriarchal religions have fostered conflict in many contemporary women. Feminists often feel that they must abandon the faith of their childhood, which indeed they must. Christian feminists then choose to affirm the unpreached feminist teachings of Jesus. Jewish feminists choose to revise religious ritual and language. Some feminists are choosing the goddess as a source of spirituality, while others have abandoned all religion. Nonfeminist women also can experience a great deal of mental anguish while trying to adhere to an oppressive religious belief system that negates their personhood.

A feminist therapist is most likely to be able to provide the therapy and role model that women with religious/spiritual conflicts need. The therapist also can suggest appropriate feminist reading material for the client.

The most important affirmation the woman in these situations needs is to be supported by the therapist, whatever choice she makes in regard to her spirituality. If the working-through process has been done at the client's pace, with respect for her belief system, she usually will make a choice that is most livable for her at that time. Affirming her choice, which still may keep her in an oppressive situation, can be done by giving a summary of her growth and an offer of availability for future work on further growth.

REFERENCES

Beit-Hallahmi, B. (1975). Religion and suicidal behavior. *Psychological Reports*, 37, 1303–1306.
Cantor, A. (1979). Jewish women's Haggadah. In C. P. Christ & J. Plaskow (Eds.), *Womanspirit rising*. New York: Harper & Row.
Christ, C. P. (1979). Why women need the Goddess: phenomenological, psychological, and political reflections. In C. P. Christ & J. Plaskow (Eds.), *Womanspirit rising*. New York: Harper & Row.
Christ, C. P., & Plaskow, J. (Eds.).(1979). *Womanspirit rising*. New York: Harper & Row.
Clark, E., & Richardson, H. (1977). The Old Testament. In E. Clark & H. Richardson (Eds.), *Women and religion*. New York: Harper & Row.
Collins, S. D. (1981). Feminist theology at the crossroads. *Christianity and Crisis*, 41(20), 342–347.
Fiorenza, E. S. (1979). Feminist spirituality, Christian identity, and Catholic vision. In C. P. Christ & J. Plaskow (Eds.), *Womanspirit rising*. New York: Harper & Row.
Greenberg, B. (1981). *On women and Judaism*. Philadelphia, PA: The Jewish Publication Society of America.
Gross, R. M. (1979). Female God language in a Jewish context. In C. P. Christ & J. Plaskow (Eds.), *Womanspirit rising*. New York: Harper & Row.
Hart, A., Ames, K. A., & Sawyer, R. N. (1974). Philosophical positions of nuns and former nuns: a discriminate analysis. *Psychological Reports*, 35, 675–678.
Hunt, I. (1960). Commentary. *Genesis* (Vol. 2). Pamphlet Bible Series. New York: Paulist Press.
Janeway, E. (1980). Who is Sylvia? On the loss of sexual paradigms. *Signs*, 5(4), 573–589.
Janowitz, N., & Wenig, M. (1979). Sabbath prayers for women. In C. P. Christ & J. Plaskow (Eds.), *Womanspirit rising*. New York: Harper & Row.
Kertzner, M. N. (1978). *What is a Jew?* New York: Collier Books.
McGrath, A. M. (1976). *Women and the church*. New York: Image Books.
Meadows, M. J. (1980). Wifely submission: Psychological/spiritual growth perspectives. *Journal of Religion and Health*, 19(2), 104–120.
Miller, J. B. (1976). *Toward a new psychology of women*. Boston: Beacon Press.

146 : : *Women's Issues across the Lifespan*

Murray, S. R., & Harrison D. D. (1981). Black women and the future. *Psychology of Women Quarterly, 6*(1), 113–122.

New Woman, New Church (March 1981). Spirituality, prayer, call, renewed priestly ministry, bonding, pp. 4–5.

New Woman, New Church (July 1982). Report of the last three sessions of the dialogue between Women's Ordination Conference and the bishops committee on women in society and in the Church, p. 406.

O'Faolain, J., & Martines, L. (Eds.).(1973). *Not in God's Image*. New York: Harper & Row.

Plaskow, J. (1979a). Bringing a daughter into the covenant. In C. P. Christ & J. Plaskow (Eds.), *Womanspirit rising*. New York: Harper & Row.

Plaskow, J. (1979b). The coming of Lilith: toward a feminist theology. In C. P. Christ & J. Plaskow (Eds.), *Womanspirit rising*. New York: Harper & Row.

Porter, J. R., & Albert, A. A. (1977). Subculture or assimilation? A cross-cultural analysis of religion and women's role. *Journal for the Scientific Study of Religion, 16*(4), 345–359.

Sheinfeld, M. (June 1982). *Infertility and Orthodox Judaism*. Belmont, MA: Resolve, Inc. Newsletter.

Stoudenmier, J. (1976). The role of religion in the depressed housewife. *Journal of Religion and Health, 15*(1), 62–67.

Wilson-Kastner, P. (1982). Christianity and new feminist religions. *New Woman, New Church*, January, pp. 4–5.

RESOURCES

Association for the Rights of Catholics in the Church, P.O. Box 3932, Philadelphia, PA 19146. (215) 623–0590.

Daughters of Sarah, 2716 W. Cortland, Chicago, IL 60647.

Women's Ordination Conference, 48 St. Marks Place, New York, NY 10003.

15

Feminist Therapy with Women and Couples Who are Infertile

MAUREEN CALISTA HENDRICKS

In an era when women are finally being recognized as equal with men, women taking control of their own lives is an important issue. Thus, the choice and the timing of motherhood are planned carefully in light of career opportunities. Even women who are not career oriented generally plan when and how many children they will have. This paper will deal with feminist therapy as it relates to women who are unable to follow through with their carefully made motherhood plans because of their own infertility and/or that of their partner.

CURRENT DATA ON INFERTILITY

The inability of a woman to become pregnant after one or more years of unprotected, regular sexual intercourse is the American Fertility Society's definition of female infertility (Albrecht & Schiff, 1982). The inability to carry a fetus to viability, as in repeated spontaneous abortions, is also considered infertility (Shane, Schiff & Wilson, 1976). Male infertility may be defined as the inability of a male to successfully impregnate a healthy fertile female regardless of the quantity and quality of his semen. There has been a gradual rise in the incidence of infertility in the United States in the past decade. In 1976, Shane et al., estimated the incidence to be 10 percent (p. 2), and by 1982 it was cited as 10 to 15 percent (Albrecht & Schiff, 1982, p. 990).

Male infertility ordinarily is diagnosed by the findings of inadequate and/or abnormal sperm and sperm count. Female infertility is more complex in its causes and diagnosis than male infertility. Ovarian function, hormonal balance, patency of fallopian tubes, and the condition of all pelvic organs and tissues contribute to a woman's degree of fertility. In the treatment of infertility, hormone therapy for both women and men may be used to correct hormonal imbalance. Often the therapy is with a combination of drugs. In spite of all the diagnostic tests and treatment presently available, only about 50 percent of infertile couples will achieve a pregnancy (Albrecht & Schiff, 1982, p. 1000). In addition, Shane et al. (1976) report an ectopic pregnancy rate in infertile women to be "five times the normal rate" and the possibility of perinatal mortality as double the normal rate (p. 40).

Accurate references to ethnicity and the impact of infertility cannot be made here because current material cannot be found in the literature. The three studies reported about black women and childbearing did not mention infertility (Crovitz & Steinmann, 1980; Murray & Harrison, 1981, Stokes & Ritchey, 1974). The only statement that may infer infertility rates was; "White and black women nearing the end of their reproductive years, ages 30–39, displayed surprisingly similar levels of childlessness" (Stokes & Ritchey, 1974, p. 208).

EMOTIONAL ASPECTS OF INFERTILITY

On the basis of the preceding data it is quite apparent that infertility, solely in terms of diagnosis and treatment, is a time-consuming process. Since both partners need to be evaluated for a complete picture of the degree of infertility, even a fertile woman or man must undergo study to validate fertility.

Once the diagnosis is made, clients need to go through a grieving process, whether they finally achieve a pregnancy or not. The emotional impact of infertility can be devastating. Although most of the literature on the emotional impact of infertility deals with couples, Williams and Power (1977) have an excellent article on infertility in single women.

There is a uniqueness to the grieving process in infertility because the recurrence of the menstrual cycle, until menopause or a hysterectomy, is both an ongoing reminder and an indicator of the infertility. The length of time it takes a client or a couple to deal with their infertility grief is related not only to their personal psychological status and the manner in which the health care team relates to them, but also to the repeated hope–despair experience of the menstrual cycle. How the couple deals with the "crisis" of menstruation is an indicator of their degree of distress.

When first seen in the acute stages of their grieving, couples tend to present with fairly similar patterns of response. The women tend to vacillate between anger and/or rage and depression, a cycle their partner frequently calls "irrational behavior." The men tend still to be denying the infertility and putting their energy into trying to minimize the woman's distress or protect themselves from it. Long before this critical time the woman herself may have denied the infertility, by waiting a number of years before having a work-up or by persisting in testing and treatment long after it was evident that most likely a pregnancy would not occur. Four years is the outer maximal limit in which treatment is likely to be successful (Albrecht & Schiff, 1982, p. 1000). Her anger may be aggravated by the years of denial and/or failure to conceive.

It is with painful regularity for most women that they are reminded once more of their infertility and must care for their menstruating bodies while perhaps experiencing physical discomfort of some degree. They usually rage at everyone and everything, a phenomenon described by Wright as "spread" (Williams & Power, 1977, p. 329). Their persistent pain on seeing pregnant women or newborn infants becomes more acute, and they may plunge into depression. The man often withdraws from her because he feels so helpless in trying to relieve her distress. He may aggravate her anguish by attempts at denial such as, "We still have next month."

Whether the woman is the infertile partner alone or with the man, she is the one who is subjected to the most frequent invasive, distressing, and perhaps painful procedures and experiences: repeated pelvic examinations, usually done by men; painful biopsies and/or x-rays during which it is made clear that "this will hurt only a bit," which tells her that she is expected to "grin and bear it"; painful hormonal injections that cause both physiological and psychological changes; having to sit in medical-office waiting rooms filled with women in various stages of pregnancy while she waits to be seen; extensive corrective surgery that may not be effective; and the possibility of a life-threatening ectopic pregnancy or fetal loss if she does conceive.

Studies of infertile men who, with their wives, chose donor artificial insemination (AID) revealed a high incidence of temporary impotence (Berger, 1980) and a strong sense of guilt about depriving the wife of his child while subjecting her to the AID (Berger, 1980; Czyba & Chevret, 1979; David & Anidan, 1976). In the three studies just cited, the wives, while experiencing varying degrees of anger toward their husbands, tended to take on the infertility onus, to protect the man. Czyba & Chevret (1979) refer to this finding as "The Secret" (p. 244). Keeping "The Secret" is so powerful a contract between the couple that the authors predict a dissolution of the marriage should there be any violation of this secret.

Couples who are diagnosed as "normal infertile" (no specific cause for infertility can be diagnosed), who make up 10 to 20 percent of infertiles (Albrecht & Schiff, 1982, p. 999) have, in reality, "infertility of unknown etiology" (Shane et al., 1976, p. 18). The medical profession, however, has tried for years to demonstrate that such couples' infertility has a basis in personal psychopathology. Denber (1978) reviewed 50 studies, and Noyes and Chapnick (1964) reviewed 75, all of which attempted to prove a psychological basis for female infertility. The authors found that the data reported did not support the theory of psychological causation.

This prevalence of the concept of the emotionally unbalanced woman can be powerful enough to lead women to question themselves about what is wrong with them or what they have done wrong that they cannot conceive. This sense of guilt is very often present in the women who have experienced repeated spontaneous abortions and attempt to determine each time what their mistake was.

Related to such sexist attitudes is the degree to which the medical community tends to minimize the side-effects that are experienced by women who take Clomid or other hormones to improve ovulation and/or hormonal balance. These side-effects often greatly distress the women. An increase in depression or agitation when taking Clomid, as well as fluid retention and up to a 10-pound weight gain on Danazol, have been reported to me by clients as well as in anecdotal literature (Nixon, 1980). Clients need to be reassured that these hormonal side-effects are not imaginary or uncommon.

Three other factors compound the grieving process of the infertile woman. Two are the history of one or more previous therapeutic abortions or a pregnancy carried to term and the child relinquished for adoption. The latter experience also can be a factor for men. The infertile client knows that somewhere "out there" is their birth child and that now they are infertile. Their distress may be compounded by the lack of availability of an adoptive child for themselves.

Finally, what I have found to be, for the infertile woman, the most emotionally devastating experience is an early hysterectomy. When pelvic disease is so extensive and/or painful that an infertile woman requires a hysterectomy, her ego strength is taxed to the maximum. Women as young as their early twenties may require hysterectomies. An attempt at suicide is always a possibility during the depths of their despair.

UTERINE SOCIALIZATION

Many women define themselves as persons in what I call uterine terms; they see their ultimate purpose in life as being conception of children and motherhood. As previously noted, even women who choose lifetime careers usually plan their education and practice around the biological clock of the reproductive years. This uterine socialization is based on years of exposure to the societal requirements of women to reproduce.

At puberty the female child normally begins her menstrual cycle. The explanation usually given is that her body is preparing itself for pregnancy. From then until menopause or a hysterectomy she lives with this cyclical reminder of her reproductive ability. In adolescence she is cautioned against sexual activity, to avoid pregnancy. She is always assumed to be fertile. Religious organizations will speak of motherhood as a redeeming feature of being a female. It is often implied that women, because they are descended from Eve, must atone for Eve's sin by enduring the birth process. Motherhood, then, is not only a societal mandate but also is perceived by many women to be a command of God. Their anguish in not being able to fulfill this command can be overwhelming. An example of the religious perspective can be found in an article about Orthodox Judaism and the issue of infertility (Sheinfeld, 1982).

Since the advent of widely available and fairly effective contraception has given women the choice of when and whether to fulfill their reproductive mandate, the few women who choose not to fulfill this mandate may be studied to determine the psychological basis for their choice. The pathology of a childless choice, implied by Kaltreider and Margolis (1977) in the women they studied, is further evidence of the powerfulness of the mandate. It is still a question of "when," not "whether to."

The combined mandates of society, religion, and female anatomy and physiology have prepared the infertile woman to choose "when" and not "whether" to reproduce. Men also are well conditioned. Infertility robs both women and men of the choice element in reproduction. For some this is their greatest area of distress. Career women who have planned their lives around "when" are suddenly faced with "maybe not." Their success in their education and careers makes their deprivation of choice more acute. They feel externally controlled and their anger (Why me?) is expressed often (Williams & Power, 1977, p. 328).

Women who have defined their femininity in uterine terms and cannot choose to complete their image through achieving one or more pregnancies (secondary infertility is most acute in these women) feel stripped of their self-worth. Many infertile women hate their bodies for failing to function reproductively and abuse the body through overeating, improper care, or neglect. The powerfulness of the reproductive mandate and the issue of choice are well presented by Russo (1979), while the femininity conflict has been studied by Gordon and Hall (1974).

THERAPEUTIC INTERVENTIONS

The client who most frequently initiates the therapeutic contact is the acutely distressed infertile woman. Since I believe that infertility is a couple issue and that working with the woman alone puts the onus of identified patient on her, I also believe it is essential to attempt to get the man involved in the therapy. Requesting his presence because of the distress that the grieving places on the relationship often will be the nudge he needs to come, even if somewhat reluctantly at first. Usually direct contact with the man by phone to explain the need for his presence and also express concern for his grief facilitates a positive response. Derdeyn and Waters (1981) have done a paper on the destructive effects on the marital relationship of unshared loss. They also refer to the divisiveness that individual therapy can have on marital distress. It is usually most therapeutic to work with the couple together. If, however, it is not possible to do couple work, much can be achieved with one partner alone. Most of what will follow, therefore, also can be applied to individual therapy with an infertile client, female or male.

The initial assessment of the infertile couple involves a determination of

1. The stage and amount of grief that each partner is experiencing
2. Whether the infertility is present in one or both
3. How distressed the relationship is
4. How long the infertility has been known
5. What diagnostic work-up and/or treatment they have had
6. What they have been told about their chances for a pregnancy
7. What options they are considering, such as AID or adoption
8. What support systems are available to them in their grieving
9. How depressed and/or suicidal each client is.

Usually each partner is at a different stage of the grief process, and support for each one with an explanation of uniqueness in grieving will begin to narrow the rift in the relationship. The therapist's respect for the acknowledgment of each partner's distress can facilitate their ability to accept what the other is experiencing as valid. This process needs to be repeated often. When both are infertile, the process is usually less difficult. When only one partner is infertile, the fertile partner may deny being angry at the infertile partner, so the process will be slower and more difficult.

The practical information contained in the assessment just cited helps the therapist to determine if the couple is getting or has had competent medical care. A basic infertility work-up consists of (1) the semen analysis, (2) documentation of normal ovarian function, (3) the postcoital examination, and (4) patency of the fallopian tubes (Albrecht & Schiff, 1982, p. 991). If the basic work-up has not been done or the couple is dissatisfied with the results or the manner in which it is handled, referral to an infertility clinic or specialist is indicated, unless the couple has "shopped" from specialist to specialist. One way to evaluate the quality of the care they receive or the health care providers they use is to contact the nearest RESOLVE branch. RESOLVE is a national support organization for infertile people, and local as well as national offices can help a therapist evaluate the adequacy of infertility work-ups, as well as provide information on competent referral sources.

If the couple is in the midst of diagnosis and/or treatment in a competent facility, then a focus on dealing with the reality of the uncertainty and disappointments that they may experience is necessary. In some ways it may seem to the therapist that the crises never end. Often, as soon as the couple has come to terms with one reality, another hope is dashed. Therapy with the infertile couple in the midst of diagnosis and treatment may consist of repeated crisis intervention.

Due to the cyclical nature of infertility grief work, as well as the repeated crises experienced by the infertile couple, there is no smooth, sequential process in therapy. The anger and depression stages of grief may need to be worked through a number of times. A major clue the therapist can use to gauge the beginning of final acceptance is when the couple start to talk about "enough is enough" and how they want to get on with their lives. At that point they are able to look at options such as adoption or child-free living. Their readiness for adoption needs to be accompanied by preparation from the therapist for some resurgence of old grief feelings during the adoptive process.

If AID and/or adoption are being considered or pursued, an evaluation of the degree or resolution of the grief process is important. Successful adjustment to and adequate parenting of an AID or adopted child requires a maximal degree of acceptance of the infertility (Berger, 1980; Polisky, 1968; Wiehe, 1976). Part of the bargaining stage of the grief process in infertility involves beginning to look at options other than a birth child. Zimmerman (1982) has done a comprehensive paper on current options such as AID, surrogate motherhood, and *in vitro* fertilization that would be most useful to the therapist working with infertile clients.

It is important to note again that the adoption process itself usually will reactivate the grief of the infertility to some degree; acknowledging this and working it through again is necessary (Polisky, 1968). In my practice I have found the anger stage to be the one most often reactivated and projected onto the adoption caseworker. The sense of loss of control can become quite acute, especially if the caseworker is not highly sensitive to the reactivated grief. During this time the infertile clients will be reminded by any number of persons of the old myth: "once you adopt you're sure to get pregnant." It is very helpful to share the fact that so far no studies have proven that any more pregnancies occur after adoption than would have occurred without adoption (Denber, 1978).

At an early point in the therapeutic process a support system assessment is essential. The sense of aloneness that most infertile people experience is intense. Few friends really are able to appreciate the pain that the infertile client experiences. If the friends have children, the infertile client may have withdrawn from contact during the time of acute grief, perhaps without an explanation for the withdrawal. Families are often just as unsupportive; fortunate are the few whose families understand the grief. In the presence of this aloneness and lack of support, referral to an organization such as RESOLVE, which was founded by and is run by infertile persons, is an important therapeutic intervention. Local RESOLVE chapters throughout the country offer support groups to infertile persons (Menning, 1977).

This support is critical, even if a pregnancy is achieved, for the pregnancy experiences of formerly infertile women tend to be fraught with apprehension and/or anxiety about the health of the fetus and their ability to carry to term. These women often do not reflect the joyful anticipation or periods of euphoria that frequently are seen in planned pregnancies. Formerly infertile pregnant women defensively guard themselves from too much hope; they usually know that fetal loss rates are higher in pregnancies among once-infertile women, and they do not trust their infertile bodies to carry a pregnancy successfully or deliver a healthy baby. As noted early in the paper, they also have a higher rate of perinatal mortality.

Bonding with the birth child may be somewhat delayed for the formerly infertile woman. Disbelief that she finally has had her frequently fantasized child can be coupled with disappointment about a difficult labor, use of medication during labor, and/or a cesarean delivery. She had expected to feel euphoric and instead feels let down and ambivalent. Preparation for the possibilities of the unexpected feelings is important anticipatory guidance in therapy, since they can be quite distressing to the woman and/or couple.

Bonding with an adoptive child is a somewhat similar experience. The reality of not having a birth child hits with a powerful sense of finality. When the infertility grief has been worked through well, support of the slow bonding is usually all that is needed. If the infertility has not been well grieved, the woman, man, and/or couple may not be able to bond with the infant. They will be unwilling to share such feelings with the adoptive agency and will need to work with a therapist to complete their grief process and/or determine if the adoption is appropriate for them. A fear of never being offered another adoptive child can prevent a couple from dealing with this lack of bonding and result in psychological harm to the child as well as the couple, especially if viewed by them as another failure.

The recurrent crises that an infertile person may experience, such as failure to respond to treatment or AID, not being approved for adoption, or difficulty in bonding with a birth or adoptive child, often lead to severe depression. A higher rate of completed suicide has been found among childless married women than unmarried women of the same age (Wenz, 1976). With each new disappointment it is necessary to reevaluate the suicidal potential of the infertile client.

In spite of the fact that the infertile client may work through her grief to a satisfactory level of acceptance at a given time, there is always the possibility of some degree of recurrence throughout her lifetime (Kraft, Palombo, Mitchell, Dean, Meyers & Schmidt, 1980). For example, menopause for some women will reactivate the pain and more working through may be necessary, but not all infertile women will have this experience (Notman, 1979).

A final therapeutic issue is the fertility of the therapist. An infertile therapist is seen by clients as more able to understand their grief. The issue of countertransference needs to be acknowledged by the infertile therapist and appropriate supervision and/or consultation sought. A once infertile therapist who has conceived successfully might tend to be more optimistic than one who has not. This is not too likely, however, for the majority of once-infertile women who do conceive will consider themselves as infertile women who happened to get pregnant. The fertile therapist who is knowledgeable and empathic also can be most effective but will have to put time into dealing with the infertile clients' anger about the therapist's fertility.

SUMMARY

Infertility for the majority of people is a loss experience that needs to be grieved. Only 1 to 2 percent of marriages today are intentionally childless (Kaltreider & Margolis, 1977, p. 179). Most couples choose "when" to have children, not "whether" to have them. The denial of that choice, imposed by infertility, creates a degree of emotional distress that varies according to the basic personality of the person and, for women, the degree of uterine socialization they possess. Only after the acute stages of the grief and grieving process have been worked through is it possible for the infertile person to look at options beyond a birth child.

Couple therapy is preferable to individual therapy so that the couple relationship may be healed of the rift that the infertility usually creates. The feminist therapist can help both partners to understand their differing responses in relationship to sex-role socialization and stereotyping. Each then can be an advocate and support for the other, especially when sexist medical behavior is encountered.

Since support systems are usually weak or absent in the family and/or friendship circle of the infertile person, a referral to an organization of infertile persons, such as RESOLVE, is warranted. At varying times in life, the infertile person may experience a resurgence of grief, which may require a reworking through in therapy or simply a support group experience in RESOLVE. Even after the reproductive years have ended, the infertile person may experience the steady presence of grief like a glowing ember in a finished fire.

REFERENCES

Albrecht, B. H., & Schiff, I. (1982). Infertility. In W. T. Branch (Ed.), *Office Practice of Medicine*. Philadelphia, PA: W. B. Saunders.

Berger, D. M. (1980). Couples' reaction to male infertility and donor insemination. *American Journal of Psychiatry, 137*(9), 1047–1049.

Crovitz, E., & Steinmann, A. (1980). A decade later: black–white attitudes toward women's familial role. *Psychology of Women Quarterly, 5*(2), 170–176.

Czyba, J. C., & Chevret, M. (1979). Psychological reactions of couples to artificial insemination of donor sperm. *International Journal of Fertility, 24*(4), 240–245.

David, A., & Anidan, D. (1976). Artificial insemination donor: clinical and psychological aspects. *Fertility and Sterility, 27*(5), 528–532.

Denber, H. C. (1978). Psychiatric aspects of infertility. *Journal of Reproductive Medicine, 20*(1), 23–29.

Derdeyn, A. P., & Waters, P. B. (1981). Unshared loss and marital conflict. *Journal of Marital and Family Therapy, 7*(4), 481–487.

Gordon, F. E., & Hall, D. T. (1974). Self-image and stereotypes of femininity: Their relationships to women's role conflicts and coping. *Journal of Applied Psychology, 59*(2), 241–243.

Kaltreider, N. B., & Margolis, A. G. (1977). Childless by choice: A clinical study. *American Journal of Psychiatry, 134*(2), 179–182.

Kraft, A. D., Palombo, J., Mitchell, D., Dean, C., Meyers, S., & Schmidt, A. W. (1980). The psychological dimensions of infertility. *American Journal of Orthopsychiatry, 50*(4), 618–628.

Menning, B. E. (1977), *Infertility*. Englewood Cliffs, NJ: Prentice-Hall.

Murray, S. R., & Harrison, D. D. (1981). Black women and the future. *Psychology of Women Quarterly, 6*(1), 113–122.

Nixon, S. (1980). For want of a child. *Chicago Magazine, 29*(12), 214–219, 242, 244.

Notman, M. (1979). Midlife concerns of women: Implications of the menopause. *American Journal of Psychiatry, 136*(10), 1270–1274.

Noyes, R. W., & Chapnick, E. M. (1964). Literature on psychology and infertility. *Fertility and Sterility, 15,* 543.

Polisky, G. K. (1968). Adoption and relinquishment as experienced in loss and mourning. Paper presented at the meeting of the American Orthopsychiatric Association Conference, Chicago, March 1968.

Russo, N. F. (1979). Overview: Sex roles, fertility and the motherhood mandate. *Psychology of Women Quarterly, 4*(1), 7–15.

Shane, J. M., Schiff, I., & Wilson, E. A. (1976). The infertile couple. In Trench, A. H. (Ed.), *Clinical Symposia* (vol. 28, no. 5 pp. 1–40). Summit, NJ: Ciba.

Sheinfeld, M. (1982). Infertility and Orthodox Judaism. *Resolve, Inc. Newsletter,* June 1982, pp. 1–40.

Stokes, C. S., & Ritchey, P. N. (1974). Some further observations on childlessness and color. *Journal of Black Studies, 5*(2), 203–209.

Wenz, F. V. (1976). Psychological reaction to infertility. *Psychological Reports, 38,* 863–866.

Wiehe, V. R. (1976). Psychological reaction to infertility. *Psychological Reports, 38,* 863–866.

Williams, L. S., & Power, P. W. (1977). The emotional impact of infertility in single women: some implications for counseling. *Journal of the American Medical Women's Association, 32*(9), 327–333.

Zimmerman, S. L. (1982). Alternatives in human reproduction for involuntary childless couples. *Family Relations, 31*(2), 233–241.

■ 16

Stepmothering: Fairy Tales and Reality

APHRODITE CLAMAR

> When I think of a stepmother, I think of someone mean and someone who doesn't love you as much as your own mother. But I know that isn't true. All I know is that I want my own mom—*Nine-year-old girl, quoted in the* New York Times, *January 3, 1983*

The stepchild has been an engrossing theme in folklore, poetry, fiction, drama, and the movies for years. Yet there has been an absence of interest in the stepmother/stepchild relationship among psychologists and others concerned with the American family. The rising number of divorces and remarriages today, and the growing proportion of stepmothers among women, make this a particularly appropriate time to deal with this long-neglected issue.

Stepfamily relationships, as characterized by wicked stepmothers, go back to the dawn of recorded history. Their victimized stepchildren are legendary—Snow White, Cinderella, and Hansel and Gretel. Cinderella just missed becoming a professional drudge; Snow White almost died of apple poisoning; Hansel and Gretel were dumped unlovingly in the witch-infested woods. In every case the stepmother was synonymous

159

with calculated wickedness. Indeed, even the dictonary definition of stepmother implies unparentlike behavior or neglect and deprivation of one's stepchildren ("one that fails to give proper care or attention," Webster has it).

The effect of these stories on children who turn out to be stepchildren is incalculable. Even Freud (1913) observed, "It is not surprising that psychoanalysis confirms our recognition of the important place that folk fairy tales have acquired in the mental life of our children" (p. 59). Children, hearing these tales, will often enact in their play the role of the inconsiderate stepmother in dealing with younger children. It should therefore come as no surprise that when a woman assumes the role of stepmother she is at once enveloped in a hostile atmosphere created not by her own actions but by folklore. "Fairy tales," Hannah Kuhn (1960) remarked, "do not know a good stepmother. Her maliciousness needs no explanations. She is wicked because she is a stepmother or she must be a stepmother because she acts wickedly." The evil character created for the stepmother by the fairy tale follows her about like a shadow. The fact that the stepmother herself, as a child, was steeped in the same old lore affects her behavior when she acquires the title. The whole situation is charged with this notion.

Margaret Mead (1970) suggests that the child in contemporary American culture develops an overdependence on the parents. "Each American child learns early and in terror that his [or her] whole security depends on that single set of parents," she writes. "We have never made adequate social provision for the security and identity of the children if that marriage is broken" (p. 109). The result, Mead argues, is the child's inability to be committed to a stepparent in a manner that will permit a meaningful relationship.

The prefix *step* in this case derives from an old English term, *astepan*, meaning bereaved or deprived. In the past, a man or woman remarried following the death of a spouse and the stepparent was considered a replacement parent, someone who stepped in to rescue a bereaved family. Today, a marriage is more likely to be ended by divorce (one out of every three marriages) than by death, and the new marriage partner often assumes the role of a significant other adult in the child's life, an add-on rather than a replacement. It is now estimated that close to 50 million individuals are, in one way or another, involved in a "step" relationship.

Thus, as the divorce rate spirals ever upward, the very nature of the stepchild has changed. No longer a child with one dead parent and a remarried surviving parent, the stepchild now has one or two remarried parents, new family relationships, new mores, new customs, and, sometimes, new siblings to contend with.

This chapter limits its discussion to a heterosexual stepmother; in today's society it is also possible that a stepmother may be living in a lesbian relationship. While some issues in the stepmother/stepchild relationship are similar regardless of the parent's sexual preference, other issues arise when two women are in a lesbian relationship, especially when each of the women may be a stepmother to the other's child.

Even the kinship vocabulary these days is astounding in its multiplicity of roles: biological or natural parent, custodial parent, nonresident parent, stepparent, stepchild, stepsibling, half-sibling, father's wife's children, mother's husband, father's wife, stepgrandmother, father's wife's mother, mother's husband's brother, stepmother-in-law, quasi-kin, and on and on.

A further complication/variable is the child's original mother. No longer conveniently dead but rather having graduated to the status of "ex," she serves as a living reminder to the new stepmother of a previous life, a previous marriage, a previous family system. The ubiquitous "ex" appears everywhere in the new family, especially in the children's behavior, dress, personalities, and general appearance. Because a divorced man who remarries is likely to choose a younger wife than his first wife; because the exwife's chances of marrying again are considerably less than her husband's; because the divorced wife is almost always in an inferior economic position to that of her former spouse; and because society teaches women to compete for men, it is a rare "ex" who wishes happiness for her former mate's new marriage. She is more likely to be jealous and competitive, if not actively engaged in undermining her husband's new marriage.

Most studies of adjustment to the role of substitute parent view the role of stepmother as the most difficult, particularly if the stepchildren are adolescents. The role adjustment of the stepfather appears to be significantly easier (Bernard, 1956). A number of reasons are offered for this discrepancy: (1) the stepmother enters a situation that historically defines her role as cruel; (2) stepmothers are stigmatized even when they are good and loving surrogate mothers, because of the emotions that are associated culturally with not trusting those without blood ties; (3) a stepmother tends to spend more time with the children than the stepfather does, creating greater opportunities for conflicts; (4) generally, children in our culture are closer to their mothers, so it becomes difficult for an "outsider" to assume mothering tasks without appearing to displace her; (5) society is apt to offer more acceptance and assistance to stepfathers for "trying" than it does to stepmothers, who are more likely to be judged; (6) women still are expected to be involved in child care, an expectation that stepmothers themselves share, even when they do not see the family in terms of traditional roles; and (7) contemporary stepmothers often tend to be childless and younger than original parents, making it more difficult to straddle the role of parent, nonparent and/or older friend.

The stepfamily often provides ample opportunity for sexual games. Children of remarried parents are highly aware of the sexual side of the new relationship ("Somebody new is sleeping in Daddy's bed"), especially if the stepmother is not married to their father and is younger and more overtly sexual than the original mother or becomes pregnant. While signs of affection between parent and child are seen as positive, especially for children whose earlier family experience has been one of hostility and conflict between parents, it is important for the stepmother to remember that she has an audience watching her every move, and excessive displays of affection can be provocative.

During adolescence, father/son relationships are particularly liable to be strained. A stepmother who joins the family at this time may inadvertently serve as an object of sexual competition between father and son—something that, while not unheard of, is socially taboo in a primary family when the mother and son are biologically related.

Thus the stepson who flaunts his physicality or who makes an announcement every time he gets undressed is giving off obvious cues of sexuality. Fondling, hugging, and kissing between stepmother and adolescent stepson may alternate with embarrassed avoidance of any intimacy, causing undue pressure, false hostility, and a blurring of the parameters of parental responsibility.

Adolescent girls may be particularly troubled by a stepmother whom they see as direct competition for the attention of their father, especially if the father was unmarried for a period of time and the daughter served as surrogate wife/housekeeper. Competition may be played out in subtle and not-so-subtle attempts to appear sexual and provocative, for example, the daughter who walks around the house in see-through nighties or tries to emulate the stepmother's sexuality in other ways.

In the majority of families, years of familiarity lessen the novelty that enhances sexual stimulation. As Dr. Richard Gardner (1976) observes, "Stepparents and stepchildren are very 'new' to one another and are thereby more likely to be sexually stimulated by one another" (p. 77). Consequently, the situation becomes "hotter and more highly charged, and the maneuvers to decompress them more formidable" (p. 77). Arguments between stepmother and stepson are a common way to defuse sexual feelings; frequently, these bitter arguments are love fights that mask sexual titillation, rivalries, guilt, frustration, and hostility produced by sexual feelings.

Another potentially difficult area for the stepmother is discipline. Some stepmothers feel timid about punishing their stepchildren or even delineating the limits of unacceptable behavior, leaving this thorny area instead to the original parents. Should the stepmother impose discipline, however, such efforts may be seen as evidence of the wicked stepmother syndrome at work, particularly when the children balk at a stepparent's discipline.

Every household has a different set of rules and regulations. How does the stepmother handle a stepchild who drops clothes on a chair at night, whereas her own children must hang theirs up? How does a stepmother handle a stepchild who uses language that is unacceptable to her, or has poor table manners, or fights constantly with a sibling, or challenges every statement with, "You're not my mother; you can't tell me what to do!"

Children want to do what they want to do when they want to do it, preferably "right now." This self-centeredness is what often makes child-rearing exhausting and stressful. Add to this potent brew the ambivalence that is a natural outgrowth of the stepparent relationship, plus fear of disloyalty to the original mother, and you have the basis for the kind of conflict that causes problems not only between the father and his new wife but also with his first wife as well.

Stepmother and spouse need to discuss and clarify disagreements on discipline, preferably out of the children's earshot. It behooves the stepmother not to appear uncertain about her beliefs or position in front of the children; uncertainty will merely generate and intensify their insecurity. It is particularly important for the stepmother and spouse to present a unified front, precluding manipulation and fights instigated by the children. Feelings of frustration, anger, and impotence by the stepmother ultimately may erode the marriage and destroy any possible relationship with the stepchildren. Children need to be disciplined not only by their original mother but by the stepmother as well; anything else gives them a distorted view of the power structure within the household and encourages them to defy the stepmother.

In this vein, the stepmother will have to accept the fact that her stepchildren constantly are comparing her to their original mother. Children are generally unhappy when a divorced parent remarries, since such a step destroys their fantasy of an eventual reunion of their parents and a return to the original, whole family—no matter how unrealistic. Invariably, comparison to the original mother will be unflattering to the stepmother. Stepmothers may need help in not taking these comparisons personally.

Should the stepmother marry a man with grown children, her role with them will be quite different. Since these young adults do not need mothering, the role open to her is one of friend and confidante—a role that, if handled sensitively, can be rewarding. Since the new stepmother comes to such a family arrangement with a clean slate, she may develop a warm, supportive relationship with her adult stepchildren that is free of the historical conflicts and misunderstandings that are the baggage of any child/parent relationship.

Now, to get back to fairy tales. Their message is clear-cut: real mothers are good; stepmothers who replace them are bad; and father, who just stands by passively as his new wife does his children in, is blameless. Fairy tales present perfect and final solutions; the child, unfortunately, lives in an imperfect world with few readily apparent solutions. Yet the child has an intense need to experience mother as good—loving, nurturing, present at all times, and preferably consistent. On the other hand, what can we do with feelings of anger, hate, and rage? In the stepfamily, the stepmother becomes the perfect target for these feelings and she is not immune to them.

It is axiomatic that human relationships are marked by some degree of ambivalence. In the stepchild/stepmother relationship, the contradictory feelings of love and hate usually directed toward one parent may be divided between the original mother (living or not) and the stepmother, with the stepmother receiving only hostility and the biological mother only adulation (Radomisli, 1981). This splitting of the ego as a defense against unbearable aspects of reality may stem from guilt over being disloyal to the original parent (Baer, 1972) or incomplete mourning for the "dead" original family.

Bowlby (1961) stresses the importance of expressing what he calls "protest" as a reaction to loss—that is, a vehement demand for the lost object, strenuous efforts to regain it, and a rejection of its replacement. Rather than decathecting from the lost love, which is what generally happens in mourning, children and adolescents tend to develop a hypercathexis to the loss. Children experience their parents and family as part of themselves, an inalienable possession without which they are incomplete. They are often ashamed of having lost this precious possession and feel inferior to children who have an intact family. Since the process of learning to love and be loved is interrupted, confusion and withdrawal result (Wolfenstein, 1966).

From the incomplete mourning, the fantasy that the original parents will return to each other may take hold. The stepmother, however, is the barrier to the realization of this fantasy. She is also experienced as a threat to the child's relationship with its father, who has probably been paying less attention to his children anyway since the new woman—now his children's stepmother—appeared in his life.

This situation, not uncommon in stepfamilies, challenges the stepmother both to understand and overcome it by using all of the skills, perceptions, and ways of connecting she has acquired in dealing with her own parents, her peers, and possibly her own children.

One of the assumptions of developmental psychology is that maturing is a process of separation: A child is attached to its mother, whereas an adult is independent and thinks for herself (Mahler, Pine, & Bergman, 1975). The fact is, however, that women's socialization does not encourage separation. The lives women lead, even as adults, are embedded in relationships; their identities are tied up with other people. As Carol Gilligan (1982) discovered in her recent research, "the highest moral value for women is not justice, as it is for men, but care, . . . to take care of people and to try to avoid hurting, . . . how to talk to people and respond, . . . how to relate to others, . . . a joining of the heart and eye" (p. 171). Empathy is built into their definition of self; closeness is essential. For women, life is a network of connections, a web of interactions. Not only do women define themselves in the context of their relationships, but they judge themselves in terms of their ability to care and the response of those for whom they care.

Stepmothers are also women, and they, too, have an ability to connect and interact with their stepchildren and to make this network of connections work for them. Unfortunately, their stepchildren, because of their unique set of problems and circumstances, are not always responsive to reaching out. The result: a feeling of rejection, often by both sides.

Thus, because of the special set of circumstances that stepmothers face, they need a special kind of help. I should like to propose a system of mentoring as a way of helping stepmothers resolve the problems created by mythology, literature, society, and the psychological needs of stepchildren and spouse.

I see the mentor not as a teacher or guide, but rather a companion; an older, more experienced woman who has already gone through stepmotherhood and has the perspective, distance, and credibility to help the younger woman. I see mentoring as a relationship between two women, adult peers, but with one wiser and more experienced than the other. (Support groups have long been available to stepparents; what I am recommending is a one-to-one, closer relationship.) The stepmother shares her concerns, frustrations, fears, and angers with the mentor, who listens, encourages, and offers herself as a role model who has been down this road before. Stepmotherhood need not be a totally isolated and negative experience; millions of women have been through it and survived. Their experience—what worked and what didn't—should be made available to their younger peers.

Society is just beginning to understand that a mentor, as well as a father or mother, is a fundamental part of normal adult development. Is it not time for stepmothers to take advantage of the expertise of other women who have "graduated" to the position of stepmother emeritus?

In those situations where mentors are not available or the problems are too complicated for peer support only, feminist therapy, with its belief in the potential of all women and in each woman knowing what is best for her—is recommended. A feminist therapist, with a commitment to equality between the sexes and to a woman's right to self-actualization without restrictions due to gender roles, is ideally suited to helping stepmothers sort out their family roles, commitments, and future decisions.

Stepfamily relationships are more complicated than those in intact original families, yet they can be richly rewarding, deeply satisfying, loving, and caring. To make them work requires patience, insight, and commitment—in greater measure, I believe, than in the difficult task of raising a family unaffected by divorce.

Among the complicating factors is the self-conscious feeling stepmothers develop when they assume the role of parent. Toward one's own children, a parent behaves—most of the time, at least—spontaneously and naturally. Dealing with one's stepchildren, however, often involves carefully weighing the implications of every action, every word, every tone of voice. That is because stepchildren do a lot of thinking about who said what or did what to whom, and what everyone involved meant by everything they did or said. The result is an overly thought-through, too-carefully calibrated kind of response to one's stepchildren, complicating still further a complex relationship.

Women are traditionally the "keepers of the flame," the ones most commited to maintaining traditions and rituals. Feminist therapy, sensitive to the sex-role stereotyping and sex discrimination experienced by women, can help them close the gap between society's and their own expectations and the practical realities of their situation. It can help them to understand what they can realistically expect to change within themselves and within their stepfamilies, and what they simply cannot.

Feminist therapy also can be helpful in premarriage counseling that helps the couple decide such basic questions as who pays for what, whose house they live in, where the children sleep, who is responsible for discipline, whether the new couple plan to have children, which ethnic or religious holidays they will observe, the moral and religious upbringing of the children, whether the parents will attend church or synagogue (and which one), and so forth. This can occur because feminist therapy is accepting of women who demand equality in male/female relations.

Thus, the feminist therapist will help the couple to share responsibility more equitably and to involve the husband in many of the household decisions traditionally delegated to women. Feminist therapy also will enhance the stepmother's role in decisions affecting the family's finances and investments, once thought to be the exclusive domain of the husband. Because the feminist therapist is oriented toward encouraging the stepmother to become an individual with her own rights within the family, this affords the stepmother the opportunity to serve as an effective role model for her stepchildren. The idea of genuine equality of husband and wife, when implemented by a father and his new wife, can serve as a tremendous boon to the new marriage and as a real help in resolving the built-in difficulties of the stepmother/stepchild situation.

Therapeutic intervention usually occurs at the time that stress begins to appear in the stepfamily. The objective is to help the stepmother

168   : : *Women's Issues across the Lifespan*

and the family clarify the areas of difficulty and restructure family relationships so as to minimize conflict and open lines of communication
among all the members of the family.

The mentoring relationship or supportive group is a viable alternative to therapy for some stepmothers. I believe that the practical support, the encouraging word, the help in coping—even the shoulder to
cry on—can help many a distressed stepmother through the inevitable
crisis of the new family.

A final note: The difficulties, complexities, and inevitable frustrations of the woman who becomes a stepmother need not and should not
overshadow the pleasures inherent in stepmotherhood. Strangers can
and do learn to love and respect one another, even if their relationship
has the prefix "step" in it. Often the stepmother will add a flavor, a zest,
an insight, and a way of looking at life that the original family could
never hope to enjoy. The stepchildren, in turn, are afforded the opportunity to experience a variety of lifestyles and flexibility of roles, and
then to select from each that which suits them best.

With creativity, stamina, and a sense of humor, stepmotherhood
can be rewarding for all. As Aristotle observed, "Those who guide children are more to be honored than those who produce them."

REFERENCES

Baer, J. (1972). *The second wife*. New York: Doubleday.

Bernard, J. (1956). *Remarriage: A study of marriage*. New York: Dryden, 1956.

Bettelheim, B. (1976). The uses of enchantment: The meaning and importance of fairy tales. New York: Random House.

Bowlby, J. (1961). Processes of mourning. *International Journal of Psychoanaly-sis, 42*, 317–340.

Freud, S. (1953). The occurrence in dreams of material from fairy tales. In J. Strachey (Ed. and Trans.), *The standard edition of the complete psychological works of Sigmund Freud* (Vol. 12, pp. 281–287). London: Hogarth Press. (Original work published 1923)

Gardner, R. A. (1976). *Psychotherapy with children of divorce*. New York: Jason Aronson.

Gilligan, C. (1982). *In a different voice: psychological theory and women's development*. Cambridge, MA: Harvard University Press.

Mahler, M. S., Pine, F., & Bergman, A. (1975). *The psychological birth of the human infant*. New York: Basic Books.

Mead, M. (1970). Anomalies in American post divorce relationships. In P. Bohannan (Ed.), *Divorce and after*. Garden City, NY: Doubleday.

Radomisli, M. (1981). Stereotypes, stepmothers, and splitting. *The American Journal of Psychoanalysis, 42*(2), 121–127.

Wolfenstein, M. (1966). How is mourning possible? In *The Psychoanalytic study of the child* (Vol. 21). New York: International Universities Press.

17

Can a Feminist Therapist Facilitate Clients' Heterosexual Relationships?

DORIS C. DE HARDT

> On the day when it will be possible for woman to love, not in her
> weakness but in her strength, not to escape herself, not to abase
> herself, but to assert herself—on that day will love become for her, as
> for a man, a source of life and not of mortal danger.—*de Beauvoir*
> *(1952, p. 629)*

De Beauvoir must have had my clients in mind, because a great
majority of them love out of weakness rather than strength and use
partnering with a man to try to escape the responsibilities of creative
adulthood (which requires finding and asserting the self). I also notice
that these clients' male partners usually actively participate in, if not
promote, the dependency paradigm thus described, whether or not
they themselves are also emotionally underdeveloped and dependent
personalities.

If my observations are correct that women often become less rather
than more the persons they are capable of becoming when struggling to

develop or maintain a relationship with a man, how can I, a feminist therapist, committed to empowering women, facilitate my client's heterosexual relationships? I find nothing in the literature to help me sort out this countertransference problem.

How can I insist that the search for a man must not be the pivotal adventure in women's lives, when a client insists that for her it is? This is especially troublesome when the man she has in mind is limited and limiting. In this situation she needs to separate out the problems she has in connection with this particular man from the problems of being male-defined in general.

It is much easier for a woman with a (reasonably) whole male partner to discern the benefits to both partners of her activities and experiences separate from him, than it is for a woman with an emotionally and socially deficient partner. Naturally, it is the latter class of women who come to therapy to work on partnerships with men.

Out of my struggles to work with the kind of client I have described here and at the same time be authentic about my own concerns about the limitations of any male-defined relationship, I have developed a series of questions for these women clients. The questions are intended to place the locus of responsibility for exploring the dynamics of her male partnership relationship with the client, while at the same time explicitly conveying my conceptual analysis of heterosexual relationships.

TEN QUESTIONS TO ASK YOURSELF ABOUT HIM *AND* YOURSELF

1. a. *Does he think he knows what's best for you?*
      Interests and values of women and men are not the same (Bernard, 1981). Men seldom know what is best for us. They may know what's best for us in terms of what's best for themselves, but that is quite another matter.
   b. *Do* you *think he knows what's best for you?*
      Some women genuinely no longer experience any awareness of their own needs, so frequently have they been usurped by the needs of others (Miller, 1976). For such women, doing something not involving significant others feels selfish or unpleasant. Yet, personal awareness of

needs is necessary to creative self-expression and wholeness as a partner.

2. a. *Does he translate or explain your feelings, thoughts, and/
    or behaviors for you?*

    This question, an extension of question 1, requires explo-
    ration of the dynamics of discounting. Discounting is usu-
    ally insidious and pervasive. It happens to most of us
    daily, even if we are strongly self-affirmed. It requires
    our energy, even if only to "process it out." Discounts
    illustrate the problem "subordinates" in general have.
    People of color and minority culture report this same
    wasteful expenditure of energy just for being "the
    other"—something other than the frame of reference.

    b. *Do* you *need him to translate or explain your feelings,
    thoughts, and behaviors for you?*

    You may see intellectually how harmful this is to you, but
    at the emotional level, you may succumb to this takeover
    of your experience, because avoiding conflict is some-
    thing women have been well taught (Miller, 1976). *Caus-
    ing* conflict is even harder for us. Even if *he* created the
    conflict by discounting you, for example, by not letting
    you have your anger ("You're so cute when you are an-
    gry!"), you get blamed for the conflict if you make an
    issue of the discount.

    Storing up resentments from constant discounts is a
    factor in depression. "Going crazy" may not be designed
    to win friends, but it *does* influence people. It renders
    discounts irrelevant. In the field of mental health, many
    well-known "experts" are also experts at discounting
    women and other perceived subordinate persons (Ches-
    ler, 1972). Listening to male "experts" tell us what's
    wrong with our mothering is a good case in point.

3. a. *Does he confuse sexual activity with nurturance and/or
    love?*

    Because men have been taught that being vulnerable is
    sissy, and because love makes you feel vulnerable (as well
    as powerful), many men have separated sex from love. In
    order to experience a women sexually, a prime requisite of
    masculinity (David & Brannon, 1976), many men have

learned to have sex but not to nurture or express love. One way to tell whether he distinguishes sex and love is to examine whether he sometimes nurtures you when sex is not on the agenda. If they choose, men can learn to nurture (Bell, 1981; Lamb, 1980). Is yours willing to learn?

b. *Do you confuse sexual activity with nurturance?*
Have you accepted this second-rate definition of love because you feel sex without love is all there is? Can you experience the vulnerability that comes from accepting genuine expressions of affection and warmth? If you don't really love yourself, you may feel uncomfortable with someone else's genuine love feelings for you.

4. a. *Does he really* like *women?*
It is important to distinguish here between "liking" and "loving." It is far easier to fall in love with a subordinate than it is to like one. Indeed, few men (or women) really like women. Only a man who really works for our equality and who does not merely have an immediate payoff in mind (e.g., making it with a feminist) has a right to say he likes women. And by *really work*, I mean put himself out, give up some of his princely advantages, suffer the pain of association and identification with lower castes. Does he belong to a CR group or men's liberation organization? Does he call himself a feminist and/or read feminist work? Does he have real friendships with women of equal or greater power, rank, intelligence, or moxie?

All right, you say, he likes *you*, even though he doesn't like women in general. This is a tender trap—seductive and dangerous. It is seductive because it falsely affirms your belief in your specialness to him, and it is dangerous because it is so tenuously based. He may like you and perceive you as special at the moment, but as time passes he will accumulate a reservoir of experiences with you, many of which involve your behaving like most or all other women. It is important to insist your man see you as being more like other women than you are different from them, because in fact you are (Bernard, 1981). He also may say he likes you and not other women because he is sleeping with you. Would he like you as well in the boardroom as in the bedroom? Does he like you to stimulate his brain as much as his penis?

b. *Do* you *really like women?*

Many women don't like and/or respect women, either, which is rational on the surface, since the cultural perception of females is negative (Chesler, 1981). Women who do not *work* on liking women bear the risk forever of retaining immigrant status within the dominant (patriarchal) culture and, more tragically, never learn to really like themselves.

5. a. *Does he validate your existence apart from his?*

Until quite recently, psychologists (and other scientists) failed to examine the nature of *male* experience. The reason is that males (who did most of the psychology) were unaware there was a need to examine and discuss male experience, since it was taken to be a given, the only reality there was. Why then would one need to *examine* male reality? A male who grows up learning that his reality *is* reality is cognitively and emotionally limited (Pearson & Pope, 1981).

Men are believed to be more "rational" than women, but in fact they are not, because the "facts" with which they reason are limited and/or distorted by their incomplete experience of others' reality. Like the blind man trying to describe an elephant, men who do not validate (experience) the reality of those unlike themselves are doomed to live in a world that is static, self-serving, judgmental, and unenriched.

How does this relate to your man? If he says, "I *let* you answer the phone" or "I'm trying to give you your rights" or "Work is not as important for you as it is for me," or if he leaves you because you are unable to have his children or if he does not really listen while you talk, you are not your own person but only a mirror set up to reflect the projected images of his desires.

b. *Do* you *see yourself only in relation to his existence?*

Women who reject or deny their own experience also wear male glasses. We women and other subordinates living within the dominant male culture learn male reality because it is taught in school, on TV, in books, and in the home. Female reality is learned before we have learned male reality, before we learn the message that *our* experiences are not culturally acceptable. We start out valuing girls as much as boys, for example, but eventually most of us come to regard male persons as more valuable. Some girls never transform their earlier female reality into male reality. As women they are role models for other women who want to learn to re-experience female reality. In relation to a man with whom we wish to share our lives, the question is whether self-transcendent experience is possible with him or merely diminished perceptions of self and the world. Ask yourself: "Can I actualize my potential with this man?"

6. a. *How committed is he to traditional concepts of masculinity and femininity?*

Threats to humanness derive from endorsement of traditional sex roles (Batlis, Small, Erdwins, & Gross, 1981; O'Neil, 1981). Nowhere is the loss more evident than in the context of male/female relationships. Some ways to look at this problem in relation to men are

i. *Does he read* Playboy, *watch porno movies, and/or take you to topless bars?*

All of these behaviors reinforce exaggerated versions of traditional male and female roles, wherein woman is primarily sexual and an object for consumption and man is a lusty animal whose cravings for flesh obliterate awareness of women as persons.

ii. *How much does he "get off" on violence? Does he enjoy movies and music that depict brutalization of women? Does he create violence? Does he believe that violence is man's natural tendency?*

It is psychologically difficult, perhaps impossible, for a person to restrict his violence to socially acceptable spheres and not have it generalize to others. Research suggests that watching violence, rather than being a healthy outlet for "natural" tendencies, increases arousal for violence (Green, 1981; Russell, 1981). If your man likes to watch women being beat up on TV, it is *more* likely he will expose you to brutality, not less. If he believes violence is the solution to political conflicts, he may donate your son to the battlefield. If he favors that special *mucho macho* image of sex and violence together, your daughter may learn she can expect to have her body assaulted in the name of "love."

iii. *If he lost his job (money, status), what kind of relationship would you have? Does he see his primary value to you as breadwinner, caretaker, or source of identity?*

A man who thus defines himself as success object, a derivative of the definition of masculinity, limits the relationship you have with him, even when all is going well. But when all is not well and he loses his job or erectile capacity, his consequent loss of selfhood augurs destruction of your relationship with him. Believing he has nothing to give makes the fantasy a reality.

iv. *Does he value your strengths and adult qualities?* Mr. Nice Guy seldom values strengths in women. His role of protector of women is threatened by women who do not need to be rescued. Such a man also does not perceive what value he has to women who are not needy. Sadly, he really does not experience his own worth as a person, and, just as sadly, his woman must stay needy and dependent to bolster his failed sense of worth.

Mr. Not Nice Guy, on the other hand, devalues, ignores, and fails to recognize women's strengths, too. He prefers women weak, dumb, and hapless because he can dominate them and feel superior. Traditional masculinity requires relatively greater potency of males. Female self-expression and power thus is constrained by partnering with a masculine male. So it is that most men marry women who are less of everything that conveys power and status in society: educated, strong, tall, old, financially secure, sophisticated.

v. *Does he ever say, "I don't know" or "I made a mistake" or "I'm sorry"?*

Masculine males are supposed to be smarter and more competent than females and most other males (David & Brannon, 1976). Carried to extremes, masculinity requires men always to have the answers and be in control and on top of things. This terrible burden causes men truly to lose track of their frailties as humans, imperfect and without answers to many questions. They especially lose track of intrapersonal and interpersonal experience, particularly as it pertains to themselves. If you are working on a relationship with a man and he does not conceptualize the possibility that he might not have an answer or his answer might be wrong, you are in for big trouble. Of course, he will deny his role in the relationship needs to be worked on in the first place.

b. *How committed are you to traditional concepts of masculinity and femininity?*

If you endorse traditional feminine and masculine roles, you will expect your man to be more sexual than yourself, justifying his need to look at other women's naked bodies and even to cheat. You will expect him to be violent, perhaps even to you. You will expect him to support you and will lose respect for him if he loses his job or decides to quit to stay home with the children. You also will see yourself as needy and dependent, requiring a man for a sense of security. You will play dumb if you know more than he does and even if you don't. You will be threatened by other women and, as they get older, even your own children. Commitment to traditional femininity is commitment to deficiency and inflexibility (Wiggins & Holzmuller, 1981). Even in the bedroom, femininity fails. Donnenfeld (1981) found that feminists are more likely to be orgasmic, while nonfeminists more often fake orgasm.

7. a. *Is he a biological or cultural sexist?*

Biological sexists are people who dislike aspects of women which are, for the most part, biologically determined (sagging breasts, wrinkles, liver spots). Cultural sexists, on the other hand, have negative attitudes and beliefs about women's behaviors that, for the most part, depend upon social factors (unreliable on the job, less competent, too emotional to be given responsible positions). It is far more difficult to feel valuable and beautiful when your partner is a biological sexist. Cultural sexists aren't so great either, but at least you do not have to acknowledge the charges— you can be as competent and responsible as *you* choose. Biological sexists get women to risk health with cosmetic surgery, harmful diets, and poisons on their hair, face, and nails. This involved denial of our physical selves, our secretions, our body fat, our skin texture, our suckling of the young—anything not male; in short, the true essence of femininity: womanliness.

I once dated a man who made a bemused comment about my stretch marks. I wonder how he would have felt if I had called the cellulite in his chest to his attention? Personally, I find such biological sexists hopeless. If you've got one, find a constant way to stay in touch with your *real* beauty, the beauty of personality that is uniquely yours.

b. *Are you a biological sexist?*
In order to keep biological sexists afloat, we women participate in great numbers in the mutilation of our bodies with unhealthy diets, surgeries, and poisons. Are you willing to stop this gynecide?

8. a. *How well does his verbal behavior correlate with his other behaviors?*
Does he tell you he cares for you only in words? Does he frequently say he did not really mean to hurt you and then go on hurting you? If you accidentally run over and kill someone you might avoid a jail sentence, because you are not held responsible since it was an accident. But if you accidentally run over and kill a person on each of 10 separate occasions, no one would pretend these 10 deaths were accidental. Yet, your man may hit you or step out on you or stay out late without calling or put you down,

repeatedly, and you are expected to forgive because he says he really cares for you and didn't mean to hurt you. Repeated behaviors are not accidents; in fact, often a single harmful incident is no accident.

b. *How well do you* want *his verbal behaviors to correlate with his other behaviors?*

Do you get payoffs from continually forgiving or accommodating him? Does it make you feel superior, martyred, or more moral than he? Does it give you the right to scold him like a little boy? More important, are you getting away with something in return? Psychic bargaining is a feature of many relationships. If he cheats on you and you keep forgiving him, is it because that way you get to let yourself go? If he puts down your strengths, are you secretly grateful because that way you don't have to risk developing your strengths? If he drinks to excess every day, do you thus get to avoid dealing with your sexuality? In a society in which direct rewards to healthy women are rationed, it is easy to fall into the trap of settling for second-rate verbal expressions of love and devotion without corresponding loving and supportive behavior.

9. a. *How does he feel about his mother?*

I recently attended a feminist men's conference. Most of the 100 or so men in attendance were genuinely able to relate to the women there as whole persons and were caring with each other and with the women. There were a few men who stood out from all the others. These few seemed to have angry, unfinished business with their mothers. Their mothers were characterized as destroyers, creatures who ate little boys alive, demons with such power even adult men were helpless to defend themselves. The twin demons of fear and hatred of mother, a woman, may generalize to you as partner. A man who fears (hates) his mother may hold you responsible for some of the feelings he has, which really derive from unfinished conflicts with her. If you love such a man, do both of you a favor and urge him to work with a counselor who can help him identify and accept his mother as human and flawed like everyone else. (This can be done even if his mother is deceased.)

b. *How do you feel about his mother?*

Do you see his mother as an evil force in your life, someone to outwit, compete with, control? Accepting the cruel myth of the wicked mother-in-law keeps us from seeing her strengths in the context of her life and denies us intimacy with the mother of the man we love.

10. a. *How committed is he to personal and partner self-awareness and growth?*

Does your man see himself as the breadwinner and you as responsible for the relationship, including his sense of well-being? This may appear fair and reasonable, this division of responsibility into spheres, but it isn't at all, whether or not you are also working. It would not be fair and reasonable even if the two spheres were equally rewarded by society.

It is not fair to expect another to make up one's psychic deficits, because to do so requires we have both knowledge about and the power to change someone else's feelings of vulnerability. Nobody has this kind of power; only the self can truly know and appreciate the self. Others can help, but the essential responsibility remains one's own. In addition to being unfair, partnerships in which only one member of the team is held responsible are unreasonable, even absurd. Imagine a business luncheon in which only one of the two men is asserting his needs and the other is responsible for the success of the meeting. Imagine two people playing tennis in which only one person is responsible for the progress of the game and the health of the players.

Ask yourself, are you a top priority in his life, independent of his work and children? Does he "own" his deep need for affiliation, which all men and women have but only women are allowed to confess to? Do you get "upkeep" fatigue trying to keep the partnership running smoothly? Has he conned you into thinking you *are* responsible for his behavior and sense of well-being?

b. *How much do* you *need for him to be committed to personal and partner self-awareness and growth?*
We women are easily conned, partly because alternatives to identifying ourselves in relationship to a man are limited, and partly because feeling we are responsible for our man's well-being keeps us from having to risk our own selfhood.

DISCUSSION

Very few men (or women) measure up to the qualities implied by these questions. Many women who read them thus feel justified in trying to get or stay with a particular toxic partner. Real and inevitable comments from clients include, "I will never get my intimacy needs met if I require all this!" "Do you hate men?" and, "I don't feel strong enough to work on these." It is a struggle to pursue these questions with so many clients, but how else can I function as a feminist therapist? I would be no more willing to try to help a homosexual convert to heterosexuality than I would be willing to "facilitate" a client's relationship with an abusing partner. Yet at times there is obviously an all-too-fine line between "my trip" and the client's wishes. Referring a resistant client to another therapist whose values are more congruent is not a satisfactory alternative, because I do not refer clients to any therapists who reinforce powerless, self-abasing, dependent roles for women.

In a culture that defines heterosexual intimacy as the *sine qua non* of intimacy, how do we unscript ourselves and our clients so we can embrace a vision of intimacy that does not specify gender or kind or amount of physicality? Bernard (1981) presents a good review of studies showing that marital (heterosexual) intimacy is the exception rather than the rule. Still our clients urge us to help them find or keep a man.

Is it because many of us therapists, even feminist therapists, still feel incomplete without a primary relationship with a man?

I still am struggling with the issues raised here. I currently am working on the concept of the intimate friendship (which may or may not involve sex). What I tell clients is something like this:

The intimate friendship is a relationship between a man and a woman who, as partners, have achieved genuine intimacy and joy, and have learned to share one another's psychological and physical environments. They have learned to share commitment, trust, affection, intellectual stimulation, solidarity and supportiveness, common values, honesty and authenticity, spontaneity, respect for one another's uniqueness, empathy, and mutual desire for intimacy. They have learned to be friends.

Only when women's psychological and physical environments are based on strength, individuality, and self-expression will love truly become for a woman a "source of life."

Proposition: It is harder, not easier, for a woman to achieve wholeness with a man. Woman's wholeness is her responsibility, not his.

REFERENCES

Batlis, N., Small, A., Erdwins, C., & Gross, R. (1981). Sex-role and need configuration. *Multivariate Experimental Clinical Research, 5,* 53–65.

Bell, R. R. (1981). Friendships of women and men. *Psychology of Women Quarterly, 5,* 402–417.

Bernard, J. (1981). *The female world*. New York: Free Press.

Chesler, P. (1972). *Women and madness*. New York: Avon.

Chesler, P. (1981). Women as patients. In S. Cox (Ed.), *Female psychology: The emerging self* (2nd ed.). New York: St. Martin's Press.

David, D. S., & Brannon, R. (1976). *The forty-nine percent majority: The male sex role*. Reading, MA: Addison-Wesley.

de Beauvoir, S. (1952). *The second sex*. New York: Knopf.

Donnenfeld, H. (1981). Personal communication from Michael Evans, University of California, Berkeley.

Green, R. G. (1981). Behavioral and physiological reactions to observed violence: Effects of prior exposure to aggressive stimuli. *Journal of Personality and Social Psychology, 40,* 868–875.

Lamb, M. E. (1980). The father's role in the facilitation of infant mental health. *Infant Mental Health Journal, 1,* 140–149.

Miller, J. B. (1976). *Toward a new psychology of women*. Boston: Beacon.

O'Neil, J. M. (1981). Patterns of gender role conflict and strain: Sexism and fear of femininity in men's lives. *Personnel and Guidance Journal, 60,* 203–210.

Pearson, C., & Pope, K. (1981). *The female hero*. New York: Bowker.

Russell, G. W. (1981). Spectator moods at an aggressive sports event. *Journal of Sport Psychology, 3,* 217–227.

Wiggins, J. S., & Holzmuller, A. (1981). Further evidence on androgyny and interpersonal flexibility. *Journal of Research in Personality, 15,* 67–80.

∎ 18
Beyond Homophobia: Learning to Work with Lesbian Clients[1]

RACHEL JOSEFOWITZ SIEGEL

A special kind of learning can take place between lesbian and non-lesbian[2] women within the therapy relationship. All therapists, lesbian and nonlesbian, have absorbed the pervasively heterosexual assumptions of our society, the fear of homosexuality, the ignorance and denial of lesbian existence. Male-centered cultural messages insist on an uneven division between homosexual and heterosexual, female and male, consistently oppressing and devaluing the homosexual and the female. The resulting polarization permeates our experience, keeping women separated from each other in mutually exclusive categories and denying our rich and caring connections with each other. Inner conflicts and denials mirror the external divisions and keep us from enjoying the full range of human sexuality and creativity.

1. Many thanks to Sandra F. Siegel for her help in clarifying my language and ideas; also to Marilyn Frye, Candace Widmer, Beverly Burch, and Lauree Moss for critical and responsive readings of early drafts.
2. The terms "lesbian" and "nonlesbian," ambiguous as they are, are used quite simply according to the client's or therapist's self-definitions.

Working together in therapy relationships, we have an opportunity to integrate the polarized parts of our personalities and to name and eliminate some of the ways in which we project them. This chapter, written by a nonlesbian feminist therapist, focuses on the growth and development she has experienced in the first 10 years of her work with lesbian clients. Her goal, beyond the best interests of her clients, has been to overcome her own ignorance and fear of lesbian reality, to lift the veil of invisibility imposed by the male heterosexual power structure, and to break the taboo of silence that helps to perpetuate the myths and distortions surrounding our love of women and our fear of that love. This writer's lesbian clients have had a chance to form a deep, nonsexual relationship with a caring, nonlesbian therapist, based on the kind of trust and respect that society, and often their own family, have denied them.

The therapist's learning, alternately frightening, painful, or exhilarating, took place in four modes: in her own therapy, through literature, with lesbian colleagues, and from lesbian clients. This last and most important mode will be explored most fully.

LEARNING THROUGH THERAPY

In her own therapy the therapist can best uncover the complexity of her sexual feelings and the particularity of her attractions and aversions to women. She can sort out the feelings and issues triggered in her by lesbian clients. However, if her own therapist is not a lesbian, the therapy will be reduced to the limits of lesbian consciousness in both therapists. In my therapy, the uncovering and exploration of sexual feelings toward women produced a deeper level of comfort with myself and eased my initial communications with lesbians in and out of therapy. The courage to explore the topic further grew out of my therapy; a fuller understanding of the lesbian experience came from other sources.

LEARNING FROM THE LITERATURE

I found the older literature about lesbians of limited use; it is based on heterosexist assumptions and on inferences drawn from studies of male homosexuals (Escamillo-Mondanaro, 1977; Ries, 1974). Although lesbianism is no longer officially considered a pathological entity, the bulk of current psychiatric literature does not reflect any significant change in attitude (Goodman, 1977; Sang, 1977). Some recent studies aim to dispel the myths of lesbian pathology. Ries (1974), surveying psychological studies of lesbians, finds no research evidence of increased pathology among lesbian women or their families of origin than among heterosexual samples of women in similar circumstances. Kirkpatrick, Smith, and Roy (1981) find that lesbian mothers treat their children very much like other mothers; gender development problems and types or frequency of pathology are similar for children of lesbian mothers and nonlesbian mothers. Hoeffer (1981) finds no significant differences among such children in acquiring sex-role behavior. Goodman (1977) observes that lesbian mothers "have helped their children to be more sensitive and accepting of differences between people and to have respect for these differences" (p. 20). Lyons (1983) finds the fears surrounding custody issues to be the only significant differentiating factor.

Research that consistently finds more similarities than differences between samples of lesbian women and heterosexual women in similar circumstances is obviously important in counteracting the still-prevailing attitudes and traditional training of mainstream psychiatry. Yet the need to disprove "lesbian pathology" and to prove the lesbian mother's harmlessness to her children indicates how far we are from seeing each other as equally human and complex, in a world that divides us into "normal" and "other," "deviant," "queer," and "unacceptable."

Recent feminist publications identify some of the blatant offenses perpetrated against lesbians in the name of therapy, such as denial of the client's reality, coercive cures through aversive therapy (Litwok, Weber, Rux, DeForeest, & Davies, 1979), and therapists collaborating with parents in the involuntary treatment of lesbian adolescents (Escamillo-Mondanaro, 1977). Lesbian accounts of homophobic persecution are often trivialized or misdiagnosed as paranoia. Psychiatric hospitalization can be especially harmful to lesbians, as the heterosexist milieu is bound to increase her sense of alienation from the world at a time when she is most in need of affirmation for her own feelings and lifestyle (Frye, personal communication, November, 1982).

More subtle are the errors of therapists who attribute all of a woman's problems to her lesbianism or who refuse to focus on her lesbianism because they consider it a symptom that will disappear when other underlying problems are resolved (Sang, 1977).

Lesbian therapists offer new insights and helpful suggestions. Litwok et al. (1979) state, "The lesbian faces problems and stresses not encountered by any other group of individuals in our society. . . . Lesbians may *act* just like everyone else, but the stressors which they face are unique to their situation" (intro.). Other writers (Cummerton, 1982; Escamillo-Mondanaro, 1977; Goodman, 1977; Litwok et al., 1979) advocate changes in clinical training programs and in mental health agencies that would educate therapists to the needs of lesbian clients and would make the atmosphere in these institutions hospitable to lesbian colleagues as well as clients. They urge nonlesbian therapists to confront their own biases, to become comfortable with all aspects of their own sexuality, and to learn as much as possible about the complexity of lesbian existence and the available lesbian community resources.

Gradually, my own reading moved beyond the professional literature and into the richness of lesbian culture. I began to appreciate the immense contributions to feminism made by lesbian thinkers. Adrienne Rich (1979, 1980) and Marilyn Frye (1981) had profound effects on me. I began to read lesbian novels, short stories, and biographies. I absorbed a deeper, more direct sense of the lives of lesbian women by reading such varied fare as *Rubyfruit Jungle* (Brown, 1978), *Sappho Was a Right-On Woman* (Abbott & Love, 1973), *The Coming Out Stories* (Stanley & Wolfe, 1980), *Nice Jewish Girls* (Beck, 1982), *The Color Purple* (Walker, 1982), and *Sinister Wisdom*, a lesbian literary quarterly. A Meg Christian concert introduced me to the sense of humor and joyousness of a lesbian celebration.

LEARNING FROM LESBIAN COLLEAGUES

Learning among colleagues, in consultation, supervision, or at professional meetings, entails an engagement and dialogue between lesbian and nonlesbian therapists that is essential to our work with lesbian clients but often has been avoided. Difficulties emerge. The risk of self-exposure and rejection are felt deeply. It is easier to interact within the safe territory of our commonalities or to avoid each other than it is to identify and explore our differences. It appears easier to deny expression to important aspects of ourselves and to maintain the distance between each other through "lies, secrets, and silence" (Rich, 1979). This kind of avoidance is a familiar survival tactic for women in a male world and for lesbians in a heterosexual world. The growth and healing that occurred when I learned to interact more openly with lesbian therapists has deepened and facilitated my therapeutic work with lesbian clients more effectively than any amount of reading or personal therapy.

LEARNING FROM LESBIAN CLIENTS

I learned most directly from lesbian clients, listening carefully during the therapy hour, asking for clarification when the client's needs called for it or when I felt confused or uninformed. Gradually, as I learned to identify the homophobic and heterosexist content of the psychological theories and assumptions that had been part of my professional training, I grew more open to factual input from lesbian clients.

Together, within the safety of the therapy room, we began the slow process of exposing the layers of clichés, myths, fears, and fantasies that surround the taboo of homosexuality.

My lesbian clients unfolded the day-to-day patterns of their lives, the innumerable denials, exclusions, and insults that engulf them individually and as couples and diminish their sense of worth and well-being in the world. I became aware of my own heterosexual privileges. I recognized the immunity conferred upon me by my married state, the public support and acceptance of being coupled that increases my sense of worth by association and opens the door to daily advantages. I learned to appreciate the complexities, fears, and rewards of the long coming-out process as well as the consequences of not coming out, and to respect each client's individual pattern and timing in making these decisions. I also learned to sort out the many aspects of a woman's concerns that were related to heterosexist oppression from those that were not.

There were changes in my attitude toward lesbians as my feminist consciousness became more sophisticated and my identification with women more profound. Early on, I accepted and validated the sexual preference of women for women as an alternate lifestyle and offered my lesbian clients a benign therapeutic antidote to the "heterosexual imperatives" (Rich, 1980) of our culture, along with large doses of consciousness raising about the politics and economics of institutionalized homophobia. I then went through a phase of envy and admiration, idealizing lesbian women who had the courage to separate themselves from the aggressively sexist relationships that prevail in the heterosexual mainstream of society.

It was a long time before I sensed that the bestowing of idealizations can be a way of holding onto the power of defining the other person. No matter how well intentioned, it can still interfere with the client's process of self-discovery and self-definition.

THE LESBIAN COUPLES GROUP

Recently, I came to the emotional and intellectual realization that our mutual learning and acceptance was limited to the degree that my interpretations of lesbian reality came out of my own reality. Like male definitions of women, my heterosexual observations of lesbians are necessarily self-limited. They may fall short of the individual lesbian's reality and run the risk of being experienced as external and judgmental, even when not intended to judge or to define. I began to search for more sensitive and equalitarian ways of interacting that would allow us to work through the varied aspects of the lesbian/nonlesbian, woman-loving/fear-of-woman-loving split.

I am indebted to the six women who trusted me to facilitate a lesbian couples group, for confronting me and challenging me to move beyond my familiar and unintentionally condescending leadership style.

Group interaction was intense. We played out an inverted version of the ancient female drama of not living up to each other's idealized expectations. There was much pain and anger. One member said, "I am not the lesbian you want me to be," and I felt, "I am not the perfect therapist/mother/friend you want me to be." My urge was to try harder, to provide a "strong woman" model capable of contradicting the "not-good-enough" messages. I wondered if the drama we were reliving was that of the "inadequate mother" being blamed for her daughter's "deviant" sexuality, by a society that misunderstood and devalued both. Another lesbian client in individual therapy was able to express similar feelings when she blamed her mother for not teaching her to be more feminine, more "normal." The roles were reversed in the group: The therapist/mother/heterosexual was excluded—she was the deviant, the other—but the interaction was the same. We worked through the "not-good-enough" feelings that every woman experiences in being "other than" the male norms of our society, and which every woman internalizes and then projects onto mother, daughter, lover, sister, colleague, friend. We challenged each other, became real to each other in our individual complexities, and began to deal with our differences in a more honest and accepting way.

I began to sense how deeply and how often we treat ourselves and each other as society has treated us. We reject, criticize, or fail to acknowledge or to value in each other those aspects of our lives and of our personalities which society devalues in women, including our friendships with and our love of women. In matters of sexuality and sexual choice especially, we mirror society's values by imposing silence and invisibility on the reality of our sexual feelings and activities. When lesbians interact with nonlesbians, this can take the form of imposing social or political judgments on each other's sexual choices.

It also seemed more difficult to be specific about sexual activity with lesbian clients than with most other clients, even when sexual functioning had been identified as a reason for seeking therapy. When I opened the subject, asking the usual questions, I was at times perceived as seductive or as a voyeur; when I did not mention sex, my silence was interpreted as disapproval. Aware of the sexual tension between women in the therapy room and the enormous silence that surrounds it in a heterosexual environment, I learned to respect the special sensitivity of lesbian women to being seen as sexual oddities, depicted in ways that are intended to arouse and titillate or in ways that deny their sexuality and reject it as odious. Language was also a problem, since the words we use in describing sexual functioning are based on a male-centered and heterosexual perspective, and the language for describing sexuality is inadequate.

REFLECTIONS

When the doors that seal off the lesbian experience are opened, women find new ways of relating to each other, of making significant connections.

The dialogue between lesbian and nonlesbian women in individual or group therapy, in consultation and supervision, at conferences and among friends can build a bridge of trust and understanding, overcoming some of the barriers between us. The opportunity to recognize and accept the differences and commonalities between us in a supportive atmosphere can facilitate the process of differentiating ourselves from the stereotypes imposed by a patriarchal heterosexual culture and lead to a deeper level of self-awareness and self-acceptance.

190   : : *Women's Issues across the Lifespan*

REFERENCES

Abbott, S., & Love, B. (1973). *Sappho was a right-on woman: a liberated view of Lesbianism*. Briarcliff Manor, NY: Stein & Day.

Beck, E. T. (Ed.).(1982). *Nice Jewish girls: A lesbian anthology*. Watertown, MA: Persephone Press.

Brown, R. M. (1978). *Rubyfruit jungle*. New York: Bantam Books.

Cummerton, J. M. (1982). Homophobia and social work practice with lesbians. In A. Weick & S. T. Vandiver (Eds.), *Women, power, and change*. Washington, DC: National Association of Social Workers.

Escamillo-Mondanaro, J. (1977). Lesbians and therapy. In E. I. Rawlings & D. K. Carter (Eds.), *Psychotherapy for women*. Springfield, IL: Charles C Thomas.

Frye, M. (1981). To be and be seen: Metaphysical misogyny. *Sinister Wisdom, 17*, 57–69.

Frye, M. Personal communication, November 1982.

Goodman, B. (1977). *The lesbian: A celebration of difference*. Brooklyn, NY: Out & Out Books.

Hoeffer, B. (1981). Children's acquisition of sex-role behavior in lesbian-mother families. *American Journal of Orthopsychiatry, 51*(3), 536–544.

Kirkpatrick, M., Smith, C, & Roy, R. (1981). Lesbian mothers and their children: A comparative study. *American Journal of Orthopsychiatry, 51*(3), 545–551.

Litwok, E., Weber, R., Rux, J., DeForeest, J., & Davies, R. (1979). *Considerations in therapy with lesbian clients*. Philadelphia: Women's Resources.

Lyons, T. (1983). Lesbian mothers' custody fears: Facts and symbols. In Robbins, J. H., & Siegel, R. J. (Eds.), *Women changing therapy: new assessments, values & strategies in feminist therapy*. New York: Haworth Press.

Rich, A. (1979). *On lies, secrets and silence*. New York: W. W. Norton.

Rich, A. (1980). Compulsory heterosexuality and lesbian experience. *Signs: Journal of Women in Culture and Society, 5*(4), 631–660.

Ries, B. F. (1974). New viewpoints on the female homosexual. In V. Franks & V. Burtle (Eds.), *Women and therapy*. New York: Brunner/Mazel.

Sang, B. E. (1977). Psychotherapy with lesbians: Some observations and tentative generalizations. In E. I. Rawlings & D. K. Carter (Eds.), *Psychotherapy for women*. Springfield, IL: Charles C Thomas.

Stanley, J. P., & Wolfe, S. J. (Eds.). (1980). *The coming out stories*. Watertown, MA: Persephone Press.

Walker, A. (1982). *The color purple*. New York: Harcourt Brace Jovanovich.

■ 19

Feminist Therapy with the Woman over 50

MARY RESH

One morning in 1982, television feminist Phil Donahue presented several nontraditional, blue-collar women: a carpenter, a heavy-equipment operator, and an electrician.

A woman in the studio audience spoke her piece bravely in that nest of feminists: "I just don't see it. Women *don't belong* in these jobs. It isn't right. They're not made for it." She had salt-and-pepper hair, short and curly, blue eyes, fair skin beginning to let go. She was wearing a white blouse with a blue ribbon tie at the neck. She looked to be about 50, and I imagined her name to be Lucille. I suspect she is representative of a large minority, that group of women who firmly reject, or even attack, the changes in sex roles that are occurring.

I assume that Lucille was born in 1930 or a few years later. How did she get to be so certain about what's right? How shall I understand her if she shows up in my office tomorrow morning?

LUCILLE'S CHILDHOOD WORLD

When Lucille was a little girl, this country was in the midst of a period known as the Great Depression, a psychological as well as an economic description of the times. Even if Lucille was a planned, wanted child at her birth, her existence likely became more problematic to her parents as the Depression worsened. Her mother may have envied the flappers of an earlier decade, but by the time Lucille started school, there was little gaiety, little playfulness or daring in most families. The foundations of Lucille's personality were established during that grim period when families taught caution, helplessness, and despair. She learned that life is serious, security is important, and the greatest pleasure is in service to others. "Woman's duty" was not then a joke.

By 1948, when Lucille was graduating from high school, the economy had enjoyed the stimulus of a major world war and the United States was a robust world power. Lucille could view present and future joyfully and with optimism. The ideal young woman was perky and sweet—June Allyson, Peggy Anne Garner. The heroic men had returned from the war, and the valiant women could retreat from shipyards and hospitals back to their kitchens and bridge clubs. Back where they belonged, some said.

Although there were radical undercurrents, as there have always been in the United States, these were minor and far from Lucille. In that year, 1948, there was near uniformity of belief among young women and it was easy to be insulated from divergent viewpoints. Here are some of the convictions that were held by Lucille and her girlfriends:

- Too much makeup or clingy clothing makes a girl look cheap.
- Nice girls don't "do it" before they are married. (Boys always want to go all the way; it's up to the girl to set the limits.)
- An unwed, pregnant girl should marry—anyone—immediately.
- Abortion is illegal, dangerous, and wrong.
- Girls should not compete with boys. If you are better at chess or tennis than your male partner, don't let him know it or *you may never have another date*.
- Having a date is all-important, and getting married is ultimately important.
- A girl should seek a man she can look up to. He should be taller, stronger, smarter, older, and earn more money than she.

- It is a compliment to be called a girl. The older you get, the more generous the compliment.
- Working is secondary to marriage, that is, something to do until you marry or something to fall back on if your husband dies.
- If something goes wrong and you never find a husband, you may be forced to have a career. Choose one of these: teacher, nurse, secretary.
- Policemen, doctors, and priests can always be trusted to be wise and kind.
- A diamond is forever. Even if married people don't like each other, they should stay together for the sake of the children.

The language of that period often carried a value message that reinforced already strongly held beliefs:

- Anyone who has smoked marijuana is a *dope fiend*.
- Unmarried persons sharing home and bed are *living in sin*.
- Persons who love others of the same sex are *queer*.
- An unmarried woman over thirty is an *old maid*. A childless woman over thirty is *barren*.
- Genitals are referred to as *it, them, down there,* and, most of all, *privates*.

LUCILLE'S ADULT WORLD

Lucille was a good girl and did what was expected: She curled her hair, padded her bra, plucked her eyebrows, and found a husband. She became a wife and mother.

Where is she now?

She may be one of a large minority who still hold most of the beliefs just listed.

She is probably undereducated for her IQ level, and if she is college-educated her coursework is out of date or irrelevant to today's marketplace. She is likely to be vocationally inexperienced. Self-help books tell her that she can claim experience as a chauffeur, interior decorator, nurse, chef, governess, educator, and administrator, but when she writes this on application forms, employers smirk and ask her where she worked last. Lucille is emotionally dependent on her husband for her sense of security and probably is economically dependent as well.

It is likely that Lucille was (technically) a virgin when she married and has never had an affair. Even if she finds satisfaction and joy in having had a sustained, affectionate sexual relationship with her husband, she is likely to feel cheated, curious, and envious when she reads just the cover, never mind the articles, of *Cosmopolitan Magazine:* EVERY GIRL CAN HAVE IN-CREDIBLE SEX POWER OVER MEN . . . THE FINE ART OF MAKING YOUR MAN FEEL UNTHREATENED BY YOUR UNBRIDLED LUST . . . SEX SURROGATES—HOW DOES IT FEEL FOR THEM AND THEIR PARTNERS?

She has a beginning awareness of aging. No matter how sophisticated her approach to health and nutrition, she is being forced to acknowledge arthritis, far-sightedness, and thinning pubic hair. A woman whose self-evaluation emphasizes being young and perky will have special grieving to do as time remodels her. The previous generation, Lucille's parents, are aging too, underlining her own mortality by their frailty.

LUCILLE IN THERAPY

Initial Conflicts

As she enters my office for the first time, what are Lucille's conflicts, what does she expect, what does she fear?

She's afraid she'll be criticized, humiliated. Her husband tells her all about affirmative action and the capable, competent women he meets at the office. Her daughter is living with a lover and limits her filial conversation to "Ohhh, Mother, you've got to be kidding." Lucille anticipates that I, too, will demean her deeply held (and/or shaky) values, and she's ready to defend.

She doesn't like the Ph.D. after my name. Even if she's not entirely sure what it means, it signifies a life she has not lived and potential distance between us. She also likes the Ph.D. because she's used to consulting experts and seeking authority, and she hopes I'll be able to tell her what to do.

She's glad to see I'm not 30.

She's confused by the discrepancies between what she was taught and what she sees. She finds it disorienting that so many of her old beliefs are being challenged or quietly ignored:

Sexual Behavior. People talk about and engage in sex before marriage, they have affairs, they have same-sex partners. Unmarried women proudly and deliberately bear children, the double standard is shaky if not entirely gone, and people are naked everyplace.

Roles. Mothers are not expected to sacrifice all for their children. Husband/wife are not necessarily permanent commitments ("as long as they both shall *love*," the kids say now—if they bother to get married at all); being a "real man" is no longer synonymous with being a good provider; the two-income middle- and upper-class family is becoming standard, with or without children, meaning that everyone wants a career and thus all work is being divided up in new ways.

Meaning. Mental health equals self-actualization, or so it seems. It's important to do your own thing, express your anger, let it all hang out. "Have a nice day" has superseded "Be a good girl." Where young women used to learn table setting, they now learn assertiveness because nobody likes a doormat.

I have presented the conflicts as external to Lucille because this is likely the way that she experiences them, but of course they are not entirely external any longer, and this is a primary source of her psychological difficulties. Friedan's *The Feminine Mystique* was not published until 1963; by then Lucille was nearly 35 years old, she had widespread cultural support for the life choices she had made, and it had been possible to ignore the changes that were occurring in our shared beliefs. That has become less possible with each year since then, so radical and widespread have the changes been. (These changes are beautifully elucidated in Daniel Yankelovich's 1981 book, *New Rules*.)

Most likely, Lucille will present with standard reactions (anxiety, depression, phobias, somatic symptoms) to her life quandary, and she will respond with improvement to the usual methods of symptom reduction (behavior modification, insight, hypnosis, cognitive restructuring, as you prefer).

A therapist with a feminist bias will be sensitive to the following feelings:

Anger. Initially, Lucille probably will be angry at present-day figures whom she feels threaten her well-being. She is likely to defend herself and her values by attacking those who seem to attack her—the "radicals."

Awe and Envy.   One layer under this anger, often there is awe and envy over the attitudes and behavior of the current generation. Lucille may be the most loving of mothers and be glad to see her daughter do what was earlier out of the question for women, but regret for her own missed opportunities is likely to be mixed with this well-wishing.

Sadness.   Careful exploration of these attitudes leads to uncovering the sadness Lucille feels as she reviews her 50 years; and often there is a return of anger, this time directed at figures from her past, for the narrowness of the choices they made known to her.

Comforts: Resolving the Unresolvable

In the course of therapy, Lucille will make cognitive changes that will interact with her feeling changes and eventually will interact with changes in her behavior:

1.   *I did the best I could. (Corollary: So did they.)* All therapy clients, and particularly those at midlife, face the dual tasks of forgiving themselves for the past and also of coming to see significant others as having been virtuous/flawed individuals, neither saints nor monsters. Admonitions originate and are perpetuated because we need them so desperately: What's done is done; it's no use crying over spilt milk.

For Lucille, it is useful to help her explore the cultural context in which she made early life decisions: Exactly what did her high-school counselor say when she told him she wanted to be a lawyer? What female role models were available to her in person, in books, in movies? What actions were labeled bold, wicked, forbidden? She may wish now that she had taken other options then, but in many ways they were not available to her; she need not assume total guilt (or responsibility) for never having learned to pilot an airplane or become a doctor.

2.   *Values clarification and tolerance for deviance*. Among the present generation, the high-school and college years are the time of greatest tolerance for deviant behaviors. Lucille is far from that time herself, and her own youth was not characterized by such tolerance. She is likely to believe now, as she did then, that there is a Right Answer out there someplace. Either abortion is right or wrong—it can't be both. And the same goes for drug use, homosexual behavior, women taxi drivers, and cohabitation without marriage.

I think we all get a little rigid as we age, even those of us who pride ourselves on our flexibility, spontaneity, and openness. After long years of experience and habits, we feel our own biases to be wisdom and others' wisdom to be foolishness. In the course of therapy, Lucille should be encouraged to formulate, express, and examine her own beliefs. As she gains confidence in deciding what is right for her, she will have less need to attack those who have different values. She also will adopt a tolerant view of the diversity in our culture, insofar as this is modeled by her therapist.

3.   *Many roads not taken.* As Lucille faces aging and her own foreshortened future, she will begin to confront her own existential regrets. Everything she did eliminated an infinity of other possibilities at that time, and that time will never come again. If she lived in Duluth, Minnesota in 1955, she missed living in Chicago or any other place in the world during that year. Her present satisfaction depends in part on her recognition of the joy and the pain of that year in Minnesota, as well as recognition of the alternatives it eliminated.

Whatever the state of her health, whatever her religious beliefs, Lucille is facing a shrinking future and must tolerate her regret for past time and her anxiety over present choices.

4.   *So what? What now?* Lucille is not a member of the Me Generation. She's a lifetime member of the "I Should" Club. (She also may be a past member of the "After All I've Done for You" Sorority, or of the "If It Feels Good It's a Sin" Association.)

With careful encouragement, Lucille can learn to say, "I want" or "I believe," and then act on that basis. Her activism at best will be an integration of her old attitudes and her new ones: She may choose to work for peace, to drive disabled persons to doctors' appointments, to promote alternatives to abortion. A felicitous therapy outcome would be an excited recognition of her present options and her commitment to a satisfying future.

Living well is the best revenge.

REFERENCES

Friedan, B. (1963). *The feminine mystique*. New York: W. W. Norton.
Yankelovich, D. (1981). *New rules: Searching for self-fulfillment in a world turned upside down*. New York: Random House.

■ four

VIOLENCE AGAINST WOMEN: AN OVERVIEW

ELIZABETH RAVE, Editor

Physical, sexual, and psychological assault, sexual harassment, sexual exploitation by professionals, incest, genital mutilation—are all forms of men's violence against women. Yet until the resurgence of the feminist movement in the late 1960s very little discussion on these topics occurred in the professional literature. What writings there were supported the victim-blaming myths prevalent in psychology as well as in the larger society. The effects of direct and potential victimization have become an integral part of the feminist movement ever since the first speak-out on rape in the late 1960s in New York City. By the mid 1970s when federal funding became available through the National Center for the Prevention and Control of Rape, "with infuriating speed and seemingly out of nowhere, traditional agencies and professionals showed up to work on rape" (Schechter, 1982, p. 42). In the 1980s, with funding for social programs scarce and patriarchy marketed on an hourly basis, there is still a need for a feminist analysis of violence against women.

Such a feminist analysis is built on the concept that violence is an unacceptable act of intimidation and the aggressor is responsible for his violence. The "rape myth" and the "masochism myth"—that women both invite and enjoy violence—is absolutely rejected. Recent research (Malamuth, in press) successfully predicts men's aggressive behavior toward women: Those men with high scores on the scales measuring the Acceptance of Rape Myth and the Acceptance of Interpersonal Violence toward Women were the men who in a laboratory situation were more punitive toward women. Others (Stock, 1984, Malamuth & Check, 1981) express concern about what they label the "eroticization of aggression." They believe that the depiction of violence as erotic, and hence satisfying, contributes to a cultural climate that sanctions acts of aggression against women.

Mainstream psychology has not provided the necessary support for individual victims of violence. The APA Task Force on Sex Bias and Sex-Role Stereotyping in Psychotherapeutic Practice (1975), in their survey of the direct effects on women as students, practitioners, and consumers found that one of the main biases is in expectations and devaluation of women. One of the recurring themes that received criticism was use of theoretical concepts, such as masochism, "to ignore or condone violence toward and victimization of women" (p. 1172). Several years later, after an analysis of the research literature, Sherman (1980) concluded, "Data provide evidence that therapists' sex role values are operative during therapy and counseling. Data indicate there is sex-role stereotyping in mental health standards and that sex-role-discrepant behaviors are judged more maladjusted" (p. 60).

Such a judgment places the woman victim of violence at a disadvantage when she seeks therapy. "Sex-role-discrepant behavior" is often what the individual survivor of interpersonal violence needs to experience as she attempts to integrate the violence she has experienced into her daily life. She is working to take control of her life and to make decisions for herself. She is actively attempting to become more independent and to develop strategies for meeting her own needs. She is learning to speak for herself and not let others define her existence for her. Feminist therapists who accept assertive, independent, self-defined women as being "adjusted" rather than "maladjusted" can provide a strong environment for victims to become survivors of interpersonal violence. Through a feminist analysis of data, new theory regarding victimization of women and children has been developed. The feminist therapist sees connections between the external and internal world of the survivor and facilitates her development of strategies for improved survival.

This part describes some of the latest feminist research, theory, and techniques in the study of violence against women.

Lenore Auerbach Walker describes, in Chapter 20, therapeutic work with victim/survivors of interpersonal violence. Although her main focus is on working with battered women, Walker emphasizes that the principles and strategies are applicable to survivors of other types of violence. She also discusses some of the needs of individual feminist therapists working with victims of violence.

Lynne Bravo Rosewater, in Chapter 21, describes her research with the MMPI and battered women. She shows the similarities between the behavioral characteristics of the diagnostic criteria for schizophrenic and borderline individuals and those behavior characteristics of battered women. Thus she cautions clinicians about rushing to a diagnostic category without first discovering whether a history of battering occurred toward the victim.

Elizabeth Rave's Chapter 22 analyzes the sexist and racist myths perpetuated by pornography. In addition, Rave describes some of the emerging research on pornography which analyzes the effects from a social learning model. She challenges the previously held belief that pornography is harmless and she demonstrates how it sets the stage for further violence against women.

Until society as a whole agrees to work toward stopping violence against women, the need for feminist therapists to provide intervention strategies will continue. The importance of separating the individual woman's own issues from those imposed by a society that does not stop men's violence is crucial to providing good therapy. Only through such an analysis can women learn to heal after being abused.

References

American Psychological Association. (1975). Report of the task force on sex bias and sex-role stereotyping in psychotherapeutic practice. *American Psychologist, 30,* 1169–1175.

Malamuth, N. (in press). Aggression against women: Cultural and individual causes. In Malamuth, N., & Donnerstein, E. (Eds.), *Pornography and sexual aggression.* New York: Academic Press.

Malamuth, N., & Check, J. V. N. (1981). The effects of mass media exposure on acceptance of violence against women: A field experiment. *Journal of Research in Personality, 15,* 436–446.

Schechter, Susan. (1982). *Women and male violence: The visions and struggles of the battered women's movement*. Boston: South End Press.

Sherman, Julia A. (1980). Therapist attitudes and sex-role stereotyping. In A. Brodsky & R. Hare-Mustin (Eds.), *Women and psychotherapy*. (pp. 35–66). New York: Guilford Press.

Stock, W. E. (1984, August). *The effects of violent pornography on women*. Paper presented at the annual meeting of the American Psychological Association, Anaheim, CA.

■ 20
Feminist Therapy with Victim/Survivors of Interpersonal Violence

LENORE E. AUERBACH WALKER

The current women's movement, with its accompanying scrutiny of the traditional practice of psychotherapy for reinforcing the harmful effects of sex bias toward women (Brodsky & Hare-Mustin, 1980), has given rise to the development of a more sex-fair woman-oriented feminist therapy. Nowhere has feminist therapy been more needed than in helping victim/survivors of violence heal from the assault trauma. Feminist analysis of interpersonal violence has revealed a predominant theme of woman-hating, fueled by the need to keep intact the male-dominant patriarchial structure of family and social relationships (Brownmiller, 1975; Butler, 1978; Chapman & Gates, 1978; Dobash & Dobash, 1981; Gelles, 1972; Jones, 1980; Martin, 1976; Pizzey, 1974; Russell & Van de Ven, 1976; Walker, 1979).

Most of the violence in this country is committed by men and directed against those who are weaker than themselves. Women and children are often their targets. The Straus, Gelles, and Steinmetz (1980) epidemiological study of 2000 American families found that spouse abuse had occurred during that year in almost one-third of the homes surveyed. While their data suggest that women also committed aggressive acts against men, much of it occurred in the categories of biting and other acts that could be considered self-defense. Unfortunately, they do not analyze their data for this interaction effect but, rather, raise its possibility while acknowledging they did not measure antecedents to the violent act reported. Rape, incest, and other forms of sexual assault reportedly occur most frequently by men against women (Brownmiller, 1975; Finkelhor, 1979; MacFarlane, 1978; Martin, 1976). Sexual behavior between clients and therapists, professors, and other professionals also has been reported as usually occurring between male professionals and their young, attractive, vulnerable, women clients (Holroyd & Brodsky, 1977). The harmful effects of such behavior are documented in 90 percent of the cases reported by almost 400 psychotherapists in a recent study by Buhoustos, Holroyd, Forer, and Greenberg (1983). The battered women interviewed in my research study tell ghastly tales of the high levels of violence committed by the men with whom they and their families lived (Walker, 1979, 1981a, 1984). Leidig (1981) presents a compelling feminist analysis of the similarities between all these violent crimes against women. Rave, in Chapter 22 of this book, links them together with the degradation of women in pornography. Whatever analysis is applied, unless the violence is seen as a function of a sexist and violent society—which ultimately only can be controlled and eliminated by changing the very structures of that society which reinforce individuals' violent behavior—we cannot be helpful to the victim/survivors.

Despite all of the new knowledge about battered women, there are some who still believe that the woman's personality dynamics caused her to be abused rather than clearly placing the blame on the violent man (and/or society). Masochism, though sometimes redefined (Blum, 1982; Shainess, 1979) has not been eliminated from the psychoanalysts' theory of why battered women stay in an abusive relationship. Empirical evidence indicates that battered women do not stay with their men longer than nonbattered women, as is often believed. The average length of a battering relationship is six years (Walker, 1981a). The average length of marriage reported by the 1980 U.S. Census is six years. Most battered women report that they don't leave as quickly as they would prefer because they can't do so without evoking further violence to themselves and others (Martin, 1982; Walker, 1984). Systems theory that proposes that violence occurs as a result of the family interaction is only correct after the violent behavior begins. Once the family interactions all become regulated by the violent behavior, its potential becomes obvious. If the man's violent behavior becomes the focus of treatment, family therapy sometimes can teach members better skills for postponing the unleashing of the violence or for avoiding being in its path (Margolin, 1979).

The interrelatedness of all forms of intrafamily violence only recently has been documented (Finkelhor, Gelles, Hotaling, & Straus, 1983). Once the child neglect cases are eliminated from child abuse statistics, it is clear that more men are the abusers (Gelles, 1983). In fact, the overlap involving men who abuse their wives as well as their children then becomes obvious (Fagan, Stewart, & Hansen, 1983; Walker, 1983). Men who physically abuse their wives often also rape them, yet the majority of state laws do not define spousal sexual assault as a crime (Martin, 1982). Children are at a higher risk for being sexually molested or assaulted if they live in families where violence occurs (Finkelhor et al., 1983; Straus, et al., 1980; Walker, 1984). Despite empirical evidence that men who admit to committing incest have a penile erectile response to sexually explicit pictures of children which is similar to that of known child molesters (Abel, Becker, Murphy, & Flanagan, 1981), many treatment programs still are based on helping the mother deal with her emotional and/or sexual inadequacies which, presumably, forced her husband to turn to their (sexually provocative, of course) daughter to meet his needs (MacFarlane, 1978).

Unfortunately, unless a feminist analysis is included when developing treatment programs for both victim/survivors and offenders, we as professionals will continue to perpetuate family violence and retraumatize the victims (Walker, 1980; 1981b). Therapy is a primarily verbal mode of treatment. We expect people to tell us what is bothering them and deal with their perceptions of reality as we explore possible avenues of change. Empirical data indicate that neither the men nor the women who experience violence can describe it easily. Both tend to minimize, deny, and rationalize the behavior.

Victims often use dissociation as a technique to separate their minds from experiencing the pain to their bodies. Offenders often can't own or describe their violent behavior but instead explain what it was the victims did or did not do to cause them to lose control. Some lie outright and deny they beat her, saying that she lost her balance and fell against the table, wall, door or down the stairs to explain her injuries. Unless carefully questioned as to what happened immediately preceding her fall, one gets the impression that there was a minor family spat in which she became so emotionally upset it caused her to act irrationally and get hurt.

Similar seemingly logical explanations are given by other assaulters who know their victims. Groth (1979) describes a group of convicted rapists who also use this verbal explanation pattern to justify or excuse their behavior. The same men whose deviant sexual excitement was measured by penile tumescence also emphatically denied verbally any sexual attraction to their daughters or other children in the research program (Abel et al., 1981). From my own research, I postulate that there is a violence-prone personality pattern that exists in some men, which has been resistant to traditional psychotherapy (Walker, 1984).

The inability to trust what is being said presents major problems for a therapist, particularly when concerned for people's safety. It also poses grave problems for the legal system. Again, empirical evidence demonstrates that, under certain supportive conditions, the women victims are able to describe the horrible details of the violence they experienced (Armstrong, 1978; Butler, 1978; Dobash & Dobash, 1981; Kilpatrick, Veronen, & Resick, 1979; Martin, 1982; Pagelow, 1981; Walker, 1981a). The atmosphere needed for women to talk is the same as the one created by the tenets of feminist therapy (Lerman, 1976). Similar reports come from rape crisis centers and battered women's shelters all over the country. Women fear being labeled "crazy" and thus cannot discuss the "crazymaking" features of such victimization until they believe they really will be understood. Then they reveal that they are not as passive as was once thought, and they talk about the many survival skills they have developed to protect them and keep them alive. Some of these survival skills also may be symptomatic of mental disorders (Rosewater, 1982). Therapists must take care not to confuse them.

Victims of violence cite being misunderstood as their most frequent complaint against therapists whom they felt were not helpful (Walker, 1980). No matter how hard the victims have tried, they know they have failed in keeping themselves totally safe from harm. While they do view the violent acts as the responsibility of the man, they also feel guilt for not having done whatever it would have taken to prevent him from unleashing his violence toward them personally. These feelings are far more complicated than originally were theorized. In feminist therapy, their complexity can be more easily revealed, accepted, and validated and the implications for how such feelings influence cognition and behavior can be understood better.

CRISIS INTERVENTION ISSUES

Short-term crisis intervention techniques are often sufficient for victims who have been assaulted by a stranger. It is important for sexual assault victims to be able to talk with a feminist woman psychotherapist about the details of what was done to her sexually. Often she does not understand why her body reacted in various ways. Those women who may have experienced sexual arousal or even orgasm need reassurance that such a physiological response does not mean they either liked or provoked the rape. Others need to tease out the difference between flirting and consenting to sex, to eliminate the guilt feelings that often occur following "date rapes." Support group therapy has been reported as being as useful as individual, when the therapist has feminist values. Generally eight to 10 sessions, once a week, are adequate to help the victim through the crisis period. If she is experiencing suicidal ideation, severe depression, or prolonged medical complications, the supportive therapy may need to be more frequent or last longer.

Most women do experience an acute crisis period following recognition that they have been a victim of violence. Some women block the memory of an assault incident for a period of time and thus do not experience the acute crisis phase until such time as they finally do recognize it. Often, another assault brings forth the buried memories and the impact of both crises is felt at the same time. An acute crisis period also occurs in those who have experienced repeated violence by men who love them (i.e., battered women, sexually exploited women, and incest victims), at the time they finally are able to label themselves victims and take steps to stop the violence. Once they get through this crisis period they become survivors. It is normal for them to experience all the symptoms of acute anxiety attacks, obsessional thoughts, and compulsive behaviors; terror or denial of fear for their own safety; and crying spells, irritability, hostility, anger, and rage. Often the woman must deal with her loving feelings toward the batterer, who doesn't always abuse her. Sometimes the feelings of anger are directed appropriately at the offender, but they also can be expressed indirectly toward others, including their feminist therapist. Learning to pace therapy to the woman's tolerance level is the best way to avoid sabotage.

The only demand I make is that the woman must rehearse an escape plan with me, so I feel relatively comfortable about her safety. Such an escape plan includes developing cognitive recognition of signs of an impending acute battering incident, like awareness that his face turns red, his eyes look menacing, his fingers twitch, or he starts complaining about a familiar subject. Then we discuss how she can get out of the house safely, identifying key items without which she could not effect her escape. I usually suggest having separate keys made and hidden for the car, hiding spare cash and extra clothes, and removing any material objects without which her life would be more miserable. Provisions for children, if appropriate, also must be thought through. Location of the nearest public telephone or neighbor to whom she can run for help and a decision as to whom she is most likely to call also must be made. Once all these decisions are reached, I insist the woman rehearse the escape plan with me, much like a fire drill. Then, even if she becomes immobilized by fear, her previously rehearsed escape plan still can work automatically.

Sometimes it takes a while for the woman to make the decision to leave, and some women must try it several times before they are convinced that they cannot control the batterer's violent behavior. Flowing with her own system and building on her strengths is the most useful way to develop a therapeutic relationship without encouraging more dependency. Therapists must be careful, however, not to expect the woman to think, feel, or behave in ways for which she does not have the skills, even in the interests of encouraging her independence. A careful assessment of her strengths and deficits will help avoid such problems.

LONG-TERM THERAPY ISSUES

Many women victim/survivors of violence choose to continue in therapy beyond the crisis stage. They use the therapy to help them reorganize their lives. Long-term therapy issues that frequently arise for them are similar to those for other women in transition. They need to develop trust, intimacy, and friendship in relationships with both men and women. Such social skills development can be facilitated in groups that also combat loneliness. Those who have learned to live with violence for a long period of time need to replace their survival behaviors with other more useful behaviors, once they are violence free. Learning to experience and express anger without fearing retaliation, to experience sensuality and sexuality for their own pleasure, and to reclaim their own bodies and emotional space without fear of invasion are all major tasks. The openness and honesty between client and therapist that is called for in feminist therapy helps avoid the manipulative tactics used by many abused women who learned these tactics originally to gain control and prevent beatings.

Most violence victims go through a period of depression, perhaps to help them cope with the pervasive anxiety and fear. Yet, their depression has some different characteristics than does the usual clinical depression. For example, in professional women, their depressed state may be related only to their home lives and doesn't necessarily generalize to their careers. Some women cannot function in their routine tasks but become quite involved in something new and intriguing to them. It usually doesn't take as long to tap into a victim/survivor's sense of humor as it does with other depressed clients. To understand the depression, I prefer the learned helplessness model of noncontingency in response and outcome (Radloff & Cox, 1981; Seligman, 1975). This model suggests that, when a victim believes her responses have only a 50-percent chance of working, rather than the high probability of success needed to believe in one's own survival, then certain cognitive, motivational, and behavioral distortions occur, eventually leading to a nonresponsive mode. Any cognitive-based model that also accounts for feelings, motivation, and behavior, however, is probably useful therapeutically.

Most abused women have found a way to protect their minds and souls from being as controlled as their bodies by the male abuser. It is probably the rapid chaining of aversive stimuli coming together in a bunch without any let-up that causes "fogging," which then results in wearing down the resistance of the victim. In cases of repeated abuse, the victim often has time in between the acute battering incidents to protect herself from letting him gain mind control, despite his excessive intrusiveness into her life. Often the woman puts herself into a mild hypnotic trance during the violence.

The way in which violent men learn to read their victims' minds is uncanny. Repeat offenders give the women just enough pleasurable reinforcement to keep them captive. There is a whole group of violent offenders who cause their harm through intimidation and fear of future violent acts. The subtlety through which this psychological abuse is done often can drive a woman crazy.

To heal the wounds of any physical violence, victims must learn to reclaim the sovereignty of their bodies. Some women who learned to experience physical pleasure through a man need to do so through a new relationship, even if it is temporary. Others cannot stand to have a man touch them for awhile. For some of my clients, joining a health club and learning to run, play racquetball, or do aerobics has been a useful adjunct to therapy. One client finds massage therapy her best way to get back in touch with her body, while another has become absorbed in nutrition and vitamins. One sexual assault victim has chosen to rebuild her career while still suing her former employer for damages; another remains on the same job; while another is unable to begin a new job. The technique used is less important than the goal, which is to help the woman feel less violated and have more ownership of her body.

An issue that often comes up after the victim/survivor learns to feel and deal with her angry rage at being attacked is whether or not to forgive her abuser. If the man is punished by the criminal justice system or in some other way harmed, she often feels less angry and more sorry for him. If I have been a witness to the psychological distress he has caused her, I find that I am much less willing to allow her to be forgiving. If she feels guilty, I can use my own anger to help her deal with the reality of his responsibility for her pain. Feminist therapy allows me to express my values, which include a crucial one that assigns total responsibility to the offender: No matter what the reason, no one has the right to abuse another person unless in self-defense! Thus, if she begins to justify, excuse, or rationalize his violent behavior, my value system provides an alternative way to view it.

Feminist therapists' participation in couples therapy and therapy programs for the men is another area where our special skills can be useful. Many authors (Abel, Blanchard, & Becker, 1978; Gangley, 1981; Groth, 1979; Saunders, 1982; Sonkin & Durphy, 1982) have written guidelines that are consistent with feminist tenets for doing therapy with the abusers. Most have found that violent men do not seek therapy unless they think they can win back their wives or stay out of jail. Further, unless there is a closely supervised court order mandating treatment in a highly specialized offender program, the probability of his staying in treatment is low (Walker, 1981b). Even more disappointing is that, despite all of the knowledge and technical skills available, there is little hope of changing the violent man's learned behavior patterns. The reinforcement he receives from a society that rewards sexist and violent behavior is apparent. Most of the success stories are temporary and only occur in those men who intrinsically are highly motivated enough to remain in treatment and confront their learned violence patterns.

IMPACT ON THERAPISTS

It wasn't until I had been practicing psychotherapy with victims of violence for awhile that I realized why so few therapists had been willing to work with this population previously. The recent growth of safehouses, rape crisis centers, and the beginning of some institutional support does help keep me from feeling overwhelmed along with the woman. Whether done purposely or not, police and the criminal justice system traditionally invalidate her terrifying experience. Her terror has an impact on me as a therapist. My rage at the horror to which women have been exposed finds its appropriate expression in my advocacy work. We therapists must come to terms with our own vulnerability to becoming a violence victim before we can be effective therapeutically. Former victim/survivors trained with advocacy and therapy skills can be effective if their own issues have been resolved.

I cannot work with a client caseload filled only with those having problems with violence. I need to balance my client population with those experiencing other kinds of problems. I know I need a vacation when I start seeing potential violence in all situations. To help achieve a balance of activities, I also supervise other psychologists and do some training for the various professional schools in Denver. The application of my research and therapy experience to the courts is an important part of my ability to help make social changes on a broader scale through public education (Walker, 1984).

It has been a personal triumph for me to watch the proliferation of safehouses, rape crisis centers, programs that deal with sexual harassment on the job or in the professional's office, and programs addressing child molestation, incest, rape, and battering. The growth in the sensitivity, awareness, and competence of professionals also has been rewarding. I began my interest in this area convinced that women would never be liberated until we were free from men's threats and actual violence

212   : : *Violence against Women: An Overview*

against us. I am still convinced it is up to feminists to remain strong in
our support of each other and other women so that sexism and violence
are both eliminated from our lives.

REFERENCES

Abel, G. G., Becker, J. V., Murphy, W. D., & Flanagan, B. (1981). Identifying
dangerous child molestors. In R. B. Stuart (Ed.), *Violent behavior: Social
learning approaches to prediction, management, and treatment*. New York:
Brunner/Mazel.
Abel, G. G., Blanchard, E. B., & Becker, J. V. (1978). An integrated treatment
program for rapists. In R. Rada (Ed.), *Clinical aspects of the rapist*. New
York: Grune & Stratton.
Armstrong, L. (1978). *Kiss daddy goodnight*. New York: Pocket Books.
Blum, H. P. (1982). Psychoanalytic reflections on the "beaten wife syndrome."
In M. Kirkpatrick (Ed.), *Women's sexual experiences: Explorations of the
dark continent*. (pp. 263–267). New York: Plenum Press.
Brodsky, A. M., & Hare-Mustin, R. (Eds.), (1980). *Women and psychotherapy*.
New York: Guilford Press.
Brownmiller, S. (1975). *Against our will: Men, women and rape*. New York:
Simon and Schuster.
Buhoustos, J., Holroyd, J., Forer, B., & Greenberg, M. (1983). Sexual intimacy
between client and psychotherapist. *Professional Psychology, 14*(2), 185–
196.
Butler, S. (1978). *Conspiracy of silence*. San Francisco: Glide Publications.
Chapman, J., & Gates, M. (Eds.). (1978). *The victimization of women* (Vol. III).
Sage policy studies of women. Beverly Hills: Sage Publications.
Dobash, R., & Dobash, R. (1981). *Violence against wives*. New York: Macmillan.
Fagan, J. A., Stewart, D. K., & Hansen, K. V. (1983). Violent men or violent
husbands? Background factors and situational correlates of severity and loca-
tion of violence. In D. Finkelhor, R. Gelles, G. Hotaling, & M. Straus
(Eds.), *The dark side of families*. Beverly Hills: Sage Publications.
Finkelhor, D. (1979). *Sexually victimized children*. New York: Free Press.
Finkelhor, D., Gelles, R., Hotaling, G., & Straus, M. (Eds.). (1983). *The dark
side of families*. Beverly Hills: Sage Publications.
Gangley, A. (1981). *Participant and trainers' manual for working with men who
batter*. Washington, DC: Center for Women Policy Studies.
Gelles, R. J. (1972). *The violent home: A study of the physical aggression be-
tween husbands and wives*. Beverly Hills: Sage Publications.
Gelles, R. J. (1983). *An exchange/social control theory of intrafamily violence*.

In D. Finkelhor, R. Gelles, G. Hotaling, & M. Straus (Eds.), *The dark side of families*. Beverly Hills: Sage Publications.

Groth, A. N. (1979). *Men who rape: The psychology of the offender*. New York: Plenum Press.

Holroyd, J., & Brodsky, A. (1977). Psychologists' attitudes and practices regarding erotic and non-erotic physical contact with patients. *American Psychologist, 32,* 843–849.

Jones, A. (1980). *Women who kill*. New York: Doubleday.

Kilpatrick, D. G., Vernon, L., & Resick, P. A. (1979). Assessment of the aftermath of rape: Changing patterns of fear. *Journal of Behavioral Assessment, 1*(2), 133–148.

Leidig, M. W. (1981). Violence against women: A feminist-psychological analysis. In S. Cox (Ed.), *Female psychology: The emerging self* (2nd ed.) (pp. 190–205). New York: St. Martin's Press.

Lerman, H. (1976). What happens in feminist therapy. In S. Cox (Ed.), *Female psychology: The emerging self* (1st ed.). Chicago: SRA.

MacFarlane, K. (1978). Sexual abuse of children. In J. Chapman & M. Gates (Eds.), *The victimization of women* (Vol. 3). Sage Yearbooks in Policy Studies of Women. Beverly Hills: Sage Publications.

Margolin, G. (1979). Conjoint marital therapy to enhance anger management and reduce spouse abuse. *American Journal of Family Therapy, 4*(2), 13–24.

Martin, D. (1976). *Battered wives*. San Francisco: Glide Publications.

Martin, D. (1982). Wife-beating: A product of sociosexual development. In M. Kirkpatrick (Ed.), *Women's sexual experiences: Exploration of the dark continent.* (pp. 247–261). New York: Plenum Press.

Pagelow, M. (1981). *Woman battering: Victims and their experiences*. Beverly Hills: Sage Publications.

Pizzey, E. (1974). *Scream quietly or the neighbors will hear*. London: Penguin Books.

Radloff, L., & Cox, S. (1981). Sex differences in depression in relation to learned susceptibility. In S. Cox (Ed.), *Female psychology: The emerging self* (2nd ed.) New York: St. Martin's Press.

Rosewater, L. B. (1982). An MMPI profile for battered women. Doctoral dissertation for The Union for Experimenting Colleges and Universities, Cincinnati, OH.

Russell, D. E. H., & Van de Ven, N. (1976). *The Proceedings of the International Tribunal of Crimes Against Women*. Millbrae, CA; Les Femmes.

Saunders, D. G. Counseling the violent husband. In P. A. Keller & L. G. Ritt (Eds.), *Innovations in clinical practice: A source book* (Vol. 1). Sarasota FL: Professional Resource Exchange.

Seligman, M. (1975). *Helplessness: On depression, development and death*. New York: John Wiley.

Shainess, N. (1979). Vulnerability to violence: Masochism as a process. *American Journal of Psychotherapy, 33*(2), 174–189.

Sonkin, D. J., & Durphy, M. (1982). *Learning to live without violence: A handbook for men*. San Francisco: Volcano Press.

Straus, M., Gelles, R., & Steinmetz, S. (1980). *Behind closed doors: Violence in the American family*. New York: Doubleday.

Walker, L. E. (1979). *The battered woman*. New York: Harper & Row.

Walker, L. E. (1980). Battered women. In A. Brodsky & R. Hare-Mustin (Eds.), *Women and psychotherapy*. New York: Guilford Press.

Walker, L. E. (1981a). *Battered woman syndrome study*. Report to N.I.M.H., grant #R01MH30147. Washington, DC: National Institute of Mental Health.

Walker, L. E. (1981b). Battered women: Sex roles and clinical issues. *Professional Psychology, 12*(1), 81–91.

Walker, L. E. (1983). The battered woman syndrome: Results and discussion. In D. Finkelhor, R. Gelles, G. Hotaling, & M. Straus (Eds.), *The dark side of families*. Beverly Hills: Sage Publications.

Walker, L. E. (1984). *The battered woman syndrome*. New York: Springer.

■ 21

Schizophrenic, Borderline, or Battered?

LYNNE BRAVO ROSEWATER

Susan, age 27, has been married for three years and has a nine-month-old baby. During the past year, for no apparent reason, she has become fearful, apprehensive, and suspicious. She has missed several days of work in the last six months, behavior in marked contrast to her previous attendance record. Susan has withdrawn from her family and friends. When confronted by them about her behavior, she denies any problems.

Although a number of diagnostic categories can be considered from such a brief description, it is possible that Susan could be suffering from the onset of a schizophrenic or a borderline personality disorder. A diagnostician, faced with such symptoms and given some more information, might assume one of them. But an important fact about Susan has been left out: She is a battered wife.

Misdiagnosis is a common problem for clinicians when they meet a battered woman, as unfortunately many clinicians are simply not educated about this problem. A major contribution of feminist therapy to the mental health field is the ability to view a woman and her problems in the context of the society in which she lives. However, this awareness of the impact of cultural conditioning on the emotional problems developed by women has yet to affect the diagnostic procedures used by mental health professionals. Nowhere is this lack of integration more evident than in the dearth of knowledge about the similarities between schizophrenic, borderline, and battered women and how to diagnose them differentially.

If clinicians erred in the past by ignoring problems women experience because of sexism, feminist therapists often have erred by eschewing the tools of clinical diagnosis. These diagnostic techniques have been said to reflect male-dominated values and therefore would not be useful in a feminist context (Mander & Rush, 1974). However, effective advocacy for women can be augmented by clinical sophistication in the use of diagnosis, whether that be in the courtroom or the clinic (Rosewater, Chapter 26 of this book; Walker, 1984). The proper use of standardized diagnostic techniques, combined with knowledge of battered women, can help shed light on a woman's circumstances and on understanding her behavior as a *reasonable* response to these circumstances. It also can be educational to learn to use common diagnostic tools in a feminist manner (Rosewater, Chapter 26 of this book).

BATTERED WOMEN AND SCHIZOPHRENIA

The third edition of the *Diagnostic and Statistical Manual of Mental Disorders* (A.P.A., 1980), also known as *DSM III*, uses behavioral descriptors as diagnostic criteria. Such behavioral symptoms may make the clinician's job easier diagnostically, but at the same time can lead to the possibility of misdiagnosis. In order to distinguish a battered woman from a schizophrenic (or borderline) woman, the therapist needs to have familiarity with the behavioral dynamics of battered women and be able to translate these dynamics into clinical descriptors. Sometimes a standardized test can be helpful in this process, because it provides a different sample of behavior.

Such a translation can be made with the use of a well-developed personality assessment technique such as the Minnesota Multiphasic Personality Inventory (MMPI) (Rosewater, 1982). The wide variety of scales available allow for an accurate behavioral description in clinical terms. I administered the MMPI to 118 battered women, all but 12 of whom were in currently (defined as within one year) abusive situations. These women, 58 white, 54 black, and 4 Hispanic, ranged in age from 17 to 53 and had been in an abusive relationship from one week to 23 years. The purpose of the research was to determine if a "battered woman's profile" existed on the MMPI.

The *DSM-III* lists several behavioral descriptors as being indicative of a schizophrenic disorder, but these same behaviors also relate to battered women. More specifically, they can be measured by the MMPI and yet not be understood as components of behavior of currently battered women. The behaviors are as follows:

- Delusions with persecutory or jealous content if accompanied by hallucinations of any kind
- Deterioration from a previous level of functioning in such areas as work, social relations, and self-care
- Duration: Continuous signs of the illness for at least six months at some time during the person's life, with some signs of illness at present (188–189).

Some of the beginning or residual symptoms described are as follows:

- Social isolation or withdrawal
- Marked impairment in role functioning as wage earner, student, or homemaker
- Blunted, flat, or inappropriate affect
- Digressive, vague, overelaborate, circumstantial, or metaphorical speech
- Ideas of reference (paranoid ideation)(189).

An examination of the circumstances attendant on a battering relationship shows that these same symptoms can appear in a victim of domestic abuse—a victim whose psychological needs are far different from those of a schizophrenic. The major difference is that the responses of battered women are often indicative of a clear grasp of *her* reality, as opposed to the total lack of touch with reality characteristic of the schizophrenic.

Let us now examine these behavioral and symptomatic descriptors in the context of the battering relationship.

Delusions

Fear is a very real element for battered women and a factor in why they stay in abusive relationships (Davidson, 1977; Martin, 1976; Menzies, 1978; Walker, 1979). Battering usually occurs in the privacy of one's home. The only witnesses, therefore, may be the couple themselves. The batterer tends to be a denier and blamer; he either denies that any violence has taken place or he blames the woman for causing the fight. Batterers are men from all religious and socioeconomic levels (Walker, 1979), and many men who secretly batter are respected members of their community. In many instances, the only one who knows the violence of which these men are capable are the women with whom they live.

Paranoia is clinically defined as delusions of persecution, meaning that the fears have no basis in fact. Numerous battered women are seen as paranoid and delusional because they are reporting things about which no one else is aware, or simply because they are extremely fearful with no apparent basis for that fear. The fact that the source of the fear is not obvious does not mean that it is unreal.

Deterioration from Previous Level of Functioning

Many battered women appear irresponsible; in fact, they often miss work because they are embarrassed to be seen after they have been beaten. This same embarrassment keeps them socially restricted, as does the social isolation imposed on them by the batterer (Davidson, 1977; Walker, 1984). His excessive jealousy causes him to place rigid restrictions on his wife's social activities, often virtually removing her from social contact (Martin, 1976; Roy, 1978; Walker, 1979, 1984).

A woman who is experiencing physical violence is also more likely to appear unkempt; it's hard to take care of your appearance when you can barely move your arms. The emotional stress of being in crisis also may exhaust her.

Duration of Illness

The third *DSM III* diagnostic criterion for a schizophrenic disorder involves the duration of the illness: "continuous signs of illness for at least six months . . . with some signs of the illness at present" (A.P.A., 1980, p. 189). Walker (1984) reported that the mean number of years married for the 400 battered women in her study was six years. In my own work I found that 83 percent of the 112 battered women I studied had been in an abusive situation one year or longer (Rosewater, 1982). The majority of battered women, therefore, tend to be in abusive situations for much longer than six months and may well display such symptoms for at least six months or longer.

Residual Symptoms

Some of the forewarning or lingering signs of a schizophrenic disorder are also characteristics of battered women, but, again, with far different significance for the therapist. While blunted, flat, or inappropriate affect can be a signal of a schizophrenic disorder, it also can be a means of effecting calm or avoiding potential conflict. It is important to realize that battered women tend to develop skills to postpone anticipated violence (Walker, 1979, 1984). Digressive, vague, overelaborate, circumstantial, or metaphorical speech, much like flat affect, may be an attempt by the battered woman to keep a volatile situation from exploding. Experience has taught her that straightforward, direct communication may trigger an acute battering episode.

In an effort to discriminate between a schizophrenic and a battered woman, I compared a "cookbook" mean chronic (female) schizophrenic profile (N = 133) from Lanyon (1968) with a mean composite battered woman's profile (N = 18) from my own research (Rosewater, 1982). The age range for the schizophrenic profile was 19 to 78, with a mean age of approximately 47. The age range of the battered women was 17 to 53, with a mean age of 28.5. Both battered women and schizophrenic women had statistically significant T-scores (T > 70) on scales 6 (which measures paranoia) and 8 (which measures schizophrenia). In addition, battered women had statistically significant mean elevation on scale 4 (which measures anger). The schizophrenic women had statistically significant elevation on scale F (which measures confusion and overwhelmedness) and did not have as low a mean score on scale K (which measures intactness) as did battered women, who had a statistically significant low mean T-score (T < 50). Battered women also tended to have a lower mean elevation on scale 5 (which measures masculinity/femininity according to stereotyped norms) than schizophrenic women. While these differences between the two mean profiles did exist, I concluded that

These two profiles may be indistinguishable; thus the clinician must determine if what appears to be a schizophrenic woman is not, in fact, a battered woman. It is also possible that a woman may be schizophrenic *and* battered. Given the general lack of awareness of clinicans about battered women, it is possible that some women previously diagnosed as schizophrenic may have in fact been battered. [Rosewater, 1982, p. 67]

Translating the descriptors of schizophrenic and battered behavior to MMPI terminology is facilitated by using the Harris-Lingoes and Serkownek subscales, which break the clinical scales into components. For instance, scale 4, which measures anger, is comprised of the subscales of family discord (problems with the family); authority conflict (I don't like to be told what to do); social imperturbability (things don't bother me); and alienation (feeling apart), both social (feeling estranged from others) and self (not liking myself). One individual with a high scale 4 might be sociopathic, showing a great deal of authority conflict and imperturbability, with no alienation; while another person with the same T-score on scale 4 might have elevations on family discord and alienation, a very different dynamic than a sociopathic personality.

Anger, Confusion, Paranoia: It Could Be Battery

Three clinical scales were significantly elevated for the currently battered women in the research sample: scale 4, which measures anger; scale 8, which measures confusion and overwhelmedness; and scale 6, which measures paranoia. Those battered women who had experienced the most violence also had significant elevations on scale 2, which measures depression. The actual behaviors being assessed are evident from the subscale elevations of these clinical scales.

Two Harris-Lingoes subscales of scale 4 were prominent in the configuration: family discord (problems with the family) and alienation, social (feeling estranged from others) and self (not liking myself). There was significant elevation for battered women in the research sample on alienation, with self-alienation being higher than social alienation. The next highest subscale was family discord. The clinical interpretation of this subscale configuration is that battered women are angry about what is occurring in their lives; they do not like what is happening within the family, but their anger is more directed at themselves (alienation) than at the batterer. In other words, battered women feel that in some way they are to blame for the battering that is occurring, or that they should be able to do something about stopping it, despite the fact that they are not responsible either for the beatings or the batterer's behavior. Treatment, therefore, is aimed at acknowledging the woman's anger, which should be directed toward the batterer rather than herself.

While scale 8 was developed to measure schizophrenia, this scale measures alienation, disruption in thought and behavior, and dissociation. Two significant features stand out in the Harris-Lingoes subscales: elevations on lack of ego-mastery, intra-psychic autonomy (slowed-down thought process and behavior), and object loss (feeling separate and apart). The clinical interpretation of these subscales is that battered women feel overwhelmed; they are both confused and slowed down physically, as well as alienated and feeling guilty for the beatings they receive. Treatment centers on understanding that the confusion is indicative of the real turmoil in the battered woman's life and the subsequent need to focus her anger outward rather than inward.

On scale 6, paranoia, the greatest elevation for the currently battered women tested is on the subscale of ideas of external influence (somebody is out to get me). Battered women do indeed feel that someone is after them, and with good reason! Paranoid symptoms or behavior can be a healthy element; psychiatrically, suspiciousness and hypervigilance should be considered as paranoia only if an individual's thought process is out of touch with reality, that is, there is no one after her. A battered woman is not misperceiving reality; she is seeing it very clearly. Therapy thus consists of support and affirmation of the reality of her perceptions.

Those battered women who had experienced the greatest violence had significant elevation on scale 2, depression. There were significant elevations on the subscales of mental dullness (not thinking clearly) and subjective depression (feeling sad and blue). The other battered women had the same configuration on the subscales. In addition, the latter had some important elevations on the subscales of physical malfunctioning (not feeling well physically) and brooding (ruminating). The clinical interpretation of these data is that battering takes a physical and emotional toll on battered women. They have difficulty thinking clearly and feel unhappy, have somatic symptoms, and ruminate about what is happening in their lives.

Almost all the currently battered women in the research sample had very low scores on the scales that measure intactness (how together an individual feels) and ego strength (how well an individual feels able to cope). These low scores, especially in combination, indicate that battered women do not feel they have inner strength or togetherness and are especially pessimistic about their ability to cope on their own. It may well be this dynamic that keeps the battered woman in the battering situation.

BORDERLINE PERSONALITY DISORDERS

Diagnostically, battered women are misdiagnosed not only as having schizophrenic disorders but, perhaps even more prevalently, as having borderline personality disorders. The diagnostic criteria for borderline personality disorders in *DSM-III* consists of eight behavioral descriptors of which at least five are required for the diagnosis to be given. These behaviors include:

- Impulsivity or unpredictability in at least two areas that are potentially self-damaging
- A pattern of unstable and intense interpersonal relationships
- Inappropriate, intense anger or lack of control
- Identity disturbance manifested by uncertainty about several issues related to identity, such as self-image, gender identity, long-term goals or career choice, friendship patterns, values, and loyalties
- Affective instability: marked shifts from normal mood to depression, irritability, or anxiety, usually lasting a few hours and only rarely more than a few days, with return to normal mood
- Intolerance of being alone
- Physically self-damaging acts
- Chronic feelings of emptiness or boredom [A.P.A., 1980, pp. 322–323]

These behavior descriptors can apply to battered women as well as to those with borderline personality disorders; therefore, the same caution is given here about the possibility of misdiagnosis. The transference issues generally attributed to borderline patients—defensiveness, primary rage, and dependency (Campbell, 1982)—need to be seen with battered women as understandable behaviors, given the violent realities of their lives.

SIMILAR SYMPTOMS, DIFFERENT TREATMENT

The inner turmoil, the confusion, the fear, the sense of not being intact, and the pessimism are common characteristics of schizophrenic, borderline, and battered women. The sense of defeat is a shared perception—a sense of hopelessness. Women labeled borderline or schizophrenic often are raised in homes where they are given mixed messages—what is said to them and what happens to them are *not* the same thing. These women learn to deny their own perceptions, believing that what they see is not what is really happening. What develops, therefore, is a sense of craziness, of not being okay. This incongruence often leads to an inability to distinguish between reality and illusion.

Battered women also are given mixed messages. Their perceptions are denied by the batterer (Davidson, 1978), so that eventually the woman begins to mistrust her own ability to perceive accurately. Hoffman (1983) found that 40 percent of the psychologically abused women in her research sample had their perceptions denied. Another kind of mixed message that battered women receive is the assurance that the legal system will protect them. When battered women do file for divorce, they often request a restraining order, with the assumption that it will protect them and keep them safe. In reality, the legal system does not provide protection for battered women; a restraining order is only enforced *after* it is broken. What the battered woman experiences is that she has been beaten up, she has *not* been protected, and that she *is not safe*. For some battered women, even leaving her own home permanently does not ease her vulnerability to the batterer, who will continue to pursue and harass her wherever she is. For example, one battered woman (at whose murder trial I testified) had left the batterer permanently on four separate occasions and had filed with the prosecutor's office 17 times. None of these actions gained her any greater safety. This lack of protection, this fear of being unsafe no matter where they are, explains why battered women stay in an abusive situation and why, in some extreme instances, in self-defense, they kill their batterers (Walker, Chapter 27 of this book). Again, their perception that they will not be protected is usually valid and indicative of a grasp on reality.

The basic difference in the treatment of battered and schizophrenic women is the validation by the therapist that the battered woman's fears are justified, while the schizophrenic woman's are imagined. For the feminist therapist, however, the awareness exists that, even if a woman is delusional, that quality does not lessen the actual sexist realities in her life or make her any less valuable as a woman and human being.

Treatment for the schizophrenic woman with the clinical symptoms of confusion and paranoia is based on helping her, at whatever pace is suitable for her, to deal with the discrepancies between her own perceptions and her external realities. The feminist therapist working with the woman labeled borderline also can validate the sexist realities that the woman is encountering and at the same time help that woman to be aware that other alternatives exist to coping with the dissatisfaction in her life than becoming "sick."

Treatment for the battered woman, on the other hand, is based on accepting that the violence in her life *is* overwhelming, and helping her, at whatever pace is suitable for her, to recognize that her anger, rather than being directed at herself, belongs with the man who is physically abusing her and with the system that allows such abuse to occur. The confusion and fearfulness are not treated as dysfunctional symptoms but rather as the normal consequences of living with violence. Since battered women feel so vulnerable about their ability to cope, therapy needs to be directed at helping them to get in touch with their own strengths, starting with the feminist therapist's recognition that staying alive is evidence itself that the battered woman has coping skills.

CONCLUSION

My treatment with battered women leads me to conclude that the symptoms they present are not due to schizophrenic or borderline personality disorders, although there are some women who are *both* battered and borderline or schizophrenic. I have found that a test like the MMPI, with the use of the Harris-Lingoes and Serkownek subscales, can measure and help clarify the differences between these diagnostic categories. Clinicians, especially feminist therapists, need to be sensitive to the possibility of confusion between the symptoms of emotional disturbance and of battered women. A thorough probe for a history of domestic violence is essential, therefore, with any case in which a woman presents the symptoms discussed in this chapter.

REFERENCES

American Psychiatric Association. (1980). *Diagnostic and statistical manual of mental disorders* (3rd ed.). Washington, DC: Author.

Campbell, K. (1982). The psychotherapy relationship with borderline personality disorders. *Psychotherapy: Theory, Research and Practice, 19*(2), 166–193.

Davidson, T. (1978). *Conjugal crime: Understanding and changing the wifebeating pattern.* New York: Ballantine Books.

Hoffman, P. P. (1983). Psychological abuse of women by spouses and live-in lovers. Doctoral dissertation, The Union for Experimenting Colleges and Universities.

Lanyon, R. I. (1968). *A handbook of MMPI group profiles.* Minneapolis: University of Minnesota Press.

Mander, A. V., & Rush, A. K. (1974). *Feminism as therapy.* New York: Random House.

Martin, D. (1976). *Battered wives.* New York: Pocket Books.

Menzies, K. (1978). The road to independence: The role of a refuge. *Victimology, 3*(1–2), 141–148.

Rosewater, L. B. (1982). The development of an MMPI profile for battered women. Doctoral dissertation, The Union for Experimenting Colleges and Universities.

Roy, M. (1978). *Battered women: A sociological study.* New York: Van Nostrand Reinhold.

Walker, L. E. (1979). *The battered woman.* New York: Harper & Row.

Walker, L. E. (1984). *The battered woman syndrome.* New York: Springer.

∎ 22

Pornography:
The Leveler of Women

ELIZABETH RAVE

Pornography may be the one industry that treats all women the same. In many ways pornography is totally nondiscriminatory. It dehumanizes and objectifies all women regardless of race, national origin, age, sexual preference, or physical disability. Not all women are represented equally in pornography, but all women are personally affected.

Pornography is an issue that feminist therapists must be aware of and involved in. It is my contention that pornography sets both the climate and the stage for violence against women—the individual rapist, batterer, incest perpetrator, and sexual harasser are the actors. Feminist therapists become involved with the results of the "performance" on the unwilling participant, the victim. Sometimes even the feminist therapist has become the victim, too. The crucial support that feminist therapists give victims is vital to all women's psychological survival. In addition, feminist therapists are in an ideal position to become active in destroying the stage by removing the foundation that provides the support for violent attacks on women. Feminist philosophy supports such advocacy, while protecting the individual client's rights.

Legal definitions of pornography still are being developed, so my working definition is really a series of statements: Pornography includes a display of power imbalance between the sexes with females being portrayed as less powerful and less in control. It also frequently portrays, suggests, or implies violence. The purpose of pornography is to sexually stimulate men by portraying women's bodies that are often contorted and twisted into very uncomfortable positions. Often, only parts of women's bodies are displayed, further objectifying and dehumanizing women.

My clinical observation of females' reactions upon viewing pornography also seems significant. Most women wince, sometimes gasp, and have an internal negative gut reaction. It's almost as if at some level of consciousness, the female viewer of pornography recognizes the personal risk involved. Erotic materials tend not to evoke the same negative gut reaction. Erotica implies mutuality and mutual pleasuring, almost the opposite of pornography.

One of the major limitations of the research to date on the effects of pornography is that the researchers have not defined their terms carefully. The President's Commission on Obscenity and Pornography (1970) in the United States used the terms "erotica" and "pornography" interchangeably. In fact, the commission preferred to use the term "sexually explicit," which is more appropriate for anatomy textbooks or sex-education materials than for describing violent sexual expression.

The same commission is the source for most popular beliefs about pornography in the United States. After $4 million spent in two years, the 19-member commission (which included two women) concluded,

> Empirical research. . . has found no evidence to date that exposure to explicit sexual materials plays a significant role in the causation of delinquent or criminal sexual behavior among youths and adults. . . . The conclusion to be drawn from the totality of these research findings is that no dangerous effects have been demonstrated on any of the populations studied. [President's Commission, 1970, pp. 27, 139]

Those conclusions are less than scientifically sound. To begin with, the commission used null hypotheses throughout. Yet the conclusion was stated in only one direction, thus giving that conclusion more weight than it warranted. In reality, the commission found neither harm nor *lack* of harm.

A large limitation of the report is that few studies reviewed were concerned with the linking of violence and sex. The commission did admit that fact: "Some areas of concern, as for example, the linkage of violence and sex, did not receive thorough inspection" (President's Commission, 1970, pp. 153–154). The admission, however, came in the middle of a paragraph. The commission members apparently did not consider the issue a serious limitation of their work. In addition, they chose not to deal with the contradictions within their own report. Ironically, the commission admitted that a limitation of its work was "access to populations of younger age groups. . . . Children were deemed inaccessible for direct inquiry" (p. 140). If the commission concluded there are "no dangerous effects," one has to wonder why "children are deemed inaccessible."

The commission also chose not to study the effects of pornography on women. That decision is almost beyond comprehension. If, as this author maintains, some women become the direct victims of male violence reinforced by pornography, the effect on women should be of prime significance. The more subtle influences of women internalizing the messages of pornography should have been investigated as well.

Irene Diamond (1980) has done a more detailed analysis and critique of the commission's methodology and conclusions, specifically, the attitude surveys, retrospective studies, experimental laboratory studies, and social indicator studies. Diamond concludes, "In retrospect, the conclusions of the Commission on Pornography and Obscenity that pornography is harmless are not warranted on the basis of the actual data that were available to it" (p. 697).

What has happened to pornography in the United States since 1970, when the commission completed its work? One thing has not changed. The audience for and the main consumer of pornography is still the male heterosexual. The messages given the male are the same old tired myths about women—the myths that every victim and survivor has to deal with and the same myths that feminists have attempted to change. Some of these specific myths that pornography perpetuates are that women like pain and enjoy being dominated, that women cause the sexual attacks, that women have few negative effects from that violence, that women contribute to the violence against other women, and that men cannot control their sex drives.

Pornography perpetuates victim-blaming ideology. Whether the setting is sexual assault or battering or incest, the theme consistently emerges that women like pain, particularly pain related to sex. Not only are victims presented as enjoying the pain, but they seem to enjoy it especially because they are giving the male pleasure. Thus, bondage and beating are presented as really okay. Distorted positions are seen as okay, and total degradation appears to be okay because the woman seemingly enjoys being "used" by the male. In fact, women are presented as enjoying it so much that most rape story lines twist rapidly into describing the victim's lust for more. Don Smith (quoted in Russell, 1980) did a content analysis of 428 "adult only" paperbacks printed between 1968 and 1974. The number of rapes increased with each year's output of newly published books. Smith also found that, in 97 percent of the stories having rape themes, the victim experiences orgasm. In three-fourths of these, she experienced multiple orgasms. On the other hand, less than 3 percent of the rapists experienced negative consequences. Such portrayals remove from males the responsibility for their coercive and violent behaviors.

Further absolution of male responsibility occurs with the perpetuation of the victim precipitation myth. Once the myth is established that the victim likes pain, it's a short step to believing that the victim caused the attack. Pornography readily makes that step for male consumers. It abounds with descriptions of women and girls desperately searching for sex, the bigger and harder the better. Females dress seductively, walk seductively, make up their faces seductively, go places intentionally searching, wait at home hoping—all to coerce males into relieving them of their pounding, all-consuming, driving lust. After reading pornography, one almost gets an image of the male as being a poor, overworked charity provider!

Obviously, if the victim likes and causes the sexual attack, there must not be any long-term effects of victimization. Pornography contributes to the belief that the force and coercion males use against females is really negligible. After all, as Don Smith (quoted in Russell, 1980) discovered, if 97 percent of the rape victims portrayed experienced orgasm, it must have been "fun" for the victim.

As feminists know, collusion arguments are very popular in psychology. If the victim herself didn't cause her own victimization, some other woman usually did, either the mother or wife. Thus, a researcher wishing to discover more about incest will find discussions of the cold and frigid mother who has given up her role of wife to her daughter. The literature on rape includes descriptions of the types of mothers and wives rapists have. Pornography contributes to these beliefs. Through its portrayal of women beating and torturing other women, pornography perpetuates the idea that women are the cause of their own pain. Nazi themes, as Dworkin (1981) illustrates, are prevalent in pornography, even in the portrayals of woman as tormenter of other women.

Certainly the most basic theme in pornography is that men cannot control themselves; they are controlled by their penises. One gets an image of the male walking down the street being led by his penis. Being so out of control, so irrational, so led by their hormones that they must have a depository for their sperm is, of course, a very negative image of males. Yet pornography reinforces the idea that men cannot control their "sex drive." The conflict between the image of the helpless male with no control of his raging hormones and the ideal of the rational, even-handed, objective male who can provide leadership in government, business, industry, and the home is worth further exploration at some other time.

Not only are myths about women in general reinforced by pornography, but myths that separate women are pervasive. Racism runs rampant throughout pornography. Black women are described in comparison to their "animal sexuality," while Asian women frequently are pictured literally tied down and spread-eagled. Asian women also are portrayed as dolls, almost as toys. One example will illustrate such racism. A magazine called *Black Ball* includes the following description:

> Tina is a marker for many of the black girls who have left the ghetto. Few ever settle for one person . . . to stick it through thick and thin. The black woman's natural ability to cull every subtle nuance of physical pleasure is a skill that has not gone unnoticed. . . . In overly base terms, she is the epitome of animal sexuality and her aggressive approach is more than just mildly appreciated. She may be bold, she may come on a bit strong, and she may even be demanding, but she commits herself to the task at hand, and the results of her labors are easily more intense than those of her white sisters. ["Manhandlers"]

In the last decade the market for pornography has expanded considerably. The most conservative estimate is that $5 billion are spent annually in the United States alone. Martha Langelan (1981) in *Aegis* analyzes the economics of pornography in what she calls "a case study in free enterprise, profitability, and success." Langelan estimates that 25 percent of all heterosexual material sold in Washington D.C. "adult" bookstores "depict explicit violence against women—torture of all kinds, whipping, beating, mutilation, rape, and murder" (p. 6).

As the business of pornography has expanded in the last 12 years, the barriers have fallen. There now are pornography "ghettos" such as Times Square in New York and Hollywood Boulevard and Western Avenue in Los Angeles. Almost every large city has very "chic" sex shops with all varieties of materials displayed in the most recent fashionable manner. One might say that today pornography runs from "sleaze to chic" within a few blocks in most cities. However, cities are by no means the only sources of pornography. In almost any place where magazines are sold, one can find pornography: in drug stores, grocery stores, airports, convenience stores, and gas stations. Cable television is the latest purveyor of pornography.

As the business of pornography has increased, so has the dehumanization of women in other media. Movies have discovered profit in portraying violence against women. Detective and romance magazines, as well as record covers, fashions, window displays, and advertising all use more themes of violence against women than before the commission's report.

What is considered sexually stimulating also has changed in pornography. Stated briefly, youth is "in." Not only are children still used in pornography, but older models are made to look childlike. Female models often have pigtails, suck lollipops, pout, are flat-chested, have no pubic hair, put their fingers in their mouths, wear white knee socks and patent-leather shoes, and in general present a "little girl" appearance. Incest themes are also common. Through these images pornography perpetuates the idea that the more powerless the female the more attractive a sex object she is.

Another change since the commission's report is the introduction of so-called pornography for women. *Playgirl* best illustrates this phenomenon. When one looks closely at the magazines, however, one soon discovers the same old sexist stereotypes being presented. For example, female nudes in *Playboy* are presented lying on pillows surrounded by frills and generally appearing helpless and vulnerable. Male nudes in *Playgirl* are presented at the helm of a boat, riding a horse, shooting a bow and arrow, or generally appearing strong and active, obviously in charge of the situation.

Violence has increased in pornography since the commission's report. Feshbach and Malamuth (1978) did a content analysis on five years of pictures and cartoons appearing in *Playboy* and *Penthouse*. They found that the amount of sexual violence in those popular magazines increased each year. Don Smith's content analysis of rape themes in "adult only" paperbacks also provides evidence that violence has increased in pornography (see Russell, 1980).

There have been many studies exploring the relationship between media viewing and aggressive behavior. Even preceding the commission's work, there was a report from the President's Commission on the Causes and Prevention of Violence in 1970. On the basis of this commission's report and subsequent research, most researchers conclude that media violence can induce some persons to act aggressively. The specific relationship between viewing violence and acting violently is not yet known, but it is accepted that at some level there is a connection. How can we as a society accept the connection between viewing media violence and acting aggressively—imprecise as that connection may be— and maintain there is no connection between viewing pornography and attitudes toward women or acting aggressively against women?

Such schizophrenic thinking can exist only by assuming the imitation/social learning model is appropriate for studying the effect of media viewing and the catharsis model is appropriate for studying the effects of pornography viewing. That dichotomy is less than scientifically sound, to say the least. For example, no thinking clinician would recommend that a child abuser should be treated by viewing films of children being spanked or by reading manuals on improving abusive techniques. Yet the President's Commission on Obscenity and Pornography could say that viewing pornography provides for "more agreeable and 'increased openness' in marital communications" (1970, p. 194). Whether viewing violence on television or specifically viewing other forms of violence against women, the negative effects of viewing such violence are still there.

Fortunately, feminist theorists and activists also have flourished since the commission's report and have challenged us to realize the effects of pornography. Brownmiller (1975) was one of the first to call attention to the contribution of pornography to the rape culture. Women against Violence in Pornography and Media organized the first feminist conference on pornography in San Francisco in 1978. From that conference came a collection of readings (Lederer, 1980) that provided theory, policy, and strategy suggestions for dealing with and educating others about the effects of pornography. Dworkin (1981) wrote about the "meaning of pornography and the system of power in which pornography exists" (p. 9). Griffin (1981) argued that "pornography is an expression not of human erotic feeling and desire, and not of a love of the life of the body, but of a fear of bodily knowledge, and a desire to silence eros" (p. 1). Barry (1979) defined pornography as a "practice of cultural sadism as well as a means of diffusing it into the mainstream of accepted behavior and therefore into the private lives of individuals" (p. 175). Linda Lovelace (1980) gave us a vivid first-person account of her experiences as a pornography movie "star," appropriately titling her autobiography, *Ordeal*.

Diana Russell (1980), one of the earliest feminist scholars of pornography, concluded that a large percentage of the male population has a propensity to rape. She suggests three important inhibitors to the acting out of this propensity. The first inhibitor is social controls, in other words, the possibility of being caught and punished. The second inhibitor is social norms, which define rape as unacceptable behavior. The third inhibitor is the individual male's conscience. Some men clearly abhor the idea of rape because they view it as immoral and brutal behavior. Russell points out that pornography that portrays rape releases the inhibitors by changing the social controls, makes rape appear easy to accomplish, and reduces fears of getting caught. Moreover, it also changes the social norms by making it seem that a lot of ordinary men rape and suffer no remorse. Instead they gain sexual and ego gratifications. Finally, pornography inhibits the conscience. If a man can persuade himself that a woman really likes being raped, that she doesn't really mean no, then why should he feel guilty for raping?

A body of research is developing that demonstrates these factors by using social learning theory methodology. In analogue studies, researchers are able to measure how viewing pornography affects the attitudes and behaviors of the viewer. Forerunners in this type of research, Feshbach and Malamuth (1978), found that college men who viewed pornography that fused sex and violence tended to be more sexually aroused by the idea of rape and less sympathetic to the victims than a control group. The researchers concluded, "The juxtaposition of violence with sexual excitement and satisfaction provides an unusual opportunity for conditioning of violent responses to erotic stimuli" (p. 117). In short, the message that pain and humiliation can be fun encourages the relaxation of inhibitions against rape.

Abel and his co-workers (Abel, Barlow, Blanchard, & Build, 1977) undertook research on pornography's effect on the sexual response of rapists and "nonrapists" (defined as men not convicted of rape). They found a difference in degree of arousal, as measured by the amount of erection, between rapists and "nonrapists" during what they described as "vivid, two-minute descriptions" of rape and nonrape sexual scenes. Rapists experienced a higher degree of arousal during the rape scenes.

Malamuth (1981) recently integrated a series of studies that addressed contentions that many "normal" men possess a proclivity to rape. Malamuth concluded,

> In these studies, an attempt was made to identify individuals with such a proclivity by asking male college students how likely they personally would be to rape if they could be assured of not being caught. On the average, about 35 percent indicated some likelihood of raping. To assess the validity of such reports as indicators of a proclivity to rape, the following three steps were taken: First, the literature was reviewed to identify responses that distinguished convicted rapists from the general population. The responses found to characterize rapists were greater acceptance of rape myths and relatively high sexual arousal to rape depictions. Second, the relationships between reported likelihood of raping and the responses found to characterize rapists were analyzed. The data clearly showed that in comparison with men who reported lower likelihood of raping, men who indicated higher likelihood were more similar to convicted rapists both in beliefs in rape myths and in sexual arousal to rape depictions. Third, the relationship between likelihood of raping reports and aggressive behavior was examined. It was found that higher reported likelihood of raping was associated with greater aggression against women within a laboratory setting. The overall pattern of the data is interpreted as supporting the validity of likelihood of raping ratings and consistent with contentions that many men have a proclivity to rape. [p. 138]

Research involving the impact of pornography on women is still almost nonexistent. As part of a larger study, Russell (1980) surveyed 933 women 18 years or older during the summer of 1978. Women were drawn from a random household sample obtained by a San Francisco public opinion polling firm. Among other questions, the women were asked, "Have you ever been upset by anyone trying to get you to do what they'd seen in pornographic pictures, movies or books?" Ten percent said they had been upset by such an experience at least once.

The issue of pornography is still confusing to many feminists, researchers, and people in general. While research results are being collected, it is important to become aware of what pornography is, what it contains, and why it is so dangerous. In conclusion, I would like to adapt Robin Morgan's insightful comment a bit: "Pornography is the theory; rape, battering, incest, and all forms of violence against women are the practices."

REFERENCES

Abel, G., Barlow, D., Blanchard, E., & Guild, D. (1977). The components of rapists' sexual arousal. *Archives of General Psychiatry, 34*(8), 895–903.

Barry, K. (1979). *Female sexual slavery*. Englewood Cliffs, NJ: Prentice-Hall.

Brownmiller, S. (1975). *Against our will: Men, women, and rape*. New York: Simon and Schuster.

Diamond, I. (1980). Pornography and repression: A reconsideration. *Signs, 5*,(4), 686–701.

Dworkin, A. (1981). *Pornography: Men possessing women*. New York: Perigee Books.

Feshbach, S., & Malamuth, N. (1978, November). Sex and aggression: Proving the link. *Psychology Today*, pp. 5–17.

Griffin, S. (1981). *Pornography and silence: Culture's revenge against nature*. New York: Harper & Row.

Langelan, M. (1981). The political economy of pornography: Marketing misogyny at $7 billion a year. *Aegis, 32*, 5–17.

Lederer, L. (Ed.). (1980). *Take back the night: Women on pornography*. New York: William Morrow.

Lovelace, L., with McGrady, M. (1980). *Ordeal: An autobiography*. Secaucus, NJ: Citadel Press.

Malamuth, N. M. (1981). Rape proclivity among males. *Journal of Social Issues, 37*(4), 138–157.

"Manhandlers." *Black Ball* (Baltimore: Tudor House Publications), 2(1).

President's Commission on Obscenity and Pornography. (1970). *Report*. Washington, DC: U.S. Government Printing Office.

Russell, D. (1980, April). Pornography and violence: What does the research say? WAVPAM (Women Against Violence and Pornography in the Media) newsletter.

■ five

POWER AND
ADVOCACY ISSUES

DOREEN SEIDLER-FELLER, Editor

One of the hallmarks of feminist therapy and theory is the emphatic claim that value-free social science is mythical. As a consequence of this position, feminist approaches to psychotherapy tend to view values clarification and development as essential parts of the therapeutic process and of theory building. This stance finds its logical conclusion in social advocacy in a wide variety of public arenas.

The chapters in this part reflect the diversity of feminist clinicians' concerns with the values underlying therapeutic work, from the standpoints of both clinician and client, particularly those values connected to theoretical development and critique and forms of social/psychological advocacy. Despite the range of substantive concerns found in these chapters and the scope of applications and settings to which these feminist clinicians have turned their attention, there remains one common theme in all of them—social and interpersonal power.

In Chapter 23, Douglas takes a direct and theoretical approach to power in the therapeutic relationship. She begins with the assertion that feminist critiques of psychotherapy are drawn from the broad context of patriarchal society. As a result, the critiques most often have focused on the modal therapeutic relationship of male therapist and female client. Conceptualization of feminist therapeutic approaches, on the other hand, has largely addressed the relationship between a female client and female therapist. Thus, other relationship types, varying in sexual balance and other potential sources of power discrepancies, have been investigated only marginally. Douglas' chapter, then, represents a theoretical attempt to systematize predictions about the relationship type as a function of therapist and sex-role power variables. The chapter is valuable, moreover, for its additional focus on the recognition of power and its implications for feminist therapy, especially in light of ideology exhorting the virtue and necessity of equalitarianism in the therapeutic relationship.

Lasky, in Chapter 24, undertakes a discussion on the taboo topic of psychotherapists' fees. She describes the central conflict articulated by psychotherapists in her interviews with them (the need to earn a living versus the desire to help people), as well as many subsidiary issues, illustrated in a series of well-considered and enlightening vignettes. The brief portraits follow an introductory look at the dearth of professional literature and training devoted to financial management issues, sex differences in the meaning and handling of money, and the special position of feminist therapists in this context. Provocatively, her conversations with women psychotherapists revealed that approximately 75 percent of them charged lower fees than males in the same geographical area with the same level of experience. Like the aspects of interpersonal power frontally addressed by Douglas, I suspect that writing that focuses on the relationship between money, power, and feminist therapy practice will multiply and find an attentive audience.

In line with this trend toward closer and more critical examination of issues such as power and money is a slowly developing critical perspective on technologies and methodologies used in treating women. In Chapter 25, Fodor questions the popular assertiveness training approaches by looking at the available data on their impact in women's lives in the field at large, and by returning to basic assumptions, for example, do women have assertiveness deficits? Recent research, Fodor shows, may render assertiveness training highly problematic and paradoxical as a technique in the feminist therapist's armamentarium. Finally, she illuminates her interest in new conceptualizations and applications of assertiveness training in larger, transpersonal milieus. While she doesn't solve any of the questions she raises, themselves in stark and spare terms, the reader is introduced to the puzzling ironies in this area, seen with a feminist eye.

In Chapter 26, Rosewater re-examines standard assessment methods from a different ideological direction. Feminist therapy, she rightly notes, has had an antitesting bias. Her chapter is devoted to generating a framework in which feminist therapists can reconsider the value and parameters of traditional assessment forms. She has prepared a prototype by using the MMPI to cull a profile of battered women. Its value is that, in combination with a thorough clinical interview, including probes for domestic violence, the profile helps establish and distinguish a battered woman from a schizophrenic one. The basic strategy then, she argues, is to create feminist interpretations for traditional tests, interpretations that can serve as concrete, objective advocacy instruments in a variety of court settings. It is also, importantly, a means of cultivating and using "expert power" in a socially useful and interested manner.

Chapter 27, the final chapter in this part, by Walker, continues to reflect the serious attention feminist writers give to social action and advocacy. The paper represents a distillation of the author's own involvement with a wide variety of empowerment and advocacy efforts in the legal system, ranging from women's self-defense cases to rape cases, other sexual assault cases, and child custody and visitation disputes. She pays special attention to the intricate considerations in women's self-defense cases, including the preparation and delivery of professional testimony, the preparation of the defendant and her testimony, strategy development and consultation with defense attorneys, consideration of insanity or self-defense pleas as issues, and various other matters that may call on a variety of skills and talents psychologists are expected to have. In important ways, Walker emphasizes the special issues and context that the feminist forensic psychologist faces in the courtroom.

■ 23

The Role of Power in Feminist Therapy: A Reformulation

MARY ANN DOUGLAS

The nature of the power relationship between therapist and client has been central to the development of feminist therapy (Gannon, 1982; Gilbert, 1980; Rawlings & Carter, 1977; Sturdivant, 1980) as well as to feminist analyses of psychotherapy (A.P.A., 1975; Chesler, 1972). There is considerable support for the idea that power is used and abused in nonfeminist psychotherapies (cf. Chesler, 1972; Gannon, 1982), primarily by male therapists working with female clients. One conclusion that has followed from this premise is that the client/therapist relationship in feminist therapy should be equalitarian or should at least represent an effort toward equalizing power (Gannon, 1982; Seidler-Feller, 1976; Sturdivant, 1980), or perhaps should be one that does not involve power at all (Rohrbaugh, 1979).

A feminist critique of psychotherapy has at its root a feminist analysis of sexist society in general. It is suggested that the modal therapeutic relationship, one between a male therapist and female client, parallels other patriarchial male/female relationship forms, for example, husband/wife and father/daughter (Chesler, 1972). The focus of feminist criticism of psychotherapy has been male therapists' abuse of power in relationships with female clients (cf. Gannon, 1982). For example, Chesler (1972) states that psychotherapy and marriage "both control and oppress women similarly" (p. 108), by fostering traditional sex-roles for women, by maintaining negative bias and devaluation of women, or by responding to women as sex-objects (A.P.A., 1975). The manner in which power operates in other therapeutic relationship types, for example, same-sex therapist/client dyads, has yet to be well articulated. Hence, within the analysis of power in feminist therapy relationships, therapist/client gender-related sources of sexism must be recognized as but one source of power that may affect the therapeutic relationship.

The purpose of this chapter is to re-examine several issues involving power in feminist therapy. The impetus for so doing is generated by two concerns. First, with the exception of Seidler-Feller (1976), insufficient attention has been paid to the various ways in which the concept of power can be applied to the analysis of the client/therapist relationship in feminist therapy. The second concern relates to the conceptualization of equalitarianism as it applies to the therapeutic relationship and the extent to which it is possible, even within feminist therapy. The following discussion of power in feminist therapies will encompass two major issues: (1) an analysis of the potential sources of power in feminist therapy and (2) the implications of power for feminist therapy. The focus of the entire discussion is directed toward feminist therapy in particular, although material may apply to nonfeminist therapies as well.

ANALYSIS OF POWER IN FEMINIST THERAPY

Feminist therapy has been defined as a "perspective to be applied to theories, techniques, and ethical standards of traditional therapies" (Marecek, Kravetz, & Finn, 1979, p. 734) and as a feminist value system that forms the basis for the belief that the socialization of men differs from that of women and that it is destructive and oppressive to women (Marecek et al., 1979; Sturdivant, 1980). The integration of a system of feminist values and beliefs with a model of psychotherapy thus forms the basis for the theory and practice of feminist therapy. It is this conceptualization of feminist therapy to which the analysis of social power is addressed.

A major working assumption of this chapter is that the feminist therapy relationship is defined as one of temporary inequality (Miller, 1976), that is, one based on service to the client. It is the client's dependence on receiving something from the therapist that contributes to defining this relationship as one of inequality (Miller, 1976), even if temporarily. Accordingly, this or any discussion of power in feminist therapy begins with the idea that the therapist is in a position of greater power. Calls for equalizing power or empowering the client originate from the feminist therapist's relatively greater power to facilitate or "allow" such a process. Therefore, that the feminist therapist retains greater power than the client in the therapeutic process is assumed; that is, "power exists and it has to be taken into account, not denied" (Miller, 1976, p. 5).

Two general models of power provide the theoretical underpinning for the discussion of power in feminist therapy. One model accounts for six potential bases of power (French & Raven, 1959) and the other provides a two-dimensional basis for power strategies in intimate relationships (Falbo & Peplau, 1980).

Bases of Power

The potential for the feminist therapist to validate the female client's experience (cf. Gilbert, 1980) and to provide support and encouragement (cf. Sturdivant, 1980) suggests sources of *reward power*. Reward power may be used in this way to enhance the client's sense of personal power (Gilbert, 1980), although it may function also to diminish a client's sense of power to validate her/his own experience. A feminist therapist's potential to disapprove of a client's actions (e.g., to remain in an oppressive marital relationship) or to devalue a client's attitude or belief system (e.g., traditional sex-role values) provides a base for *coercive power*. Expressions of anger, annoyance, or impatience, if they are perceived as punishing by the client, are other potential sources of therapist coercive power. The competent feminist therapist possesses knowledge concerning the detrimental effects of traditional sex-role socialization for women and men (*informational power*), has the ability (*expert power*) to facilitate resocialization experiences, and holds a contract with the client to do so (*legitimate power*). A feminist therapist's influence in helping the client with decisions regarding medication, hospitalization, and so forth is based partially on legitimate, expert, and informational power. Role-modeling and self-disclosure by the feminist therapist (cf. Gannon, 1982; Sturdivant, 1980) are methods likely to increase the therapist's potential for *referent power*. Further attention is needed, in the development of feminist therapies, to the processes of power and the outcomes of its use.

Dimensions of Power

Feminist therapy can be defined by its emphasis on *bilateral power* strategies, away from "the *unilateral control* exercised by the therapist in traditional psychotherapy models" (Sturdivant, 1980, p. 157). The use, and perhaps effectiveness of bilateral power strategies may rest on the expectation of responsiveness to them, however (Falbo & Peplau, 1980). Even the feminist therapist may find it necessary to utilize unilateral power strategies in some instances in which, for example, a suicidal client refuses treatment, a battered woman wishes to remain in a situation that is imminently dangerous, or a mother supports an incestuous father's re-entry into the house in spite of continued risk to the daughter.

Feminist therapy involves the use of both *direct* and *indirect* forms of power. A therapist's assertiveness or matter-of-fact manner in addressing a topic that is difficult or taboo for the client are examples of direct power. Indirect power may be expressed by the feminist therapist in nonverbal communication of affect, silence, or role-modeling.

Gender as Power

At the base of a feminist analysis of society generally and of nonfeminist psychotherapy is the idea that the status of male is more powerful than the status of female (Bernard, 1972; Johnson, 1976). Miller (1976) defines this as permanent inequality and suggests that the difficulty in managing heterosexual relationships of temporary inequality may generate from the fact that they exist within a context of permanent inequality between the sexes. The difference in power between the sexes has been attributed to sex-role socialization processes (cf. Falbo & Peplau, 1980) and to greater ascribed power for men than women in our society (cf. Frieze, Parsons, Johnson, Ruble, Zellman, 1978). The context of permanent inequality may overwhelm our ability to learn to operate within any relationship defined by temporary inequality.

A third perspective from which to view therapist power in general, and feminist therapist power in particular, is to address the gender structure of the therapist/client relationship. As noted earlier, previous criticism of power in psychotherapy has focused on male-therapist/female-client relationships, while, at the same time, discussion of power in feminist therapy has (either explicitly or implicitly) focused solely on the female-therapist/female-client relationship. Thus, the issue of power as it originates from gender status has not been articulated as independent from power that stems from the role of therapist.

A further issue is embedded within the question of gender as power in feminist therapy. Whereas the principles of feminist therapy do not preclude men from practicing feminist therapy (Gilbert, 1980), it has been suggested that "most feminist therapists agree that feminist therapy can be done only by women" (Sturdivant, 1980, p. 82). Thus, it is assumed, conceptually at least, that feminist therapy may involve either female or male therapists working with either female or male clients. Further, although this chapter does not address the issue directly, it is suggested that the principle of feminist therapy also may be applied with couples and families, including both male and female adults and children. Given the premise that feminist therapy need not be limited to female therapists providing individual therapy to female clients, it is possible to examine how gender and its interaction with the therapist role may contribute to the understanding of power in feminist therapy. Taking into account both gender role and role of therapist simultaneously is necessary, since neither occurs in isolation.

Table 23–1 presents the cumulative effect of these two variables of power in feminist therapy. In three relationship types, the cumulative effect of therapist and gender role results in greater therapist power than client power. However, the cumulative effect in the female-therapist/male-client relationship type is uncertain, depending upon the relative power of each role. If the goal of the power structure in the therapeutic relationship is toward equalitarianism, divergent methods are required by which to accomplish that end, depending upon the gender structure of the relationship.

IMPLICATIONS OF POWER FOR FEMINIST THERAPY

Rohrbaugh (1979) suggested that "if the therapist is indeed inherently powerful, it can even be dangerous to pretend that the client–therapist relationship is totally equal (p. 446)." Denying the potential power in-

Table 23–1 Relative Power of Therapist vis-à-vis the Client, Based on Therapist and Gender Roles

Sources of Power	Female Therapist		Male Therapist	
	Female Client	Male Client	Female Client	Male Client
Therapist Role	GT	GT	GT	GT
Gender Role	EQ	GC	GT	EQ
Total relative power of therapist vis-à-vis client	GT	?	GT	GT

Key: GT = greater therapist power
GC = greater client power
EQ = equal client/therapist power

herent in feminist therapy can be likened to the response of traditional psychotherapists, suggested by Gannon (1982), which is either to fail to acknowledge that power exists or to deny that they make use of it. Gannon further suggested that acknowledging power is the first step toward sharing it or toward changing the power structure. An analysis of the implications of power for feminist therapy must begin from a position that fully acknowledges the inherent and varied power in the therapeutic relationship.

Balance of Power

An issue central to the discussion of power is that of power balance, or the relative (potential or utilized) power of the therapist and client. "Although attempts to systematize feminist therapy are not yet definitive" (Marecek et al., 1979, p. 734), one principle common to most formulations of feminist therapy is that of equalitarianism in the client/therapist relationship (cf. Gilbert, 1980; Rawlings & Carter, 1977).

Miller's (1976) distinction between temporary and permanent equality allows for an examination of equalitarianism in the therapeutic relationship based on service provided by the therapist to the client, separate from equalitarianism based on gender-related issues inherent in sexist society. Miller further describes the eventual goal of the temporarily unequal relationship as being the termination of it. That is to say, the basis for the inequality, namely, service by the therapist and need by the client, is no longer inherent in the relationship structure. Thus, one principle guiding the balance of power in feminist therapy is to define the therapeutic relationship as one of temporary inequality with the eventual goal one of terminating it and/or redefining it as equalitarian.

A second principle suggested here concerning the balance of power based on the therapist role in feminist therapy is to make the inequality as least disparate as possible while still allowing for the achievement of therapeutic goals. These goals may be resocialization, amelioration of detrimental effects of oppression and empowerment of the client, and, finally, termination of the therapeutic relationship altogether. What defines the least inequality in the balance of power between therapist and client in order to achieve the client's goals in feminist therapy is based on judgment by the feminist therapist. This judgment is one for which the therapist is accountable.

Types of Therapeutic Relationships

The following discussion addresses each of the therapeutic relationship types identified earlier in Table 23–1.

Achieving the least disparate balance of power overall in the feminist therapeutic relationship is, initially, facilitated by reliance on same-sex client/therapist pairing. Gender-based power imbalance in opposite-sex therapeutic relationships seems unlikely to facilitate change toward feminist therapeutic goals. At worst, this imbalance is devastating to women clients (cf. Chesler, 1972). Thus, efforts toward equalizing power, either in the direction of decreasing (male) or increasing (female) therapist power, seems imperative. Generally, androgynous behavior on the part of both male and female therapist in opposite-sex therapeutic relationships would facilitate the effort toward equalizing power, as would an indication of an active therapist effort toward modification of the social forces that lead to (different types of) oppression for both women and men.

The importance of achieving the least disparate balance of power, based on the therapist role necessary to achieve therapy goals, applies equally well to all relationship types. Theoretically, the competent feminist therapist ultimately determines this delicate balance, since it is she who is in a position to give up power, thus attempting to equalize it, whether it be from either or both the gender and therapist roles. A number of "power-sharing strategies" (cf. Seidler-Feller, 1976) have been suggested by other authors.

Two clear alternatives present themselves as means for minimizing the inequality in the feminist therapy relationship: (1) further examination of ways to equalize power between women and men, for example, in female-therapist/male-client and male-therapist/female-client relationships, and in therapy with heterosexual, lesbian, and gay male families by male and female therapists, and (2) limitation of feminist therapy to same-sex therapist/client dyads.

CONCLUSION

A number of research questions are generated from the previous discussion. Attention should be given to the empirical investigation of various issues in feminist therapy (Gilbert, 1980), to aid in further development of the field. For example, questions concerning the actual use of power strategies in feminist therapy, power balance issues, types of power used, effectiveness, and accountability require answers based on empirical research.

REFERENCES

American Psychological Association. (1975). Report of the Task Force on Sex Bias and Sex-Role Stereotyping in Psychotherapeutic Practice. *American Psychologist, 30,* 1169–1175.

Bernard, J. S. (1972). *The future of marriage.* New York: World.

Chesler, P. (1972). *Women and madness.* Garden City, NY: Doubleday.

Falbo, T., & Peplau, L. A. (1980). Power strategies in intimate relationships. *Journal of Personality and Social Psychology, 38*(4), 618–628.

French, J. R. P., Jr., & Raven, B. (1959). The bases of social power. In D. Cartwright (Ed.), *Studies in social power.* Ann Arbor, MI: Institute for Social Research.

Frieze, I. H., Parsons, J. E., Johnson, P. B., Ruble, D. N., & Zellman, G. L. (1978). *Women and sex roles.* New York: W. W. Norton.

Gannon, L. (1982). The role of power in psychotherapy. *Women & Therapy, 1*(2), 3–11.

Gilbert, L. A. (1980). Feminist therapy. In A. M. Brodsky & R. T. Hare-Mustin (Eds.), *Women and psychotherapy: An assessment of research and practice.* New York: Guilford Press.

Johnson, P. (1976). Women and power: Toward a theory of effectiveness. *The Journal of Social Issues, 32,* 88–110.

Marecek, J., Kravetz, D., & Finn, S. (1979). Comparison of women who enter feminist therapy and women who enter traditional therapy. *Journal of Consulting and Clinical Psychology, 47,* 734–742.

Miller, J. B. (1976). *Toward a new psychology of women.* Boston: Beacon Press.

Rawlings, E. I., & Carter, D. K. (1977). Feminist and nonsexist psychotherapy. In E. I. Rawlings & D. K. Carter (Eds.), *Psychotherapy for women: Treatment toward equality.* Springfield, IL: Charles C Thomas.

Rohrbaugh, J. B. (1979). *Women: Psychology's puzzle.* New York: Basic Books.

Seidler-Feller, D. (1976). Process and power in couples psychotherapy: A feminist view. *Voices, 12,* 67–71.

Sturdivant, S. (1980). *Therapy with women: A feminist philosophy of treatment.* New York: Springer.

■24

Psychotherapists' Ambivalence about Fees[1]

ELLA LASKY

Many psychotherapists are ambivalent about setting fees. This fact has been discussed at various professional workshops over the past several years (Lasky, 1980, 1981), but in general not much attention has been paid to fee setting in our professional literature. To explore the conflicts involved in this issue further, I conducted an informal survey of 60 psychotherapists from various parts of the country whose experience ranges from 2.5 to 20 years. While not a representative sample, it contains lively and useful anecdotal data that provide the basis for a discussion of the issues.

One fact is certain: Ambivalence about setting fees exists, and it is not confined to novices. Two-thirds of those surveyed expressed considerable intrapsychic conflict about setting fees and establishing the other parameters of the therapeutic contract. The most commonly expressed confusion centers on a conflict over balancing a sense of profes-

1. I would like to express my appreciation to Aphrodite Clamar, Ph.D., and Paul Trudeau, Ph.D., for their careful reviews of several drafts of this paper. I appreciate the loving editorial assistance and moral support my husband, Jonathan Cardon, extended to me throughout this project.

sional worth and the necessity to earn a living with the desire to help people. Many therapists feel uncomfortable about being in "business" as a psychotherapist when their original motivation for entering the field was a desire to help others. Some therapists reported feeling like oppressors for wanting to take money from people who are upset and need therapy; others expressed concern that they feel excited, powerful, apologetic, or embarassed when setting a high fee, and guilty, annoyed, or resentful when setting a low one. Some feel greedy if they refuse to work with a particular client because of his/her inability to pay a reasonable fee; others report that they feel "too good" or "too powerful" when the fees they charge allow them to earn a comfortable living.

Unfortunately, the psychology profession provides little or no training concerning money matters. The reasons why the area of financial management is so blatantly neglected in our training are complex. It may be that psychologists stay away from addressing the issue of money because, like other professionals, we feel it is beneath our dignity. It also may be that, since our training takes place in clinics and hospitals where patients pay a secretary or cashier and not the therapist directly, there is simply no motivation to discuss or adjust fees. The beginning therapist usually feels relieved by this arrangement and typically doesn't discuss the fee again unless the patient brings the topic up. This is unfortunate, because we are losing a fertile training opportunity by our avoidance of this issue.

The matter of money and what it represents confronts everyone. Our society instills in us conflicting values about money. While the American credo tells us that "we are all created equal," we also learn that "some people (the rich) are more equal than others (the poor)" (Lindgren, 1980). Money has other symbolic meanings which vary from person to person. The individual meanings are determined by each person's life circumstances: the religion, culture, and social class of one's family; the attitude of one's parents toward money; and the way money actually was handled in the family.

All of us are influenced by the cultural and familial issues that money presents; however, there are some important differences in the ways men and women approach the issue of making money. These differences are demonstrated by the following studies.

A study of 202 MBA's (Jellinek & Harlan, 1979) found that a significant percentage of women assessed themselves at a considerably lower market value than their male peers. The males surveyed expected to receive higher salaries at their first jobs and at the peak of their careers than the women, this despite the fact that the MBA candidates were similar in age, marital status, prior work experience, and prior salary.

Men and women pay themselves differently, according to a series of experiments by Callahan-Levy and Meese (1979). Males and females, ages six through college age, were asked to do age-appropriate tasks and to pay themselves individually, in total privacy, from an envelope containing some money. There were no significant gender differences in each subject's evaluation of his/her own performance; however, there were significant differences in the payments: At each age the females paid themselves *significantly* less than the males. The researchers suggest that females perceive money as a less salient reward for work.

A recent study of college students (Orlofsky & Stake, 1981) found no significant differences between males and females in terms of their achievement strivings or their interpersonal desires. There were, however, highly significant differences when it came to financial matters. The majority of the males said they expected to be the primary financial support for their families, while most of the females expected to be supported primarily by their husbands. Thus it is apparent that gender differences with regard to money and financial responsibility have been internalized by both females and males early in life; they still exert their influence in later years, although career planning is taking place simultaneously. These differences are reflected later in men's desires for higher salaries and women's intrapsychic conflicts about their salaries.

My interviews with psychotherapists revealed that 75 percent of the women charge lower fees than males of the same level of experience in their geographic area, 15 percent charge the same fees, and 10 percent charge more than their male peers. This suggests that many women psychotherapists, like the women in the aforementioned studies, undervalue their professional services or that men overvalue theirs. Other women psychotherapists simply felt that providing excellent professional services was more important to them than earning high fees.

The viewpoint of feminist therapists reflects a humanistic orientation when it comes to setting fees. One of the two key principles of feminist therapy is that the therapist/client relationship is equalitarian (Gilbert, 1980). In light of this, most feminist therapists use a sliding scale and negotiate a fee that will be fair to both client and therapist. This is especially important because the goal of feminist therapists is to provide professional services to as many women as possible. Women, Third World women in particular, are concentrated in lower-paying jobs and earn approximately one-third less than their male counterparts in every occupational category (U.S. Department of Commerce, 1978) and therefore would suffer from the insistence on a fixed fee.

My interviews indicate that it is particularly difficult for most women psychotherapists to be clear about their fees. While two-thirds of both men and women interviewed have conflicts about determining fees, the focus of these conflicts differs. Many men revealed that they glossed over the conflict (internally) and resolved it by focusing on how much income they need to support their families. Women psychotherapists, on the other hand, tend to be acutely aware of the conflict about setting fees. They feel a three-way conflict: (1) feeling the need to support themselves and their families, (2) feeling torn between working additional hours to earn more money and wanting to spend the time with their friends and family, and (3) finding themselves focusing as much, or more, on the patient's financial needs than on their own. These different conflicts are understandable, since men are responding to years of conditioning to earn money while women only recently have begun to think about it as a choice.

Some conflicts about fees that are common among women therapists emerged from these interviews.

Therapist Jones is an overly nurturant female therapist. She agrees to see Ms. A at a fee lower than her usual one. As a result of their work together, Ms. A gets a promotion and raise. When Therapist Jones suggests increasing the fee, Ms. A says she is reluctant to do so. Therapist Jones does not counter her reluctance forcefully and subsequently feels resentful, used, and foolish for having lowered her fee for this client. When she calms down, she realizes that she has just learned something new about Ms. A's psychodynamics and the way Ms. A treats others. In fact, Therapist Jones realizes that she feels just like Ms. A's lover often is described to feel, and therefore sees that the issue presents a good opportunity to explore with Ms. A how she often tries to manipulate others through her helplessness, greed, self-centeredness, and contempt for them. Addressing the issue this way proves fruitful for both the client and the therapist.

For Therapist Smith the most difficult circumstance regarding fees takes place when a client who has created a self-defeating circumstance asks for the fee or number of sessions per week to be reduced. Her patient, Mr. B, recently has arranged a nearly impossible work situation for himself that commits him to longer hours and more travel, thereby reducing the time available for therapy. He asks Therapist Smith to lower the number of sessions per week because of his situation. Therapist Smith finds the request difficult to deal with because she feels manipulated, hurt, and angry; she is uncertain if her reaction is appropriate, and she decides to consult a colleague on the matter. As a result it becomes clear that the client had a role in creating the problem and can rearrange his work hours and return to the original therapy schedule. When this is pointed out to him, he feels relieved. Therapist Smith then uses this opportunity to point out that the way he's treated her relates to the often unilateral way he makes and breaks contracts with other people; she is able to use this event to look at other aspects of his character structure.

Therapist Adams reports taking into treatment at a reduced fee a young woman in her late thirties, Ms. C, whose economic circumstances are poor. After several months, Ms. C brings in some insurance forms and mentions that she hadn't realized she'd had these benefits. She doesn't propose adjusting the fee, and Therapist Adams feels exploited and manipulated. She blames herself for failing to ask about insurance in the initial interview and this self-blame makes it difficult to decide how to handle the situation. Many women therapists are particularly vulnerable to charming, needy young clients who "forget" about their own resources. Some therapists identify with them, others want to love and care for them. Unfortunately, this often leads to unconscious collusion between the client's style and the therapist, and blocks the client's progress.

Therapist Green works long hours but doesn't have the commensurate income. She feels she can't ask any of her clients for higher fees because she doesn't want to "burden" them, nor does she want to seem "greedy." Ironically, she has never explored money matters fully with her clients and doesn't know who can and who cannot afford higher fees. It is her own reaction formation against greed that stands in the way of a fuller exploration of this issue.

Among the benefits of being clear in your own mind about your fee structure is an ability to be comfortable rather than defensive when you discuss money matters with your clients. This is of significant value to the therapeutic relationship. As we know, almost every client, no matter what the presenting symptom, has ambivalence about money. By being clear about your own fee you will offer the client, perhaps for the first time, the refreshing experience of having a frank, open, and unambiguous discussion about money. Second, if your client is angry about something related to money, your own comfort with the topic may allow you to understand the patient's emotional pain and hostility without your being defensive, doctrinaire, or apologetic. Finally, setting an appropriate fee for your clients will help make it more difficult for them to relax into passively dependent help-seeking.

Setting fees that are too low for a particular client often will elicit gratitude, humiliation, or shame reactions and may inhibit expressions of hurt, anger, love, or resentment toward the therapist. Fees that are too high often will elicit anger, resentment, humiliation, or shame reactions and often result in premature terminations of therapy. They also may inhibit the expression of dependency, closeness, appreciation, hurt, or love toward the therapist. Establishing your fee structure requires careful thought and consideration. Fees that are too high and too low both can be countertherapeutic.

It is clear that therapists undermine the treatment when they become flustered about their position on fees. These are some practical steps one can take to deal with conflicts about money:

1. Take notice of when and with which types of clients these conflicted feelings arise. Try to assess whether you are being overly nurturant, sometimes self-blaming, or sometimes narcissistic when it comes to setting your fee. After having gathered the data about yourself, you can identify your pattern and then work on each situation as it arises.

2. Include in your initial interview questions about income, assets, expenses, loans, insurance benefits, and so forth. This will set the stage for money to be an ordinary topic of discussion in the therapy and will help in setting a proper fee.

3. Review your caseload and income before a consultation with a potential client. This will help clarify your decisions about whether to take additional clients and about what kind of clients to take, and will help you to make a rational decision about your fee.

4. Review the cost of running your office. Understand that you do have an overhead, just like anyone else in business; this may help you focus on setting fees that are appropriate.

5. Consult with a colleague if it seems that you cannot resolve your fee problems. Occasionally one might go back into therapy or analysis to explore this issue.

Clarity about what you charge for your professional services has many benefits for clients and also for therapists. Among the benefits is the freedom to think and speak about a taboo topic, so that it does not control you. This freedom will enhance your sense of professional and personal worth.

REFERENCES

Callahan-Levy, C. M., & Meese, L. A. (1979). Sex differences in the allocation of pay. *Journal of Personality and Social Psychology, 37,* 433–446.

Gilbert, L. A. (1980). Feminist therapy. In A. M. Brodsky & R. T. Hare-Mustin (Eds.), *Women and psychotherapy* (pp. 245–266). New York: Guilford Press.

Jellinek, M., & Harlan, A. (1979). *MBA goals and aspirations.* (Working Paper No. 19). Wellesley: Center for Research on Women.

Lasky, E. (1980, September). The therapist as socialized female. Conversation hour at the annual convention of the American Psychological Association, Montreal.

Lasky, E. (1981, March). Money and fees. Conversation hour at the midwinter convention of the Psychotherapy Division of the American Psychological Association, San Antonio, TX.

Lindgren, H. C. (1980). *Great expectations: The psychology of money.* Los Altos, CA: William Kaufman.

Orlofsky, J. L., & Stake, J. E. (1981). Psychological masculinity and femininity: Relationship to striving and self-concept in the achievement and interpersonal domains. *Psychology of Women Quarterly, 6,* 218–233.

U. S. Department of Commerce, Bureau of the Census (1978). *Current population reports: Consumer income.* Washington, DC: U.S. Government Printing Office.

25

Assertiveness Training for the Eighties: Moving Beyond the Personal

IRIS GOLDSTEIN FODOR

Since the early 1970s, assertiveness training has been one of the most popular feminist therapy programs (Jakubowski-Spector, 1973; Osborn & Harris, 1975). Large numbers of women have participated in assertiveness training workshops all over the United States and Europe. They have been the consumers of at least 20 popular self-help books and have sought training not only from professional therapists at clinics but from trainers of diverse backgrounds at a variety of community centers and continuing education programs. Articles about assertiveness training have been written in almost every U.S. woman's magazine, and there has been widespread coverage in newspapers as well (Stringer-Moore & Jack, 1981).

Given the widespread popularity of assertiveness training during this last decade and its acceptance into the mainstream of feminist therapy, it is now time to pause for thought and review. Since assertiveness training for women was developed as a feminist therapy and since most women appear to enter workshops hoping to become more assertive in order to achieve personal as well as professional goals, we must ask ourselves how effective assertiveness training programs are in meeting such goals. In particular, we need to ask (1) Do women have a deficit in assertiveness? (2) Do we know what effective assertiveness is? (3) What are the consequences of being assertive? (4) Is assertiveness training for the individual the most desirable method for enabling women to achieve their personal and professional goals? Or, put another way, is assertiveness training yet another "treatment" that is directed at the victim of societal injustice, placing the burden for social change on the backs of individual women?

THE ISSUE OF ASSERTIVENESS DEFICITS

Most work on assertiveness training is based on the assumption of a female assertiveness deficit. Alberti & Emmons (1970) provide the standard definition of assertiveness as being "behavior which enables a person to act in his (her) best interest, to stand up for himself (herself) without feeling undue anxiety, to express his (her) honest feelings comfortably or to exercise his (her) rights without denying the rights of others" (p. 2).

Indeed, women, upon entering an assertiveness training workshop, are asked to state, "I am unassertive" (Fodor, 1980). Broverman, Broverman, Clarkson, Rosenkrantz, & Vogel (1970) found that mental health professionals rated assertiveness as an appropriate trait for a healthy male and its opposite, unassertiveness (passive, submissive behavior), as appropriate for a healthy female. Most feminist therapists also would argue that the traditional female role reinforces such nonassertive behaviors as passivity and dependency. For example Osborn & Harris (1975) write, "Women are reinforced in many interpersonal situations for being agreeable, conciliatory, and reticent. This submissive posture limits their opportunity for self-expression" (p. 20).

However, when we look at self-report scales for assertive behaviors, we do not find that males are assertive and females are unassertive. Rather, we find that women demonstrate greater difficulty than men in refusing requests, expressing negative feelings, and setting limits. On the other hand, women more easily than men give expressions of love, affection, and approval to others (Chandler, Cook, & Dugovics, 1978; Hollandsworth & Wall, 1977).

A large body of research and training has centered on women's problems in refusing requests. Rathus and Nevid's review (in press) suggests that females demonstrate conflict between acting in their own self-interest and being nurturant in refusal situations. This is problematic behavior if we follow male values, but is it problematic if we adhere to Gilligan's (1982) conclusion from research on moral development? She claims that, for women, caring for others is more highly valued than caring for self, and she places a positive value on such a trait. Instead of asking broadly whether women have an assertiveness deficit, we need to ask our questions more carefully: In what ways or under what conditions is a female nonassertive? What are female assets in assertion? Are we following the male model of values when we assume that acting in one's self-interest or being too expressive of feelings is a deficit? Since males do not tend to value free expression of feelings, this assertive female strength is underplayed. What is needed is further systematic study of female vocabularies before we can claim that most women require assertiveness training.

WHAT IS EFFECTIVE ASSERTIVE BEHAVIOR?

While female assertiveness difficulties have not been delineated carefully, trainers have gone on to assume that there is an appropriate assertive behavior that can be taught. Most studies use graduate students or published experts as judges who determine what such appropriate assertive behaviors are for various problematic situations, while in workshops group consensus typically defines appropriate assertion. In fact, little work has been done to study assertive behavior in the real world and its effectiveness for women. Let us consider the following clinical case:

> A young woman attorney was to have her first appearance in court. She had long been fearful of such an appearance and had successfully managed to avoid court for years. At her superior's insistence, she had to prepare for court presentations. We worked via role play, behavior rehearsal, and desensitization on what seemed to both of us an effective courtroom style. The client went into court feeling more confident and prepared but was unnerved by the hard, attacking, abrasive style of the opposing male attorney. Even though she had performed in the way we had rehearsed, she

did not feel strong or effective and was often on the verge of tears. [Fodor & Epstein, 1983, p. 420]

If we focus on the issue of shaping an assertive response for this particular situation we are presented with many problems. What is effective assertive behavior for a female lawyer in the courtroom? If women do not wish to model the attacking mode of many male lawyers, what are the alternatives? Therapists, before beginning an assertiveness program for a particular client who has been assessed as unassertive, need to think through what is appropriate assertive behavior for each situation. We need to ask ourselves who we want to be like, and who we do not want to be like. It would be helpful to videotape assertive women who are considered effective in various settings, to study what aspects of their assertive behavior might be modeled for client study.

CONSEQUENCES OF FEMALE ASSERTIVENESS

From the beginning, work in assertiveness training focused on consciousness raising as a form of cognitive restructuring in identifying the socialized, apparently irrational beliefs that inhibited assertive responding. It sought to replace those beliefs with feminist and more rational belief systems. Following this reasoning, many assertiveness trainers viewed unassertiveness as irrational behavior. After a decade of following our female clients from their training groups into the real world, however, we must conclude that beliefs that inhibit assertive responding may not be so irrational or maladaptive as once thought (Fodor, 1980; Linehan & Egan, 1979).

There is now a growing body of research that suggests that there is a strong bias against assertive women (Solomon & Rothblum, 1984). Linehan & Egan (1979), for example, claim that "even if women are appropriately assertive if they model themselves after assertive effective men, the results of their interactions may well not be positive . . . ; behaviors which are effective for men are not necessarily effective for women" (p. 5).

Research by Bellack, Hersen, and Lamparski (1979), Fiedler and Beach (1978), and Rich and Schroeder (1976) suggests bias against assertive behavior in females. For example, Rich and Schroeder report that both expert and peer male and female judges identified comparable assertive behaviors, when enacted by men, as assertive, but aggressive when performed by women.

Hence, in training individual women to become assertive, we run into a paradox. Given the nature of prejudice in our society about assertive women (shared by both males and females), we may be training individual women to be even more ineffective and frustrated. To return to the example of the woman lawyer, if we help her to develop the humanistic style of assertiveness proposed by Alberti and Emmons (1970) (strong, but respectful of others), we may fail to help her develop effective courtroom behavior, for that style of assertiveness might reinforce the prejudice that women attorneys cannot fight for their clients like their more attacking male colleagues. If we help our client to model even a toned-down male style, she is most likely to be perceived as too aggressive and hence ineffective. When the client was near to tears in court, maybe she was reacting to this no-win situation.

To help women lawyers develop alternatives to traditional male-defined courtroom behaviors, female lawyers may need to work together to develop such alternatives and provide support for an acceptable female-defined assertive courtroom style.

ASSERTIVENESS TRAINING AND SOCIETAL CHANGE: GOING BEYOND THE PERSONAL

While the goal of trainers and individual clients has been to enhance personal power, the underlying assumption of assertiveness training was that, if individual women changed, societal attitudes toward them would change. However, while thousands of women have chosen to encounter their environment with an assertive stance, the response to the change often has been negative. Attitudes toward granting women full equity have not changed enough. Critics of assertiveness training who are feminists have suggested a shift from individual work because it focuses on symptoms and blaming the victim to a societal focus that addresses the larger issues and treats the system (Henley & Nancy, 1980; Linehan & Egan, 1979). For example, Linehan & Egan argue that "when half the population is targeted as needing to change their behavior in order to gain fair treatment by the system, we have to ask what system are those individuals trying to fit."

Going beyond individual work, toward creating an environment receptive to strong, assertive women, we need to take our methodology into a broader, more difficult arena and address power issues and male domination. In present society, males still control the political and economic structures. Further, as we see from the preceding discussion, they resist accepting and relating to assertive women and mislabel female assertion as aggression. Most likely, they view assertive women as a threat to their continuing power monopoly. Hence we need to go beyond work with individual women and their personal assertiveness issues and begin to use assertiveness techniques to challenge male patriarchal structure.

What I am proposing is a four-pronged program that supplements the individual work.

1.　We need to go beyond treating individual women. As a group, women need to be educated about assertiveness in order to understand what assertive strengths they already possess and to work together to develop female-defined assertive behavior. Women also must educate each other, since many women are among the most negative evaluators of female assertive behavior (Solomon & Rothblum, 1984).

2.　We need to view the male's negative response to female assertiveness as a problem requiring change. When individual women complain about problematic interactions, we need to view the negative climate for female assertive behavior as a problematic area for male/female relations and work with the male as well. We need further to develop appropriate assertiveness techniques, research, training materials, and support groups for those courageous women who stand alone and challenge the system.

More women need to be encouraged to follow the example of Christine Craft, who sued her employer after she was fired as anchorwoman because she was considered unattractive and not deferential to men. Mental health professionals should be taking the lead in providing resource materials as well as supporting the follow-up for women in similar situations.

3.　We must enter the business and corporate sectors as trainers. Women are finding opportunities for advancement in formerly male arenas and are getting mixed messages. Collins (1982), in an article surveying issues for women in management, states, "Middle-management supervisors give the highest rating to older, less aggressive women, . . . those women who didn't rock the boat, who were less threatening, less dynamic. Yet, they wanted a different kind of person to fill high level spots. [They wanted] young aggressive dynamos and the women who might fit that pattern weren't being promoted" (p. 14).

Solomon, Brehony, Rothblum, and Kelly (1983) investigated corporate managers' perceptions of assertive males and females. The managers rated female empathic/assertive models as most favored, yet the research suggests that, in practice, the aggressive style is favored for top management. Thus, research and training workshops within the business community are needed to promote acceptance of an appropriate female-defined assertive style.

4.   We must focus on the media. The male-dominated media play a leading role in perpetuating negative female assertiveness stereotypes (Segal, 1977). Women's developing assertiveness often is presented as a form of "me-ism" that emphasizes giving up women's traditional nurturing role (Henley & Nancy, 1980). Further, political women often have been singled out for negative attention for their abrasive/aggressive qualities (Berman, 1977). Assertiveness trainers often have not been able responsibly to control negative reporting about aggressiveness training. For example, *New York Magazine* consulted with numerous assertiveness trainers about a feature cover story on assertiveness training for women and still chose to put on its cover a cartoon showing a woman slapping a man after attending such a workshop (Dubrow, 1975). We need to develop strategies for dealing with the media, particularly when they persist in distorting our work. We need to be resourceful in the development of materials suitable for presentation in the media, for example, articles, television programs, and fiction scripts. We again must be willing to use our voices and economic power to counter many of the negative, female stereotypes still presented daily by the media. Research and training programs for media executives, similar to those proposed for the business community, seem warranted.

SUMMARY

Before appropriate individual treatment packages can be designed for women, assertiveness trainers must study female assertiveness deficits and strengths properly and present clients with female assertiveness models that include effective strategies for coping with various situations they encounter in real life. Further, research needs to be conducted on the consequences of assertive responding, particularly the negative responses of men and prejudice within the wider community. Going beyond individual work, trainers must address societal misperceptions and mislabeling of female assertiveness. We need to bring our assessment and training materials into the wider community. We need to train supervisors, corporate executives, and media personnel about women's assertiveness, so we can create an environment receptive to the assertive woman.

REFERENCES

Alberti, R. E., & Emmons, M. L. (1970). *Your perfect right*. San Luis Obispo, CA: *Impact*.

Bellack, A.S., Hersen, M., & Lamparski, D. (1979). Role play tests for assessing social skills: Are they useful? *Journal of Consulting and Clinical Psychology, 47*, 334–342.

Berman, S. (1977, November 14). Bess Myerson is one tough customer. *New York Magazine,* p. 7.

Broverman, I. K., Broverman, D. M., Clarkson, F. E., Rosenkrantz, P. S., & Vogel, S. R. (1970). Sex-role stereotypes and clinical judgments of mental health. *Journal of Consulting and Clinical Psychology, 34,* 107.

Chandler, T., Cook, B., & Dugovics, D. (1978). Sex differences in self-reported assertiveness. *Psychological Reports, 43,* 394–402.

Collins, G. (1983, May 31). Unforeseen business barriers for women. *The New York Times,* p. 14.

Dubrow, M. (1975, July 18). Female assertiveness: How a pussycat can learn to be a panther. *New York Magazine.*

Fiedler, D., & Beach, L. R. (1978). On the decision to be assertive. *Journal of Consulting and Clinical Psychology, 46,* 537–546.

Fodor, I. G. (1980). The treatment of communication problems with assertiveness training. In A. Goldstein & E. Foa (Eds.), *Handbook of behavioral interventions*. New York: John Wiley.

Fodor, I. G., & Epstein, R. C. (1983). Assertiveness training for women: Where are we failing? In P. Emmelcamp & E. Foa (Eds.), *Failures in behavioral therapy*. New York: John Wiley.

Gilligan, C. (1982). *In a Different Voice*. Cambridge, MA: Harvard University Press.

Henley, N., & Nancy, M. (1980, February). Assertiveness training in the social context. *Assert,* 1–2.

Hollandsworth, J., Jr., & Wall, K. (1977). Sex differences in assertive behavior:

An empirical investigation. *Journal of Counseling Psychology, 24* (3), 217–222.

Jakobowski-Spector, P. (1973). Facilitating the growth of women through assertive training. *The Counseling Psychologist, 4,* 76–86.

Linehan, M., & Egan, K. (1979). Assertion training for women: Square peg in a round hole? Paper presented at Symposium on Behavioral Therapy for Women, at the Annual Meeting of the Association for Advanced Behavior Therapy, San Francisco.

Osborn, S. M., & Harris, G. G. (1975). *Assertive training for women.* Springfield, IL.: Charles C. Thomas.

Rathus, S. A., & Nevid, J. S. (In press). Multivariate and normative data pertaining to the Rathus Assertiveness Schedule with the college population. *Behavior Therapy.*

Rich, A. R., & Schroeder, H. E. (1976). Research issues in assertiveness training. *Psychological Bulletin, 83,* 1081–1096.

Segal, J. L. (1977). The steamroom at the Yale Club: Women news editors and the newspaper industry. Unpublished manuscript.

Solomon, L. J., Brehony, K. A., Rothblum, E. D., & Kelly, J. A. (1983). The relationship of verbal content in assertive responses to perceptions of the businessperson. *Journal of Organization Behavior Management, 4,* 49–63.

Solomon, L. J., & Rothblum, E. D. (1984). Social skills problems experienced by women. In L. L. Abate & M. A. Milan (Eds.), *Handbook of social skills training and research.* New York: John Wiley.

Stringer-Moore, D., & Jack, G. B. (1981). Assertive behavior training: A cross-referenced annotated bibliography. San Luis Obispo, CA: *Impact.*

◼ 26

Feminist Interpretation of Traditional Testing

LYNNE BRAVO ROSEWATER

Most feminist literature in psychology to date has been opposed to testing. One reason for this position is that tests contain the values of a patriarchial culture and, as such, reflect sexist views. In addition, diagnostic testing has been rejected because of the belief that testing itself places the therapist in an expert position vis-à-vis the client and hence refutes the notion of an equalitarian relationship (Rawlings & Carter, 1977).

The idea that this relationship can be equalitarian, however, has itself been challenged (see Chapter 23 of this book, by Douglas), as the existence of a therapist/client relationship in and of itself signifies a power differential. Douglas argues that what separates feminist therapy from others is how that power is utilized; that is, a feminist therapist has an obligation to use her power to effect change. Brown (Chapter 29 of this book) furthers this argument in her comments on feminist ethics by saying that as feminist therapists we must "consciously and actively share our power and privilege."

Ironically, perhaps, a way for feminist therapists to challenge the status quo and act on Brown's charge is to develop feminist interpretations for standardized tests. Such interpretations can be used to advocate effectively for change on women's behalf. One example is the use of feminist test interpretations in the defense of battered women charged with aggravated murder who, in self-defense, have killed their batterers. Feminist interpretations of testing also can be important in helping women retain (or regain) custody of their children.

This chapter will address two issues: (1) arguments for the importance of developing feminist interpretations of standardized tests, along with some case examples of how such testing can be used as feminist advocacy; and (2) the feminist ethics of sharing test information with clients.

IMPORTANCE OF FEMINIST
INTERPRETATIONS OF TESTS

A repetitive theme in feminist literature is that women must learn how to use power more effectively (Brodsky & Hare-Mustin, 1980; Mander & Rush, 1977; Rawlings & Carter, 1977; Wycoff, 1977) and that it is consistent with feminist ethics to use our own power to effect change (see Chapters 23 and 29 of this book). One way for feminist therapists to use power is to develop alternative interpretations for widely influential test instruments, interpretations that would be consistent with the philosophic base of feminism. Such interpretations would develop from a blending of our expertise about test instruments with the psychology of women.

The concept of alternative interpretations is grounded historically in the decisions of the U.S. Supreme Court. Using the same document—the Constitution of the United States—as a basis for interpretation, the court, at different times, supported the position that slaves were property (Dred Scott) and the position that separate, but equal, is inherently unequal (Brown *vs*. Topeka Board of Education). The justices on the court are professionals who use a basis of standardization (the Constitution) but also their own judgment and discrimination, which are influenced by current cultural values. In the same vein, the psychologist, a trained professional, uses testing that is based on standardization but also uses personal judgment and discrimination that are influenced by the existing culture.

An example of applying such judgment to standarized testing is illustrated by my research in developing a Minnesota Multiphasic Personality Inventory (MMPI) profile for battered women (Rosewater, 1982). I found that the mean MMPI 3-point code type (486/468) for the 118 battered women in my study was markedly similar to a "cookbook" chronic female schizophrenic profile obtained from a study of 133 women (Lanyon, 1968). The fact that these two profiles may be indistinguishable led me to raise the question of whether many women previously diagnosed as chronic schizophrenics may not, in fact, have been battered women. I concluded that, in order to make an accurate diagnosis, clinicians must have a thorough and accurate client history, with a direct probe for a history of domestic violence. (For further discussion, see Chapter 21 in this volume). Thus, a feminist interpretation of a standardized test could be used to refute a misdiagnosis.

Using Feminist Test Interpretations in Advocacy Cases

Statistical data and respected standardized psychometric measures represent not just the opinion of an expert, but tangible evidence. In a 1980 murder trial of a battered woman who shot and killed her husband while he was sleeping, I testified as an expert witness on battered women and used this woman's MMPI profile as part of my testimony. I learned of the not-guilty verdict from a woman juror who called me immediately to say she felt she had participated in one of the most significant events in her life in helping acquit the defendant. The juror told me, "[She] is the same age I am. That could have been me. I'm so glad that you had a *test* (emphasis mine) that showed she was a battered woman." Without such testimony this woman presently might be in prison.

In the most unusual custody case in which I have testified, a 23-year-old woman with two young daughters fled from Cleveland to her parents' home in another city, after her husband held a gun to her head and threatened to kill her. The husband, in his wife's absence, requested an *ex parte* hearing[1] and was awarded custody of the girls. Prior to these incidents, the wife (after her husband threatened to kill her daughter if she didn't comply) had pleaded guilty to child abuse charges in connection with her husband's son by a previous marriage. The plea then was used against the woman when she tried to regain custody of her daughters. Her husband's lawyer told the court that the woman was

---

1. An *ex parte* hearing is one in which only one party is represented.

an unfit mother because she had a record of child abuse. As an expert witness, with an MMPI as supportive evidence, I testified about how a woman could plead guilty to a charge of which she was innocent. The wife was awarded custody of her daughters; without advocacy on her behalf the abusive husband might have retained custody.

In both of the cases just cited, the use of a widely respected test like the MMPI helped give the judge (and the jury in the first case) a concrete basis for grasping the dynamics of the victimization of domestic violence; hence, a standardized test, as interpreted by a feminist psychologist, facilitated a finding in favor of the woman victim of violence.

Another example of advocacy with feminist interpretation of testing is illustrated by my therapeutic relationship with a bright woman in her mid thirties who had been psychiatrically hospitalized twice and diagnosed as having a borderline personality disorder with brief psychotic episodes. After six months of therapy the woman was offered a high-paying job as a technical editor, but in order to keep the job she had to get a national security clearance. This woman feared that her hospitalization record would keep her from passing a security check. Since I had done testing with her, I suggested that she include my name as her current therapist and that I, with her permission, would use this testing to argue in her favor, as she was perfectly capable of managing a responsible job. Subsequently I was interviewed, and I used her MMPI test results to advocate for the woman. She was given the national security clearance, which most likely would have been refused without this feminist intervention.

One of the advantages of feminist test interpretation is its ability to explain seemingly adverse behavior. An example is an assessment I did for a woman who had been battered for 20 years and who, in self-defense, had killed her husband by cutting his throat with a knife. Despite two eyewitnesses who saw the woman get the knife, the woman insisted her husband had gotten the knife. On her MMPI this woman had a significantly high T-score on the repression scale ($R = 80$). Such a high score usually is interpreted as an indication of extreme denial or deceit (Graham, 1977). This was a religious woman who had never been in any trouble with the law; hence, my test interpretation was that she could not accept her behavior, however necessary it was to save her own life. She dealt with this conflict by denying the part of the incident that was morally unacceptable to her and by insisting that her husband had caused the fatal wound. The greatest problem for the lawyer representing the defendant was that the woman was obviously lying. The lawyer feared that the judge would be harsher with the woman because of her unwillingness to admit the truth. Her MMPI, however, was admitted as evidence and discussed with the judge in chambers, who afterward put the woman on probation with no jail sentence.

Developing Feminist Interpretations

Developing feminist interpretations for testing has to evolve out of clinical use of such tests by feminist therapists. In my own clinical practice I regularly use the MMPI, which is probably the most widely used personality inventory in the country.[2]

Objective personality tests like the MMPI have been labeled sexist (Rawlings & Carter, 1977). One critical item on the MMPI is question #74: "I have often wished I were a girl," or "I have never been sorry that I am a girl." If either a man or woman answers "true," this response is considered indicative of psychological maladjustment. With the inclusion of this and other such similar items, the MMPI certainly can be labeled sexist. Depending on the test, the therapist may have to discard certain questions or subscales or challenge the standard interpretation of the response. In this case, for example, a woman's response that she's never been sorry that she is a girl would be considered by a feminist a healthy rather than pathological one. While nonsexist test interpretation is a relatively new concept for objective personality assessments, such nonsexist test interpretations have been used for vocational tests (Dewy, 1977).

THE FEMINIST ETHICS OF PERSONALITY TESTING

In addition to how tests are interpreted, criticisms have centered on how results are handled as the property of the therapist. This power is seen as placing the therapist in the role of expert and as enhancing the therapist's interests rather than the patients' (Rawlings & Carter, 1977). Yet, as Brown points out (Chapter 29), expertise need not be seen

---

2. A written copy of a feminist interpretation of the MMPI is available from the author, at 23360 Chagrin Blvd., Suite 202, Cleveland, Ohio 44122.

negatively. The feminist ethic in handling the data gathered from personality testing is that such results be shared. The therapist needs to explain the test data in a way that makes the results comprehensible to the client. The client's feedback then becomes as integral a part of the test sharing as the therapist's explanation. The decision about how the test data should be utilized as part of the therapy process is also a joint effort.

Empowerment is dependent upon self-awareness. Women seek therapy because they want to change. As feminist therapists, our job as facilitators of that process of change is to help raise clients' awareness in a manner that does not further the victimization of the women with whom we work. The practice of double victimization, blaming the victim for the problem, adds to clients' sense of guilt and self-blame (Chapman & Gates, 1978). Women often tend to blame themselves for the problems they encounter. This dynamic has been found with battered women (Rosewater, 1982) and may partially explain why battered women remain in an abusive situation: Their anger becomes converted to guilt. Many battered women, in the past as well as the present, who seek outside help from a counselor or religious leader, are asked what they are doing to cause the violence (Davidson, 1978). Such questioning in itself tends to reinforce self-alienation and guilt. A feminist therapist, avoiding such victimization, can use data from a personality test such as the MMPI to help a client focus her anger on the conditions that create her victimization, rather than on herself.

As a feminist therapist, my assumption in interpreting testing is that a woman's behavior is reactive rather than pathological. As Gilbert (1980) states, "The basic assumption underlying feminist therapy is that ideology, social structure and behavior are inextricably woven" (p. 274). My research with the MMPI and battered women (Rosewater, 1982) showed a significant correlation[3] between the score elevation on the subscale that measures ideas of external influence (Pa1) and the frequency of beatings, severity of injury, and extent of violence. For a victim of domestic violence, an elevation on the Pa1 scale may be considered as an indication of her level of fearfulness. In testifying as an expert witness in the murder trials of battered women who have killed their batterers, I use these data to substantiate the legal concept of fear of imminent bodily harm.

3. The Frequency of Battering and Violent Hurt were significantly correlated with pal, ideas of external influence, at the .01 level, while violent action was significantly correlated at the .05 level.

A feminist ethic for interpreting personality assessments can and does exist. Essential to that ethic is sharing information, refusing to be part of the victimization process, and accepting behavior as reactive rather than pathological. It is my belief that good therapy is feminist therapy, but what distinguishes competent therapy from feminist therapy is that feminist therapy has a commitment both to an equalitarian therapist/client relationship and to equal opportunity for women and men for personal, political, institutional, and economic power (Rawlings & Carter, 1977). If in fact we believe that the personal is political, that we are facilitators in the process of social change, then using feminist interpretations of traditional testing is merely an extension of the philosophical tenets we already hold.

CONCLUSION

Feminist test interpretations are ethically consistent with feminist therapy and the political tenets of feminism in that feminism demands social action as an integral part of its philosophy. Feminist test interpretation is one way that the feminist therapist can use her power to help effect constructive social change for women. Numerous examples have been given in this chapter of the effectiveness of using such feminist test interpretations in the courtroom. To effect change we must heighten awareness; feminist interpretation of tests can be helpful to the individual woman seeking to change, as it can raise her awareness about her own behavior. It also can raise the awareness of others in society—attorneys, judges, and members of the jury, in the cases cited here.

The feminist ethic of using test data is that test results need to be shared with a woman client in a joint effort to evaluate the accuracy of the interpretation of those results. As feminist therapists we can and should use our power and privilege to effect change. Changing the system is a tiresome task; feminist interpretation of tests may aid considerably in that endeavor.

REFERENCES

Brodsky, A. M., & Hare-Mustin, R. (Eds.). (1980). *Women and psychotherapy.* New York: Guilford Press.

Chapman, J. R., & Gates, M. (Eds.). (1978). *The victimization of women.* Beverly Hills: Sage.

Davidson, T. (1978). *Conjugal crime: Understanding and changing the wifebeating pattern*. New York: Ballantine.

Dewy, C. R. (1977). Vocational counseling with women: A non-sexist technique. In E. I. Rawlings & D. K. Carter (Eds.), *Psychotherapy for women: Treatment toward equality*. Springfield, IL: Charles C Thomas.

Gilbert, L. A. (1980). Feminist therapy. In A. M. Brodsky & R. Hare-Mustin (Eds.), *Women and psychotherapy*. New York: Guilford Press.

Graham, J. R. (1977). *The MMPI: A practical guide*. New York: Oxford University Press.

Lanyon, R. I. (1968). *A handbook of MMPI group profiles*. Minneapolis: University of Minnesota Press.

Mander, A. V., & Rush, A. K. (1977). *Feminism as therapy*. New York: Random House.

Rawlings, E. I., & Carter, D. K. (Eds.). (1977). *Psychotherapy for women: Treatment toward equality*. Springfield, IL: Charles C Thomas.

Rosewater, L. B. (1982). The development of an MMPI profile for battered women. Unpublished doctoral dissertation. The Union for Experimenting Colleges and Universities, Cincinnati, Ohio.

Wycoff, H. (1977). Radical psychiatry for women. In E. I. Rawlings & D. K. Carter (Eds.), *Psychotherapy for women: Treatment toward equality*. Springfield, IL: Charles C Thomas.

■ 27
Feminist Forensic Psychology

LENORE E. AUERBACH WALKER

Within the past 10 years, feminists have issued important challenges to the law, especially as we became more knowledgeable about past discrimination and the legal profession's potential to help us gain equality. These challenges came from women attorneys and judges as well as those outside of the system, much the way the challenges have arisen in psychology. As feminist psychologists we have used our research methods to document sexist practices in psychology and create sex-fair psychotherapy. Feminist attorneys have used legal research to document sexist legal practices and create new ways for the courts to protect women's rights. Forensic psychology, the combination of law and psychology, has the potential to integrate both legal and psychological professional concerns. Feminist forensic psychology has the power to utilize both professions' skills to further promote equality for women, by combining the talents of advocates to assure sex-fair legal procedures and outcomes. Nowhere is that more needed than in the area of criminal law.

Psychotherapists rarely think of themselves as advocates, believing that the neutrality learned in our training is essential to being a good

274

therapist. Feminist criticism has demonstrated that neutrality is a myth in therapy; moreover, it has gone on to demonstrate that an equalitarian relationship with appropriate self-disclosure about personal values even enhances the therapeutic outcome. It follows then, that being an advocate in the courtroom as an expert witness can allow for the objectivity of scientific psychology to be utilized on behalf of a client. It also allows the feminist psychologist to utilize her psychology skills to educate the community about particular social issues that oppress women.

WOMEN'S SELF-DEFENSE

In some ways, women's self-defense cases have provoked the criminal justice system to become more relevant to women's legal rights. The role of the psychologist in criminal proceedings is to explain behavior that otherwise might seem deviant. The classic Broverman study (Broverman, Broverman, Clarkson, Rosencrantz, & Vogel, 1970) demonstrated that the same behaviors considered normal when committed by men were seen as deviant for women. Many of the emotions thought to be present when an aggressive act is committed were measured in that study. Women who are not excused for such criminal acts, usually by use of the legal insanity defense, are seen as more violent than a man who commits the same offense. Thus, a feminist psychologist has the opportunity to correct the expected bias and educate the court as to why a woman would behave in an aggressive manner.

Women who kill represent less than 15 percent of all the homicides in the United States (Jones, 1980). Most of these are women who kill their attackers, usually trying to defend themselves or their children. It is more frequent, according to United States Department of Justice statistics (cited in Berk, Berk, Loeske, & Rauma, 1983), for the woman in an abusive relationship to be the one who is injured or killed. This occurs even in those cases classified as mutual combat by other researchers (Straus, Gelles, & Steinmetz, 1980). The sexist bias in the criminal courts makes it more difficult to see justifiable or mitigating circumstances for women who use violence than for men who commit the same violent act. For example, it has been my experience that women are likely to be charged with premeditated murder after having killed their batterer. Men who batter their victims to death are likely to be charged with committing manslaughter in a heat of passion.

Given this sex-biased attitude, it is important for the forensic psychologist to meet appropriate professional standards. This is especially critical for the feminist psychotherapist, so that her credibility as a psychologist is not diminished by her political views, should they become known and challenged in the courtroom. My experience is that each attorney wants to win and will use any information that can be obtained to try to shake the expert's credibility. Questions trying to portray me as too man-hating and biased because I am a feminist are a common ploy. The American Psychological Association entered an *amicus* brief in a Florida case (State *v*. Hawthorne) to support my own methodology as being appropriate in the sufficiently well-developed field of study of the psychology of the battered woman. Brodsky (1977) suggests minimizing the impact of difficult questions by giving brief and unemotional responses. I find that by giving a definition of who a feminist is quickly takes the punch out of such courtroom tactics. The definition I use states that a feminist is someone who believes in equality for women in economic, political, and social areas and who takes some kind of action to work toward such equality. I also dress in regulation courtroom attire, usually a business suit or dress. Most important, however, is the ability to appear unruffled, knowledgeable, confident, and professional.

PREPARATION FOR TESTIMONY

The responsibility of giving professional opinions based upon reasonable judgment makes it imperative that the forensic psychologist be well prepared, know all the relevant details, and be able to defend such judgments with appropriate psychological theories and practice. Psychometric testing and behavioral assessment augment the standard clinical interview. I attempt to corroborate my professional opinion in battered woman self-defense cases with other factual evidence, such as reading police reports, witness statements, defendant's statements, autopsy findings, descriptions of physical evidence, previous medical and psychological records, and preliminary hearing or grand jury testimony, when available.

A behavioral assessment of the client is conducted, with the assistance of my associates, using the questionnaire format developed for my NIMH-funded research project (Walker, 1984). We spend approximately 30 hours in face-to-face interviewing and reading of documents.

If other mental health professionals also are scheduled to do an evaluation or testify, it is important for us all to discuss our findings prior to giving testimony. My associates and I also spend valuable time assisting the attorneys in trial preparation. Since I travel all over the country, they educate me in the customs of their courtroom, while I provide educational material about battered women. The feminist approach is less threatening to even the most chauvinistic defense attorneys when it is implicit in providing a defense for their client.

If appropriate, I also will assist in preparing a client to testify by trying to help her feel more comfortable in the court. Taking an optimistic and nonthreatening attitude while providing the client with information about what to expect helps demystify the process for her. Most of the women with whom I work have never been in criminal court before, and so a process of desensitization is most helpful. It is important to provide support so that the defendant can explain her story in believable terms. Battered women have the expectation that they will not be heard, so they often minimize, deny, or simply omit relevant facts essential to their cases. The male-dominated courtroom atmosphere also seems to render women less verbal. These problems, together with the effects of traditional socialization that teaches women that what we have to say isn't that important, make special preparation for women's testimony advisable.

Stating psychological theories and conclusions in an understandable manner is the way the psychologist expert witness educates the jury. While technically the expert is said to be a neutral witness for the court, that is not usually possible, given the adversarial nature of the criminal or civil trial. In self-defense cases, I first complete the forensic evaluation, to determine whether or not the cumulative effects of abuse impacted upon the defendant's behavior. The decision to testify at a trial is made after the evaluation findings are discussed with the attorneys. Testimony centers around presenting a general theory of violence against women, a description of the typical behavioral characteristics of battered women and batterers, and, finally, findings specific to the defendant that match the theory. If the findings do not match the general theory, then I usually do not testify. The defense attorney and I work together to choose the best questions to ask on direct examination, in order to elicit this information.

Using the psychological construct of learned helplessness as applied to battered women (Walker, 1979) allows me to organize my evaluation findings to demonstrate that things which happen to women in child-hood and in a violent relationship influence the behavior for which they are being held accountable. Most women who are repeatedly violated learn that they cannot control their own victimization; thus, they lack free will. Psychologically, they learn to develop survival skills that do not include the ability to terminate a battering relationship. Since the threat of leaving or the actual separation is the time when the batterer becomes most likely to kill her or the children, her perception of an inability to escape a life-threatening attack without using deadly force herself is usually accurate. When a battered woman kills her attacker, she is usually desperate, focusing upon a survival instinct in order to keep herself and perhaps her children alive.

Helping the courts to understand the nature of the extreme amount of violence in a battering relationship is an important task of the expert witness in a self-defense case. Most people believe that the truth lies somewhere between two different stories about a fight. Judges and ju-rors must be convinced that the woman's version is usually the most accurate picture available, and even so, her description of the beatings is probably a minimized version of its true horror. In cases where the abuser has survived and also testifies, his version is more likely to be filled with rationalizations for why he had to beat her or with outright lies of denial.

Explanations for why women stay in such horrible marriages, why they don't call the police or follow through with prosecutions, and how specific traumatic events affect individual women are most useful in both criminal and civil cases involving battered women. I explain how rein-forcement techniques in the social learning framework of the cycle the-ory of violence keep the woman hoping he'll change enough to become the loving man she wants and to make the relationship violence free (Walker, 1979, 1984).

DISTINGUISHING BETWEEN INSANITY AND SELF-DEFENSE

Historically, women who behave in antisocial ways are labeled crazy and are punished by confinement to mental institutions rather than jail (Ches-ler, 1972). This may not be an advantage to women in criminal cases. At a recent Colorado American Civil Liberties Union conference, Colorado

Supreme Court Judge Jean Dubofsky cited data she has collected illustrating the differential treatment of women and men offenders. She said, "Women are less likely to be arrested than men and more likely to be released into the custody of a relative or friend rather than on their own recognizance. Women, while less often held, are more often treated harshly. Women have a greater chance of facing solitary confinement than men and female juvenile offenders fail to receive the counseling and placement in work assignments afforded their male counterparts" (Hickman, 1983).

The rise in punishment by the criminal justice system seems to correlate with the rise in women's demands for equality (Jones, 1980). It sometimes seems as though feminists are being encouraged to retreat by men who wish to show us that equality has its price. Approximating an androgynous ideal for human behavior may include equal punishment as a response to crime for both sexes. Despite Justice Dubofsky's grim data, it is apparent that the criminal justice system may have more benefits for women offenders than the mental health system. There is a set of procedural rules in prison programs that mental hospitals lack, resulting in longer confinement times for women in state hospitals. Women can attend school and job-training programs while in prison, inadequate as they may be, but not usually when in hospitals. They are more likely to receive counseling when they are assigned to community-based halfway houses of correction, as opposed to those run by mental health departments. In either place, however, women are vulnerable to being physically and sexually assaulted again, this time by their wardens, guards, staff, or other inmates (Jones, 1980).

Thus, deciding whether or not to use a plea of not guilty by reason of insanity or diminished capacity, as a defense to criminal charges, needs careful consideration. For many women, killing their abuser may be thought to be a mentally and physically healthy act, even though they were able to act to protect themselves only after the cumulative effects of the abuse caused them to have a break with reality. The *DSM III* (A.P.A., 1980) diagnostic categories of Post Traumatic Stress Disorder, Chronic or Delayed Type; Brief Reactive Psychosis; Depression; and Dissociative Disorders are most useful in these cases.

Most of the 60 trauma victims I've evaluated suffered from some memory loss after they committed a violent act in self-defense. Many also confuse time in the past, resulting in a telescoping and merging of violent acts as they report them immediately following the killing. Using the *DSM III* explanation and criteria for Psychogenic Amnesia explains the psychological reasons for the memory loss and distortions. It helps convince juries that women are not just manipulating or malingering to get out of trouble. My experience has demonstrated that it is therapeutic for many of the women to understand the diagnostic categories, for their own ability to cope with what they have done. Most of them do accept the fact that they resorted to violent behavior, only because they were pushed beyond their breaking point.

Nonetheless, the final decision for whether or not the facts of the incident suggest legal insanity or self-defense (in some states both defenses can be asserted simultaneously) is one that needs to be decided by the attorney, psychologist, and woman together. Legal strategy often weighs the decision in a particular way. Using a special interpretation of the MMPI that compares defendants to other battered women has been a helpful tool in making the decision (Rosewater, 1982). Despite the need to keep the larger feminist picture in perspective, an individual woman's needs always must be the primary focus. Thus, the feminist therapist must be careful to allow the woman to participate fully in making the choice, after helping her to understand all of the alternatives.

OTHER AREAS FOR EXPERT WITNESS TESTIMONY

There is potential for the feminist perspective to be heard in court proceedings other than self-defense cases. Recently I have been involved in interpreting rape-trauma syndrome effects to the court. I have been asked to testify as to the psychological damages suffered by women who were sexually assaulted. Such testimony assists the jury in putting a dollar value on her psychological trauma. In another case, the prosecutor used my testimony describing the rape victim's psychological trauma as evidence of aggravating circumstances, with the result that the judge used his rights under the law to double the convicted assailant's jail sentence. Several states have admitted a psychologist's testimony as to the presence of rape-trauma syndrome in victims to rebut a defendant's assertion that the victim consented to have sexual intercourse with him. This testimony has been found to be most helpful in gaining convictions in acquaintance or date rapes.

The state attorney general's office can hire psychologists to testify to trauma suffered by victims who have been sexually assaulted by licensed professionals. I testified at one such administrative hearing where the medical examining board was deliberating about removing a doctor's license to practice. It was important to explain to the board that even fondling without genital penetration can and did have serious psychological repercussions for the victims. Providing copies of the latest literature in the field can boost the psychologist's credibility and support the primary role, which is to educate the court.

In domestic violence cases, psychologists can assist attorneys in filing for restraining orders and can assist prosecutors in gaining assault convictions against men who batter women (Patterson, 1979). Battered women may commit other criminal offenses under duress, such as forgery, burglary, assault, arson, and drug offenses. Interviews with women in prison indicate that they usually committed these acts as a way to meet their batterer's demands and avoid another beating (Walker, 1981).

Not all cases result in actually providing expert witness testimony in a trial or sentencing hearing. Some prosecutors have agreed to negotiate a plea or even dismiss charges, once they have read a psychologist's report. Judges may make their decisions upon reading the report rather than listening to testimony, especially if they have appointed the psychologist to make the evaluation. I also have been hired by attorneys, on behalf of their clients, to read and interpret other psychological reports to them and assist in developing effective courtroom strategy for helping their client's position. Occasionally I have been hired to apply psychological principles to creating an effective courtroom atmosphere for presenting a case in the most favorable setting. This can include what clothes to wear, where to sit, how to deliver an effective argument, what materials to carry into the courtroom, and how to select jurors.

Courts are relying more and more on psychological evaluation and testimony for help in making decisions about children's futures. Feminist psychologists can add an important perspective when child custody disputes are decided. This is most critical when a lesbian mother must defend her ability to parent her children. It is also important in determining both custody and visitation in domestic violence cases. The move toward presumption of joint custody in some states represents a step backward from the hard-won women's rights to parent their children. Most women cannot negotiate from a position of equality with men, which often forces the child to try to equalize such power differences.

Psychological evaluation and treatment planning from a feminist perspective is also useful in child dependency, neglect, and delinquency hearings. Children who have been psychologically neglected and physically and sexually assaulted need the special sensitivity that feminist psychology brings to developing an evaluation and treatment plan for them.

In Colorado, a joint task force of attorneys and psychologists appointed by the Colorado Women's Bar Association and Colorado Women's Psychology Association is studying the issues involved in sexual assault of children and is preparing a report of its findings to be presented to its respective organizations. There is also a coalition, of which I am a member, that prepared evidence for use in a possible class-action law suit against the Denver Police Department for failure to protect battered women by not having promulgated rules and regulations for enforcing an arrest policy as an alternative to the ineffective mediation of family disputes currently in effect. Instead, the new Denver mayor has negotiated a settlement that is to everyone's satisfaction. Thus, feminist therapists also can engage in community advocacy issues. Actually, we can be of assistance in most legal proceedings where someone's state of mind is at issue.

CONCLUSION

The feminist therapist who chooses to work within the court system needs to be prepared to deal with sexist legal values and practices. Our sensitivity to separating individual from societal issues can assist the courts in keeping sexist issues from clouding the individual legal issues in question. Since sexist courts often hold racist and homophobic views as well, the feminist forensic psychologist often must sort out various forms of discrimination.

This means it will be necessary to rethink some cherished ideals, like expecting equal justice for all. I have concentrated on describing some of the difficult areas I've experienced when working within the criminal justice system. Undoubtedly there are many others. Translating the psychology of women into the general field of forensic psychology represents a challenge that, if met, can satisfy the feminist therapist's need to advocate for social change as well as use psychotherapy skills to help individual clients learn to live more effectively.

REFERENCES

American Psychiatric Association. (1980). Diagnostic and statistical manual of mental disorders (3rd ed.) (DSM. III). Washington, DC: Author.

Berk, R. A., Berk, S. F., Loeske, D. R., & Rauma, D. (1983). Mutual combat and other family violence myths. In D. Finkelhor, R. Gelles, G. Hotaling, & M. Straus (Eds.), *The dark side of families*. Beverley Hills: Sage.

Brodsky, S. L. (1977). The mental health professional on the witness stand: A survival guide. In B. D. Sales (Ed.), *Psychology in the legal process*. New York: Spectrum.

Broverman, I., Broverman, D., Clarkson, F., Rosencrantz, P., & Vogel, S. (1970). Sex-role stereotypes and clinical judgments of mental health. *Journal of Consulting and Clinical Psychology, 34* 1–7.

Chesler, P. (1972). *Women and madness*. New York: Doubleday.

Hickman, F. (1983). With liberty and justice for women: An ACLU conference on women and the law. *Colorado Civil Liberties, 30*(3), 3.

Jones, A. (1980). *Women who kill*. New York: Doubleday.

Patterson, E. J. (1979). How the legal system responds to battered women. In D. Moore (Ed.), *Battered women*. Beverly Hills: Sage Publications.

Rosewater, L. B. (1982). An MMPI profile for battered women. Doctoral dissertation for Union Graduate School, Cincinnati, OH.

Schneider, E. (1980). Equal rights to trial for women: Sex bias in the law of self-defense. *Harvard Civil Rights–Civil Liberties Law Review, 15*(3), 623–647.

Straus, M., Gelles, R., & Steinmetz, S. (1980). *Behind closed doors: Violence in America*. New York: Doubleday.

Walker, L. E. (1979). *The battered woman*. New York: Harper & Row.

Walker, L. E. (1981). *Final Report: The battered woman syndrome study*. NIMH grant #R01MH30147. Washington, DC: National Institute of Mental Health.

Walker, L. E. (1984). *The battered woman syndrome*. New York: Springer.

■ six

FEMINIST ETHICS

LAURA BROWN AND HANNAH LERMAN, Editors

Concern with ethics has implicitly influenced the development of feminist therapy since its beginnings. Feminist therapists also have influenced therapy by expanding the definition of ethics to include, for example, the practice of discrimination against women.

Although some feminist therapists have participated in the promulgation of ethics statements within different mental health professions, in this volume many assumptions are questioned. It is apparent that some of the boundaries and distinctions fostered by standard ethical codes reflect and reinforce patriarchal reality and do not necessarily represent feminist principles. With the realization that both our chosen therapy modalities and our beliefs about what occurs in therapy create new questions and special concerns, feminist therapy has begun the slow and complex process of developing a code of ethics that reflects the concerns of women.

The two chapters in this part speak to two broader ethical issues that arise in feminist practice. The authors do not offer solutions that all feminist therapists would agree with, nor does either author assume that to be her task. Often the issues discussed in these chapters raise more questions than they answer. These chapters, however, serve to open discussion and discourse on some ethical concerns that have always been present in feminist therapy.

Joan Saks Berman addresses herself to the issue of overlapping relationships in feminist therapy. She examines the multiple possibilities for the ethical conduct of what traditionally have been described as "dual" relationships, and the special considerations that arise for feminist therapists in taking on overlapping roles. Using the situation of the small rural community as her starting point, she asks us to reconsider our assumptions about the kinds and degrees of boundaries we create between our own lives and those of the people we work with.

Laura Brown discusses the emotionally charged issue of the business aspects of feminist therapy. She raises the question for feminist therapists of how they can actively integrate their feminist beliefs into the ways they do business. In particular, she examines the difficult balancing act that the feminist private practitioner must do when attempting to achieve both a personally satisfactory lifestyle and an ethically satisfactory style of doing business.

We shrink from any posture of rigidity or "rightness." These chapters are offered in the feminist spirit of criticism/self-criticism that assumes that the opening up of such difficult issues can result in the development of new ways of seeing, doing, and relating that are more truly woman centered.

28
Ethical Feminist Perspectives on Dual Relationships with Clients[1]

JOAN R. SAKS BERMAN

Feminist therapy begins with an inherently ethical stance in that it raises questions about the sexist biases of the field of psychology, particularly about the quality and practice of traditional psychotherapy. Professional standards of conduct, however, can conflict with, or may not be complete enough to include, the specific goals, principles, and strategies of feminist therapy.

Psychologists are expected to adhere to the A.P.A. Ethical Principles of Psychologists (1981), which discourage working therapeutically with someone with whom one may have another relationship, such as employee, student, supervisee, and so forth. It also prohibits having sexual relationships with clients. I, as a feminist, can find no fault with prohibitions against sexual intimacies with clients, or against

1. The author wishes to thank Elaine Sachnoff, Jill Bellinson, Laura Brown, Hannah Lerman, Alice Simmerman, and the others who took the time to read earlier versions of this chapter and offer their comments and suggestions.

treating individuals who are under one's authority in an employment situation. Abuses of this kind have been brought to public attention largely through the efforts of feminists. I want to focus here on other kinds of possible dual relationships that also generally are discouraged. Perhaps it would be more accurate to consider them as *overlapping relationships*.

Any therapy offered on a fee-for-service basis is essentially an over-lapping relationship, whether acknowledged as such or not, in that it is both a business arrangement and a relationship on a personal level. It is likely, too, that the overlap of therapy with other relationships is proba-bly more prevalent than is commonly thought, or, as Roll and Millen (1981) stated, "the injunction against seeing friends and acquaintances in therapy has been almost universally accepted and almost as universally violated." Also, the instance where a therapist agrees to barter for an exchange of services in place of cash payment has been judged to be unacceptable by the A.P.A. Ethics Committee unless an objectively priced product is part of this exchange (Hall & Hare-Mustin, 1983). Barter, while problematic in many instances, has been accepted among feminist therapists as an alternative mode of exchange. It accentuates the overlapping relationship issue that is already present in all therapy for hire.

Roll and Millen (1981) recommend avoiding overlapping relation-ships to the extent that they can be avoided. They recognize, however, that in small towns, and for those therapists who have a contract to do therapy for a subcommunity (e.g., on a university campus or at an in-house clinic at a large industrial plant), such overlap will be difficult to avoid. They also consider emergency situations to be valid exceptions. Outside of the mentioned instances, however, they say that "the likeli-hood is that the therapist's own pathological needs for power, affection, or control are determining factors in the decision" to maintain dual relationships (p. 182).

While the A.P.A. Ethical Principles' stand on dual relationships attempts to diminish the abuse of power in the therapy relationship, the detachment with which it does so seems, at the same time, to be perpetu-ating the artificial aspect of the relationship. Inherent in it is the model, derived from medicine and psychoanalysis, of the "Total Professional," whose identity is narrowly defined by his work and who presents himself as ostensibly value free so that the patient's interaction with him becomes the basis for the interpretation of the transference.[2] His public reputation is based on his professional relationships and work, and patients are referred to him by physicians and other professionals.

The Total Professional as described remains in the "ivory tower" of his consulting room. If he ventures forth into community activity, it is from the perspective of noblesse oblige, and he speaks to groups such as the P.T.A., men's clubs, women's clubs, church groups, and the like, representing the profession to the public, still with the mask of value-free objectivity.

In contrast to this image, Kozol (1975), in his critique of education, a related profession contended that

> Teachers never can be non-political or neutral. They are political when they say: "Good morning." They are political when they sneeze, break out in tears or roar with laughter. Gide said: "Style is character." In the classroom, life-style is the heart of education. . . . What the teacher "teaches" is by no means chiefly in the words he [sic] speaks. It is at least part in what he *is*, in what he *does*, in what he seems to *wish to be*. The secret curriculum is the teacher's own lived values and convictions, in the lineaments of his expression and in the biography of passion or self-exile which is written in his eye. [p. 101]

Can we speak differently about a psychotherapist?

Overlapping relationships might be considered to be defined on a continuum, from those in which there is a pre-existing emotional intimacy that might lead to a new kind of emotional relationship, to those in which the pre-existing relationship is task-oriented (e.g., co-workers) and the therapy relationship requires a kind of shifting of gears to a different level.

Let us consider some situations. A psychologist has been involved in feminist and other political activities since the sixties. There is considerable overlap between her social relationships and her political relationships, as one might expect from a well-integrated identity, and she applies her political analysis to her professional work. If her sisters in the struggle seek to engage her professional services because they see

2. Throughout this paper, the male pronoun is used generically when referring to traditional psychologists and psychotherapists. The female pronoun is used generically when referring to feminist therapists and their clients.

her as someone they can trust because she shares their values and as someone who knows about the activities and relationships that are important to them, must she refuse to enter a professional relationship with them, knowing that there are few others who meet the clients' criteria? If a communal household seeks her consultation for a group problem, or an activist couple asks her to mediate their dissolving relationship because they respect her grasp of the personal as political, must she refuse because she was in a radical therapist collective with some of them and feminist consciousness-raising group with others?

What if our feminist therapist lives and works in a small town in a remote area? The nearest psychological services outside of the agency in which she works are 80 miles in any direction. The feminist therapist works at a public hospital that charges no fees for eligible clients, and the group of eligible clients includes most of the 300 employees of the hospital. These 300 employees are also the people with whom she is most likely to have her social relationships. The other members of the mental health department staff include a male psychiatrist, traditionally trained and medically oriented, and three paraprofessionals belonging to the ethnic group indigenous to the area. Given this situation, suppose one of the professional employees makes an appointment because she needs to talk to someone about her relationship with her lesbian lover. Should our feminist therapist refuse to provide her with a service that she is legally entitled to, because, since they are both feminists, and have discovered they have acquaintances in common in other cities, they have become friends in a town that doesn't acknowledge the existence of feminists, much less lesbians? Should she likewise refuse to see the young nurse, recently arrived from school in a large city, whose experience of culture shock is exacerbated by the need to return to the closet because of the homophobia of the other young men in the area? What about an employee's wife, who is in the therapist's exercise class and whom she sees at Saturday night parties, who became upset because the ongoing conflict with her mother worsened to the point where she struck her?

The clients in these examples, although in some ways limited in their choices, are making an informed choice of therapist. They have chosen someone whom they feel they can trust not to mess them up with psychiatric jargon and mystification, who will not diagnose their politics as pathology, and who will, they feel, maintain their confidentiality. Is this choice then to be denied because of the ethical principle, or can the potential difficulties be negotiated as part of the therapeutic contract?

In my present small-town situation, my circumstances are such that it is quite likely that I will bump into people who have come to see me for therapy and they will be quite friendly and not try to hide the fact that they know me. They will say hello to me in the bank or the post office or at community events, and introduce me to their families. I've even been invited to a Tupperware party by a client. Although for many there is a concern about privacy when they come to see me in my office, because they are likely to have relatives who work in the hospital and rumors grow like weeds, it doesn't seem to extend to the idea of knowing me as a person. This is in contrast to when I lived in a big city, where I would meet one of my clients at a party or in some other social context and they weren't even sure they wanted to talk to me. Somehow, by doing that, they felt they would be giving it away that they knew me in a professional sense (as if psychologists didn't have any other kind of acquaintances). The difference may be in the degree of openness one finds when there is a greater or lesser sense of community or when there are cultural differences or urban, rural, or regional differences. Perhaps I should also state that my examples of overlapping relationships have not, with a few exceptions, included long-term, high-intensity therapeutic contacts. Nevertheless, once again I come to the thought that the sense of community or common values may be an important characteristic. Those clients whom I knew previously from social and/or political activities did not tend to avoid me in public places once therapy began.

As a therapist, I continue to have a heightened sense of confidentiality when I meet clients in public and must remain aware of the power I have because of what I know. It is necessary for me to be aware always of what the source is of what I know and to censor what I say to people in public, whether clients or others. A client often is willing to reveal considerable personal information in public, which is, of course, her privilege, but it is not mine to decide for her.

Roll and Millen (1981) recommend that one be prepared to lose the extratherapeutic friendship. They further point out that, when the role of therapist conflicts with the other role, we have more responsibility toward someone we decide to treat than toward someone who is an acquaintance or friend, and that we must respect the vulnerable role in which a friend-as-patient is placed.

The therapist probably needs, first of all, to be aware of her own comfort or discomfort with the potential relationship. One feminist therapist I know routinely refuses to take on as clients other feminist therapists or those *she* identifies as valued friends, but on occasion has seen her students as clients. She has said that she usually prefers to keep them as friends, which to her means a two-way relationship in which she can call on them for things for herself, which she feels a therapist would not be able to do.

My own feelings on the matter are somewhat different from those of my colleague. If someone I know socially or from shared political activity seeks my services as a therapist, I tend to interpret their choice as an affirmation that I have achieved some success in my goal of attaining integration in my personal, political, and professional development. For my part, the decision to enter into such an arrangement, an extension of a previously existing relationship, is based on a faith in others, or perhaps it is better stated as a reciprocity of respect. Especially in the case of those who are known through political activity, there is a basic unity of shared values that governs our behavior toward one another. For some, the political values are more important in choice of therapist than friendship.

I believe that we must try not to see ourselves as separate from or better than other people because of our education and status, but rather recognize that we are one with them. In this respect, the way we relate to our clients and our friends is very much the same. Perhaps this is another way of stating that we attempt to equalize the power in the relationship. When working with clients whom we did not know previously, we often have to educate them to this idea. They are accustomed to thinking of the professional as an authority, by definition better than they, and as the holder of the power; and they assume a learned, submissive role. On the other hand, those who come with a pre-existing relationship are more likely to come as equals.

Empathy is perhaps even more important than power in therapy and is the critical element of any close relationship. Where there are overlapping relationships involved in therapy, one must be sensitive to the needs of the individual person, both as a client and a friend. Rather than approaching the situation with a predetermined set of rules, we need to be open to letting the client set the rules and the terms of the contract, subject, of course, to the limits of our own comfort. We also must be ready, when therapy is terminated, to resume a friendship on its usual terms. At that point, we can stop monitoring self-disclosure and share our personal feelings more openly.

During the process of writing this paper, I spoke to a former client, the employee's wife mentioned previously, about how she saw the experience of therapy when there is an overlapping relationship. As I have mentioned, she had entered therapy to deal with an ongoing conflict with her mother. At the beginning of therapy there was no prior discussion of the implications of the overlapping relationship. She began her response to my post-therapy questions by stating that she had not considered entering therapy before because the psychiatrists who had been on the staff during the eight or nine years previous were all "weird" in their idiosyncratic ways. Furthermore, although she is not actively a feminist, she felt that she needed a woman to talk to because a man wouldn't understand this kind of problem. She said that she had thought about how it would be when we met in social situations but decided that she wouldn't be uncomfortable, because she talks to her friends about her concerns, anyway, and she recognized that there was no anonymity in our small town. She recalled that in the therapy sessions we would sometimes "chat" about other things of mutual interest, as well as common experiences (appropriate self-disclosure), and that her feeling of being "more equal" helped her to feel more comfortable. I remarked that, while some people feel more comfortable talking about their problem with someone they know, others purposely seek out a professional stranger. She thought that the nature of the problem was important. For example, she said, if the problem were one of peeking into windows or having sex with small boys, problems that would be associated more with shame, that perhaps a "white-coat approach" would be more comfortable.

There is obviously some discrimination on the part of the potential client as to whether she feels more comfortable working with a stranger (with or without white coat) or someone she knows. The therapist also may discriminate in her decisions regarding who to treat, based upon her knowledge of the potential client's ego strength and self-differentiation, as well as the therapist's own needs for personal space and distance. While my own approach to therapy is not one that relies heavily on diagnostic labels, I think it is probably more difficult to work in an overlapping relationship with clients who would be seriously enough disordered to be diagnosed as schizoid, narcissistic, or a borderline disorder.

While considering the positive possibilities of overlapping relationships, feminist therapists also must guard against misusing those relationships. The ability to resist the pull to a destructive or exploitative relationship is difficult but important if we are to avoid being the victims or perpetrators of unprincipled trashing, which has occurred too often in the women's movement in the guise of sisterhood. It is imperative, as a feminist, not to ignore the danger of exploiting a client, which our critical analysis has said occurs all too frequently. One must guard against this by knowing oneself, by seeking consultation when appropriate, and by being involved in a supportive network that allows for both criticism and self-criticism. This cannot be emphasized enough!

Furthermore, beyond the use of appropriate self-disclosure as a therapeutic technique, in an overlapping relationship the client is likely to be more aware of the therapist's personal and social relationships, and the therapist must be prepared to respond to scrutiny and challenge with openness. Temerlin and Temerlin (1982) referred in a recent study to psychotherapy cults as iatrogenic perversions. They found that the cult-creating therapists of the five groups they studied were "charismatic, authoritarian, and dominating men with narcissistic, grandiose features and a strong tendency to paranoia, characteristics typical of leaders of religious cults" (p. 132). These therapists, who treated their friends, students, lovers, relatives, employees, and colleagues, did not maintain "clean, fee-for-service relationships." They controlled their patients' personal lives with dictatorial authority, regarding the spouse who was not in therapy as a threat to group solidarity. Other therapy and therapists were viewed with hostility and condescension, as if the leader's own conception of personality and psychotherapy was the only valid one. This phenomenon represents a potential danger for a therapist who does not look inward or receive feedback about her unconventional behavior.

The described characteristics of psychotherapy cults are clearly incompatible with the values and strategies of feminist therapy. Among other things, they are contrary to ideas about the equalization of power, flexibility in the use of innovative techniques, openness of variations in lifestyle, and encouragement of autonomy of the client.

Some therapists work extensively with transference with their clients. In this case, an overlapping relationship may be too confusing, perhaps more for the client than for the therapist. In a long-term therapeutic relationship in which transference issues become salient, it may become difficult for either the client or the therapist to separate out which relationship issues belong to the therapy interaction and which belong to the social interaction. This becomes even more complicated when the client is testing the relationship and exploring issues of trust.

In the opinion of Roll and Millen (1981), "the transference relationship is real and the 'real' relationship is real." Treating all interactions as transference will negate the reality of the patient's observations, while avoiding dealing with transference runs the risk of confusing the real, that is, nontransference, relationship.

In an overlapping relationship, one risks sabotaging therapy by failing to confront a client out of fear of ruining the friendship, or by denying or glossing over strongly negative information in the service of the friendship. This is a danger, however, that exists in therapy without overlapping relationships as well, whenever the therapist does not want to hear certain kinds of information. We know that, all too often, professionals similarly have denied negative information, for example, by refusing to acknowledge the validity of a woman's claim that she is a victim of incest. Furthermore, in individual therapy, with clients with whom there is no overlapping relationship, when the therapist is involved for too long, she runs the risk of losing her objectivity. If she sees the same client in group therapy, especially when aided by a cotherapist, she is likely to become aware of and observe different things.

In this chapter, I have dealt with some of the problems surrounding the controversial issue of overlapping relationships between therapists and clients. As feminist therapists, we may find that we need to define our ethical standards in a different way from traditional practitioners of psychotherapy, to the extent that our theory, and therefore our practice, diverges from that which is conventional and established. In making our theoretical and political values explicit, including our intention of equalizing power in the therapeutic relationship and our attempts to diminish alienation and resist oppression, we may attract as clients women who already know us and who are making a choice as informed consumers.

If our community is limited by geographical isolation or by definition as a specific subcommunity, we are more likely to need a way of dealing with overlapping relationships. We need to be exquisitely aware of the potential problems, including our own misuse of power, breach of confidentiality, possible loss of the pre-existing relationship, difficulties in transference and limerance (Tennov, 1979), and loss of privacy for the therapist. At the same time, it perhaps is not necessary to forego, in every case, the possible therapeutic benefits of an overlapping relationship. We also must be aware that we may engender criticism from our colleagues and must judge the consequences of doing so.

In each case of an overlapping relationship, we are defining our role at some place on a continuum that extends from intimate helping friend to distant professional stranger, and this must be redefined with each client. In order to do so effectively, we must make use of peer consultation and supervision whenever possible and be open to considering constructive criticism seriously. We must be involved actively in the continuing process of clarifying our own values as therapists and feminists and our own needs and limits regarding role differentiation and ego-integration, as well as those of our clients.

In this short discussion, I feel that I have only touched on the surface of the issue, without delving into the essence of the process. I have written about role differentiation and setting limits, which now seems in some way contradictory to my earlier remarks about a well-integrated identity. I think that perhaps it is a dialectical relationship, in which the separate aspects are constantly in juxtaposition, in a constantly changing balance. Once more, I find myself coming back to my definition of a feminist therapist, which is that she is simultaneously a healer, a social change agent, and a taker of risks. She actively involves herself in the world around her. It is perhaps in this context that we must view the ethics of overlapping relationships and work together to resolve the dilemma that is raised.

REFERENCES

American Psychological Association (1981). Ethical principles of psychologists. *American Psychologist, 36*, 633–638.

Hall, J. E., & Hare-Mustin, R. T. (1983). Sanctions and the diversity of ethical complaints against psychologists. *American Psychologist, 38*, 714–729.

Kozol, J. (1975). *The night is dark and I am far from home*. Boston: Houghton Mifflin.

Roll, S., & Millen, L. (1981). A guide to violating an injunction in psychotherapy: On seeing acquaintances as patients. *Psychotherapy: Theory, Research and Practice, 18*, 179–187.

Temerlin, M. K., & Temerlin, J. W. (1982). Psychotherapy cults: An iatrogenic perversion. *Psychotherapy: Theory, Research and Practice, 19*, 131–141.

Tennov, D. (1979). *Love and limerance*. New York: Stein & Day.

■ 29

Ethics and Business Practice in Feminist Therapy[1]

LAURA BROWN

I have often heard that it is a difficult contradiction for a businesswoman to pursue a feminist political stance in her work. This statement has always seemed odd to me, for a feminist therapist in private practice is a businesswoman. The striking difference between this businesswoman and others is that the coin in which she trades is the pain of women's lives in the patriarchy. Our position as healers has been a part of our reluctance, as a profession, to clarify our rights and responsibilities as feminist businesswomen.

Some early feminist writers questioned whether feminist therapists should charge for services that ought to flow freely from the context of good social networks (Gearhart, 1979; Mander & Rush, 1974).[2] It has

---

1. My thinking on this topic has been stimulated by my encounters with Evie Litwok of Women's Resources Distribution Company, who was the first feminist psychologist I encountered who spoke of the importance of women's economic autonomy. Miriam Vogel, who is my partner in both life and work, demonstrates to me by her daily example how to run a business by feminist principles. Her loving support creates the environment in which I can think and write.
2. I am indebted to Joan Saks Berman for identifying the written sources of this phenomenon.

297

only been more recently that we feminist therapists have become publicly comfortable saying that our work goes beyond friendship and that we are indeed practitioners of a healing art that is neither intuitive nor naturally present in all women. The questions and guilt of earlier years do linger in the philosophical background, leading to some unclear thinking about how to do business as a feminist therapist.

Our feminist ethics can be expressed very radically, powerfully, and subtly by our business practices. After all, the values of patriarchal culture are quite apparent in the ways that nonfeminist therapists work. The diplomas hanging on the wall to remind the client who the "real expert" is, the inflexibly high fees, the use of "doctor" when referring to the therapist, the sexist and pejorative system of diagnostic nomenclature, all have been targets of earlier feminist critiques of psychotherapy (Chesler, 1972; Mander & Rush, 1974).

It is particularly important to integrate ethics into our practice because feminist therapy remains more a philosophical system than a prescription of technique. Ethical issues must loom large when our conscious choices as feminist therapists reflect our own hard-won ethical stance. Because the ethics of feminism are developmental and multi-layered, there is no one clearly defined feminist ethic. There is, instead, a way of seeing that holds that many perspectives on one event all can describe reality. This chapter will illustrate that vision by being a step in the developmental process rather than a promulgation of unassailable rules of conduct.

I immediately encountered a contradiction when I began this chapter. When I began to reread the ethics casebook of the American Psychological Association, I was re-minded (Daly, 1978)—as in "to come again to my mind and intellect"—that patriarchal institutions imbue even their best efforts with values that, as a feminist, I will find objectionable. While I subscribe, in practice, to the provisions of the A.P.A. ethical code,[3] I find within it many philosophical points of departure. The most significant such point lies in the description, in that code, of the importance of the psychologist's awareness of and compliance with the values and standards of the community.

Feminists are, and must be, "disloyal to civilization" (Rich, 1979). We are very aware of patriarchal standards and values. Our perspective

---

3. For example, the principles against sexual contact between therapist and client were placed in the A.P.A. ethics code by the long efforts of feminist psychologists within the structure of the A.P.A.

as the universal phenomenological "Other" (Daly, 1978) allows us adequate distance from which to observe those rules, and our oppression as women requires that we know that code well to survive. But our feminist community of the heart has been redefined as the community of womankind. Our values and standards are often a repudiation of the devaluation of women we see in the culture around us.

What constitutes the ethics of a feminist? Most centrally, feminism implies equality of power and value among all people, a reality where gender, race, class, age, able-bodiedness and affectional/sexual preference are not salient variables in the assessment of human worth. A feminist values equally the lives and work of all women, regardless of privilege accruing to race, class, education, or title. A feminist values her own work and competency in the light of those principles of equality, striving for her own ultimate growth rather than competing and comparing with others. A feminist is acutely aware of how power operates among and between people and uses her own power and privilege conspicuously and responsibly. She celebrates all the possibilities and realities of womankind in her life and work, honoring and acknowledging the differences of our gifts. Being a feminist means living with a radical re-vision of ourselves, saying, "What injures women injures men; what heals and advances women does so for me as well." The embrace of a feminist ethic moves us into the phenomenological space where women become "we " rather than "they."

It follows that feminist therapists will reject the task of social controller given to therapy professionals by patriarchal culture. Early feminist critics of traditional therapy often singled out this social control aspect when elucidating the destructive potentials that psychotherapy held for women when practiced without a feminist consciousness (Chesler, 1972; Weisstein, 1970).

In rejecting that social controller role, the feminist therapist finds herself re-evaluating everything from diagnosis and assessment to the structure and dynamics of the therapy session. In working to create the equal power dynamic, a feminist therapist, while often being the mirror image of the mythical "any good therapist" also may engage often in behaviors that would invite questions, if not censure, in the traditional settings where she was trained.

Creating that equal power dynamic is a paradoxical challenge. If the therapist has the power to "create" a framework of equality, if we can "allow" our clients the right to their personal wisdom and perceptions of reality, then the meta-message of that assumption also must be examined. The "creator" is in fact the more powerful person; the permission-giver is unequal to the one to whom permission is given. Feminist therapists must be aware of the power differences that are thus inherent in any therapy setting. To deny differences in power between ourselves and our clients on the grounds of shared womanhood is as naive a belief as the notion that there exists a value-free therapist. The therapist will continue to have greater privilege in the world by virtue of her training, her heightened verbal and interpersonal skills, and her income. While we cannot create absolute equality in a context where there is none, we can share our power and privilege consciously and actively. We can work toward the creation of equalitarian environments in which enhanced possibilities for the growth of equality exist. Being equalitarian means not colluding with the culture by passively ignoring the factors that can create power differences between ourselves and our clients. Thus, a feminist therapist needs to analyze the factors in both her business and therapy styles that either can bring home a message of inequality or can be reshaped into an opening to shared and equalized power.

The setting of our practice is an initial factor in communicating our equalitarian intent. Are we situated within the community we serve? Is our office located in a setting in which it is comparatively safe for women to walk? Are we accessible by public transportation and to women whose abilities to be mobile are different from our own? Does our office furniture say "Designer Showplace" so loudly that our working-class clients fear soiling the sofa? Or is our work setting more class-neutral? (I use this term to avoid implications that we should be shabby.) Do we display our credentials in such a way as to confront our clients continually with our greater educational privilege, or are they in sight without being the *pièce de résistance* of the office walls? Are we aware of the messages about class and appearance that we communicate through our mode of dress? Many of those ways of being that have been considered acceptable, "professional" behaviors can be seen, on closer analysis, to be reinforcers of patriarchal norms of inequality.

Fee scales and payment schedules are ethical issues and business concerns that always have been present in feminist therapy. Most traditional therapists have high, fixed fees. Were feminist therapists to adhere to this norm, we would become unavailable to many of the women with whom we desire to work. Some feminist therapists, however, have raised concerns that a sliding fee scale is a devaluation of women and women's work. This question is raised often in connection with concerns about the negative impact of downward mobility on women and the possibility that sliding scales are a version of the rescue effort practiced by some therapists.

Such concerns are problematic from a feminist ethical perspective. It is unclear how the work of a therapist is intrinsically more valuable than the work of a lesser-paid schoolteacher or house cleaner. Rather, it seems that a sliding fee scale serves a feminist ethical function. It confronts the assumption that the tasks of the privileged, educated classes are in fact more valuable and that women should accept the dregs from the bottom of the barrel because of their generally less secure economic position in society.

A kernel of truth does lie in the notion that some sliding scales are the reflection of a desire to rescue or of guilt over privilege. I do think that a therapist is ethically bound not to create situations that will lead her to resent her clients, as will happen inevitably when behavior is motivated by guilt. Thus, a feminist therapist must examine honestly her own sense of what is the lowest pay at which she will feel well compensated and use that as the bottom of her scale. We do not value the equality of other women when we model the process of selling our own work short. Likewise, we must not recreate structures that reinforce the idea that women and their work are less than equal because they come unequipped with an advanced degree or a large paycheck.

Some feminist therapists have chosen to resolve this ethical dilemma by offering a percentage of their services for free. I have some concerns about how such a solution affects power dynamics in therapy. *Pro bono* work may sabotage our intent to create structures that will lend themselves to equal power. Maimonides, the twelfth-century Jewish sage, contended that, when both the giver of charity and the extent of the gift are known to the recipient, then giver and receiver are both most acutely aware of their difference in status. Clients who are aware that they are our tithe to charity may have a less equal opportunity to develop the equalitarian relationship that we seek to create.

A related issue with both business and ethical overtones is that of the acceptance of barter payments for psychotherapy services. Barter creates an overlapping relationship where the therapist is working with her employee. Anecdotal evidence suggests that barter exchanges are most often a source of friction and hassle. Clients report feeling abused, therapists report feeling a loss of privacy or being ripped off. In addition, it is unclear whether or not barter is expressly forbidden by the ethics codes of many professional groups. Yet barter has a place in the question of a feminist approach to fees, and thus deserves examination.

Several patterns emerge when the stories of bad barter arrangements are analyzed. Problems seem to develop primarily when the ethical principle of striving toward equality is violated. Either the therapist accepts a barter from the client that the former neither wants nor values, or the client accepts barter terms that require a task that she feels is demeaning to her sense of self-worth or she is underpaid for. In the first case, the therapist has not honored the value of her own work or the equal importance of her feelings in the transaction. In the second, the work and feelings of the client have been devalued. In both cases, the meta-message of the barter exchange is that one of the participants in the arrangement is clearly less equal than the other.

Barter is not an ethical imperative of feminist business practice; it is, rather, one possible solution to the problem of fees. There are, however, ethical and feminist ways to do business in this fashion, guided by the intent to create situations in feminist therapy that will lend themselves to the development of an equalitarian dynamic. In barter, the recipient must be getting something she values and the giver must be providing goods or services that she feels a sense of personal worth for doing or creating. Rates of exchange need to be negotiated mutually, with respect for both client and therapist insofar as is possible.

A third business and ethical issue related to fees is the use of third-party payments for psychotherapy and the requirements of third-party payers that a formal diagnosis be given before payment will be rendered. Many, although not all, feminist therapists have objected to the use of formal diagnostic nomenclature on the grounds that it is sexist, racist, classist, and generally unreflective of women's realities. Many clients are unaware that insurance companies have this requirement and are equally unaware that a diagnosis, once given, may have long-term negative effects on how they are perceived by others.

An inequality of power exists here. The therapist has knowledge of the nomenclature and its implications, while the client does not. An ethical stance for a feminist therapist is to inform clients of the outcome of their use of insurance and to discuss the diagnosis that will be used. I believe that it is also a reflection of a feminist perspective when the therapist seeks the least pejorative diagnosis she can find. Given the inaccuracy of the diagnostic process and the medical-model bias of the *DSM-III*, this is not an avoidance of the "truth" on the part of the therapist, but rather a feminist analysis and commentary on the true usefulness and meaningfulness of the diagnostic system. It is also a feminist ethical stance to give clients the option not to use their insurance if they have concerns regarding the impact of a psychiatric diagnosis.

It is important to stress that I am not advocating a life of downward economic mobility for feminist therapists. I do not think that a therapist who uses feminist ethics as a guideline for setting fees and billing will suffer negative consequences economically. The concept of economic scarcity, conceptualized psychologically as a "stroke economy" by the Berkeley Radical Psychiatry Group (Steiner, 1976) permeates our culture so thoroughly that we often believe that we will achieve economic success only by following patriarchal rules of competitive striving. If feminist therapists examine their beliefs regarding finances and identify the sources of their fears, they more easily will allow themselves the integration of business and politics that is operationalized in the sliding fee scale and its conceptual relatives.

I am aware of how important it is that feminist therapists confront their female socialization regarding money and the doing of business, particularly when I reflect upon how uncomfortable my own words would have made me feel a decade earlier. Making money and doing business were long in the realm of things that "nice" women did not do. In a setting where financial acumen is a primary source of political power, that socialization to be "nice" has had the effect of cutting women off from power and control over their lives, in both personal and political spheres. To be both good businesswomen and ethical feminist therapists, we must learn to examine our assumptions and developmental process regarding money, business, and financial success, every bit as much as we have examined our internalized oppression on other matters. We must come to confront the subtle messages we give ourselves that we cannot deserve our good fortune when we achieve it or that, once it is achieved, we must work compulsively to avoid the joys that can come from work well done and its fiscal rewards.

What feminist therapists can do is be ethical and conscious in the practice of business as well as in the practice of therapy. When we use feminist ethics as guiding principles for our business decisions, we give ourselves permission to know about business, to empower ourselves, and thus to set the stage for the sharing of power that is at the heart of feminist therapy.

REFERENCES

Chesler, P. (1972). *Women and madness*. New York: Doubleday.

Daly, M. (1978). *Gyn/Ecology*. Boston: Beacon Press.

Gearhart, S. (1979). *The wanderground*. Watertown, MA: Persephone Press.

Mander, A. V., & Rush, A. K. (1974). *Feminism as therapy*. New York: Random House/Bookworks.

Rich, A. (1979). *On lies, secrets, and silence*. New York: W. W. Norton.

Steiner, Claude (1976). *Scripts people live*. New York: Bantam Books.

Weisstein, N. (1970). Kinder, kuche, kirk as scientific law: Psychology constructs the female. In R. Morgan (Ed.), *Sisterhood is powerful*. New York: Vintage Books.

■ seven

THE TRAINING OF FEMINIST THERAPISTS

NATALIE PORTER AND
PATRICIA SPENCER FAUNCE, Editors

The practice of feminist therapy has moved into its second decade at the same time as the training of therapists about the mental health issues of women has become an important priority. Feminist therapists must be concerned about the dissemination of the theory and practice, both to established and prospective therapists. The inclusion of feminist therapy courses and supervision at all levels of training will mark its coming of age.

Therapists with feminist concerns have increased dramatically, as witnessed by the rapid increase in enrollments in feminist psychological organizations. Feminist therapists now are represented in public and private outpatient and inpatient facilities, medical centers, and universities. They hold training positions in graduate programs, internships, and practicum sites. Never before have feminist therapists had such an opportunity to train and supervise others about the treatment of female clients.

The need to educate mental health professionals about women has been demonstrated consistently. The A.P.A. Task Force on Sex Bias and

Sex Role Stereotyping (1975) documented the complaints that therapists possessed negative expectations and values toward women, were sexist in their theoretical conceptualizations, fostered traditional sex roles in their clients, and interacted with female clients as sex objects, including having sexual relations with them. Sex biases against women (Broverman, Broverman, Clarkson, Rosenkrantz, & Vogel, 1970; Fabrikant, 1974; Tanney & Birk, 1976), sex stereotypes (Abramowitz, Abramowitz, Jackson, & Gomes, 1973; Miller, 1974; Neulinger, Stein, Schillinger, & Welkowitz, 1970), and ignorance about the psychological, physiological, and sociological concerns of women (Bingham & House, 1973; Sherman, Koufacos, & Kenworthy, 1978) have been found to pervade the mental health field.

The Task Force on Sex Bias and Sex Role Stereotyping (A.P.A., 1975) recommended that therapists be educated in an effort to improve mental health care for women. Specialized workshops, seminars, and practicum training were recommended as remedies for the effects of sex bias and stereotyping. Thirteen guidelines were delineated for therapists, including specifications that the therapy process or outcome not be constricted by gender roles and stereotypes, that therapists be aware of their own sex biases and cease using sexist language and theories, that therapists not attribute the situational and cultural factors of their female clients' problems to personality factors, and that therapists facilitate their clients' explorations of the effects of sexism on their lives (A.P.A., 1978).

Training in therapy with women, however, has been limited, available only in a few select graduate programs, through conferences, postgraduate workshops, and seminars, or through informal networks such as peer supervision of feminist therapists. Typically, the individuals receiving training in these settings represent a select group of therapists—those who recognize and are attempting to rectify their deficits in treating women. The participants are typically more sensitive and sophisticated with regard to nonsexist and feminist alternatives to traditional therapy than the average therapist. These training opportunities are an important beginning but are insufficient for improving the general treatment of women by mental health professionals. Feminist therapy supervision must move into the mainstream of therapist training, to be part of the training of all potential therapists.

The following three chapters focus on training students in graduate programs in feminist therapy. Patricia Faunce provides in Chapter 30 a conceptual framework for the integration of teaching feminist therapy with feminist pedagogy and scholarship. She argues that feminist scholarship requires the learner to relearn and redefine the world, using a women-centered paradigm. This paradigm must be reflected in feminist therapy courses through the pedagogical process as well as the course content. Faunce offers 11 principles that illustrate how a feminist therapy course can provide this synthesis. The principles are organized around four themes that serve as the foundation for integrating political, economic, and scholarly analyses: power and cooperation, resocialization and transformation, holistic subjectivity and diversity, and woman-focus.

Sharon Kahn and Gisela Theurer present in Chapter 31 an evaluation study of their course on counseling women. They conceptualize course objectives based on feminist therapy principles, including greater empathy for female clients, an understanding of mental health issues from a less gender-stereotyped perspective, and the treatment of women through developing with them a greater range of options. The article outlines an evaluation/research methodology that improves significantly on the more common strategy of collecting only attitudinal, self-report data. Instead, the authors have developed simulated counseling situations that measure changes in participants' attitudes and abilities. Finally, this research demonstrates that a course in counseling women does meet the stated objectives of increasing students' sensitivity and skills in counseling women.

Natalie Porter, in Chapter 32, provides strategies for supervising therapy trainees on feminist issues. She views the quality of the supervisor/trainee relationship as pivotal in teaching feminist therapy. The supervisor must develop a trusting, relatively equalitarian relationship with the trainee, in order to model the aims of feminist therapy and to create an unthreatening atmosphere conducive to the trainee's self-examination. Porter outlines the stages through which effective supervision often progresses and describes alternative approaches to individual supervision.

REFERENCES

Abramowitz, S. J., Abramowitz, C. V., Jackson, C., & Gomes, B. (1973). The politics of clinical judgment: What nonliberal examiners infer about women who do not stifle themselves. *Journal of Consulting and Clinical Psychology, 41,* 385–391.

American Psychological Association (1975). Report of the task force on sex bias and sex-role stereotyping in psychotherapeutic practice. *American Psychologist, 30,* 1169–1175.

American Psychological Association. Guidelines for therapy with women. (1978). *American Psychologist, 33,* 1122.

Bingham, W. C., & House, E. W. (1973). Counselors view women and work: Accuracy of information. *Vocational Guidance Quarterly, 21,* 262–268.

Broverman, I. K., Broverman, D. M., Clarkson, F., Rosenkrantz, P., & Vogel, S. R. (1970). Sex-role stereotypes and clinical judgments of mental health. *Journal of Consulting Psychology, 34,* 1–7.

Fabrikant, B. (1974). The psychotherapist and the female patient: Perceptions and change. In V. Franks & V. Burtle (Eds.), *Women in therapy.* New York: Brunner/Mazel.

Miller, D. (1974). The influence of the patient's sex on clinical judgment. *Smith College Studies in Social Work, 44,* 89–100.

Neulinger, J. Stein, M. I., Schillinger, M., & Welkowitz, J. (1970). Perceptions of the optimally integrated person as a function of therapist's characteristics. *Perceptual and Motor Skills, 30,* 375–384.

Sherman, J. A., Koufacos, C., & Kenworth, J. A. (1978). Therapists: Their attitudes and information about women. *Psychology of Women Quarterly, 2,* 299–313.

Tanney, M. F., & Birk, J. M. (1976). Women counselors for women clients? A review of the research. *Counseling Psychologist, 6,* 28–32.

■30

Teaching Feminist Therapies: Integrating Feminist Therapy, Pedagogy, and Scholarship

PATRICIA SPENCER FAUNCE

Women's work is always toward wholeness.—*May Sarton*

The teaching of feminist therapies requires that the classroom be an integration of feminist therapy, pedagogy, and scholarship. It should be a laboratory of feminist principles, that is, the feminist belief system should be its framework and working tool. Feminism is an advocacy system for women. Feminism insists that women must have personal autonomy and both the freedom to direct and the responsibility for directing all areas of their lives; they must decide for themselves what it means to be a woman; and they must define themselves as independent persons, separate from their relationships. Feminism fosters pride in being female, emphasizes the commonality of the female experience across cultural and socioeconomic lines, and develops a sense of community among women. Feminism holds that all roles are open to all

309

people and that every woman is entitled to the opportunity to develop her potential fully. Feminism recognizes the culturally and experientially based perspective differences between women and men, assumes women and men are more alike than not, and insists that possible differences not be conceptualized in terms of "superiority/inferiority." Finally, feminism strives to equalize personal power, asserts that no person should have noncontractual dominion over another, and encourages equalitarian relationships (Sturdivant, 1980).

A feminist analysis requires the learner to examine the social, political, and economic systems within which females develop and to understand their effects on therapeutic and educational practices and on female functioning. The development of therapeutic, pedagogical, and social-change strategies with the goal of maximizing female development is a natural outgrowth of such an orientation.

Feminists have brought this revolutionary, women-centered paradigm to the realms of psychotherapy and academe (Boxer, 1982; Denny, 1983; Lord, 1982; Richardson, 1982; Spender, 1982; Tyler, 1983). Both feminist therapy and feminist pedagogy (1) recognize "truth" to be value-based and hence political; (2) view traditional conceptualizations of truth as elitist, exclusionary, myopic, and oppressive; and (3) seek to transform radically the values that determine how we view self, others, history, and the world—that is, "reality." Striking process analogies also are evident: Both feminist therapy and feminist pedagogy seek, within an equalitarian, reciprocal mode, to question traditional assumptions, validate personal experience, and examine the political implications of how truth is defined.

The pursuit and process of scholarship itself has healing and wellness value for women. As a feminist helping form, scholarship represents a radical re-education and philosophic transformation of the client/student and an education in the art of rethinking and redefining the external world, a process that becomes an ongoing strength. The scholarship process also contributes to the creation of an intellectual, integrated, active view of the world and a redefinition of ourselves as active, demanding, and whole.

Eleven principles that illustrate the integration of feminist therapy, pedagogy, and scholarship into a feminist therapies course are presented in this chapter. These principles are organized around four themes: power and cooperation, resocialization and transformation, holistic subjectivity and diversity, and woman-focus.

POWER AND COOPERATION

Three of the 11 principles are discussed in this section, focusing on power dissemination, reciprocal influence, collective learning, and woman-as-resource as necessary ingredients in the teaching/learning models of feminist therapies.

Reflecting a Reciprocal Model of Influence

Patriarchal or traditional, unilaterally grounded educational/therapeutic modes are of particular disadvantage for women and other minority-status groups (Boxer, 1982; Rawlings & Carter, 1975; Tyler, 1983). A reciprocal model of influence (equalitarianism) is compatible with feminist therapy and pedagogy. Its governing variables emphasize openness, freedom, consensus, cooperation, questioning, and personal commitment. These are operative values/principles in feminist classrooms and therapeutic settings, and similarly these encounters integrate consciousness-raising techniques and values into a fluid assortment of other practices intended to encourage self-revelation, interpersonal sharing, equalitarianism, intellectual provocation, cooperation, and political awareness. Various techniques are used to restructure the classroom experience: circular arrangements of chairs, small-group sessions, first-name use for everyone, journal keeping, reflection papers, cooperative projects, and student/faculty collective teaching modes. The goal of these and similarly revolutionary pedagogical and therapeutic practices is to help the woman become less alienated from her own experience; increase her self-esteem and her ability to assert and fulfill emotional, physical, and intellectual needs; attain satisfying roles; develop positive conceptualizations of sexuality; and work effectively toward political and social change. Identification and solidarity with other women is basic and essential for female growth.

Providing Clarity regarding Power for Women and an
Affirmative Classroom Power Approach

Power is a feminist issue and an analysis of power differentials is pertinent to both psychotherapy and the academy (Lord, 1982; Richardson, 1982; Schaef, 1981; Sturdivant, 1980). In the female system, power is conceived of as personal power as well as limitless: When power is shared it increases, regenerates, and expands. This also is true with ideas: If they are freely given and exchanged, ideas change and expand constantly, remaining alive and fresh.

Power distribution in the feminist therapies classroom is tied intimately to the subject matter and is especially salient for the instructor. How learning is to take place is a vital question. The teaching/learning process must be shared by students and instructor. Such dissemination of power can lead to instructor dilemmas, for example, possible abandonment of the syllabus, a lecture topic, or other instructor desires. Tension and conflict may accompany open, candid dialogue with students. Thus, awareness regarding power as an issue in women's lives and a feminist rationale for power dissemination in the classroom are necessary in a feminist therapies course.

Cultivating a Cooperative/Collective Learning Approach, with Each Person Valued as a Teaching Resource

The feminist's valued achievement style, both in the classroom and therapy, is based on cooperation, mutual respect, and interdependence. The instructor/therapist and student/client are both learner and expert: They teach each other, and knowledge, information, and experience are shared. Women pooling their information and resources, presenting/ teaching selected sessions, and learning from others are engaged in a salient process that is an extension of the equalitarian, cooperative, and considerate turn-taking talk arrangement normally engaged in by women.

Underlying the view of the student/client as both learner and "expert" is the feminist view (Lord, 1982; Rich, 1979) that each student is responsible for her own learning and growth. That responsibility affects the quality of her life and of the classroom/therapy milieus because she claims her education in both settings and is responsible for herself. She refuses to let others do her thinking, talking, and naming; she respects and uses her brains and instincts; and grapples with hard work. She demands to be taken seriously, seeks out criticism, and recognizes that the most affirmative thing anyone can do for her is to demand that she push herself further.

A teaching/learning process that both demands and facilitates such input and involvement from all participants has many positive effects (Faunce, 1982, 1983; Lord, 1982). First, power is disseminated. Second, less anxiety is experienced. Third, material, information, and issues are grappled with in a manner relevant to students' interests and needs.

Fourth, learners demonstrate that they are also experts and that they can pose questions and find answers. Fifth, initiating, independent, active learners are fostered. Sixth, students feel that being treated as resource/expert is one of their most positive learning experiences.

RESOCIALIZATION AND TRANSFORMATION

Two more principles are included here: (1) emphasis on the personal as political and (2) the integration of scholarship and politics.

The Personal Is Political

The Women's Movement is a radical movement that bases its politics on concrete personal experiences. Feelings and politics are intertwined: the personal is political. One's relationship to power in any group or system comprises what is meant by *political* or *politics*. Women's experiences are shared by every woman and are therefore political. What was thought to be a personal problem has a social cause and probably a political solution.

Teachers of feminist therapy must make explicit this "personal-is-political" concept. Women students of feminist therapies must learn how social structures and attitudes have molded and limited their opportunities and those of other women since birth. They must ascertain the extent to which women have been denigrated in this society and how they have developed prejudices against themselves and other women. Until women students see the connections between what happens both to them as individual women and to all women, they have not experienced the necessary ingredient of consciousness raising in their work as feminist therapists.

Integrating Scholarship and Politics

A commitment to broad sociocultural transformation is explicit in much of the feminist educational and psychological literature (Boxer, 1982; Richardson, 1982; Spacks, 1981; Spender, 1982; Tyler, 1983). A feminist transformation of therapy and of academe through heightened awareness, minority-group bonding, and social action would lead ultimately to a world free from sexism, racism, ageism, class bias, and heterosexual bias—that is, free from those ideologies and institutions that have oppressed and exploited some for the advantage of others.

Feminist therapists and educators are change agents: Their task is to question and reshape personal and, ultimately, sociopolitical values. The task is not merely one of eliminating sexism from the therapist's office or the university classroom, the "add-women-and-stir" method (Boxer, 1982), but rather a profound revision of all we know and believe, the full integration of feminist values into our world belief systems. Feminist therapy facilitates change by providing a resocialization process through making values explicit, affirming individual perceptions of experience, enabling individuals to comprehend the sociocultural origins of psychological distress, providing opportunities for validating experiences and learning new social/interactional skills, and offering the therapist as a resource and role model.

Resocialization by similar means is the aim of feminist pedagogy. Feminist courses attempt to integrate scholarship and politics, and feminist curricula challenge the male hegemony over the content of college courses and the substance of knowledge itself. The feminist classroom focus is on re-visioning classical conceptualizations of truth and reality, particularly those relative to females. Both feminist educators and therapists seek to effect a breakthrough in consciousness and knowledge that would transform the social order from the single individual to the whole society (Tyler, 1983).

The transforming revolutionary potential rests on the fusion of feminist process with content. Feminist educators emphasize the multidisciplinarity of feminist courses and seek to break down the traditional, specialized, compartmentalizations into "departments" and "disciplines." Hierarchical arrangements are frowned upon in program organization and the classroom setting. Feminist criticism of authoritarian control and power differentials translates into equalitarian, consensus-based classrooms. The feminist debunking of the prized masculine thought modes (rationality, intense abstraction, the passive voice) leads to feminist discourse modes that stress attention to the relation of art and life, commitment, and flexibility and seek to be inclusive and holistic and to incorporate intuitive insights into the exploration of intellectual ideas.

Thus, a social-activist component is inherent in teaching feminist therapies. This, in turn, constitutes a threat to established personality theory and therapeutic and educational practices. The status quo is challenged on several levels. The knowledge base and the definition of the field are challenged first. The feminist interdisciplinary perspective challenges the traditional emphasis on specialized and highly defined knowledge in a specialty area while it encourages the feminist therapy instructor to draw upon other fields in her attempt to understand women's behavior. She can find herself needing advanced knowledge and expertise in various areas, but, given limits of time and energy, she is likely to find that she and her students are unfamiliar visitors in new territory. This acceptable and desirable nontraditional image clashes with the traditional image of the highly specialized expert. The knowledge base of the field is eroded even more radically through addressing the interactive oppressive forces of sexism, homophobism, racism, ageism, and classism.

Second, traditional patriarchal assumptions and definitions about women are challenged. Third, research methodology and resulting data about and treatment methods for women are challenged. Fourth, there is a redefinition of the means by which data on women are examined, validated, and used; a redefinition of what it means to be female. Fifth, social activism/transformation/revolution are supported.

HOLISTIC SUBJECTIVITY AND DIVERSITY

Three more of the 11 principles are holistic consciousness, women's subjective experience, and women's diversities and strengths.

Fostering a Holistic Consciousness

Both feminist teaching and therapy models must embrace a holistic consciousness that comprehends the mind/body mutuality, sees woman's existence as a potentially harmonious mind/body interaction, and sees a woman as a dynamic, integrated, complex being with the capacity for self-healing. The mind and body work in unison to heal or hurt, and we can learn to control their interaction. A holistic focus stresses that, since a person's mind and body work as a single unit, health exists when they are in harmony, while illness results from conflict and stress. Thus, the holistic approach emphasizes healing, the maintenance of optimum health, and the prevention of illness.

In the female system (Schaef, 1981), the healer/teacher's role is to facilitate the flow of helpful knowledge, energy, healing, and learning that comes from the client/student. The healing/learning process is based on the relationship between the healer/teacher and the client/students. The healer/teacher must be knowledgeable and use her knowledge to allow healing/learning to occur, and she must have a good relationship with herself in order to release the healing/learning flow within the student/client. A woman's ability to control her mind and body enables her to become an active participant in both the classroom and healing processes. Moreover, methods of preserving her own health become the moral objective and prerogative of each woman, student/client, and teacher/therapist.

Encouraging and Validating the Subjective, Personal Experiences and Perceptions of Women

Each one of us is an expert on what it means to be a woman, once we get in touch with our experiential knowledge. Women must be encouraged to question critically, on the basis of their personal experiences and feelings, the so-called "objective" facts and belief systems that require women to believe that a so-called scientific statement is always more valid than a statement regarding their own belief. Feminist analysis assumes that an objective, value-free, universal reality does not exist. The assumptions and beliefs that underlie prevailing cultural and scientific "truths" are predicated on subjective values that reflect and perpetuate the interests of the dominant male cultural group. Recognizing that an objective, value-free reality does not exist and identifying dissonance and discrepancies between one's own perceptions and existing theory is a process through which critical questions can be framed and investigated.

The nontraditional frame of reference views the process of emotional/personal knowledge acquisition as being just as important, if not more important than, the cognitive/impersonal process. The nontraditional value perspective revalues the emotional and personal modes and recognizes them as strengths buried in women's reality.

The validity, value, and power of the emotional and personal becomes quite pronounced when dealing with the kinds of life-structure issues addressed in a feminist therapies course and in therapy itself. Change or potential change in life structures strikes at basic foundations in the lives of both students/clients and instructors/therapists and engages some level of emotional response, thus opening the door for the occurrence of personal and emotional learning.

Time and energy devoted to one kind of knowledge acquisition may detract from others. The feminist therapy instructor, as part of her responsibility for class management and time allocation, faces recurring decisions regarding the priority to be placed on emotional/personal processes versus cognitive/impersonal issues. In the time-limited academic context, however, perceptions and experiential knowledge demand use, validation, and response.

Identifying and Making Use of Women's Diversities and Strengths

Differences and divisions among and between women undeniably exist and are a positive basis for exploration, validation, and gaining a perspective on women's common experience. They are a starting point within a feminist framework that views the differences as a resource. The feminist therapies course must examine how these divisions and differences have been construed; what their purposes and roles are in perpetuating patriarchy; and how they contribute to women's common, shared experience.

Sensitivity to the interacting forces of other social/cultural/sexual statuses and roles with that of gender demands new conceptual tools for a critical and radical revision of what is known. For example, what might look to some as a radical analysis of the female role may seem to others as containing implicit white, middle-class bias (e.g., Miller's 1976 analysis of the role of power in women's personality development). Sexism, in feminist terms, is part of an interactive nexus of oppressive categorical "isms"; feminists cannot legitimately disentangle gender-based oppression from that based on race, class, age, and sex. The perspectives of black, Third World, working-class, or lesbian women must permeate all aspects of a feminist therapies course. Special, ghetto-ized topic sessions are simply not adequate.

Woman-Focus

The final three principles focus on the need to study the female species, to include the female in the human model, and to provide a female instructor, and female-focused language.

Studying the Female Species and the Female Human Model

The study of only the female species is critical because almost all helping professions, courses, therapeutic strategies, and personality theories are about males. A woman-focus also is important in preventing women from backing off from their own perceptions (Lord, 1982; Schaef, 1981). We must avoid the temptation of both female and male students to spend their time comparing women with men (engaging in the games of "Who's worse off?" and "Everyone is human"), feeling sorry for the men, and/or participating in other "stoppers" that appear in both therapeutic and educational settings. To facilitate a female focus, instructors/ therapists and students/clients must learn to recognize those techniques that are used to make women back off from the use of their female-centered personal perceptions and experiential knowledge.

The same is true regarding a strong female focus as the normal human model. Overwhelming justification (e.g., Doherty, 1973; Faunce & Phipps-Yonas, 1979; Frieze, Parson, Johnson, Ruble, & Zellman, 1978; Lord, 1982; Sherman, 1973; Sturdivant, 1980) exists for viewing and treating women only as a normal human model; no justification exists for doing otherwise.

Providing a Female and Feminist Therapies Course Instructor

The gender and political ideology of the feminist therapies course instructor/therapist is a critical variable because the teaching and therapeutic settings are microcosms of society's sexist ills (Lord, 1982; Sturdivant, 1980; Tyler, 1983). Respected criteria for effective feminist therapists and educators include female gender, value-consciousness and honesty, working toward optimal functioning in her life, and social activism.

We must do everything possible in a feminist therapies course, as in feminist therapy, to provide strong feminist (which includes female) role models. Many female students feel they learn as much from the role model(s) of feminist instructors (Faunce, 1982, 1983; Lord, 1982) as from any aspect of a course. Exposure to confident, initiating, verbal women who know the field/topic as well is a prime ingredient in their growth, self-concept development, achievement, and pursuit of career options. The feminist instructor/therapist has the greater ability to empathize with women students because of shared experiences of being a woman in this society and greater sensitivity to women's issues because they are

more personally relevant to her. Further, having a feminist instructor/
therapist provides the woman student/client an opportunity for developing peer-relationship skills.

Using Female-focused Language

Speech and sex are linked (Key, 1975; Lakoff, 1975; Lord, 1982; Miller &
Swift, 1976; Thorne & Henley, 1975). Our feelings about the world color
the expression of our thoughts; therefore, we can use our linguistic behavior as diagnostic of our hidden feelings about things. Everyday words we
speak and write have a great deal to do with the way women and men
conceptualize and relate to each other, socially, politically, and sexually.
Language usage reflects the deep bias in our culture against women: It
has deprecated, ignored, and set women apart. Words are relevant and
significant because they are the secondary-symbol system that labels the
concepts in our brain, the human computer. The experience of using, for
example, "woman" and female pronouns generically is a critical consciousness-raising exercise and provokes rethinking. The replacement of
female referents in the secondary-symbol system results in making the
concept of "femaleness" visible in the brain: Linguistic visibility equals
conceptual visibility.

SUMMARY

Feminists in both education and psychotherapy must work within the
female system. They must create their lives and work out of women-
centered values and provide women with affirmative milieus for resocialization, self-validation, woman-bonding, and limitless growth. These are
exciting revolutionary processes.

REFERENCES

Boxer, M. J. (1982). For and about women: The theory and practice of women's
    studies in the United States. In N. O. Keohane, M. Z. Rosaldo, & B. C.
    Gelpi (Eds.), *Feminist theory: A critique of ideology* (pp. 237–272), Chi-
    cago, IL: University of Chicago Press.
Denny, P. A. (1983). Scholarship as therapy: Feminist learning as a response to
    women's psychological distress. Unpublished paper. Minneapolis, MN:
    University of Minnesota.

320   : : *The Training of Feminist Therapists*

Doherty, M. A. (1973). Sexual bias in personality theory. *Counseling Psychologist*, 4(1), 67–74.

Faunce, P. S. (1982). Summaries of student course evaluations for WoSt 5-377: Feminist therapies and Psy 8-120: personality, therapy and women. Unpublished paper. Minneapolis, MN: University of Minnesota.

Faunce, P. S. (1983). Summaries of student course evaluations for WoSt 5-377: Feminist therapies and Psy 8-120: Personality, therapy and women. Unpublished paper. Minneapolis, MN: University of Minnesota.

Faunce, P. S., & Phipps-Yonas, S. (1978, January/February). Women's liberation and human sexual relations. *International Journal of Women's Studies*, 1(1), 83–95. Also reprinted in J. H. Williams (Ed.), (1979), *Psychology of Women: Selected Readings* (pp. 228–240). New York: W. W. Norton.

Frieze, I. H., Parson, J. E., Johnson, P. B., Ruble, D. N., & Zellman, C. L. (1978). *Women and sex roles*. New York: W. W. Norton.

Key, M. R. (1975). *Male/Female language*. Metuchen, N.J.: Scarecrow Press.

Lakoff, R. (1975). *Language and woman's place*. New York: Harper & Row.

Lord, S. B. (1982, Fall). Teaching the psychology of women: Examination of a teaching-learning model. *Psychology of Women Quarterly*, 7(1), 71–80.

Miller, C., & Swift, K. (1976). *Words and women*. Garden City, NY: Anchor Press/Doubleday.

Miller, J. B. (1976). *Toward a new psychology of women*. Boston: Beacon Press.

Rawlings, E. I., & Carter, D. K. (Eds.). (1975). *Psychotherapy for women: Treatment toward equality*. Springfield, IL: Charles C Thomas.

Rich, A. (1979). Claiming an education. In *Lies, secrets, and silence* (pp. 231–236). New York, NY: W. W. Norton.

Richardson, M. S. (1982, Fall). Sources of tension in teaching the psychology of women. *Psychology of Women Quarterly*, 7(1), 45–54.

Schaef, A. W. (1981). *Women's reality*. Minneapolis, MN: Winston Press.

Sherman, J. A. (1973). *On the psychology of women*. Springfield, IL: Charles C Thomas.

Spacks, P. M. (1981). The difference it makes. In E. Langland & W. Gove (Eds.), *A feminist perspective in the academy: The difference it makes* (pp. 7–24). Chicago, IL: University of Chicago Press.

Spender, D. (1982). *Invisible woman: The schooling scandal*. London: Writers and Readers Publishing.

Sturdivant, S. (1980). *Therapy with women: A feminist philosophy of treatment*. New York: Springer.

Thorne, B., & Henley, N. (Eds.). (1975). *Language and sex*. Rowley, MA: Newbury House.

Tyler, K. M. Feminist pedagogy: Parallels with feminist therapy. Unpublished paper. Minneapolis, MN: University of Minnesota.

■31
Evaluation Research in a Course on Counseling Women: A Case Study[1]

SHARON E. KAHN AND GISELA M. THEURER

Much attention has been directed toward raising the consciousness of helping professionals about the specific needs of female clients and the concomitant changes necessary in educational programs. The call for innovative training programs spans at least a decade from Gardner's (1971) demand that "sexist counseling must stop" (p. 705) to Worell's (1980) proposal for training specialists in counseling women. Moore and Strickler (1980) noted the discrepancy between the widespread attitudinal support given and the lack of training and continuing education programs designed for decreasing sexist treatment practices. Recently, the Counseling Psychology Division of the American Psychological Association (1981) initiated a project designed to identify innovative curriculum models in the field in order to develop an educational package that

1. We would like to express special appreciation to Janice Birk, Patricia Faunce, Clara Hill, Natalie Porter, and Nancy Schlossberg for their reviews of an earlier draft of this chapter.

321

could be disseminated to academic programs and training sites, with the purpose of improving training for counseling women.

Descriptions of workshops and courses designed to train counselors in gender-fair counseling are available (Moore & Nelson, 1981; Nickerson, Espin, & Gawelek, 1982; Thomas, Moore, & Sams, 1980), yet the number of published evaluations of the effectiveness of training in these procedures remains small (Gilbert, 1979; Gilbert & Waldroop, 1978). Scott and McMillan (1980) concluded their survey of counselor education departments in the United States with the recommendation that research be done to determine the most effective approach to training counselors in sex-fair counseling. Johnson (1982) suggested that instructors teaching the psychology of women were in an excellent position to develop and/or to assess instruments designed to measure sex-role attitudes.

The purpose of this chapter is to describe a multistage project in counselor education that centers on a course entitled "Counseling Girls and Women." First is a description of the course, followed by a report on the development and use of a research measure for evaluating attitudes and awareness of gender-role issues. This tool was used to measure the impact of the course on graduate students. An assessment of this impact makes up the core of this chapter. Finally, future directions for the evaluation and training of counselors who work with female clients are discussed.

COURSE DESCRIPTION

The course, "Counseling Girls and Women," is a one-semester course available to all graduate students in the Department of Counseling Psychology. It has been offered at The University of British Columbia since the academic year 1976–1977. The course is designed to be a cognitive and affective experience, with the goal of improving counseling with female clients. Class time is spent in lecture, discussion, and experiential learning. Structured exercises and role plays are used to increase the students' awareness of the psychological experiences of female clients and demonstrate how knowledge and attitudes affect the counseling situation.

Traditional and contemporary theories of psychology and the mental health of women, the female socialization process, female educational and vocational development, and the changing roles of women are examined. Specific course content covers consciousness raising, the effects of gender on counseling theory and practice, gender differences in socialization and development, the concept of androgyny, and nonsexist and feminist counseling interventions. All assignments combine the acquisition of knowledge of the psychology of women with the personal exploration of one's own values, attitudes, and beliefs about women. Students are encouraged to integrate personal interest and experience with course assignments and to work collectively with one another.

DEVELOPMENT OF A RESEARCH MEASURE

To measure counselor bias, videotaped counseling vignettes were developed in four areas of perceived sex bias and sex-role stereotyping that affect women as clients (A.P.A., 1975): (1) fostering traditional sex roles, (2) bias in expectations and devaluation of women, (3) sexist use of psychoanalytic concepts, and (4) responding to women as sex objects. Each vignette depicts a client discussing her or his problems with a counselor who is not seen by the viewer—indeed, the vignettes were taped so that the client appears to be addressing the viewer as a counselor. The average length of each vignette is just under three minutes.

Vignettes were selected as preferable to trait scales to measure changes in sex biases because (1) the transparency of attitude measures allows subjects to misrepresent themselves in the more liberal direction (see review by Sherman, 1980), (2) vignettes depict a situational context that has been suggested to be important in sex-role stimulus materials (Whitley, 1979), and (3) vignettes more realistically approximate a counseling interview and depict degree and appropriateness of affect. For these reasons the counseling field traditionally has used videotaped vignettes for training and measurement of growth in counselor training (e.g., Campbell, Kagan, & Krathwohl, 1971; Danish & Kagan, 1971). For example, Gilbert and Waldroop (1978) used videotaped vignettes to measure upper-division students' (male and female seniors in psychology or related areas who had preregistered in a course in individual counseling) sensitivity to sex bias in their clinical evaluation of female clients.

A videotape questionnaire was designed to accompany the vignettes. The open-ended questions were derived from the "Principles Concerning the Counseling and Therapy of Women" developed by the A.P.A. (1979). Areas covered by the questions included a primary component of effective counseling; empathy; an understanding of, information about, and attitudes toward gender-role issues; and counseling intervention. A subjective or free response style was selected based on the finding that a forced-choice format maximizes stereotypic responses (Lunneborg, 1970; Whitley, 1979).

EVALUATION OF THE COURSE

Method

Subjects. The experimental group consisted of 17 female graduate students who were enrolled in the 13-week "Counseling Girls and Women" course at the University of British Columbia. They had a median age of 30 (range = 23–47), and their mean number of years of background experience in the helping professions was 8.1. Men were not included in the study, as only two male students enrolled in the course. The control group consisted of 17 female students who indicated on a survey asking about elective course planning that they planned to take the course at a later date. They were matched with the experimental group on background training and years of experience. The small size of the available population did not allow for random selection and assignment to treatment groups, but having students who planned to take the same course at a later date provided a motivated baseline control group.

Procedure. During the first week of classes, both experimental and control groups filled out the Therapists' Attitude toward Women Scale (TAWS) as a pre-test. For the post-test, the experimental group filled out the TAWS at their second-to-last classroom meeting and did the Videotape Questionnaire at the last class meeting. Since the control group subjects were not in one class together, they completed the TAWS and the Videotape Questionnaire in small groups during the last month of classes. Another questionnaire was completed by all subjects at pre- and post-testing, to disguise the nature of the study.

Six months following the completion of the course, five subjects randomly selected from each of the experimental and control groups were interviewed. Subjects were asked to recall the vignettes and to relate what they remember thinking, feeling, and responding to each vignette. In addition, the five experimental subjects were interviewed to determine personal and professional changes that might have occurred as a result of the course.

Measures: The Therapists' Attitude toward Women Scale. The TAWS (Sherman, Koufacos, & Kenworthy, 1978) is a 32-item Likert scale, where possible responses range from 32 to 160. Lower scores on the TAWS represent a greater endorsement of liberal and less-stereotyped attitudes toward women. Coefficient alpha for the scale was .86.

The four videotaped counseling vignettes (Kahn, 1980) were chosen for the present study from a pilot study using 20 practicing counselors, half of whom identified themselves as feminist counselors. The four vignettes present female and male relationship issues. The female clients were not able to express their feelings to their partners, nor to get their needs met. In all four cases, whether it is the lack of self-definition, meaningful contact, or support for career or family plans, the clients did not identify their struggle as the result of societal pressure to conform to traditional gender-role behaviors. Three graduate students in counseling psychology agreed that the four vignettes were equivalent in technical quality.

As determined by responses of feminist and nonfeminist counselors in the pilot study, five questions were selected for the Videotape Questionnaire (Kahn & Theurer, 1981):

1. As a counselor, what would you say to this client?
2. What beliefs seem to be in conflict for this client?
3. As a counselor, what is your understanding of the environmental issues as presented by this client?
4. As a counselor, what beliefs, values, and attitudes do you have about this client's issues?
5. As a counselor, what goals and strategies would you have for your work with this client?

The authors constructed a four-point scale ranging from zero (no awareness of female gender-role issues mentioned in the responses) to three (at least two explicit and specific female gender-role issues mentioned). This scale was used to rate responses to questions 2 through 5. Question 1 was rated using Carkhuff's (1969) five-point scale for discriminating levels of empathy.

Three graduate students who previously had taken the course in counseling women and who were not informed of the questions in the present study were trained as raters, using the pilot data. The responses of the subjects were typed, coded, and randomly ordered to eliminate any rater bias that might arise from form or style. Each question was rated separately for all subjects before the next question was considered, and all questions were rated independently by the three raters. The Pearson Product–Moment coefficient between each of the rater pairs was calculated. Interrater reliabilities between pairs of raters were .83, .83, and .80, showing that the raters had a high level of agreement.

To establish a validity check, the Videotape Questionnaire was administered to three known groups: 30 undergraduate students with no experience or training in counseling (all female), 33 counseling psychology students who had some experience and training in counseling (22 female, 11 male), and 14 counseling psychology faculty members (6 female, 8 male). The construct validity of the Videotape Questionnaire was demonstrated by the differential response elicited by those three groups. Counseling psychology faculty members (X = 1.65; S.D. = 1.10) and students (X = 1.24; S.D. = 1.13) consistently responded to all questions over all vignettes with more awareness of gender-role issues than did the undergraduate students (X = .65; S.D. = .75).

Results

Therapists' Attitude toward Women Scale. Means and standard deviations for the experimental group were X = 63.53 and S.D. = 8.68 pre-test and X = 56.41 and S.D. = 7.38 post-test. For the control group, X = 72.70 and S.D. = 6.77 pre-test and X = 68.47 and S.D. = 8.18 post-test. Results of a *t*-test on the pre-test means revealed that the experimental group held more liberal attitudes from the beginning than did the control group (*t* = 3.40, *p* < .01) and maintained their more liberal beliefs upon post-testing, as indicated by a one-way analysis of covariance between groups (F = 5.58, p < .025).

Videotape Questionnaire. A median test was used to measure the differences between the experimental group and the control group, using the median of the combined groups as the basis for dichotomizing the scores. A chi-square test was used to test for differences between the two independent groups on the five questions, as shown in Table 31–1.

Question 1 required an understanding (empathic) or directive response. Both the students in the course and those who did not take the course had received similar training in empathy skills; therefore, no

Table 31-1 Median Scores and Chi-square Results* of the Five Questions on the Videotape Questionnaire

	Groups			
Question	Experimental	Control	Combined	Chi-square
1	3.10	2.86	2.98	2.16
2	1.07	1.17	1.14	.24
3	1.63	.47	1.09	6.78[b]
4	1.82	1.50	1.77	.32
5	2.09	1.50	1.82	5.72[c]

*a. All chi-squares tested with one degree of freedom.
 b. $p < .01$
 c. $p < .02$

difference was expected between the two groups on that question, and none was found.

Question 2 required that the students demonstrate their understanding of the issues presented by the client, rather than an analysis about the causes of the conflict. No significant difference was expected or found between the two groups, as all subjects tended to paraphrase the clients on this question.

On Question 3, the experimental group raised significantly more gender issues than did the control group. On Question 4, however, no differences were found. This finding was unexpected.

The experimental group mentioned gender-related goals significantly more often than the control group on question 5. The subjects in the experimental group tended to advocate assertiveness training, work on anger, women's support groups, power analysis, and consciousness raising, as well as the more "traditional" therapeutic strategies of exploration of feelings and needs, couples counseling and work on self-esteem. The subjects in the control group chose only the traditional counseling interventions.

An inter-test correlation was done between the TAWS and the Videotape Questionnaire, to examine convergent and discriminant validity. The Pearson Product–Moment correlation coefficient showed a statistically significant correlation ($r = .52$; $p < .001$), strengthening the evidence for validity of each of the two measures.

Interviews. Six months following the post-testing, five students who had taken the course in counseling women discussed the clients' problems in terms of sexism, gender-role expectations, and the effects of the socialization process on women. Students in the control group who had not yet taken the course also viewed these clients as fighting to achieve self-hood and equity. They talked about "generational problems" or "old versus new values." The treatment strategies of the students who had taken the course included consciousness raising through teaching about women's issues, women's support groups, confrontation, and assertiveness training. None of the students in the control group selected any of these interventions and repeatedly suggested listening, exploration, clarification, and decision-making as potential interventions.

The five students who took the counseling of women course were asked to describe their own personal and professional changes that might have resulted from the course. One student said she was aware of believing in women and their potential. This positive evaluation of women was echoed by several students who reported increased self-esteem and acceptance of themselves as competent women. Two women students said that they had begun to see the effects of sexism, both in their work with clients and in their own personal relationships. For example, one student said, "I am aware now to look for explanations in the sociocultural environment." A student who since has decided to conduct her thesis research in an area related to women's gender-role development reported, "My antenna is tuned for sexism." Other trainees talked about acquiring a more directive stance with clients.

Discussion

The results show that specific training in counseling women improves students' awareness of and attitudes toward female clients. Those students who completed the course held liberal attitudes toward women, both before and after the course, demonstrated an awareness of sociocultural influences on client concerns, and indicated a wide range of active counseling interventions they would employ with female clients.

From the responses it becomes clear that the students who took the course gained a significant awareness of the cultural influences on women clients. Members of the control group remained unaware (or less aware) of the difficulties caused for women by not conforming to sex-role stereotypical behaviors. The TAWS did detect a significant awareness difference between the two groups; therefore, on the question concerning counselor's attitudes (question 4), a similar difference was expected to emerge. From studying the subjects' answers, two points stand out that may be explanations for the results. The first is that subjects seem not to have differentiated between the client's beliefs (question 2) and the subject/counselor's beliefs (question 4). Second, the subjects provided in-depth analyses to question 3, frequently including their attitudes toward the presenting issue. Subjects may have had nothing left to state for question 4.

The differences found at pre-testing between the experimental and control groups may indicate that students who are interested in women as a special client group already hold more liberal attitudes toward women. Nickerson et al. (1982) found that those students in a regular master's program responded more stereotypically to attitudes toward women and self-report measures of psychological feminity and masculinity and were less changed as a result of their year of training than those students who elected a specialization in counseling women. Students who elect to take a course in counseling women early in their graduate programs may do so because of their greater interest in women's issues or involvement in social analysis, either through reading, discussion, or participation in a consciousness-raising group. A post-test difference between the two groups on the TAWS indicates that the course may have strengthened and reinforced the already existing liberal attitudes toward women, a process that may not occur for trainees in other courses.

FUTURE DIRECTIONS FOR RESEARCH AND CURRICULUM

Several issues that require further investigation are raised in the development of the videotape measure. The rating scale at present is too open to individual rater interpretation. Although raters usually come to similar scores, they may have reached the score through different means. The instructions on the Videotape Questionnaire also warrant reconsideration. Subjects may have hurried through the questionnaire; therefore, the written answers may reflect less complexity than the students are aware of and may not reflect how they actually would behave. The Videotape Questionnaire measures individuals' ability to identify gender-role issues; it does not measure their ability to use this understanding effectively in promoting positive client growth in a counseling relationship.

The issue of internal consistency of the vignettes remains to be explored and needs to be validated against behavior in counseling situations. The questions of whether and how to develop vignettes where age and problem are standardized, whether to develop a variety of different vignettes, and what issues to portray (lesbian relationship, career, homemaker) are open for further investigation. Sex bias may take on covert forms that research studies can track down within the context of specific situations or cases.

Questions concerning low male enrollment, lack of male faculty involvement, and the systematic inclusion of issues of race, class, and sexual preference in a course on counseling women require further attention. Similarly, longitudinal studies of training outcomes are recommended, to determine the effective components of these courses.

As educational programs expand to include special material on counseling women and as specialists in counseling women are trained, planned evaluations should be added to Worell's (1980) plea for "carefully planned training programs that expose counselors to information, experiential activities, and feedback on their behavior in real and simulated counseling situations" (p. 479). Developing and evaluating the course, "Counseling Girls and Women," has been an exciting way to learn about gender bias and social change within the university. The authors hope that counseling psychology students will be stimulated to shape the field of counselor education and training by their involvement in their own research and practice with female clients.

REFERENCES

American Psychological Association. (1975). Report of the Task Force on sex bias and sex-role stereotyping in psychotherapeutic practice. *American Psychologist, 30,* 1169–1175.

American Psychological Association. (1979). Principles concerning the counseling and therapy of women. *The Counseling Psychologist, 8,* 21.

American Psychological Association. (1981). *Division 17 Committee on Women Task Force report on training for counseling women.* Washington, DC: Author.

Campbell, R. J., Kagan, N., & Krathwohl, D. R. (1971). The development and validation of a scale to measure affective sensitivity (empathy). *Journal of Counseling Psychology, 18,* 407–412.

Carkhuff, R. R. (1969). *Helping and human relations* (vol. 1). New York: Holt, Rinehart & Winston.

Danish, S. J., & Kagan, N. (1971). Measurement of affective sensitivity: Toward a valid measure of interpersonal perception. *Journal of Counseling Psychology, 18,* 51–54.

Gardner, J. (1971). Sexist counseling must stop. *Personnel and Guidance Journal, 49,* 705–714.

Gilbert, L. A. (1979). An approach to training sex fair mental health workers. *Professional Psychology, 10,* 365–372.

Gilbert, L. A., & Waldroop, J. (1978). Evaluation of a procedure for increasing sex fair counseling. *Journal of Counseling Psychology, 25,* 410–418.

Johnson, M. (1982). Research on teaching the psychology of women. *Psychology of Women Quarterly, 7,* 96–104.

Kahn, S. E. (1980). *Adult clients talk to counselors.* Videotape. Vancouver, British Columbia: University of British Columbia, Faculty of Education.

Kahn, S. E., & Theurer, G. M. (1981). Videotape Questionnaire. Vancouver, British Columbia: University of British Columbia, Faculty of Education.

Lunneborg, P. W. (1970). Stereotypic aspects in masculinity–femininity measurement. *Journal of Consulting and Clinical Psychology, 34,* 113–118.

Moore, H. B., & Nelson, E. S. (1981). A workshop for developing awareness of sex-role bias in counseling students. *Counselor Education and Supervision, 20,* 312–316.

Moore, H. B., & Strickler, C. (1980). The counseling profession's response to sex-biased counseling: An update. *The Personnel and Guidance Journal, 59,* 84–87.

Nickerson, E. T., Espin, O., & Gawelek, M. A. (1982). Counseling women: A graduate master's degree specialization for training mental health professionals to work with women. *Counselor Education and Supervision, 21,* 194–199.

Scott, N. A., & McMillan, J. L. (1980). An investigation of training for sex-fair counseling. *Counselor Education and Supervision, 20,* 84–91.

Sherman, J. A. (1980). Therapist attitudes and sex-role stereotyping. In A. M. Brodsky & R. Hare-Mustin (Eds.), *Women and psychotherapy* (pp. 35–66). New York: Guilford Press.

Sherman, J., Koufacos, C., & Kenworthy, J. A. (1978). Therapists: Their attitudes and information about women. *Psychology of Women Quarterly, 2,* 299–313.

Thomas, M. B., Moore, H. B., & Sams, C. (1980). Counselor renewal workshop in sex equality. *Counselor Education and Supervision, 20,* 57–61.

Whitley, B. E. (1979). Sex roles and psychotherapy: A current appraisal. *Psychological Bulletin, 86,* 1309–1321.

Worell, J. (1980). New directions in counseling women. *Personnel and Guidance Journal, 58,* 477–484.

■ 32

New Perspectives on Therapy Supervision[1]

NATALIE PORTER

Feminist therapy arose from the recognition that traditional forms of therapy often have not helped and frequently have harmed women (Chesler, 1972). Feminist supervision has arisen from the recognition that traditional forms of supervision do not prepare therapists to counsel women effectively. This chapter focuses on feminist models of supervision: the goals and process of feminist supervision, the relationship of feminist supervision to the principles of feminist therapy, and the similarities and differences between feminist and traditional models of supervision. Feminist supervision is discussed from the perspective of a feminist therapist supervising trainees in a university clinical psychology training program. This training differs from a site where trainees are self-selected because of their own feminism. My goals are to raise the consciousness of all trainees and improve the overall quality of therapy for women.

1. I would like to thank Patricia Faunce and Deb Sanchez for their invaluable critiques of an earlier version of this chapter.

THE TRADITIONAL SUPERVISION PROCESS

Therapy supervision serves several purposes for the trainee, including giving opportunities for learning therapy, receiving feedback with which to evaluate one's strengths and weaknesses, receiving support, and enhancing personal growth (Greenberg, 1980). The literature on supervision emphasizes two supervisory functions with regard to the trainee's learning of therapy: to teach the requisite techniques and skills of therapy and to help the trainee understand the interpersonal process of therapy. All schools of therapy focus on both aspects, although to differing degrees.

The relationship between supervisor and trainee determines whether or not the tasks of supervision will be accomplished. Conditions that facilitate growth in trainees correspond to those that facilitate client improvement, including the development of a positive relationship, empathy, respect, genuineness, concreteness, and self-disclosure (Pierce, Carkhuff, & Berenson, 1967; Porter, 1979). The type of self-disclosure necessary for self-examination requires a safe climate where the trainee feels protected from retribution (Greenberg, 1980). These characteristics could be present in all supervision. Too often, however, they are absent, just as they frequently are absent from therapy.

Several types of conflicts exist in traditional supervision. Unequal power and authority distribution in supervision comprise an inherent conflict between supervisor and trainee (Greenberg, 1980; Marshall & Confer, 1980). The trainee is caught in a bind: One's learning involves exposing one's weaker moments to an authority figure with evaluative powers. Kadushin (1968) has argued that two debilitating supervisory attitudes occur regularly in supervision. First, the supervisor attempts to mold the trainee into the supervisor's image, ignoring the trainee's own personal characteristics and strengths. Second, the supervisor expresses a subtle condescension toward the trainee. This may be manifested in several ways. The trainee may be treated as the patient by a supervisor who focuses primarily on the trainee's anxieties and defenses. When the trainee, usually more attuned to power differentials, balks at self-disclosure, she or he is labeled resistant. The trainee who disagrees with a supervisor's interpretation is called defensive. An overly active or authoritarian supervisor using a didactic approach widens the expert/trainee gap by fostering a climate where all good ideas emanate from the supervisor. Supervisors can close down the communication process by (1) focusing on the trainee's weaknesses and attempting to "flush out" her or his mistakes, (2) forcing self-disclosure, particularly one-sided disclosure, and (3) focusing primarily on the psychopathology of the trainee. In such cases, supervisors are exploiting their power and status, inhibiting the trainees' learning, and modeling a destructive therapeutic style.

Furthermore, supervision suffers from the same sexist biases as does therapy. The A.P.A. Task Force on Sex Bias and Sex Stereotyping (1975) identified concerns for supervisor/trainee relationships as well as therapist/client ones, including sex biases, stereotyping, and sexual exploitation of female graduate students by their male supervisors.

PRINCIPLES, OBJECTIVES, AND MECHANICS OF FEMINIST SUPERVISION

Principles

Feminist supervisors have the responsibility to apply the basic tenets of feminist therapy to the supervisory process. Feminist supervision can be described by paraphrasing a statement by Maracek and Kravetz (1977) that feminist therapy is a philosophy that can be integrated with other therapeutic approaches rather than a distinct therapeutic system. Feminist supervision focuses on many of the same content and process issues as traditional supervision but incorporates feminist principles. These principles include the beliefs that (1) women's conflicts, poor self-esteem, and feelings of powerlessness stem from sociocultural factors, namely, the sexist, second-class treatment of women; (2) self-determination, autonomy, and equal status in society are essential for women's mental health; (3) the relationship between therapist and client must be equalitarian in order to model and foster self-determination and autonomy; and (4) therapy is a political process, and the therapist must work for social as well as individual change (Gilbert, 1980; Holroyd, 1976; Lerman, 1976; Maracek & Kravetz, 1977; Rawlings & Carter, 1977). The application of these tenets to supervision addresses and reduces many of the power conflicts and abuses endemic to traditional forms of supervision.

Objectives

The objectives are derived from those of feminist therapy. The supervisor must respect the unique goals and autonomy of each trainee, just as feminist therapy promotes the development of independent women free to define their own goals. She must strive for the trainee's awareness of her or his attributes, values, and behaviors with respect to gender, and the impact of the social structure on both the trainee's and the client's behavior and "personality." She must establish the type of climate that will facilitate the trainee's exploration of issues relevant to therapy with women, including her or his own sex stereotypes, socialization, and biases. Just as feminist therapists view the personal as political (Gilbert, 1980), so must the supervisor facilitate the trainee's understanding of the political impact of therapy, each individual's role in society, and the need for collective social action. Just as feminist therapists view the therapist/client relationship as an attempt to be more equalitarian and nonhierarchical than in traditional therapies (Butler, 1982; Gilbert, 1980), the supervisor must model greater equality and respect for the trainee. Furthermore, feminist supervision must educate the trainee in areas of special concern to women, including menstruation, pregnancy, childbirth, rape, incest, body image, eating disorders, lesbianism and female bonding and friendships.

The basic tenets of feminist therapy with regard to power must apply in supervision. The primary goal of the feminist supervisor must be to model an equalitarian therapeutic relationship. The supervisor must focus on the trainee as learner rather than patient, demystifying the role of power in the relationship, and conducting a continual evaluation of the trainee's work with the client (adapted from Guidelines of the Philadelphia Feminist Therapy Collective, cited by Butler, 1982).

Power cannot be denied or erased in supervision. To deny power is to deny responsibility: the supervisor's responsibility to introduce new information and methods of analyses, to give useful feedback to the trainee, and to ensure quality care for the trainee's clients. Trainees consider laissez-faire supervision to be as dissatisfying and ineffective as authoritarian methods (Cherniss & Equatios, 1977).

The feminist supervisor, however, can use power constructively. She can empower the trainee by listening to and working with the trainee's goals and jointly establishing supervisory objectives and criteria for performance. Specific feedback aimed at increasing the trainee's self-awareness can be provided; inductions of guilt feelings should be avoided. Furthermore, the supervisor can solicit ongoing feedback from the trainee regarding the process and content of supervision. Insight-oriented supervision may be undertaken profitably, providing the trainee has given consent. The supervisor's sensitivity to and respect for the trainee's self-disclosures, as opposed to a psychopathology hunt, must be apparent to the trainee.

Mechanics

Audio- or videotaping is essential to supervision. Most of us are unaware of the myriad ways we express our misogyny—through facial expressions, interruptions, not listening, and taking too patronizing and protective a stance with a "helpless female" or a contemptuous, punitive stance with an "aggressive" one. Only actual representations of the therapy sessions will allow supervisors access to this information. Taping also provides an avenue for examining the trainee's perceptions and biases, for they will be far more apparent to both supervisor and trainee.

STAGES OF FEMINIST SUPERVISION

Feminist supervision can be conceptualized as having four stages. The process of supervision generally progresses most effectively when the stages are introduced in the following sequence: 1) the discussion of specific topics and information relevant to the trainee's female clients; 2) a more general exploration of the effects of socialization, stereotyping, and sexism on the development of personality and psychopathology in women; 3) the more focused exploration of the trainee's socialization including sexist biases, stereotypes, and behaviors and their impact on therapy with women; and 4) the recognition that individual solutions are inadequate for societal problems and that social action is necessary. The supervisor must begin at the level of each trainee, helping each one achieve greater awareness of these issues. Some trainees may proceed through all four stages. The goals may remain more modest for others; e.g., increasing their awareness that sexism exists or of the effects of sex-role stereotyping on behavior. Some trainees will explore their own attitudes and biases; others will shy away from this challenge, and still others will maintain their own self-serving, sexist viewpoints.

Stage 1: Introduction of a Feminist Perspective

The supervisor introduces a feminist analysis of therapy by comparing and contrasting this perspective to the more traditional ones familiar to the student. In effect, this stage has a more didactic focus than the others. The student is referred to the literature discussing the feminist perspective related to a client's problems. I focus supervision by discussing with the trainee the similarities and differences between the feminist and traditional literatures and the implications of each view for treat-ment interventions. We formulate hypotheses and develop treatment plans based on the feminist therapy literature. Workshop attendance is encouraged.

Beginning the supervisory process by educating on specific topics has several advantages. The personal distance afforded by emphasizing more intellectualized issues allows the supervisor the opportunity to introduce new and potentially controversial material in a relatively un-threatening fashion. The trainee may approach the harsh realities of women's experience without feeling personally overwhelmed and re-treating into her or his own defenses. The supervisor has the opportu-nity to develop the climate appropriate for more personal exploration and to discover the attitudes and values of the trainee. The trainee has the chance to determine whether the supervisor will be supportive and nonpunitive as she or he takes more risks in self-disclosure.

Furthermore, personal and institutionalized sexist attitudes are harder for individuals to recognize and admit than is ignorance about a specialized area of therapy. Most individuals at least monitor the expres-sion of overtly sexist biases, recognizing the social undesirability of such behavior, especially with a female supervisor. Ignorance about "women's issues" appears not to be considered a sin, however (Sherman, Koufacos & Kenworthy, 1978), and trainees appear less inhibited in admitting their lack of information than their negative attitudes about women. Feminist supervision may be the first time the trainee has had access to accurate or complete information about the psychological and sociological issues per-taining to women. This knowledge often motivates more serious contem-plation or exploration of women's issues. Finally, sexist attitudes, how-ever pervasive, are generally nonconscious and subtle (Brodsky, 1980; Porter & Geis, 1981) and may be perceived by the trainee only after concentrated examination.

Stage 2: Exploring Sexism and Socialization in Society

The content issues described in stage 1 tend to provide the lead-in for this stage of exploring the more general effects of sex-role stereotyping and socialization on women. The supervisor begins to direct the trainee away from purely psychological, individualized, or ahistorical analyses of behavior, toward an understanding of the role of cutural, historical, and environmental factors. The supervisor refocuses client problems away from a discussion purely of specific syndromes and symptoms to a broader societal viewpoint. During this phase, the supervisor can assist the trainee in making connections between "symptoms" as adaptive or once-adaptive solutions to societal expectations or oppression, rather than as individual expressions of psychopathology. The trainee may focus initially on the problems from a model of internalized psychopathology, tossing around terms such as passive-aggressive, passive-dependent, manipulative, or seductive with little or no self-consciousness. The role of the feminist supervisor at this point would be to place these behaviors and pejorative terms in a cultural, relational, and patriarchal context and to examine how the environment precipitates and maintains these behaviors.

During this stage of training, I may recommend more general readings by feminist theorists or by women writing about their experiences. For example, I may suggest readings on women and power, rape and pornography, or female sexuality. Through imagery, I ask the trainee to assume the role of the client and explore her world, relationships, sense of powerlessness and helpessness, and perceptions of self and others. I actively offer alternative ways of viewing the problems and personalities of clients.

Case Example: An advanced male trainee was assigned a 24-year-old woman with a partially debilitating handicap. She used either a wheelchair or cane because walking was painful. Her body was asymmetrical. Each therapy session, she enumerated all the crises and traumas of the previous week, each one worse than the last. She appeared to be simultaneously begging for solutions and resisting those offered. The therpist felt angry and frustrated, both for being considered the all-knowing expert and for being ignored when he did intervene. He labeled the woman "dependent" and "passive-aggressive" and became somewhat withdrawn and cool in therapy.

In supervision, we focused on the cultural roots of both her behavior and his responses. We explored how the environment may have shaped her behaviors. We examined how her handicap forced her into an even more "beholden" position relative to men than is true for non-disabled women; how she learned to express compliance and suppress anger as protective measures aimed at not alienating her caretakers; and how a woman who so clearly perceives herself as not living up to societal standards of attractiveness would feel vulnerable and unworthy. We explored how hostility results from women's socialization to seek out men as experts, even when this behavior is invalidating of oneself. We discussed the trainee's tendency to overemphasize power issues in relationships and feel threatened by dependency. We concentrated on shifting his focus to greater empathy and support. We also discussed his "socialized" tendency to withdraw emotionally when uncomfortable. The trainee sought ways to encourage her to feel more powerful through validating her experiences and remaining more emotionally available.

Stage 3: Exploring the Trainee's Attitudes

The most difficult stage in feminist supervision is the trainee's exploration of her or his own internalized misogynist attitudes and behaviors and their pervasive effects on the therapy process. This stage is the most important one, particularly from the perspective of "the personal is political." We all must face our own sexism and how our assumptions based on gender lead to differing expectations, goals, and behaviors in therapy. Focusing on how the trainee's specific therapeutic interactions are a result of her or his perceptions of, biases about, and responses to women is the most challenging, fragile, and potentially productive aspect of feminist supervision.

Reviewing audio and video tapes of therapy transactions is most important when concentrating on these issues. The supervisor must listen carefully to the messages sent from therapist to client, to the nonverbal as well as verbal interactions. How does a therapist subtlely show contempt for a women's lifestyle, reinforce "traditional" albeit maladaptive behavioral patterns, or set up a hierarchical relationship? What are the therapist's attitudes and how does she or he convey them throughout the process? In this stage, we focus on making the attitudes, biases, assumptions, and beliefs of the therapist explicit, exploring how the therapist came to possess them and how they aid or interfere with therapy with a female client.

Case Example: An advanced and feminist trainee was counseling a young woman whom she described to a supervision group as having a "controlling mother." At that point I asked the group to explore the use of this concept, its usual derogatory connotation, the double binds of women as mothers, and our own ageism and sexism regarding "controlling" women. We began by examining the negative cultural connotations of the term when used to describe women and our own beliefs that "controlling" women are "nags" and "bitches"—basically very unpleasant people. We expressed our own personal fears of being viewed as controlling women and the ways society keeps us in line by punishing assertive women. We compared the negative view of "controlling" women to the positive terms used to describe "controlling" men— "leader," "in charge," "in control," "commanding," or "dynamic."

We went on to examine the alternatives left to mothers, especially single parents or those paired with peripheral fathers, as in this case. We discussed our own mother/daughter relationships, from the stand-points of being both daughters and mothers. We shared our own nega-tive and positive feelings about these relationships. We explored ways to change our own relationships as well as our distorted perceptions of mothers generally. Finally, we used our shared knowledge, experience, and feelings to arrive at potential interventions with the client, including assisting her in exploring many of these same issues.

Stage 4: Taking a Collective Perspective

The fourth stage requires that the trainee move away from an individually oriented view of treatment toward a more collective perspective. Under-standing the importance of social activism, self-help groups, and fewer hierarchies in society is the main objective of this stage. Trainees are encouraged to explore and contact the community resources that might be helpful to their clients. In supervision we determine which resources could benefit particular clients and encourage participation. We also at-tempt to offer appropriate groups for women in our training clinic.

The shift from an individual to a group perspective should be mani-fested not only in the trainee's relationships with clients but also in their own personal lives. I encourage trainees to participate in social action groups outside of training. Some trainees have developed autonomously a feminist reading group; many attend a women-psychologists' support group. I have developed three clinical activities for assisting trainees in working collectively: a feminist practicum team, cotherapy opportunities in women's groups, and experience leading consciousness-raising groups. The practicum team is a voluntary supervision team in which we discuss therapy cases and feminist issues. The group format reduces the power differential between supervisor and trainees and permits the members to learn from each other. In cotherapy, two leaders are paired to run groups dealing with concerns to women, such as eating disorders or incest. Trai-nees are either at different levels of training, experience, or awareness or are of different sexes. Much of supervision focuses on ways to alleviate power differentials or sex-stereotypic behavior between the leaders. Cotherapists take much responsibility in confronting their partners and accepting feedback. In the consciousness-raising groups, trainees lead groups for undergraduates taking a course on the psychology of women. The trainees then meet to discuss the issues that evolve in their respective groups. The consciousness-raising groups are same-sex, but the trainees' discussion groups are mixed and include the trainees who lead both the female and male consciousness-raising groups.

Case Example: A 30-year-old lesbian sought treatment to assist her in coping with a new relationship. Her partner had three children and was fearful that a disclosure of this, her first lesbian relationship, would jeopardize her custody rights. This secrecy and the parenting issues appeared to be major sources of conflict in the relationship. The client had been seen at the clinic previously. In supervision, we noted that, although the client had been "out" as a lesbian for several years, she kept her distance from lesbian support groups and friendships. She tended to focus her attention on a current partner, with few other relationships. When her relationships ended, she did not have back-up relationships and felt isolated. We developed two objectives for therapy that were successful: (1) to assist this client in becoming more involved in the activities and groups sponsored by the community's organization of lesbians and (2) to encourage the participation of the client and her partner in a group for lesbian parents.

Although the supervision stages are sequential, the boundaries between them are quite fluid. Supervisors and trainees typically move back and forth between the four stages. Stage 1, introducing a trainee to a feminist understanding of cases, and stage 2, exploring the role of society in shaping women, tend to occur almost simultaneously. With every piece of information acquired by the trainee, a discussion of cultural factors is likely to ensue.

CONCLUSION

Now that feminist therapy has moved into its second decade, we must develop models for supervising and training students. Feminist therapy has an organized body of principles that can be passed on to trainees systematically. We must develop training methods congruent with our therapeutic philosophy. As in the initiation of any creative endeavor, our early attempts will be based on trial and error. We must scrutinize them rigorously, searching for more effective training methods.

The stages of supervision proposed in this chapter evolved with experience. Initially I used a different sequence. Intuitively, starting with an understanding of sexism in society and oneself, moving to an analysis of the role of sociocultural factors on women's development, and then learning interventions specific to the issues at hand seemed a more sensible supervision sequence. In fact, this sequence may be appropriate for a trainee with a feminist consciousness, one who possesses awareness but lacks particular information or technique. My initial beliefs, especially when working with male trainees, was that they would have to raise their consciousness about sexism and understand their own socialization and sexist attitudes before they could understand the feminist therapy literature. Philosophically I still believe that therapists must be sensitive to their own participation in misogyny before seeing female clients or attempting a feminist analysis of therapy. However, pragmatically I have learned that for the less-informed or nonfeminist trainee, attempting to raise the more personal issues first results in defensiveness, externalization of the problem, an inability to see the issues, and the tendency to remain stuck at an intellectual level. The process works as ineffectively as interpreting a client's behavioral patterns before she or he is aware that such patterns even exist.

REFERENCES

American Psychological Association. (1975). Report of the task force on sex bias and sex-role stereotyping in psychotherapeutic practice. *American Psychologist, 30,* 1169–1175.

Brodsky, A. (1980). Supervising therapy with women. In A. K. Hess (Ed.), *Psychotherapy supervision: Theory, research and practice.* New York: John Wiley & Sons.

Butler, M. (1982, April). Feminist therapy: A second look at a working definition. Paper presented at the meeting of the Advanced Feminist Therapist Institute, Vail, CO.

Cherniss, C., & Equatios, E. (1977). Styles of clinical supervision in community health programs. *Journal of Consulting and Clinical Psychology, 45,* 1195–1196.

Chesler, P. (1972). Patient and patriarch: Women and the psychotherapeutic relationship. In V. Gornick & B. K. Moran (Eds.), *Women in sexist society*. New York: Basic Books.

Gilbert, L. A. (1980). Feminist therapy. In A. Brodsky & R. T. Hare-Mustin (Eds.), *Women and psychotherapy: An assessment of research and practice*. New York: Guilford Press.

Greenberg, L. (1980). Supervision from the perspective of the supervisee. In A. K. Hess (Ed.), *Psychotherapy supervision: Theory, research and practice*. New York: John Wiley.

Holroyd, J. (1976). Psychotherapy and women's liberation. *Counseling Psychotherapy, 6*, 22–28.

Kadushin, A. (1968). Games people play in supervision. *Social Work, 13*, 23–32.

Lerman, H. (1976). What happens in feminist therapy. In S. Cox (Ed.), *Female psychology: The emerging self*. Chicago, IL: Science Research Associates.

Maracek, J., & Kravetz, D. (1977). Women and mental health: A review of feminist change efforts. *Psychiatry, 40*, 323–329.

Marshall, W. R., & Confer, W. N. (1980). Psychotherapy supervision: Supervisee's perspective. In A. K. Hess (Ed.), *Psychotherapy supervision: Theory, research and practice* (pp. 92–102). New York: John Wiley.

Pierce, R., Carkhuff, R. R., & Berenson, B. G. (1967). The differential effects of high and low functioning counselors upon counselors-in-training. *Journal of Clinical Psychology, 23*, 212–215.

Porter, M. (1979). The effects of the nature of the supervisory relationship on participant's ability to give accurate descriptions of the client. Unpublished doctoral dissertation, University of Detroit, Michigan.

Porter, N., & Geis, F. L. (1981). Women and nonverbal leadership cues: When seeing is not believing. In C. Mayo & N. M. Henley (Eds.), *Gender and nonverbal behavior* (pp. 39–62). New York: Springer-Verlag.

Rawlings, E. J., & Carter, D. K. (Eds.).(1977). *Psychotherapy for women: Treatment toward equality*. Springfield, IL: Charles C Thomas.

Sherman, J. A., Koufacos, C., & Kenworthy, J. A. (1978). Therapists: Their attitudes and information about women. *Psychology of Women Quarterly, 2*, 299–313.

Epilogue

IT'S A TRICKY BUSINESS

It's a tricky business done by you and me:
Being the eyes for others to clearly see.
Standing closely by, put our needs aside,
And keep on giving.

Wisdom overflowing and ears that never close,
Expected to understand all that's posed.
Never in a mood; selfless, calm and cool,
And always giving, always giving.

CHORUS:
But what about us? Who's gonna tend us?
What about us? We hear so much sadness
Our hearts could break.
What about us? We tend others' gardens,
While ours shrivel up, thirsty and starving
For tenderness. It's craziness.

What a way to make a living, off of people's pain;
Selling umbrellas in the midst of rain.
Caring by the hour; if you pay us now,
We'll keep on giving.

344

Friends and close relations have a heavy load.
Our well is usually dry at home.
Strangers get our best, for dear ones little's left
Of us for giving, always giving.

CHORUS:
But what about us? Who's gonna tend us?
What about us? Our needs are tremendous
By the end of the day.
What about us? We feeders need feeding;
Vacations and such, and time for retreating
From others' needs—for nourishing.

Yes, it's a funny business, yet one we have to trust.
We're someone to come to when bubbles burst.
When people lose their dreams, they come to you and me.
We keep on giving.
We're always giving.

—*Judy Eron*

I'M A FEMINIST

CHORUS:
I'm not a Freudian, I'm not a Jungian,
I'm a feminist.
I'm not Adlerian, nor a Skinnerian,
I'm a feminist.
I'm not a Perls Gestalt, though I like what he taught,
I'm a feminist.
I'm not an Ellis fan, or Harry Sullivan,
I'm a feminist therapist.

Those boys and their theories have helped us a lot,
But a problem with a woman each one of them's got.
Envying penises is not where I'm at.
Face it—only a man could have come up with that!

(CHORUS)

Years on the couch as the analyst sits,
Listening to memories and dreams erotic.
Taking his notes on the pad on his lap,
To cover the stirring big bulge in his slacks.

(CHORUS)

Needing new heroes, we've found a new crew,
Choderow and Dinnerstein to mention a few.
And if our colleagues in psych don't agree,
We'll leave them behind in our dust, don't you see.

(CHORUS)

—*Judy Eron*

Index

Date Due

ILL (PKT) 9726937		
NOV 1 3 1996		
MAY 0 2000		